SIXTH EDITION

Argumentation and Critical Decision Making

Richard D. Rieke
University of Utah

Malcolm O. Sillars
University of Utah

Tarla Rai Peterson
University of Utah

Boston   New York   San Francisco
Mexico City   Montreal   Toronto   London   Madrid   Munich   Paris
Hong Kong   Singapore   Tokyo   Cape Town   Sydney

Executive Editor: *Karon Bowers*
Series Editor: *Brian Wheel*
Editorial Assistant: *Jennifer Trebby*
Marketing Manager: *Mandee Eckersley*
Composition and Prepress Buyer: *Linda Cox*
Manufacturing Buyer: *JoAnne Sweeney*
Cover Administrator: *Joel Gendron*
Editorial-Production Service: *Omegatype Typography, Inc.*
Electronic Composition: *Omegatype Typography, Inc.*

For related titles and support materials, visit our online catalog at www.ablongman.com.

Between the time Website information is gathered and then published, it is not unusual for some sites to have closed. Also, the transcription of URLs can result in unintended typographical errors. The publisher would appreciate notification where these errors occur so that they may be corrected in subsequent editions.

Library of Congress Cataloging-in-Publication Data

Rieke, Richard D.
    Argumentation and critical decision making / Richard D. Rieke,
Malcolm O. Sillars, Tarla Rai Peterson. — 6th ed.
        p.   cm.
    Includes bibliographical references.
    ISBN 0-205-41793-0
        1. Debates and debating.   I. Sillars, Malcolm O. (Malcolm Osgood),
II. Peterson, Tarla Rai.   III. Title.

PN4181.R47 2005
808.5'3—dc22

                                                                    2004050567

Printed in the United States of America

10 9 8 7 6 5 4 3 2 1   09 08 07 06 05 04

CONTENTS

16   Argumentation in Government and Politics   293

PREFACE

This is the sixth edition of a book that first appeared in 1975. In the first edition, we dedicated ourselves to the development of an audience-centered approach to the study of argumentation that reflected the best of contemporary scholarship while holding true to the heritage that comes to us from Ancient Greece and Rome, and Europe. This edition continues that dedication.

Each chapter has been thoroughly reexamined with an eye toward new scholarship that can expand our discussion. Each chapter has been updated with examples of actual argument practices that come from contemporary decision making. As always, we approach our subject from the perspective of explaining how people really go about critical decision making. We avoid hypothetical examples and academic points that do not help the reader grow in understanding real-world processes.

In this edition, we introduce a third author, Tarla Rai Peterson, a professor in the Department of Communication at the University of Utah. She enriches the text by bringing a postmodernist and feminist perspective to the understanding of argumentation. She helps the reader understand the feminist and postmodernist critique of argumentation, and then demonstrates how, rather than making the subject obsolete, it strengthens the role of argumentation in practical affairs. A new Chapter 3 is the result of her work. Professor Peterson's extensive research background in environmental science and communication brings strong new material to the rest of the book.

This edition is structured in three sections: principles, tools, and applications. The first three chapters have been extensively revised to make them easier to teach, and they include new material reflecting contemporary thinking. The applications section also includes much new material. The applications investigate argumentation practices in law, science, religion, business, and government and politics. Chapters 13, 14, 15, and 16 are all virtually new material. For example, the era of business misbehavior that led to one company or executive after another being charged with ethical and legal violations in business decision making required a completely new chapter reflecting these events.

For more than a quarter-century, we have revised this text to reflect the movement in the field of argumentation. For example, as the importance of argumentation has grown in many academic disciplines, our writing has moved to embrace concepts and examples from each of them. The critique of argumentation as being too adversarial and reflective of modernist, male-dominated thought has moved us to strengthen the discussion of the role of dialectic and dialogue in critical decision making while removing fight- or war-based examples from such discussions as those on refutation. And the new Chapter 3 expands our scope into contemporary thought.

However much we change this book to keep up with modern trends, we do not abandon our foundation that solidly reflects the work of Aristotle, Plato, Stephen Toulmin, Chaim Perelman, C. L. Hamblin, and others. The discussion of informal logic still reflects both Aristotle's original thought and the thinking of contemporary students of critical thinking and philosophy. The tools section brings together well-established thinking about the nature of arguments and the role of evidence, values, and credibility in their support. The chapters on refutation include references to contemporary philosophical thought that combines classical with contemporary thinking.

Argumentation and Critical Decision Making is designed to contribute to meeting the need of courses in argumentation, informal logic, critical thinking, composition, rhetoric, or forensics. When we teach a course in communication and law, we have students read this text alongside another dealing with negotiation, mediation, and litigation. Any course that addresses decision processes within a specific field or discipline could well use this text as a companion to other readings.

Pedagogy and Instructional Support

As in previous editions, we provide a variety of elements designed to make this book more teachable and accessible to students. These elements include the following:

- Each chapter begins with a list of key terms.
- Important concepts are printed in italics the first time they occur in the text.
- Each chapter concludes with a summary.
- A suggested student project is included at the end of each chapter.
- Research citations in the text and a references section provide additional readings.
- An Instructor's Manual is available from the publisher. It includes sample syllabi, additional projects, and test materials.

Acknowledgments

This edition was influenced by all those whom we acknowledged for assisting us in the first five editions and many other students and colleagues over the past quarter-century. University of Utah colleagues Dennis C. Alexander, Mark Bergstrom, Marouf Hasian, Jr., and Mary Louise Willbrand as well as David Henry of the University of Nevada, Las Vegas, Markus J. Peterson of Texas A&M University, and Thomas H. Olbricht of Pepperdine University, as well as the reviewers for this edition, Dan Durbin of the University of Southern California, Ekaterina Haskins of Boston College, Sabrena R. Parton of Berry College, and Richard Pineda of CSU San Bernadino, have been particularly helpful. We have appreciated the assistance of Karon Bowers, Brian Wheel, and Jennifer Trebby from Allyn and Bacon.

R. D. R.
M. O. S.
T. R. P.

PART ONE

Principles

The domain of argumentation encompasses virtually every occasion in which people seek to make the best possible decision in spite of the inevitability of uncertainty. What are the principles that underlie the process of argumentation? How do people make critical decisions? How do people evaluate arguments, telling good ones from bad? When people perceive a problem exists, how can they move from this feeling of concern to the statement of a proposition worthy of critical decision making? How can people prepare a full argumentative case that will facilitate decision making? These are the principles we discuss in this section.

1 The Domain of Argumentation

KEY TERMS

adherence	internal dialogue
decision maker	reflective thinking
claim	argument
factual claim	support
value claim	values
policy claim	criticism
issue	critical thinking
proposition	dialectic
evidence	critical decision
credibility	rhetoric
fallacies	probability
uncertainty	audience
language	proof

Argumentation is at once a familiar and puzzling concept. It is familiar in the sense that the word is one you know, it probably appears in your conversation occasionally, and, research suggests, you have been making up reasons since you were about four years old. In fact, you still use a lot of the reasons that came to mind when you were just a child (Willbrand and Rieke). As a kid, you probably reasoned on the basis of power authority, "My Mommy said I don't have to eat green beans, so there!" As an adult, you surely still use power authority, although in a more grown-up way, "My advisor says this course will satisfy a major requirement, and she has the power to make that determination."

Argumentation is puzzling because people so rarely take time to reflect on what they mean and do under the heading of argument or argumentation. If we were to ask a group of people what argumentation means, we would get many different answers, and most of them would be fairly superficial.

The difficult part about studying argumentation is keeping your mind open to new ways of thinking about a familiar process. The objective of this book is to sensitize you to your own argumentation behaviors and provide new information and insight to help you be as effective as possible.

In the first three chapters, we will offer our perspective on argumentation for your consideration. Subsequent chapters will present information about engaging in argumentation that we expect will provide you with some valuable insights.

We begin by introducing you to the key elements of argumentation. Then we will explain how argumentation is inherent in critical decision making.

Elements of Argumentation

Argumentation is the communicative process of advancing, supporting, criticizing, and modifying claims so that appropriate decision makers, defined by relevant spheres, may grant or deny adherence. Let us briefly discuss the important terms in this working definition.

Adherence

The objective of argumentation, as Chaim Perelman and L. Olbrechts-Tyteca have noted, is to gain *adherence,* which is the informed support of others (1). By informed, we mean that people who have committed themselves to your claim are consciously aware of the reasons for doing so. By support, we mean that people stand ready to act on your claims, not just grant lip service.

We have said that argumentation is a communication process, which means it involves engaging people's minds through interaction. As we will see in the next chapter, different people make different demands on arguments before committing themselves. The responsibility for decision making is shared, including the responsibility for bad decisions.

Appropriate Decision Makers

The appropriate *decision makers* are those necessary to the ultimate implementation of the decision. You may win adherence of fellow students to the proposition that the midterm exam should count less than the final paper in grading your class, but if the professor says no, what have you accomplished?

When the George W. Bush administration in the United States initiated a worldwide debate over alleged attempts by Saddam Hussein in Iraq to acquire and perhaps use weapons of mass destruction, the administration appealed to the Security Council of the United Nations for a resolution of condemnation. U.S. Secretary of State Colin Powell presented a detailed argumentative case before the United Nations, and representatives of many other countries entered the discussion. In the end, the resolution was rejected, with such powerful nations as France, Germany, Russia, and China voting no.

In the eyes of many observers, arguments had been properly presented to the appropriate decision makers, and they had decided. The world, it seemed, had rejected war, at least for the time being, and would continue international inspections instead.

However, President Bush formed a coalition consisting mostly of the United States and Britain, and proceeded to invade and conquer Iraq without regard for the decision of the Security Council. This action revealed who the appropriate decision makers were: the leaders of the United States and the United Kingdom. While some continue to argue that the United Nations *should* have been the appropriate decision makers, the fact is the United Nations lacked the power or authority to insist that its decision be final.

The appropriate decision makers need not be powerful persons. All citizens have a part in implementing some decisions. By participating in public interest groups, by actively participating in the political process and by voting, you can become an appropriate decision maker, regardless of your position, on public questions. When you make an argument, you must address it to the appropriate decision makers if you expect to generate more than lip service.

Because argumentation functions as a social-interactive process and because people's critical decisions are the products of argumentation, we speak of argumentation as audience-centered. The word *audience* is used in its broadest sense to include all argumentative situations ranging from interpersonal interaction between two people to talk radio or chat rooms on the Internet, from readers of letters to the editor to those who watch C-SPAN.

Spheres

Spheres are collections of people in the process of interacting upon and making critical decisions. The easiest sphere to understand is that group of people who lived together as you grew up. Within that group, rules of interaction were developed and enforced, values were established, acceptable reasons were identified, and the appropriate decision makers emerged over time. People who live together learn how language will be interpreted, establish roles and hierarchies, develop relatively common perceptions of reality, and come to understand what arguments will be respected. Even though children may disagree with their parents or guardians over what counts as a good argument, they usually must adapt to those standards because of their standing in the hierarchy. As you grew up, you established different spheres with peers and other adults where standards of argumentation were different from those enforced in the home. Spheres are explained further in Chapter 2.

Claims

A *claim* is a statement that you want others to accept and act upon (to grant their adherence). It may be linked to a series of other claims that constitute a case.

When a claim is used to justify another claim, it is called a *subclaim.* "Watching TV for more than three hours a day makes children aggressive" is a claim. It becomes a subclaim when it is used to justify the claim, "The media should reduce the amount of violence in their shows."

There are three kinds of claims: *fact, value,* and *policy.* Later in this chapter we will see how they interrelate and are used to support one another. For now, let us see what they are.

Factual Claim   A *factual claim* affirms that certain conditions exist in the material world and could be observed. Decision makers are asked to adhere to a factual claim because it is confirmed by objective data from reliable sources. The following are examples of factual claims:

> Cypress College is in Orange County, California.
>
> Twenty-four species of animals run faster than humans.
>
> New Mexico became a state in 1912.
>
> The percentage of the U.S. population over sixty-five will significantly increase by the year 2020.

These are all factual claims. Each makes a claim that decision makers might verify by reference to some kind of data. The first two are claims of *present fact* and the third is a claim of *past fact.* The fourth claim about the U.S. population is worth special note as it is a claim of *future fact* (Cronkhite). A visit or a website tells you that Cypress College is in Orange County, California, a count found in an almanac confirms there are twenty-four species of animals faster than humans, and a historical record shows that New Mexico became a state in 1912. But, a future fact cannot be confirmed by looking at objective data from reliable sources. Decision makers will require more extensive reasoning to give it adherence. However, it is still a factual claim because at some point you, or someone, will be able to check it by objective data or observation. For instance, current government statistics tell us how many people are over sixty-five years of age today. By examining the percentage of people fifty and over with the general population today you can estimate the percentage who will be over sixty-five in 2020. Eventually, in 2020, you can check it, if you wish.

Nonetheless, whether of past, present, or future, factual claims all have similar characteristics. All make assertions about what a situation was, is, or will be. All can be identified by some variety of the verb "to be." Note the examples above: "Cypress College *is* . . . ," "Twenty-four species of animals *are* . . . ," "New Mexico *became* . . . ," "The percentage of the population over sixty-five *will be* . . . " And, all are analyzed in the same way.

Value Claim   A claim that asserts the quality of a person, place, thing, or idea is called a *value claim:*

> Natural gas is our best energy source.
> Drugs and alcohol are a threat to public morality.

Both of these statements make claims about the value of something; they make a value judgment that cannot be checked against data. "Drugs and alcohol are a threat to public morality" is clearly a value claim. "Public morality" is a condition that can be defined only by the participants in argumentation. It has no generally accepted means of verification. Natural gas, on the other hand, might be shown to have less pollutants, may cost less per BTU than other energy sources, and may have other characteristics that seem to make this claim as verifiable as a factual claim. But *best* means more than verifiable characteristics. Some people find gas *better* than electricity for cooking. How is that to be verified? So, value claims may vary from personal choice to definition in the strictest verifiable terms.

The value claim is frequently confused with the factual claim because it has the same form. It is built around some version of the verb "to be." Note the examples above: "Drugs and alcohol *are* . . . ," "Natural gas *is*. . . ." Furthermore, as we will show later in this book, the value claim is analyzed the same way as is the factual claim. But the value claim can always be distinguished from the factual claim because it has in it a value term ("public morality/immorality," "best/worst," "right/wrong," "just/unjust," "beautiful/ugly") that contains a judgment that cannot be objectively verified and depends on the decision makers' concepts of what is and what is not of value.

Policy Claim   A claim that tells someone or some agency how to behave is called a *policy claim*. Any statement of a rule, law, or regulation is a policy claim and is a proposed change in the way people or agencies currently behave:

> No left turn.
> Don't walk on the grass.
> The balanced budget amendment to the constitution should be passed.
> Medical marijuana use ought to be legalized.
> The United States must control illegal immigration.

Because policy claims have to do with behavior, it will help you to identify them by checking to see if they state or imply the word *should*. The first two claims do not specifically state "You should not turn left" or "You should not walk on the grass," but they are commands based on policy decisions. The last two policy claims use terms *ought* and *must* that mean the same as *should*.

Note the differences in these three related claims:

> Left turns are against the law at Fifth and Elm streets. (factual claim)
> Left turns at Fifth and Elm are dangerous. (value claim)
> You should not turn left at Fifth and Elm Streets. (policy claim)

All three claims deal with the same subject matter but they are quite different. They require different kinds of analysis and argumentation, primarily because asking for a change of behavior is more than asserting a fact or value.

Notice that a claim is a single statement, but it is possible that you could have a sentence with more than one claim in it. Consider this sentence: "The average composite U.S. College Testing Program score for U.S. high school students is 20.8, a significant drop from twenty years earlier." There is a factual claim about the scores and a value claim about their significance. You may need to separate these two for your analysis.

Issue

The term *issue,* as frequently used in our society, can be confused with the term *claim.* A politician will argue, "My opponent has missed the issue; we need a balanced budget amendment." But an issue is more than an important claim. *An issue is the clash of two opposing claims stated as a question.*

To make analysis more pointed, you should always state issues in a hypothetical form allowing only two responses: yes or no. In this way, the statement of the issue points the response either toward one claim or a continued search.

For example, you might ask, "Are current tuition rates too low?" One person says yes, another says no: there is an issue. Issues are best stated with such words as *should, will, does, can,* or *is* because such words clearly imply a yes or no answer. If the decision makers decide the answer is no, it does not mean the discussion of tuition is over; it merely means those interested in change must revise their analysis and open another issue. For example, they might move to the question,

"Will higher tuition rates improve our education?"[1]

By the same token, issues never begin with such words as *who, what, where, when, why,* or *how.* These and similar words lead to an open-ended question such as, "What is the impact of livestock grazing on federal lands?" The response to such a question is wide open and does not focus the analysis. As you will see in Chapter 4, such general questions may be the point where analysis begins, but such analysis will look to find issues.

Many political leaders in western states oppose wilderness designation for federal lands because that will restrict the economic development of those lands for livestock grazing, mining, and logging. Environmental groups favor a greater designation of wilderness to preserve more land in the natural state. They claim: "More federal land should be designated as wilderness." Others argue against such designation. Here, then, is a policy issue: "Should more public land be designated as wilderness?" No, opponents say, because designated wilderness land hurts the local economy. Supporters claim that it does not. Here is a value issue: "Does wilderness designation of federal land hurt the local economy?" "Wilderness attracts tourists who strengthen the local economy," say the supporters. Opponents say, "Tourism adds less to the economy than do mining, grazing, and lumbering." This clash of claims results in an issue of fact: "Does tourism add more to the economy than mining, grazing, and lumbering?"

Not all claims result in issues, but any claim (policy, fact, or value) may become an issue. If you say to a friend, "We should go to the basketball game tonight," you have a claim. But, if she says, "Sure, let's go," you have no issue. Issues are important because they identify the significant points where controversy exists and, therefore, where possible claim modification can be made to reach agreement. If such modification is impossible, these points become the places where you must concentrate your argument.

---

[1]In some logic systems this point is made by substituting for yes or no, yes or not yes. All you have decided to do was not to say yes to the question this particular issue poses, not to reject anything else on this subject.

Proposition

A *proposition* is a claim that expresses the judgment that decision makers are asked to accept or reject. Generally speaking, like other claims, a proposition may be of fact, value, or policy.[2] But, while other claims may serve as subclaims to one another and to propositions, a proposition cannot be a subclaim because it represents the point where you want the decision makers to be when your argumentation is finished.

Claims accumulate to form other claims. These claims support a proposition. You may change your proposition when new information is added or when your proposition is rejected. Argumentation is a continuing process of changing issues, claims, and propositions. But, at the point you choose to build a case (see Chapter 5), you select a judgment for decision makers to accept or reject. The claim that states that judgment is the proposition.

The following is a brief outline of a controversy to illustrate the relationship between a proposition and its supporting claims.

Proposition of Policy: The Associated Students of this university should provide low-cost day care for the children of students.

I. Almost 20 percent of the students have children. (factual claim)

II. Acceptable day care is expensive. (value claim)

III. Many students have to restrict their educations because they do not have affordable day care available. (value claim)

IV. The Associated Students should spend money on things that students need rather than unnecessary social events and expensive popular lectures. (policy claim)

V. A day care program would cost less than 5 percent of the annual Associated Students' budget. (claim of future fact)

Support

Whatever communication (including both words and objects) is necessary and available to secure adherence, what it takes to get others to accept and act on your claim,

---

[2]Among students of argumentation there have been attempts to define a wider variety of propositions than the three most traditional ones we have identified here. However, these show that fact, value, and policy come in a variety of forms. As long as you recognize that all fact, value, or policy claims will not look exactly alike you can be a successful arguer using these three.

There are definitional propositions (Ehninger and Brockriede 218–29) in which people argue how to define a term (e.g.: "What is a democracy?"). We treat these as factual claims. Definition is discussed in Chapter 6. Some people treat some value claims that imply a policy claim ("War is immoral") as a "quasi-policy claim." Some differentiate "comparative value claims" from value claims ("Rape victims are more important than a free press") and treat some value claims ("Television is an important literary genre") as what they call "value-object claims" (Zarefsky). "Historical/scientific claims" (Zarefsky) and "historical inference claims" (Church and Wilbanks 37) are sometimes used to identify a particular kind of claim of fact ("The Battle of the Little Big Horn was a military victory, not a massacre").

falls within the concept of *support.* Sometimes, nothing more than your statement of the claim is required:

> **JERI:**   This university should not torture animals in the name of research.
>
> **MARY LOU:**   You're right!

We often put support alongside a claim without waiting to find out if others will demand it.

> **JERI:**   This university should not torture animals in the name of research, be-cause [support] wanton cruelty to living creatures is never acceptable.

It is also common to give reasons where the claim is understood but not spoken. In their conversation, Jeri might just say, "Animals have rights against unnecessary suffering," and Mary Lou will understand from the context that it is a claim about university research. In more complex situations, where disagreement is expressed or anticipated, support of more explicit kinds is used. We will discuss the following:

Evidence   We can strengthen a claim and increase its potential for adherence if we add to it examples, statistics, or testimony, the three broad categories of *evidence.* This is discussed in Chapter 7.

Values   Claims are supported when they are identified with social *values*—generalized conceptions of what are desirable ends or ways of behaving—of the decision makers. Values are discussed in Chapter 8.

Credibility   Claims are more acceptable when the person making the claim, or the source reporting the claim, is regarded as credible, as believable, and worthy of adherence. *Credibility* is discussed in Chapter 9.

Argument

An *argument,* in our usage, is a single unit of argumentation comprising a claim and its support. Both claim and support may be explicitly stated or one or both may be implied but understood by the persons participating in the argumentation process. To qualify as an argument, the support must potentially provide justification to relevant decision makers to grant adherence to the claim.

A caution is necessary here. In English usage, *argument* can also refer to the open expression of conflict, as in, "My roommate and I had a terrible argument last night." In fact, in Western thought arguments and argumentation are often associated with competition, a form of fighting. For example, the word "trial," used to identify a proceeding involving legal arguments, started out meaning a combat or physical torture in which the winner or survivor would be seen as having the correct side in the conflict.

The idea of argumentation functioning in a competitive forum where the desire to win might overcome the search for the best answer has always been troubling. It was this concern that led Socrates to defend the dialectical approach to decisions and the need to wait for the discovery of truth. While the inherent uncertainty pervading the domain of argumentation makes Socrates' position unworkable, as we explain below, the competitive (some say masculine) character of many decision making situations continues to be a source of concern. We discuss other rationales in argumentation that are intended to diminish the competitive impulse in Chapter 3.

Our discussion will take such concerns into account by observing that people can use arguments in a cooperative search for the best decisions even when the search involves competition. Wayne Brockriede acknowledged this perspective when he spoke of arguers as lovers.

An angry exchange may well involve arguments, but the term *argument* as we use it is the antithesis of angry exchanges. For good arguments to emerge, people usually must wait until the anger is diminished. Labor–management negotiations are often delayed by what are called "cooling-off periods," in the hope of improving the quality of arguments exchanged. In this book, argument includes the argument a lawyer prepares for a trial, the argument supporting a scientific principle, or the argument of a friend that you should join her in studying for the test.

Daniel O'Keefe explains two meanings of argument other than the confusion with angry exchanges. What he calls argument1 "is a kind of utterance or a sort of communicative act" (121). This speaks of an argument as a product as we have just defined it. What O'Keefe calls argument2 is a communicative process, what we have defined as argumentation. Argumentation (argument2) refers to the ongoing process of advancing, rejecting, modifying, and accepting claims, while argument (argument1) refers to a single claim with its support. Our interest is in arguments functioning within argumentation in whatever context, ranging from informal interpersonal communication to such complex situations as law, politics, religion, business, or science.

Criticism

Argumentation involves criticism of claims with the open potential for modifying them. Dogmatic defense of positions is not argumentation, it is fanaticism. Criticism involves refutation, which is discussed in Chapters 10 and 11. Stephen Toulmin says that the test of an argument is its ability to "stand up to criticism" (9).

The recording industry, confronted with what it perceived to be an alarming increase in file-swapping (obtaining digital recordings of music online without paying either the artist or the production company), decided to fight back. The arguments were typical of a commercial enterprise that finds its product being obtained without payment: they offer a product in the expectation of making a profit; if customers can get their product without paying them, they will soon be out of business; therefore, they must stop this "stealing" of their assets by calling on the law. Napster, a company that allowed music to be obtained free over the Internet, was mostly outlawed by the courts. Then, the music industry announced a program of individual lawsuits against hundreds of file-swappers.

The arguments seemed to embody the commonsense thinking of free enterprise, and should have resulted in less file-swapping and more profits for the industry, but that did not happen. On the contrary, according to Jenny Eliscu in the August 7, 2003, issue of *Rolling Stone* magazine (15–16), the music industry experienced a severe drop in sales, 600 record stores were closed, and 1,300 label staffers were laid off. Instead of taking a traditional line of argument, Eliscu reported, the music industry should have realized they were facing an entirely new situation calling for a new way of thinking. Her example was Apple's iTunes, a program that sells downloads for ninety-nine cents apiece. At the time of her report, more than five million songs had been sold even within the restricted market of people using Apple computers. Thus, the criticism of the music industry arguments came in two forms: a pragmatic test showing negative results, and the presence of what might be a better alternative.

This example of argumentation comes from the world of business, where criticism is frequently centered on results such as earnings, market share, and product viability. In more formal spheres such as law and science, complex rules often determine the character of criticism. Argumentation in interpersonal spheres is based heavily on cooperation and the compromising of personal preferences.

As we use it, criticism does not mean excessive fault-finding or hurtful negative comments. Our sense of criticism is the antithesis of that behavior, just as argument, as we intend it in this context, is the opposite of angry exchanges.

Elements of Critical Decision Making

A critical decision is one that survives the test of a relevant set of criteria. Choice is made on the basis of clearly articulated arguments that have been held open to refutation or disagreement. It stands up to criticism, and it remains open to further criticism as long as possible. When the arguments change, when new arguments occur, when the criteria for decision change, the decision changes accordingly.

President Bush's case for war against Iraq actually was based on three lines of argument, according to Ben McGrath of the *New Yorker* (July 28, 2003, 27–31): "The nature and history of the Iraqi regime; the security of the United States; and the idea that a liberated Iraq would have a transformative effect on the region" (28). When, months after Iraq had been mostly subdued, there was still no evidence of weapons of mass destruction that would have threatened U.S. security, the debate had to adjust accordingly. The Bush administration declared that the other two lines of reasoning fully justified going to war, but others insisted on arguing the point, claiming the war had been a mistake. And, a further discussion arose over the possibility that the claims about Iraq's threat to U.S. security had been exaggerated intentionally in order to win public adherence to the war decision.

Critical decisions are the opposite of those we make unconsciously, impulsively, dogmatically. Responses to the failure to find dangerous weapons in Iraq tended to come instantly and were mostly divided along partisan lines. Republicans were inclined to dismiss the absence of weapons of mass destruction saying, "We got rid of that monster Saddam Hussein, and that's good." Democrats were inclined to claim, "The country was misled into believing Iraq might have nuclear weapons, and if getting rid of Saddam Hussein was the basis for war, there are a lot of other tyrants in the world who should be thrown out and we cannot go to war over all of them, so why did we pick on Saddam?" All of these claims carried the smell of dogmatism: those in favor of the war defended it regardless of changing justifications, and those opposed to war took every opportunity to condemn it. Possibly, there was uncritical decision making going on.

However, critical decision making does not demand certain knowledge or unanimous agreement. Within the domain of argumentation, questions have no sure answers to which all reasonable people must agree. When we say decisions must stand up to criticism, we mean that before action is taken, people must engage in a critical process and act, when the time comes, on the results of that process. While there is no single way this must be done, we will explain the process by focusing on some of the more important elements: *toleration of uncertainty, internal dialogue, dialectic, rhetoric,* and the *willingness to act* even though no certain answers or unanimous agreement have been produced.

Toleration of Uncertainty

To call decision making critical is to say that the claims of argumentation are inherently open to ongoing criticism. Decisions must be made and actions taken on them without knowing for certain that they are correct. In religion, politics, science, ethics, business, law, government, education, and many more pivotal areas of your life, you must decide and act without being able to wait until you are certain.

In ancient Greece, Socrates was sure that an absolute truth was out there waiting to be discovered, but he also recognized how very difficult it was to find. His solution was simply to continue searching, indefinitely if necessary, until absolute truth was found. Philosophers may have the luxury of an endless search for truth, but you rarely do.

Those human tasks that must be accomplished through reason within a context of *uncertainty* lie within the domain of argumentation. To engage in argumentation is to tolerate uncertainty.

Uncertainty Is Pervasive   As you proceed in the study of argumentation, you will probably be surprised to find uncertainty so pervasive. Throughout modern times, many scholars (followers of Socrates) have refused to teach argumentation because it operated in arenas of uncertainty, and they were interested only in the absolute. As those issues once thought to be susceptible to certain answers have proven to be, at best, uncertain, the study of argumentation has become increasingly important. Physicist F. David Peat characterizes the history of science in the twentieth century as moving from certainty to uncertainty. "We have left the dream of absolute certainty behind. In its place each of us must now take responsibility for the uncertain future" (213).

Uncertainty is partly the result of the constantly changing world we inhabit. The universe is expanding, the world continues to experience forces that push continents apart and mountains up and down, and living organisms are born, live, and die in continuous change. Michael Shnayerson and Mark J. Plotkin report that in 1969 the U.S. surgeon general declared, "We can close the books on infectious diseases," because of the emergence of antibiotics. But thirty years later a new surgeon general announced, "We are seeing a global resurgence of infectious diseases," because of the development of drug-resistant bacteria (11).

Critical decisions once respected can, under ongoing criticism, fall into disrespect. Until 2002, says Clifford J. Rosen, "physicians routinely urged their female patients to take hormone replacement therapy . . . at menopause, not only to protect against osteoporosis but to ward off other age-related health problems . . . including heart disease and dementia." Then, in 2003, a report from the Women's Health Initiative claimed that hormone therapy caused small increases in breast cancer, heart attack, stroke, and blood clots, "and that the risks of the therapy outweighed its modest benefits . . . " (75). Medicine cannot wait until some treatment is proved absolutely correct before using it to try to save lives. Ask your physician to identify a medicine or medical procedure that is absolutely safe and effective.

As in all other argumentation situations, medical researchers develop the best arguments possible, subject them to the best criticism possible, and then go ahead even though they are not absolutely certain the selected treatment is the right thing to do.

Language Is Inherently Ambiguous   Another source of uncertainty is the inherently ambiguous character of language. By language, we usually mean words, but the same principles apply to all signs, pictures, objects, mathematical symbols, musical sounds, and anything else that facilitates communication.

One of the things that allowed people in the past to think they could find certainty was the belief that language could convey precise meaning. They thought meaning was derived from a tight link between language and "reality," (the presumed but erroneous belief in the regularity of the universe). Aristotle's idea of *fallacies* (argument practices that are persuasive but illogical), which is still influential today, rests largely on such assumptions about language (Hamblin 50–63). Aristotle believed in language precision. He noted how many times argumentation is frustrated by ambiguity, frequently by people who intentionally hope to mislead, and so he labeled those instances as fallacies or sophistical refutations. Aristotle's system loses much of its force today, when we find language cannot be made as precise as the system requires. Language is inherently ambiguous.

Language is a collection of noises, movements, and marks people utter or set down on a surface. Language is not connected to things "in the world;" it is simply a tool people use to interact with each other. These noises and marks become language only when we use them as such, and that use defines their nature (Kent 11). Words do not have meaning; people have meaning that they try to share through language. When you seek to communicate, there are at least three meaning processes at work: (1) the meaning you intend to communicate; (2) the conventional meanings stored in dictionaries or other data bases; (3) the interpretations made by the people with whom you are communicating (Anderson and Meyer 48). The artist Richard Schmid says, "I paint what I see, but the real subject is the artist's perception, not the thing itself" (Chapman 22). A work of art is a part of language just as words are. The subject of language is one's perception, not reality.

The idea of certain language practices always being fallacious does not square with contemporary thought. Language is a human product generated through social interaction and the assignment of meanings. You make interpretations of language that are based on your understanding, and you make guesses about how others will interpret your language.

In your family, neighborhood, religious institutions, and among close friends and coworkers, you can make quite good guesses as to the meaning your words will be given because all are using a similar interpretation strategy. However, the inherent ambiguity of language, its unique meaning for each person, means that your guesses will never be perfect (Kent 31).

Take, for example, the concept of equal opportunity. In the debate over affirmative action, everybody supports equal opportunity. But for some, equal opportunity means creating an even playing field by giving added weight to those whose opportunities have been degraded by past discrimination. To others, equal opportunity means letting each individual be judged by the same criteria without discrimination in any direction. There is no single, correct meaning for equal opportunity.

We do not have to use highly abstract words such as equal opportunity to illustrate the ambiguity of language. Consider these apparently simple words, "A well regulated militia being necessary to the security of a free State, the right of the people to keep and bear arms shall not be infringed." When this statement, the Second Amendment to the Constitution of the United States, is said within a constitutional law context its interpretation is quite different from that used by the National Rifle Association (NRA) or a citizens' volunteer militia. The Supreme Court has put emphasis on the word *militia* and concludes that it applies to such state government sponsored organizations as the National Guard in opposition to a federal standing army (*U.S. v Miller*). The NRA and some constitutional historians look mostly at the words *the right of the people to keep and bear arms,* and conclude it means government cannot deny individuals' possession of firearms (Levy, 134). Whether the word *arms* includes clearly military weapons such as assault rifles is also disputed.

The Attraction of Certainty Is Powerful   History documents a search for truth and certainty. Philosopher John Dewey observed that our society is obsessed with a quest for certainty (Dewey). Whether it is a genetic characteristic of humans or something learned, people deplore doubt. It is an uncomfortable state of mind from which people seek to free themselves (Peirce 7–18). We like to think of science and mathematics as bedrock, certain reality. "We demand truths that are absolute, leaders who are blameless and doctors who are omniscient" (Salzer B5). We expect arguments that are true and valid for everyone.

Perelman and Olbrechts-Tyteca note that René Descartes, the influential seventeenth-century philosopher and mathematician, declared that anything that was not certain was false. "It was this philosopher who made the self-evident the mark of reason, and considered rational only those demonstrations which, starting from clear and distinct ideas, extended, by means of apodictic [incontestable] proofs, the self-evidence of the axioms to the derived theorems" (1). Descartes believed his certainty was divine because God would not mislead us. His ideas struck a chord with Europeans who had suffered long and terrible wars and were desperate for something secure to hold to (Kagan et al. 467–78).

The attraction of certainty seems stronger than ever today. Many of the most important debates are predicated on the presumption of self-evident and absolute rights. There is a religious fervor behind many claims, and those who disagree are characterized as evil. Issues of abortion, genetic engineering, in vitro fertilization, welfare, nuclear power, environmental protection, euthanasia, prayer in schools, world government, and many more are frequently approached in such absolute terms. An Internet search for "animal rights" reveals a debate deeply based on absolutes. The New Jersey Animal Rights Alliance recognizes the role of language in argumentation by demanding that the word *pet* be removed from the English language. They will not be satisfied that animals are being protected until nobody has a pet.

Herbert E. Meyer, a former official with the Central Intelligence Agency, believes that if political scientists would simply codify social scientific knowledge as he thinks physicists do, they could "separate true insights from false ones." Lacking such certain knowledge, Meyer writes, causes voters to "end up confused and disoriented, making decisions based on varying perceptions of reality." He wants an operator's manual for voters that would identify such maxims as, "You cannot make the poor rich by making the rich poor" (Meyer). His maxims sound a lot like value statements based on his perception of reality. He turns out to be like most of us in wanting certainty, but only on his terms.

By entering the domain of argumentation, you acknowledge the inherent uncertainty of most issues you will address. Doing so will free you from the fruitless search for certainty and will reduce the frequency with which you predicate arguments on the assertion of absolute rights or principles.

The Future is Inherently Uncertain   The primary reason for uncertainty in argumentation stems from the fact that decision making invariably commits you now to actions to be carried out in the future. Argumentation comes into play when you must choose, and choice inherently involves uncertainty. It may be uncertainty about future consequences of what you do today, future preferences, or how you will feel about today's actions tomorrow (Simonson 158). No prediction seems shakier than the weather forecast, but people seem mesmerized by the deceptive precision with which reports are cast. People tell each other, "It will go up to 30 tomorrow," because that is what was reported. Tomorrow, when the temperature reaches only 25, we have already forgotten our misplaced credulity and talk again about what will happen tomorrow. It would not hurt you to remind yourself about the uncertainty of the future by saying, "The best argument available claims it will be 30 tomorrow, but we know that is not a certainty."

Argumentation and Critical Decision Making describes a process by which you seek the best possible choices within a context of uncertainty and ambiguity. Most of the decision making people do occurs in this context. From trying to understand how your own mind works to characterizing the universe, from deciding what to do on Saturday night to pondering to what to do with your life, you engage in argumentation and critical decision making. The better you use the process, the better you are at making decisions. But unless you are genuinely willing to open your mind to alternative ideas (to become uncertain about the best decision) and accept the inevitable uncertainty of the outcome, you cannot make critical decisions.

Critical Thinking—The Internal Dialogue

A second element of critical decision making is critical thinking. While argumentation is a social process (audience-centered), it involves engaging individuals in making up their minds about how to act through communication with other people. Many people speak of critical thinking alone, as if it were an end in itself. But critical thinking that is uncoupled from behavior has little value. Argumentation theory asserts that critical thinking is one important part of the larger process of making critical decisions. There may be times when you are satisfied simply to think critically, but we are talking about the incessant obligation to make a decision and act on it.

The tension between critical thinking and the urgency of decision making is highlighted by a proposal by George H. Atkinson to put scientists into the Department of State so that foreign policy decisions can be based on scientific findings. He mentions issues such as HIV-AIDS, global warming, and dirty bombs. However, he acknowledges that scientists and diplomats are fundamentally different. Scientists are among the best practitioners of critical thinking, but they are not widely known for their expertise in making tough policy decisions. Scientists, says Atkinson, "would need to recognize that State Department decisions are propelled by the political process, not necessarily scientific data. . . .When ideology comes up against scientific understanding, it can be very frustrating" (Lehrman 26).

The term *critical thinking* calls attention to the fact that who you are, how your mind works, and what roles you play in society are inextricably linked. Self-awareness or reflection upon your own thinking and open-mindedness toward others become essential features of critical thinking (Millman 48–49). Such phrases as "sensitive to context," "reflective," "thinking appropriate to a particular mode or domain of thinking," and "to assess the force of reasons in the context in which reasons play a role" are other ways to characterize critical thinking.

Many scholars argue that critical thinking means to follow the rules of formal logic, or at least to avoid fallacies that often turn on logical errors. Courses in logic are taught with the purpose of improving critical thinking. However, even those who have studied formal logic find it difficult to follow it in their thought processes. "Over the last 40 years there has been a great deal of work in cognitive psychology on people's logical reasoning abilities. . . . The conclusion of this work was that in many areas people seem unable to reason logically" (Oaksford and Chater 2 173–4). This should not be surprising since logic is the "calculus of certainty" and it was not designed to manage our thinking in the uncertain domain of argumentation. What is needed, say Mike Oaksford and Nick Chater, is a calculus of uncertainty that they identify as probability theory (13). Michael Scriven has suggested a theory of informal logic in which he rejects most aspects of formal logic in order to provide a rationale for critical thinking (21–45). At this stage of our discussion, it is enough to say that critical thinking employs the same process of argumentation that we describe throughout this book.

Critical thinking is the *personal* phase of critical decision making. It is the first step in the conscious reconciliation between your inner thoughts and your social experience. As we explain in Chapter 2, critical decision making requires us to work with our individual thinking as well as our interaction with others in developing and testing arguments. To rely totally on either your own thoughts or social influence is dangerous. If individuals engaging in argumentation are not willing and able to think critically, they will be unable to participate effectively in critical decision making.

When we say that critical thinking is the personal phase of critical decision making, we are not suggesting that it is all that different from the social act of argumentation. Indeed, research suggests that critical thinking is really a mini-debate you carry on with yourself. What is often mistaken for private thought is more likely an "internalized conversation" (Mead 173), an "internal dialogue" (Mukarovsky), or an "imagined interaction" (Gotcher and Honeycutt 1–3). All of these concepts refer essentially to the same thing, which we will call an internal dialogue.

The idea is this: you are able to carry on a conversation in your mind that involves both a "self" that represents you and "others" who stand for those people, real or imagined, with whom you wish to try out an argument. In a sense, all of our communication behaviors are pretested in social simulations (internal dialogue) prior to being shared in actual social situations (Wenburg and Wilmot 21). It may be misleading, in fact, to distinguish between imagined and actual interactions. During any conversation, you may find yourself doing some of the dialogue mentally while some of it may be spoken aloud, and, at any moment, you may not be able to say with confidence which is which. Some societies make no such distinction (Regal 61–66).

In critical thinking, you become keenly aware of your internal dialogues. You identify and put aside the tendency to think only of how to justify your thoughts while denigrating the thinking of others. Instead, you must apply critical tests, reflect on what you are doing, and try to open your mind to the potential weaknesses in your position while truly looking for other and better ways of thinking. Ian Mitroff calls it "smart thinking" and says if you are adept at it you "know how to cut through complex issues, ask the right questions, and solve the right problems." He concludes, "The ability to spot the right problems, frame them correctly, and implement appropriate solutions to them is the true competitive edge that will separate the successful individuals, organizations, and societies from the also-rans" (Mitroff 6).

It is critical thinking that makes you able to become a working partner in the next element of critical decision making: *dialectic*.

Dialectic—The External Dialogue

Dialectic is an ancient process that is very much on the minds of contemporary scholars. As an element of critical decision making, *dialectic* is the social dialogue in which people seek to come to understanding by opening themselves to the thinking of others with an interest in learning and changing. Critical thinking is the internal dialogue and dialectic is an external, interpersonal or intertextual dialogue (Montgomery and Baxter 2). Now, instead of an imagined conversation, you actually interact with one or more other people. The objective is to continue the development of your own thoughts by learning those of others, combining personal and social influences in a creative error correction process.

Aristotle defined dialectic as the counterpart of rhetoric—a companion in the critical decision making process, a philosophical disputation. He believed that people are inherently rational: "The function of man is an activity of the soul which follows or implies a rational principle" *(Nicomachean Ethics* 1098a).

In dialectic, individuals engage in conversation, one person advances a claim tentatively, seeks to point out the logic behind it, and then responds to the probing questions of the others. "Dialectic proceeds by question and answer, not, as rhetoric does, by continuous exposition" (Kennedy in Aristotle. *On Rhetoric* 26). Michael Leff identifies four points of contrast between dialectic and rhetoric: (1) issues in dialectic are more general and abstract than those in rhetoric; (2) dialectic deals with the relationship of propositions to one another in a search for rationality, while rhetoric relates propositions to situations following social norms; (3) dialectic proceeds through question and answer with participants seeking to persuade one another, where in rhetoric there is relatively uninterrupted discourse in an effort to persuade an audience; and (4) "dialectic employs unadorned, technical language, whereas rhetoric accommodates and embellishes language for persuasive purposes" (57).

William Isaacs describes dialectic as dialogue enabling a "free flow of meaning, which has the potential of transforming the power relationships among the people concerned" (395). His program, he says, can help business organizations change their patterns of behavior in productive ways. In many meetings, says Isaacs, people feel themselves or their actions being challenged and this generates a tendency toward defensiveness. However, in dialogue, Isaacs argues, one has the choice to *"defend* or *suspend:"* to suspend one's defensiveness in order to listen and learn from others (365).

Barbara M. Montgomery and Leslie A. Baxter discuss dialectic in relation to personal relationships. They identify four core concepts typical to dialectical scholarship: *contradiction, change, praxis,* and *totality* (3–12). While there are specific disagreements over the details of these elements, we can supply elementary explanations. *Contradiction* suggests the interdependent interrelationship of opposites in our interactions. "In general, phenomena are opposites if they are actively incompatible and mutually negate one another definitionally, logically, or functionally" (Montgomery and Baxter 4). It is during the dialectical stage of critical decision making that issues (statements identifying significant clashes or opposition in points of view) are identified. *Change* calls attention to the motion and process influences on our interactions over time. *Praxis* refers to what people say to each other, most commonly the stories we share. Narrative is fundamental to human interaction and it is through stories that we become who we are at any moment. *Totality* reminds us that contradictions cannot be discussed apart from other contradictions and that contradiction cannot be separated from time, space, and cultural environments.

Some contemporary scholars suggest that failure to understand and engage in dialectic is at the heart of some of our most painful difficulties. They suggest that the dogmatic rights-based diatribes that too often replace argumentation demonstrate the absence of dialectic in our society. We need to be aware, say Floyd W. Matson and Ashley Montagu,

> . . . that the end of human communication is not to *command* but to *commune;* and that knowledge of the highest order (whether of oneself, or of the other) is to be sought and found not through detachment but through connection, not by objectivity but by inter-subjectivity, not in a state of estranged aloofness but in something resembling an act of love (6).

Hamblin suggests that the difficulty in identifying fallacies in argumentation reflects an unhealthy drive for certainty. "What is, above all, necessary," says Hamblin, "is to de-throne deduction from its supposed pre-eminent position as a provider of certainty" (250). He would replace it with dialectic through which people can determine the specific demands of the question and thereby identify what are truly misuses of logic.

Richard H. Gaskins says that argumentation runs into trouble when debates boil down to an inability to prove any position beyond question, resulting in decisions being made not on solid, critical grounds, but by default (1–11). He proposes more effective use of dialectic through which values, presumptions, and criteria can be worked out in advance (240–72).

Derek Edwards and Jonathan Potter argue that psychological research into such human cognitive behavior as perception, memory, language and mental representation, knowledge, and reasoning must proceed from the fact that these processes are socially and culturally embedded (14). They are to be understood through an examination not of the individual mind (which is all but impossible to examine) but in naturally occurring conversation, an informal dialectic. "The phenomena of thought and reasoning, of mind and memory, are best understood as culturally formed, socially shaped and defined, constituted in talk and text. . . ." Cognitive processes, they say, " . . . are ideas generated within cultures, conceptions of sense, action and motive that people invent to mediate their dealings with each other and to engage in social forms of life" (18).

Rhetoric

The fourth element in critical decision making, building on uncertainty and the internal and external dialogues, is *rhetoric.* Aristotle defined rhetoric as the "ability [of a person, group, society, or culture] in each [particular] case to see [perceive] the available means of persuasion" (*On Rhetoric* 36). To perceive the available means of persuasion is to understand an issue from all points of view and ways of thinking. It is not necessary to use all of the available means, just take them into account (13).

While the meaning of rhetoric has varied dramatically in the almost 2,500 years since Aristotle, we will discuss its contemporary relevance to argumentation and critical decision making. There are three key rhetorical elements we need to explain here: audience, probability, and proof.

Audience   Rhetoric is concerned with people, how they think, act, and communicate. When we say our perspective of argumentation is audience-centered, we are saying it is a rhetorical perspective. In dialectic, the focus is on the soundness of reasoning and availability of support for claims. In rhetoric, the focus is on the bases with which people will grant or deny adherence to claims. As we will see in the discussion of proof, people resort to a wide variety of bases in making up their minds.

In his discussion of rhetoric, Aristotle observed rhetoric occurring throughout society: deciding on public policy, resolving legal disputes, and developing and strengthening the values that underlie most arguments. He noticed that different people respond differently to arguments, so he talked about how rhetoric can be adapted to the young, middle-aged, and elderly; to the wealthy and the powerful; to those in all stations of society.

Aristotle divided knowledge into two groups: scientific demonstration, which he believed was not audience-centered, and rhetoric, which dealt with those issues not susceptible to certain demonstration and thus turning on human judgment. Today, scholars are much less likely to accept this division. Scientists of all kinds are more inclined to see their work as audience-centered, and we now read of rhetorical analyses of almost all aspects of scientific endeavor. Thomas Kuhn speaks of scientific revolutions in discussing his contention that science rests on paradigms or groups of people with common models, perspectives, problems, and procedures. When paradigms come into conflict, they work it out, says Kuhn, by using what is essentially political rhetoric.

Probability   As we have said, argumentation deals with those tasks that require decision under uncertainty. In a condition of uncertainty, the best we can seek is probability. We need to talk about two different meanings for the word *probability*.

In statistics and other forms of mathematical analyses of frequencies or chance, objective calculations can be made of the probability with which a certain phenomenon will occur or the probability that the phenomenon that did occur was the result of pure chance. For example, serious gamblers can say with high confidence the frequency with which certain combinations of numbers will appear on dice or roulette. Weather forecasters can calculate the frequency with which certain weather patterns will occur. Experimenters can say that their results could have been explained by chance alone, say, once in a thousand times.

Rhetorical probability is a more general concept that embraces mathematical probability as well as what might be called human or subjective probability. Early research into decision making revealed that people do not necessarily stick to mathematical probability even when it is explained to them and guaranteed to produce greater profits (Edwards and Tversky 71–89). Psychologists coined the term "subjective probability" to describe the experience in which, for example, people were told to bet on a single outcome because it was certain to produce a victory where all other options would not. In spite of this information, people varied their bets because they *felt* like doing so. Feelings, intuitions, values, and emotions are part of rhetorical probability.

Economists Andrew W. Lo and Richard H. Thaler note that people are presumed to behave rationally when making such decisions as investing money. For example, before buying securities, you should "maximize utility" by seeking to receive the most satisfaction for your money, and rationally that means paying the "right price" based on the intrinsic value of the stock you are buying. Price-earnings ratios, charts of past performance, and the behavior of factors that influence stock performance can be studied to produce mathematical probabilities of future values. But, say Lo and Thaler, people regularly reject such rational probabilities to act instead on, "behavioral assumptions such as overreaction, overconfidence, loss aversion, and other human foibles that each of us exhibits with alarming regularity (Lo and Thaler 10–13)." They conclude that markets are not rational in the traditional economic sense. Investors ultimately act on the basis of rhetorical (subjective) probability.

Rhetorical probability works two ways: the extent to which one person is willing to advance a claim and be held responsible for it, and the extent to which people are willing to accept and act upon a claim. In critical decision making, both of these probability judgments apply.

We have said that argumentation deals with the uncertain, but there is no law that says you cannot *say* you are certain about a claim. People do it all the time. We use such words as "absolutely," "certainly," "unquestionably," or "without a doubt" to describe our claims. If your claim really cannot be advanced with objective certainty, how can you say it is so? Because you are not describing the mathematical probability of your claim or some other measure of reality, you are describing the extent to which you are willing to be associated with the claim and be held responsible for the outcome. You may say that mathematically the safest bet on the typical game of craps is the "come" or "pass," but the outcome is still uncertain, it is a gamble, and your certainty will likely disappear if you are asked to guarantee a high bet. The mathematical probability has not changed, just your stake in the outcome.

Consider, for example, the decision to drop atomic bombs on two Japanese cities during World War II. There were scientific probabilities about whether the bombs would work and whether they would cause extensive destruction. There were tactical probabilities about whether the Japanese would surrender once the bombs were dropped, or if they were about to surrender anyhow. The alternative, dropping the bombs on a deserted area while Japanese leaders looked on, was rejected as unlikely (improbable) to cause surrender. There was the military probability of how many lives would be lost on both sides if an invasion of the Japanese home islands occurred. There was the moral probability whether history would judge the dropping of the bombs to be justified.

The debate over this decision continues. There is sharp disagreement on most of these questions. President Harry S. Truman, however, could not wait a half-century to make the decision. He had little time and knew he would live forever with the consequences of the decision. He committed himself to those consequences, and that is rhetorical probability.

On the fifty-eighth anniversary of the dropping of the bombs, Nicholas D. Kristof reported in the *New York Times* that "there's an emerging consensus: we Americans have blood on our hands" (August 5, 2003). But he argued in reply that the consensus is "profoundly mistaken" and that the bombs helped end the war.

Proof   Mathematical calculations and experimental demonstrations constitute proof for some scientific probability claims. Rhetorical proof, which includes such scientific proof, is more complex.

Aristotle included three forms of proof in his discussion of rhetoric. *Logos* represented the use of reasoning taking the form of logic as support for claims. In Aristotle's system, examples served as the rhetorical equivalent to induction, and the *enthymeme* (a rhetorical syllogism) served as rhetorical deduction. In a symbolic format, induction and deduction are forms of logic that work on problems outside the domain of argumentation. A pure induction requires itemization of 100 percent of the elements under consideration. A rhetorical induction or example requires sufficient instances to satisfy the audience. Simply demonstrating that it satisfies the rules of internal validity proves a symbolic deduction or syllogism. A rhetorical deduction or enthymeme depends upon its link to established beliefs, values, and ways of thinking already held by the audience.

Pathos, for Aristotle, included the feelings, emotions, intuitions, sympathies, and prejudices that people bring to decisions. It suggested the fact that people accept or reject claims and make or refuse to make decisions on the basis of the values that are connected to the arguments.

Ethos identified the extent to which people are inclined to go along with an argument because of who expresses it. In contemporary research, ethos is seen as part of credibility.

In the chapters that follow, we will discuss the various forms of support that are available to prove your claims. The important point to remember here is that rhetorical proof is addressed to people (audience-centered) and the quality of proof is measured by the extent to which the appropriate decision makers find it sufficient for their needs.

Acting within Uncertainty

The final element in critical decision making is the willingness and ability to act even when you are uncertain. Philosophers are adept at thorough criticism and dialectic. They are able to express themselves with rhetorical effectiveness. But often they take the position of Socrates and refuse to act until they have achieved certainty. The result is that they are not usually identified as action-oriented people.

In many college curricula, critical thinking is taught alone, without being subsumed under critical decision making. That approach to critical thinking is similar to the philosophers mentioned above. You may have well-developed critical skills, but unless you have learned how to act on them, they are of little value in a practical sense.

We come then, in this final element of critical decision making, back to where we began—the tolerance of uncertainty. It is not sufficient to tolerate uncertainty if you allow yourself to be frozen by doubt and end up like Hamlet. Critical decision making includes ultimately the willingness to make and act upon your decision, knowing that you may later regret it, or knowing, like President Truman, that history might condemn you more than a half-century later.

Conclusion

We have introduced you to the domain of argumentation by identifying the elements of argumentation and critical decision making. In argumentation a key term is adherence, which characterizes the audience-centered focus of argumentation on the appropriate decision makers, who have also been defined. Claims, the points or propositions you offer for others' consideration and adherence, the support or materials provided to help others understand and subscribe to your claims, and the definition of argument as the intersection of a claim and its support have been discussed. Arguments serve to resolve issues of fact, value, and policy. Criticism, the give and take of making your claims and noting the weaknesses in alternative claims, has been explained as a key feature of argumentation.

To participate in critical decision making, you must understand that you will necessarily be working with uncertain knowledge, and you must keep your mind open to alternatives and resist the temptation to rush to belief. Critical thinking is a concept that describes reflective, open-minded attention to your own thinking and the search for alternatives and complete information. Dialectic and rhetoric are counterparts in the development of critical decisions. Dialectic is the question–answer process through which you and others inquire, seek to understand the values and criteria appropriate to your decision, and entertain various points of view. Rhetoric, on the other hand, is the process of persuasion through which claims are presented to decision makers (audience) with the appropriate proof to help them understand and grant adherence.

Finally, we have said that to be a part of critical decision making you must be willing not only to tolerate uncertainty but to take action in its presence. In summary, we have said that argumentation provides the mechanism that mediates the tension between individual judgment (your mind) and social judgment (your culture) to bring the most powerful and relevant criteria to bear on any decision. The product is social (audience-centered) critical decision making.

PROJECT

Read the editorials in one issue of a newspaper and answer these questions for each:
a. What adherence is sought from the reader?
b. Who are the appropriate decision makers? Why?
c. What claims does the editorial make?
d. What support is provided for the claims?
e. What criticism can you make of the arguments?

CHAPTER

2 Critical Appraisal of Argumentation

KEY TERMS

criteria
critical decision
commonsense
reasonableness
belief systems
world views
starting points
interpretation strategies

facts
probabilities
commonplaces
spheres
ultimate purpose
patterns
interaction

When you interview for a job, you and the interviewer are engaged in the critical appraisal of argumentation. The position announcement should set the broad *criteria* that will be used to judge your application, and the interview will flesh them out. A help-wanted ad that appeared in the *Salt Lake Tribune* for positions with KeyBank noted that, "Integrity is adhering to the highest standards of honesty, professionalism and ethical behavior in all that we do and is one of Key's core values." They go on to describe the client relations representative position:

> You will provide customer transaction services, process teller transactions, and balance daily work. Requires 1 year of work experience (preferably in customer service), good written/verbal communication abilities, basic math skills, ability to develop working knowledge of financial products/services, familiarity with computer/office equipment, and a high school diploma or equivalent.[1]

During your interview with KeyBank, they could well ask, "Why should we hire you?" This is an invitation for you to present arguments on your behalf, complementing those in your application. What will be the strongest arguments you can

---

[1] *The Salt Lake Tribune,* Sunday, September 19, 1999, F23.

make? At this stage, your best bet is to follow the criteria set out in the job announcement and argue the following: (1) I have 1 year of work experience (if it is customer service, point that out); (2) I have good written/verbal communication abilities; (3) I have basic math skills; (4) I have the ability to develop a working knowledge of financial products/services; (5) I have familiarity with computer/office equipment; (6) I have a high school diploma.[2]

If you can convince KeyBank of each of these points, and if they truly are the criteria being used to make this decision, it would be reasonable for them to hire you. It would be a *critical decision*. Of course, they could interview five people, all of whom meet these criteria. It would be reasonable to hire any one of them. So a critical decision does not mean resolution of uncertainty. It does not necessarily mean finding the one correct decision. It means selecting and applying a set of criteria designed to generate the best possible decision.

What will probably happen is this: during the interview, KeyBank will refine the criteria as you develop your arguments. They will try to make value judgments about the quality of your credentials compared to other applicants, and, before making a hiring decision, they will probably discuss the applicant pool with other colleagues to add their particular criteria.

Before a job offer is made, still other criteria may be applied, partly in response to arguments you make. For example, you might point out your understanding of integrity and your willingness and ability to meet this standard. While that was not a specific job requirement, the fact that KeyBank chose to say in their ad that integrity is one of their core values means that quality has importance for them in relation to this position.

In Chapter 1, we defined a critical decision as one that can survive the test of a relevant set of criteria, one that can stand up to *criticism*. We also said that argumentation and critical decision making involve choice in a context of uncertainty.

In this chapter, we will talk about how people apply criteria to arguments, and how they can use such criticism to increase the quality of their decisions even in the face of uncertainty. We introduce the term "reasonable" to describe the process through which arguments are tested and finally granted adherence because they rest on reasons and reasoning that reflect the standards of the sphere within which they are being critically examined. First, we will identify some of the forces that tend to reduce the reasonableness of decisions. Then we will give greater detail about how people make reasonable decisions.

Argumentation and Being Reasonable

Critical appraisal of argumentation applies to you in two interacting ways: (1) When you *present* an argument, the better you understand the way it will be evaluated, the

---

[2]If you have the equivalent of a high school diploma, you should come prepared with documentation in support of that argument.

stronger you can make it; (2) When you *evaluate* an argument, the better you understand the relevant criteria (tests for argument evaluation), the better (more critical) will be your decisions. These two points interact in the sense that presenters and evaluators of argumentation do their jobs best when they consciously operate within a common set of criteria (a sphere).

Why People Advance Unreasonable Arguments

What is an unreasonable argument? It is one that cannot stand up to critical appraisal, one that cannot survive criticism. People are skillful at rationalizing their beliefs and decisions—coming up with reasons is not the problem. The problem is coming up with reasons that survive the scrutiny of your own critical thinking and the dialectical and rhetorical interactions of others who are intent upon making good decisions rather than sticking tenaciously to whatever they believe or say. "We assign a moment to decision to dignify the process as a timely result of rational and conscious thought. But decisions are made of kneaded feelings; they are more often a lump than a sum" (Harris 143).

Beliefs Are Not Necessarily Reasonable

While it was said about the Communists of the old Soviet Union, it might be said of anyone, "They believe everything they can prove, and they can prove anything they believe." *The Wizard's First Rule* tells us, "Given proper motivations, almost anyone will believe almost anything. . . . They will believe a lie because they want to believe it's true, or because they are afraid it might be true" (Goodkind 560). While your beliefs are important and meaningful to you, they may not have come from a reasonable foundation or they may be applied in a way that cannot survive critical scrutiny.

Patrick Colm Hogan reports a variety of studies showing that beliefs operating in systems are behind a good deal of our tendency to conform to political and ideological positions even when the beliefs are quite untrue or at least without clear support (58–86). People develop fundamental beliefs during childhood that continue to influence their decisions throughout life. "They distort people's perceptions and even their memories, reforming individuals' experience in their image. For many years, cognitive scientists have been aware of a broad human tendency to reinterpret experience in conformity with basic beliefs . . ." (74).

Glenn D. Walters argues that criminal behavior can be best understood by examining the development of individuals' belief systems. He defines a belief system as a "group of interrelated convictions of truth or statements of perceived reality" (21). They involve, he says, not just cognitive elements but also include behavioral, sensory, motivational, and affective features. Walters says that beliefs are interactive both with the various internal elements just mentioned and with one's experience with the world. Beliefs are, says Walters, "more than what fills a person's head . . ." (21). To understand criminal behavior he says, we must understand, "that people construct their own realities and then proceed to defend these realities against alternative perspectives. Objective reality has no real value or meaning in this model . . ." (44).

Your beliefs function, as these authors suggest, in belief systems that we will call *world views*. It is from your world views that you experience stereotypes, prejudices, norms, folkways, language, and culture. World views are neither inherently reasonable nor unreasonable. They enable you to make it through life more comfortably. Having a common language is obviously important. So is sharing common narratives, scripts, or stories of how to go about your daily life: how to dress, eat, play, worship, form relationships, educate children, and care for the elderly. What you perceive as commonsense in any occasion is determined by your world views. You may have noticed, however, that your commonsense is different from that of, say, your parents or acquaintances from other parts of the world. You may feel that other people's commonsense is unreasonable; they may think the same of you.

Thinking Is Not Necessarily Reasonable

More than a half-century of psychological research supports the claim that people use a variety of biases and heuristics to guide their thinking and decision making in ways that depart from what rational theory would predict (Gilovich, Griffin & Kahneman 4–16). For example, thinking may be guided by facts that happen to be readily available or easy to access rather than those most significant to supporting your point. Your thoughts about a case at hand such as whether you should report a coworker you suspect of stealing will likely be shaped by how similar you think this case is to a stereotypical one that comes to mind. If you are asked to state the date on which George Washington became president of the United States, you might well start with some anchoring point that comes to mind, say the date of the Declaration of Independence, and then adjust the time of Washington's inauguration in relation to 1776. Your thinking may or not turn out to be correct (1789) depending on your anchor point. People presented with choice may well select on the basis of what is the most familiar—not really knowing any of the candidates for office, you may vote for one whose name looks familiar to you. Your familiarity could as easily come from reading about a serial killer as an accomplished public servant.

Thomas Gilovich and his colleagues report, "There is a long tradition of research . . . illustrating that people actively construe the meaning of a given task or stimulus . . . and that their own chronically accessible categories, habits, and experiences powerfully influence their construals . . ." (12). Moreover, people will deliberately use "less effortful procedures when the judgment is relatively unimportant and motivation is low" (16). Our thinking is irresistibly influenced by such survival needs as food, shelter, defense, and reproduction.

The Mind Is Not Necessarily Reasonable

Ever since Plato assumed a separation of mind and body, and Aristotle proclaimed human beings to be rational animals, scholars have operated on the assumption that our mind functions in an inherently logical way. Aristotle's rhetorical system is premised on the assumption that people are able to find truth, even when it is mixed in with a great deal of nonsense, because they have a rational capacity. To this day, some logicians, linguists, psycholinguists, and cognitive psychologists continue to claim that the human mind operates according to formal logical rules or probabilities (Braine and O'Brien; Oaksford and Chater).

In his 1637 *Discourse on Method,* René Descartes announced, "I think, therefore, I am," giving his support to the notion that the mind can be separated from the body so as to operate logically. In his 1994 book, *Descartes' Error,* Antonio R. Damasio, M. W. Allen Professor of Neurology and head of the Department of Neurology at the University of Iowa College of Medicine, says this about Descartes' claim: "The statement, perhaps the most famous in the history of philosophy . . . illustrates precisely the opposite of what I believe to be true about the origins of mind and about the relation between mind and body" (248). We should say, "I am, therefore I think," says Damasio. He claims the mind cannot be understood apart from a knowledge of neuroanatomy, neurophysiology, and neurochemistry. There is considerable evidence, says Damasio, that efforts to find an inherently logical function in the mind are doomed to failure.

Gerald M. Edelman, director of the Neurosciences Institute and chairman of the Department of Neurobiology at the Scripps Research Institute, agrees. He reports that people are physiological and social beings capable of thinking and feeling, but there is no evidence of a rationality of mind that can be separated from our totality as human beings.

Schizophrenia is defined by James H. Meador-Woodruff, M.D. of the University of Michigan as including dramatic hallucinations in which patients hear "voices that are clearly located outside of their heads, most often engaged in a running commentary on their thoughts and behaviors." While schizophrenia is a dramatic and rare example of how your mind can mislead you, it helps make the point that the mind is not inherently or reliably reasonable. The product of your mind may not stand up to criticism.

As you have grown up, your mind has developed so as to sort sensory stimuli you experience into meaningful units. In that way, your mind creates its own reality to serve your needs. But since your mind creates its own reality, no matter how helpful that may be, it could be seen as Philip Regal sees it, as an "illusion organ" (69). That means sometimes your reality could get you into trouble. In the summer of 1999, John F. Kennedy, Jr., his wife, and her sister died in a plane crash off Martha's Vineyard, Massachusetts. Investigation revealed that the plane dove straight into the water at a high speed, and no mechanical problems were discovered. Our friend, a retired colonel in the U.S. Marine Corps who started his flying career in World War II fighters, said what probably happened is that Kennedy's mind told him he was flying level even though the plane was on its downward course. "A pilot," our friend said, "must learn to ignore personal reality and stick totally with what the instruments say. Kennedy just didn't have enough instrument flight experience to be able to do that."

Social Influence Is Not Necessarily Reasonable

Solomon Asch reports experiments in which he asked people to judge the length of one line compared to a series of other lines. He adjusted the task until people judging alone made almost no errors. He then selected four experimenters who were instructed to announce an incorrect answer, and put them with a series of naive subjects who did not know the experimenters were being intentionally incorrect. One by one, the experimenters would announce an incorrect choice, and then the naive subject was asked to respond. Imagine the social pressure this placed on the naive subjects. They had just heard four apparently honest people give answers that seemed obviously wrong. In the research, about a third of the naive subjects chose to give the same incorrect answer rather than disagree with the others.

Some of these later said they actually saw the incorrect response as correct, while others said they just went along with the group, being unwilling to oppose the majority or deciding the majority must be right. In this instance, social influence moved people to doubt their personal judgment, which almost certainly would have produced a correct response. How many times have you abandoned what you thought was right when, one after another, your friends said you were wrong? How many times have you stubbornly insisted you were right in the face of unanimous opposition? Maybe you were. Maybe you weren't.

Characteristics of Reasonable Arguments

So, what makes one argument better, more sound, stronger, more reasonable than another argument? Why should appropriate decision makers be more influenced by one argument than another? From the examples we have just given, you should see that arguments derive their power or force either from the criteria already in the minds of the decision makers, or from criteria that emerge in the decision makers' minds during the course of the interaction.

When your arguments—claims and support—square directly with the criteria in the minds of the decision makers, the arguments will draw power from those criteria and thus be more influential. In contrast to past philosophical thought, arguments are not necessarily more powerful by virtue of their internal logical validity or by passing some scientific test of truth. As we will explain in this chapter, concepts of logical validity and scientific truth, *when they are part of the criteria decision makers apply,* will play a role in the appraisal of your arguments. But you cannot count on this process always happening.

If arguments are tested by criteria in the minds of decision makers, how does argumentation differ from persuasion in general? What makes argumentation different from what we see on TV, read on billboards, or hear from some fast-talking sales person? The answer is, first, that argumentation is a relatively distinct dimension of persuasion that includes many of the strategies found in ordinary advertising or political campaigning (Willbrand and Rieke, "Reason Giving" 57).

Second, argumentation is a *distinct* dimension of persuasion, in that people tend to use it when they want to make wise decisions, and the strategies used in argumentation tend to be different from other forms of persuasion. Arguments employ more of the forms of criteria that we discuss later in this chapter than do common persuasive messages, and argumentation occurs within spheres that demand such criteria, as we will discuss. Argumentation appeals to the reasonableness of the decision makers by consciously focusing on criteria that are carefully selected, subjected to criticism, publicly accessible, and open to continual reexamination. Many commentators on critical thinking and informal logic argue that *all* persuasion should be subjected to argumentative analysis. If this were done, they say, people would be less likely to be taken in by unreasonable persuasive efforts.

Argumentation serves as the process through which people seek to enhance the positive contributions of their personal reality while holding in abeyance its unreasonable tendencies. Argumentation is the process through which people take advantage of the positive influences in their society and culture while holding in abeyance the perilous social pressures that produce unreasonable behavior. By employing messages predicated upon carefully chosen and socially scrutinized criteria, argumentation becomes that form of persuasion dedicated to making the best possible decisions. This almost always means taking advantage of types of criteria and social processes that have proved helpful over the years in yielding reasonable decisions.

In the next section, we discuss some of those types of criteria that contribute to reasonableness. We explain the concept of spheres through which people acting together can demand reasonable arguments, and we will close by describing how spheres function to produce critical decisions. As you read this section, keep in mind that all these systems for argumentation depend upon the willingness and ability of the relevant decision makers to use them effectively.

The Bases of Reason in Argumentation

Argumentation is the product of centuries of evolution in social practices aimed at resolving or creating uncertainty. We try to resolve uncertainty by making wise decisions that cannot be held absolutely, and we create uncertainty by raising doubts about ideas that may no longer deserve support (Goodnight 215). During this evolution, people have developed a number of systematic practices designed to improve the quality of argumentation and the decisions it produces. In this section, we describe some of these processes. We identify some powerful concepts that provide the necessary common bonding for reasoned interaction to take place and that form a fundamental test of the strength of an argument.

Starting Points for Argumentation

Argumentation works by connecting that to which people already adhere with claims to which they are being asked to grant adherence. If they grant adherence to those claims, then the newly accepted claims can be used as the connectors to still other claims, leading finally to a decision. The energy or power that drives argumentation is found in people: that which they believe provides the foundation for that which they are asked to believe. In any argumentative interaction, then, some starting points (that to which participants already adhere) must be identified—those powerful concepts that will start the connecting process: language interpretation strategies, facts, presumptions, probabilities, and commonplaces.

A general focus for appraisal of arguments is to examine the nature and quality of the powerful concepts invoked. If they are mistaken—either not shared by all the relevant decision makers, or controversial—then the arguments that flow from them become suspect.

Language Interpretation Strategies   The most fundamental starting point is language and shared interpretation strategies. English is widely spoken in India because of the many years of British rule, and English is spoken in the United States for the same reason, but such sharing of a common language does not guarantee sufficient commonality for argumentation. With the development of calling centers in India, training sessions in speaking U.S. English are being conducted in India. The interactants will need to negotiate some common strategies for interpreting their common language before critical argumentation can occur.

Language is commonly referred to as human symbolic activity. The symbols that make up language are arbitrarily assigned meaning when people interpret them as part of interaction. Words do not have meanings; people have meanings. You have meanings in mind when you speak or write, but they are based on your prior experience and education. In the immediate context in which you are speaking, writing, or reading, the meanings of the words will depend upon the context in which you find yourself at the time, and the people with whom you are interacting.

Even within the close group of your friends or family, there is never absolute commonality in the interpretation of language. It is necessary to make guesses about others' interpretation strategies, and then try to understand where you must revise to improve communication.

The first step in evaluating arguments is to open up interpretation strategies for examination. Disagreements may dissolve as strategies are made to coincide, but so might agreements. Before advancing or evaluating an argument, you must satisfy yourself that you understand what is being communicated.

Facts   In the discussion of analysis in Chapter 4, we observe that facts can become issues, questions around which controversy occurs. However, as starting points of argumentation, facts are empirical knowledge derived from observation or experience over which there is no controversy.[3] The morning sun appears in the east. Caviar costs more than chopped liver. Mothers who abuse alcohol or drugs during pregnancy endanger the health of their babies. These are facts that could very well be the starting

---

[3]We do not mean to say that these so-called facts are beyond controversy. At one time, people held as fact that the world was flat. We use *fact* here to mean a powerful concept that is widely accepted without controversy, *at the time of the argument,* to the extent it can be invoked as the starting connection for further argumentation. Today, we might be able to invoke the "fact" that the universe is constantly expanding as a starting point for the argument, only to have people a hundred years from now laugh at the idea the same way we laugh at the idea that the world is flat.

points of arguments, because the decision makers regard them as facts beyond question.

There are profound differences in what is accepted as fact as you move from one sphere to another. Millions of people acknowledge the "fact" that Jesus is the Messiah, and millions reject the idea totally. Even among scientists, there is significant disagreement about what to count as fact. Colleagues who doubted there was any factual basis for such research seriously challenged a physics professor who studies UFOs.

In appraising arguments, one place to look is at the facts used as starting points, because people may accept facts that, upon reflection, they should not. First-time backpackers in the mountains whose knowledge of high country is based more on beer commercials than on serious study sometimes look at cold streams cascading over smooth rocks and conclude it must be safe to drink from them:

CURLY: "It's a fact that bacteria can't live in rapidly moving water that's almost freezing."
MOE: "Yeah, I've heard that, too."
CURLY: "So it's okay to drink it."

Unfortunately, many mountain streams contain *Giardia* bacteria that thrive in cold rushing water and cause severe intestinal distress. Curly's argument would not have led to trouble if Moe had challenged the factual starting point.

Presumptions Another powerful concept that serves as a starting point for arguments is presumption. A *presumption* occurs when one arguer occupies the argumentative ground or position "until some sufficient reason is adduced against it" (Whately 112). Like facts, presumptions may reflect considerable experience and observation, but they usually involve a broader generalization or a point taken hypothetically for the sake of argument.

Many presumptions have been formally stated in legal decisions. Children are presumed to have less ability to look out for themselves than adults, so society demands more care for them. Some mentally disabled persons are presumed to be unable to understand the difference between right and wrong, so courts may send them to hospitals rather than prisons. Property lines that have been marked by fences and have remained uncontested for many years are presumed to be correct and may be accepted even when a survey shows otherwise. People are presumed to be able to behave rationally, so the law punishes those who, for example, drive under the influence of drugs or alcohol.

U.S. criminal law presumes people to be innocent until proven guilty. As this presumption suggests, all presumptions are subject to challenge and may be overturned. In fact, people may start with a presumption they really do not believe, just to get the argumentation going. If they didn't have a presumption to work from (say, the presumption of innocence), they would not know who has to start the argument and who wins in the absence of clear superiority of one argument over another. The U.S. criminal law presumes innocence just so the state has to open with a claim of guilt.

The individual citizen does not have to prove innocence. If the state fails to win the argument, we choose to let the citizen go free rather than risk convicting the innocent. We expand the concepts of presumption, burden of proof, and *prima facie* cases in Chapter 5 during the discussion of case building.

Part of the critical appraisal of argumentation is examination of presumptions. Because presumption is more or less arbitrary, it is possible for one position in the discussion to claim presumption and use it as a tool to force others to defend their position. This may put an unreasonable burden on one point of view and lead to an unreasonable decision (Gaskins).

Probabilities   As starting points of argument, *probabilities* consist of commonly held beliefs about what is likely to happen, what is ordinary and what is to be expected. Such beliefs can be used as premises for arguments. After extensive observations, we hold powerful concepts of such probabilities as the times of the tides, the movements of the planets, the changing of the seasons, or the behavior of matter under various conditions. We reason from biological probabilities such as what plants will survive in certain climates, how animals will respond to loss of habitat, and how diseases disseminate. We hold concepts of how people will probably act under certain circumstances: they will look to such basic needs as food, clothing, and shelter before considering such abstract needs as self-fulfillment; they will seek pleasure and avoid pain; they will organize themselves into societies.

Like presumptions, probabilities vary from one sphere to another. Many hold the probability that human beings will seek to avoid death, but some spheres hold that death in a holy cause is desirable.

Where presumptions may be points that are taken for the sake of argument without solid proof of their validity, probabilities get arguments started because they are likely to be accepted as well established by proof while falling short of the confidence given to facts. Their susceptibility to challenge makes it necessary to present claims resting on probabilities with some statements of *qualification.*

Stephen Toulmin says that when people qualify claims, they "authorize . . . hearers to put more or less faith in the assertions . . . treat them as correspondingly more or less trustworthy" (*The Uses of Argument* 91). Since argument functions within uncertainty, there is always some degree of qualification on claims. Sometimes you use words: likely, almost certainly, probably, maybe. Sometimes you use numbers: 90 percent chance, $p < .05$, three to one odds. No matter how you express these probabilities, they communicate the force with which an argument is advanced, the degree of faith you authorize others to place on your claims.

Appraising arguments, then, necessarily involves an examination of the probabilities on which they rest and the qualifications with which they are presented. A point of criticism is to ask the basis of the probability statement.

In deciding what and how much higher education you need, you may turn to statistics that indicate probabilities about what kinds of majors will be most in demand when you graduate and what value advanced degrees may produce. In 2003, the major most likely to produce a job at good pay was nursing. But you must decide now on your major, based on such a probability, knowing that in two or three years conditions may change. If enormous numbers of people act on that probability and major in nursing, in a few years the field may be over-supplied, leaving no job for you. By adopting a new major and agreeing to devote several years of your life to school, you express a high confidence in the probability of that major producing what you expect; you hold few qualifications.

The probability of one team winning a championship is a function of past behavior and current performance. The loss of a key player changes the odds. But the foundation of probability is the extent to which you and others agree to commit yourselves. In horse racing, the odds of a horse winning change depending on how people bet. The horses do not vary in their ability, the people vary in their degree of commitment. The critic must always examine the basis of the probability assessment, and remember how probabilities change.

Commonplaces In argumentative practice, various ways of putting arguments together become standardized, common, widely recognized, and accepted. These *commonplaces* are lines of argument or places from which arguments can be built. Aristotle speaks of rationales such as opposites: what goes up must come down. He called them, depending upon which translation you use, *topoi,* topics, lines of argument, or commonplaces (Roberts 1396). Perelman and Olbrechts-Tyteca call them *loci* (83). We will call them commonplaces.

In appraising arguments, the commonplaces on which they are developed must be examined. We have mentioned the commonplace of opposites as an example. If one argues from this commonplace, the critic must test the assumption of opposition. Up and down do not work the same in the weightlessness of space, which Aristotle never heard of.

An argument based on genealogy was also common in Aristotle's time, but it is less likely to survive critical scrutiny today. To argue, for example, that people are suitable for high office because of the high status of their parents is not well received in a democracy. However, genealogy still functions as a commonplace in certain argumentative contexts. Some religions pay particular attention to genealogy in defining membership. The selection of a British monarch or a Japanese emperor rests on that commonplace. And, in a looser way, many people point with pride to their distinguished ancestors, however far-fetched; we pay attention to how the children of movie, sports, and music celebrities succeed or fail; we follow closely the ins and outs of distinguished families such as the Kennedys.

A fortiori (more or less) argues, for example, that if you can perform the more difficult task, you can surely perform the easier one. Or, conversely, if you can't do an easy task, you won't be able to do a more difficult one. The argument "If we can put a man on the moon, we should be able to solve the hunger problem" rests on the commonplace of *a fortiori.* So does this one: if you cannot pass the introductory course, you surely will flunk the advanced one.

Considerations of *time* work as commonplaces. Professionals charge fees based on the time spent for a client or patient. Most wages are calculated on time. Forty hours is deemed enough work for a week, and any more deserves better pay. Students argue for a better grade on the basis of how much time was spent on an assignment. We presume that a person can't be in two places at the same time, so the accused may argue an alibi based on the time to go from point A to point B.

It is impossible to list all commonplaces because they vary from time to time and from sphere to sphere. The potency of the commonplaces of induction and deduction has been the subject of much debate during this century. The commonplace of cause and effect is interpreted in quite different ways within different spheres.

Language interpretation strategies, facts, presumptions, probabilities, and commonplaces are powerful concepts that work as socially generated starting points for argument. When you make an argument, you will want to think carefully about where you can start it with reasonable assurance that there is common ground between you and your decision makers. In your critical appraisal of the argumentation of others, you must scrutinize the starting points to see whether they were well selected.

Spheres

We have spoken frequently of appropriate decision makers as the object of your argumentation. Now we will locate decision makers within decision making groups, forums, organizations, societies, professions, disciplines, generations, or other such arrangements, which we will refer to as *spheres*. We will provide a general definition of spheres first, and then discuss some of the ways spheres work in argumentation and critical decision making.

Definition of Spheres

Spheres are collections of people in the process of interacting upon and making critical decisions. They are real sociological entities (Willard 28). You cannot make a critical decision completely alone. No matter how private you believe your thoughts to be, your internal dialogue involves a myriad of "voices" from your life's experiences.

Spheres function in the present tense: they are in the process of making critical decisions. While they quite often have a history of the same or similar people doing similar activities, that history functions for the purposes of critical decision making only as construed in the present. Derek Edwards and Jonathan Potter argue that perception, memory, language, knowledge, and reasoning are neither fixed in our brains nor guaranteed in documents and protocols. They are to be found in our interactions in the present. What we recall as facts, they say, are really what we put into our present rhetorical accounts and accept as facts (44–57).

Spheres operate as decision-making groups. Although millions of people may ultimately play a part in a single decision, in practical terms, the process occurs in multiple, overlapping small groups (see Frey 4–8).

John F. Cragan and David W. Wright define a small group "as a few people engaged in communication interaction over time . . . who have common goals and norms and have developed a communication pattern for meeting their goals in an interdependent manner" (7). While the size of the group can vary widely, generally speaking at any time a group probably involves enough people to provide a diversity of opinion yet still allow the development of reasonably close interpersonal relations in which people know and react to every other member.

Donald G. Ellis and B. Aubrey Fisher describe *group structuration* as a process in which groups develop by making use of certain rules and resources while processing information. Rules control how things ought to be done in the group and resources are materials and attributes the group can use, "such as special knowledge, money, status, equipment, and relationships" (56). While groups develop highly individualized patterns of interaction and sets of rules and resources, they are still in constant tension with external constraints.

When we speak of spheres, then, we are talking about decision-making groups with recognizable goals and norms and sets of rules and resources and patterns of interaction, most often under ongoing tension (direction, control, ultimate decision power) with external entities. For example, in a business setting, a task force in research and development may be working on how an invention might be transformed into a marketable product, but they do so within the constraints of the larger company organization. In law, two lawyers and a judge may generate a ruling, but it must be done according to the dictates of the appropriate laws and subject to the review of courts of appeal.

While spheres operate in the present, their interactions observed over time demonstrate patterns that are related to one another and used time after time. In critical decision making, these patterns of interaction include the starting points of argument, the way argumentation is conducted, and the criteria used to evaluate arguments and form critical decisions. Because they are thus predictable, the patterns guide your guesses about how your arguments will be understood and criticized. Because they are predictable, patterns of argumentation come to be associated with some groups and serve to increase the likelihood that critical decisions will result. *Groups are called spheres when their predictable patterns of communicative behavior are used in the production and evaluation of argumentation.*

Spheres, then, consist of people functioning as a group who share a cluster of criteria for the production and appraisal of argumentation. People in spheres share language interpretation strategies, facts, presumptions, probabilities, and commonplaces. But remember that sharing is in the present, subject to ongoing change, and is never certain to yield a critical decision.

Location of Spheres

Spheres may consist of only a few people or may constitute groups within complex organizations involving many people. Spheres may be transitory or enduring. At any time, you may be a member of many spheres. Your *internal dialogue,* because it includes many voices, can work as a sphere. Basic *social groups* such as families, friends, or people with common interests can function as spheres. Standing or temporary *task-oriented small groups* such as committees or task forces function as spheres.

Groups working within the rubric of a religion, profession, academic discipline, vocation, civic or charitable organization, business, or governmental unit may function as spheres. Sometimes the defining characteristic of a sphere is ethnic association, a social movement, or a political entity such as a state or nation. All spheres function within a culture and during a certain time or generation, both of which supply some of the argumentation patterns of a sphere.

Spheres and Level of Activity

G. Thomas Goodnight identifies three levels of activity of spheres: personal, technical, and public. By level of activity, Goodnight means the "grounds on which arguments are built and the authorities to which arguers appeal" (216).

In *personal spheres,* the level of activity is more spontaneous, negotiated interpersonally or in your internal dialogues. The interstructured and repetitive patterns of argumentation tend to be less easily discerned and predicted, so the chances of a critical decision are lower than at other levels of activity.

Technical spheres are those in which formal argumentative patterns are enforced. The highly specialized criteria are appropriate to the nature of the decisions made by such professional groups as lawyers, managers, scholars, engineers, physicians, and technicians. Those with advanced education, possessing a special kind of knowledge, are most likely to be found in technical spheres. Toulmin (*The Uses of Argument*) uses the term *field* to describe special criteria for the appraisal of arguments within a particular technical sphere. Charles Arthur Willard notes that a technical sphere may restrict access to its patterns of argumentation by requiring decision participants to " . . . master specialized codes, procedures, knowledge, and language to limit what can count as reasonable argument. . . ." (50). This may insulate it from interacting with other spheres without substantial translation.

Public spheres usually involve those people who seek participation in public debate and are recognized by the relevant decision makers. They may be elected politicians or publicly recognized spokespersons. While politicians may use highly formalized arguments, their decision making must be comprehensible to the public. The chief problem with the public sphere is complexity. Public decision makers face complex organizations representing different values, interests, and influence.

Goodnight's idea of the personal, technical, and public spheres is useful in understanding that some issues require only the most informal and commonsense demands for support of arguments, while other issues demand highly specialized argumentation. The public sphere is neither as casual as the personal nor as specialized as the technical. Yet, as Goodnight says, "it provides forums with customs, traditions, and requirements for arguers" because the consequences of public disputes go beyond either the personal or technical spheres.

Ultimate Purpose

Each sphere involves an ultimate purpose that provides a relatively enduring set of tests of arguments. Toulmin speaks of this concept as "doing what there is there to be done" (*Human Understanding,* 485). What critical tests arguments and decisions must satisfy are themselves rooted in " . . . what we [people in the sphere] want now, constructed from our sense of purpose and what we are here for" (Willihnganz, et al. 202). This generalized sense of purpose resists change to the extent that it is unlikely that one person or one argumentative interchange will have much effect on it.

In the history of U.S. business, for example, there has been sharp debate over its ultimate purpose, and this has slowly modified the way in which business arguments are appraised. A hundred years ago, the single ultimate purpose of business was to make money. Arguments about raising wages, improving working conditions, accepting unions, protecting the environment, or contributing to the community rarely survived the test of the profit criterion.

Today, these arguments stand a better chance of passing the test because of the slow evolution of the ultimate purpose of business. Concern for the well-being of the work force is now often justified as a contributor to profit. Many businesses now see being a good neighbor as part of their ultimate purpose. And the public sphere, through laws, has required businesses to revise their ultimate purpose to include concern for safety, consumers, individual rights, and control of their hazardous by-products.

Conclusion

When you appraise argumentation, when you try to decide what arguments are acceptable, what ones are not, and what decision makes the most sense, you will necessarily make your judgments under the influence and within the limits of your genetic make-up, the environments in which you have lived, your world views, and the social interactions you have experienced. Sometimes these factors will help you act wisely, and sometimes they will get you into trouble.

Over many centuries, people have developed systematic argumentation practices that can increase the likelihood that you will make sensible decisions. When properly used, these will help you make critical decisions. Powerful concepts such as language interpretation strategies, facts, presumptions, probabilities, and commonplaces can serve as starting points for argumentation. They establish a foundation on which everyone can argue and provide some ready rationales on which to build claims.

When people functioning in groups develop communicative behaviors that are interstructured and repetitive and thus occur in predictable patterns for the purposes of producing and evaluating argumentation, they constitute spheres. In spheres, people share both common ground and an ultimate purpose that set relatively enduring standards by which argumentation is judged.

P R O J E C T

Write a description of a job interview you have had. Did you understand the criteria to be used in making a hiring decision? Did you make arguments in response to the criteria? Did the job decision rest on the criteria? In all, do you think the decision was critical or uncritical, and why?

3 Critical Approaches to Argumentation

KEY TERMS

good reasons
logic
science
narrative
postmodernism
feminism
social constructionism
master narrative
essentialize

subjective experience
feminist argumentation
patriarchal reasoning
personal testimony
cooperation
alternative dispute resolution
moral conflict
mediation
facilitator

In Chapter 2 we examined ways people appraise arguments, focusing on how they decide what is reasonable. We pointed out that criteria that are appropriate for evaluating an argument in some situations are not necessarily appropriate for all situations. Whenever people participate in an argument, they strive to present themselves as reasonable, or as making sense. Notions of what it means to be sensible, however, change as society changes. In this chapter we will describe five critical approaches to the question of how something comes to make sense. You can use these approaches to analyze arguments, as well as to become a more effective advocate.

1. Being sensible means having good reasons. We will examine the ways claims are justified through reasoned discourse. You demonstrate that you have good reasons to support your claims by employing standard patterns of valid inference, drawn from logic. You also appear to be reasonable if your arguments are consistent and are not contradictory.
2. Being sensible means being scientific. If claims are derived from systematic observation of the world through the senses of sight, sound, taste, touch, and smell, they make sense: "Seeing is believing." Scientific argument also includes systematic analysis of your observations.

3. Being sensible means telling a good story. When someone describes an event, you listen to "what happened," and decide if it makes sense on the basis of how coherent and believable the story is.
4. Being sensible means responding to the fragmented identities and relationships that characterize postmodern culture. You demonstrate the sensibleness of your argument by identifying tensions, contradictions, absences, silences, and paradoxes. This approach is especially useful when you want to identify which voices enjoy privileged status, how that has been accomplished, and how it might be changed.
5. Being sensible means recognizing that men and women have been socialized differently, and that this socialization process affects how people construct, deliver, and receive arguments. You can identify and critique these differences, using them to open new possibilities for consideration.

We will explain how these five ways of making sense of the world appear in some form or another in the communication patterns of many social interactions. After explaining the three traditional critical perspectives toward argumentation, we will briefly describe two nontraditional approaches to dispute resolution that incorporate concepts drawn from *postmodernism* and *feminism.*

Traditional Criteria

The first three approaches listed at the beginning of this chapter have been used to critically evaluate arguments for centuries. For this reason, we refer to them as traditional criteria.

Good Reasons

In the rhetorical tradition, Aristotle (Roberts) focuses on reasoned discourse. What reasons are offered in support or justification of a claim? Are they good reasons, or good enough to warrant adherence to the claim?

When children or adults are asked to generate reasons in support of a claim, they typically call upon their own authority ("I believe it"); *power authority* ("The textbook says it's so"); *moral obligation* ("It's the right thing to believe"); *social pressure* ("Everyone believes it"); or *listener benefit* ("If you want to pass this test, you will be well advised to believe it"), among other kinds of reasons (Willbrand and Rieke 420). Reasons generated in this way are learned from early childhood and reflect the enculturation each person has experienced (Toulmin, "Commentary"). Coming up with good reasons is learned in response to challenges:

"Why did you do that?"
"Because."
"Because why?"

"Just because."
"That's not good enough!"
"The teacher said I could." (power authority)
"Okay."

Some of the ways we test reasons to see if they are good enough are these:

1. **The reasons should speak with one voice.** This test advises you to look for contradictions. When the religious leader who preaches faithfulness in marriage is found in a motel room with someone other than a spouse, the sermon loses its punch. In reasons, the old cliché, "Don't do as I do; do as I say," does not overcome contradiction.
2. **The reasons should be consistent.** Here, the critic looks to see if all parts of the argumentation play by the same rules. If a politician argues for big reductions in defense spending but opposes the closure of a military base in the home district, the argument is weakened by lack of consistency. The pro-life advocate who supports capital punishment communicates inconsistency.
3. **The argument should locate starting points within the appropriate audience.** Arguments should neither patronize the audience by telling them what they already know nor presume starting points that do not exist.
4. **The reasons should be expressed in language that communicates to the appropriate decision makers.** Critics should check to see if everyone involved in the argumentation is using the same interpretation strategies.
5. **The reasons should be complete.** A critic searches for points necessary to the claim that are not addressed, exceptions or variations to the materials included.
6. **The reasons must be reasonably related to the point they support.** As we explain in our discussions of evidence in Chapter 7, there are specific tests to which reasons must be put.

Logic

Aristotle set out a pattern of formal relations by which arguments could be tested for validity. That is to say, if you begin with true premises, this logic can dictate the ways in which they can be combined to yield true conclusions. The pattern is called syllogism (deduction) and is taught, with the modifications that have been made over the years, as formal logic.

Typical examples of the validity patterns in syllogisms are the *categorical, hypothetical,* and *disjunctive.* We will give simple examples of each.

Categorical: If all A is B,
And if all C is A,
Then all C is B
Hypothetical: If A, then B

So if A exists
Then B exists
Or if B does not exist,
Then A does not exist
Disjunctive: Either A or B
So if A exists
Then B does not exist, or, again, if B exists, then A does not

Modern formal logic texts (Gensler) illustrate the various valid forms of these syllogisms and show how validity can be tested symbolically in a method closely resembling mathematics. Because of different basic assumptions and requirements, this logic deals with such tasks as computer programming, that fall outside the domain of argumentation. That is to say, this logic is the calculus of certainty. The search for mathematical certainty grounded in logic goes back at least to Euclid in ancient Greece. Throughout the first half of the twentieth century, mathematical philosophers attempted to organize every possible assumption and principle used in mathematics into logical patterns, complete with strict rules for moving from one step to the next. Mathematics was fundamentally changed when, in 1931, Kurt Gödel published a paper arguing that mathematics "is both incomplete and inconsistent" (Peat, 41). The search for a "new" logic continues to this day.

Martin D. S. Braine, David P. O'Brien and their colleagues explain in detail their theory of mental logic consisting of "a set of inference schemas. . . . For example, when one knows that two propositions of the form *p or q* and *not p* are true, one can assert *q*" (3). They provide an extensive list of such schemas, although it does not claim to be exhaustive. While we disagree with their contention that the human mind naturally employs such logic, we agree that people are quite capable of learning and using it.

During the last half of the twentieth century, there was much philosophical discussion of the viability of formal logic in argumentation (Toulmin, *The Uses of Argument;* Perelman and Olbrechts-Tyteca). At the same time, work in artificial intelligence presented computer programmers with the need for a goal-directed, knowledge-based logic (a logic of uncertainty) suited to describing how people actually go about the business of practical reasoning (Walton).

The result has been what is called *informal logic* (Johnson and Blair). In many ways, its contribution is directed toward the discussion of fallacies, as we explain in Chapter 11. In its more conservative form, informal logic employs the patterns of deductive logic to criticize arguments within the realm of argumentation. Thus, the concept of validity is retained, but the force of conclusions does not reach the certainty of formal logic. Perelman and Olbrechts-Tyteca speak of *quasi-logic,* meaning the use of syllogistic forms in presenting arguments to benefit from the widespread respect given to logic by many decision makers.

Douglas Walton offers a goal-directed pattern of informal logic appropriate for both artificial intelligence and practical reasoning. Walton sees informal logic, unlike formal logic, as working with reasoning in a problem-solving context, involving some value-laden mandate (must, should), premised on known requirements and consequences, projecting into the future, assessing costs and benefits, calling for a shift or adjustment in the collective commitments of the relevant decision makers (83).

The argumentation scheme Walton offers is this:

A is the goal.
B is necessary to bring about A.
Therefore, B is necessary.

This is used, says Walton, to convince someone to take whatever action is entailed in B. Critical appraisal of such argumentation, according to Walton, follows these questions:

1. Are there alternatives to B?
2. Is B an acceptable (or the best) alternative?
3. Is it possible to bring about B?
4. Does B have bad side effects? (85)

In his recent work, Walton has described a new dialectic that returns to the dialectical writings of the ancient Greeks "as a general perspective and way of evaluating arguments in a context of dialogue." He seeks to provide "a new theoretical basis for logic which can be used to evaluate arguments that arise in everyday conversational exchanges" (*The New Dialectic* 4–36).

Frans H. van Eemeren and Rob Grootendorst have proposed a set of rules by which critical decision making can be guided. They speak of dialectical constituents of argument as the logical or reasonable foundation. They list ten rules for critical discussion:

1. Participants must not try to silence each other to prevent the exchange of arguments and criticism.
2. If you make a claim, you must be willing to provide support if it is requested.
3. When you criticize someone's argument, you should be sure you are talking about what they really said.
4. You should defend your claims with arguments relevant to them.
5. You should not claim that others have presumed something they have not, and you should be willing to admit your own presumptions.
6. You should not try to start argumentation with a starting point others do not accept, and you should not deny a genuine starting point.
7. You should not say your claim has been established unless you have provided proper argumentative support.
8. You should stick to arguments that are logically valid or can be made valid.
9. If you fail to establish your claim, admit it; if others establish their claims, admit it.

10. Avoid unnecessary ambiguity, and try to interpret other's arguments as clearly as possible (1993).

Science

There are many versions of the "scientific method," depending on the particular sphere involved. However, we can identify the use of science as a means of evaluating arguments in a more general way. Simply put, scientific logic rests on carefully performed observations, successful predictions, and the ability of others to obtain the same results. Ronald Pine provides these essential elements (42):

1. Observations are conducted: your empirical faculties are engaged in relation to a problem or phenomenon (sight, sound, taste, touch, smell).
2. Creative thought about the observations is done.
3. A hypothesis is generated in which you state the product of your creative thought in the form of a prediction.
4. Specific tests or experiments based on the hypothesis are conducted. The effort is to see if these now focused observations still make sense in relation to the hypothesis.
5. A claim is advanced in support of the hypothesis using the exposition of the first four steps and is presented with enough detail that others can repeat your work and get the same result.

Richard Parker advanced these steps as tests of scientific logic:

1. The argument must be internally consistent.
2. Its premises must be acceptable to the decision makers for whom it is intended.
3. It must survive refutation.
4. It must survive confutation or the critical examination of all arguments for and against.

Over the past 300 years or so, science has been recognized as a particularly powerful form of argumentation. Spectacular scientific and technological advances have led some to believe, as did Aristotle, that science stands outside the domain of argumentation because it deals in certainty. In 1970, however, philosopher of science Thomas Kuhn argued that scientific arguments operate within uncertainty and should be criticized as argumentation. Part of this shift in perspective comes from within science itself. F. David Peat describes the transformation of science wrought by quantum theory as, "chairs and tables dissolved into an empty space filled with colliding atoms. Then atoms broke apart into nuclei, nuclei into elementary particles, and finally, elementary particles into symmetries, transformations, and processes in the quantum vacuum" (52–53). Postmodernist, rhetorical, and cultural studies commentators have taken the point further to show social, political, and cultural influences on scientific claims (Condit, Fuller).

Physicist Alan Sokal accepts the claim that science falls within the domain of argumentation by noting these points of agreement:

> "1. Science is a human endeavor, and like any other human endeavor, it merits being subjected to rigorous social analysis. . . . 2. Even the content of scientific debate—what types of theories can be conceived and entertained, what criteria are to be used for deciding among competing theories—is constrained in part by the prevailing attitudes of mind, which in turn arise in part from deep-seated historical factors. . . . 3. There is nothing wrong with research informed by a political commitment as long as that commitment does not blind the researcher to inconvenient facts" (10).

Having said that, however, Sokal proceeds to reiterate that the method of science is the source of powerful argumentation.

A Good Story

Recent scholarly attention (Fisher) has turned to narrative logic or storytelling as a test of argumentation. For example:

> From the stone-age Tasaday people of the Philippine rain forest to the suburbanites in Scarsdale, narrative is the only art that exists in all human cultures. It is by narrative that we experience our lives. . . . [I]maginative narrative, which in its refined and printed form we call fiction, was decisive in the creation of our species, and is still essential in the development of each human individual and necessary to the maintenance of his health and pursuit of his purposes (Morton 2).

Malcolm O. Sillars and Bruce E. Gronbeck observe that people judge the rationality or truthfulness of human behavior in terms of what actions make sense, and what makes sense to people rests upon the stories that are told within a culture. People make sense of their world in terms of the stories they tell about themselves. Stories are symbolic actions that create social reality, and so, even when stories are fiction, they are not false, because they reflect the experience of those who tell the stories and those who hear or read them.

A narrative has a sense of chronology with regard to a central subject, developed coherently, leading to a narrative closure or outcome. Narratives generally involve a *theme* (good triumphs over evil), *structure* (beginning, middle, end), *characters* (heroes and villains), *peripeteia* (a change of fortune or reversal of circumstances), *narrative voice* (the storyteller), and *style* (language including figures of speech) (Sillars and Gronbeck Chapter 10).

According to W. Lance Bennett and Martha S. Feldman, we organize our understanding around stories from early childhood. What counts as real and what makes sense is learned as central actions and the way those actions are characterized in relation to the people and motivations that make them up. People evaluate stories in part by asking whether they are coherent—whether the content and structure of the story hang together properly—and whether they are faithful to what people have come to believe to be true about the real world (Fisher). How would you evaluate the following narrative?

> Two close friends, Raffi and David, entered Carlsbad Caverns National Park and purchased a camping permit on Wednesday evening. A mile later, they filled out a backcountry card and hiked into Rattlesnake Canyon. They camped overnight and sought to leave Thursday morning, but apparently lost their way. They had little water. Sunday afternoon, a Park Ranger found the men. David was dead and buried under a pile of large rocks, and Raffi said he had killed him as an act of mercy. They were lost, said Raffi, and suffering from the heat and lack of water. David had begged to be relieved of his misery, said Raffi. An SOS of rocks had been mostly formed on the ground. While Raffi showed signs of dehydration, he was able to speak coherently and was fine within an hour of receiving a saline IV. An autopsy revealed that David showed signs of moderate to severe dehydration, but his fluids were not deficient to the point of causing death. The campsite was 240 feet from the trail head, which is marked with rock cairns, and a mile from their car. If they had hiked to a higher point, they would have been able to see the trail or the visitors' center. Raffi is charged with murder.

At the end of the twentieth century, many scholars in the social sciences concluded that narratives provided excellent data for their research. "Emphasizing the stories people tell about their lives, [they] construed narrative as both a means of knowing and a way of telling about the social world" (Montgomery and Baxter 43). Narrative, they believed, is the way people experience and understand their own lives. Other researchers (Cobb) have found that narrative plays a central role in successful mediations. For these reasons, argumentation cast in the form of narrative is a powerful way to make connections with the appropriate decision makers.

Nontraditional Criteria

The traditional rationale for studying argumentation is that if disputants are sufficiently willing and able to present their cases and respond to others thoughtfully and logically, they can achieve mutually satisfactory resolution. It assumes that, in most cases, argumentation and debate will lead to a mutually agreeable solution. Failure to settle a dispute by these methods is viewed as a symptom of unskilled communication, failure to engage in critical decision making, or just plain selfishness. The approaches we have described thus far are grounded in this rationale.

The persistent and increasingly public nature of terrorist activities, such as the September 11, 2001, destruction of the World Trade Center in New York City, have persuaded many people that traditional orientations toward political diplomacy are not only insufficient, but misguided. One response to terrorism aimed at the United States has been a proliferation of legislation that curtails individual freedom in the interests of national security. Another has been a series of military invasions in the interests of rooting out terrorism from other nations. Criticism is kept to a minimum by accusations of anti-Americanism. A traditional orientation might consider both the actions we label as "terrorist" and those we label as "war" to be outside the realm of argumentation. A postmodernist account, however, urges people to understand terrorism as the argument of the powerless. In a world where the "public screen" has replaced the "public sphere," the most significant arguments are those that grab the viewers' attention quickly, before they glance away.

Ideas drawn from postmodernism and feminism offer a way of interpreting the sensibility of radical actions, which can contribute to better understanding and more effective responses to these deeply felt conflicts. Some argumentation scholars claim postmodern and feminist insights are antithetical, and even destructive, to the process of argumentation (Rowland). We find them fundamentally consistent with the perspective toward argumentation described in Chapter 1. Despite differences between the traditional and nontraditional approaches to argument, all are loosely grounded in a *social constructionist* orientation that views human realities as products of social interaction. At the same time, we recognize that the differences between traditional and nontraditional approaches are important. For example, postmodernism and feminism offer approaches to the concept of reason that can encourage people who are engaged in argumentation to develop forms of communication that are especially appropriate to contemporary situations.

We now turn to a discussion of how postmodern and feminist thought contribute to our understanding of argumentation. First, we will discuss the postmodernist idea of being sensible by focusing on the socially constructed nature of human consciousness. Second, we will discuss feminism and its contributions to how arguments come to make sense.

Postmodernism

Unlike the assumptions of western civilization exemplified by the more traditional approaches to argument discussed earlier, postmodernism (Derrida, Docherty, Foucault) describes a cultural *zeitgeist* of crisis, desperation, anxiety, schizophrenia, nostalgia, *pastiche* (the endless recycling of old cultural forms to make new but familiar forms), apocalyptic millennialism, and lassitude (we're too cool to either feel or show that we feel desire or pain very deeply—The quintessential postmodern utterance is: "*Whatever . . .* ").

Postmodernism rejects the grand, controlling, institutionalized, and reductive *master narratives* of Enlightenment western culture, such as positivism, Marxism, liberal democracy, and Christianity. Postmodernists argue that these narratives have unified cultures by providing their members with absolute, totalizing truth and certainty. That certainty has been achieved by *essentializing* specific social structures. When you essentialize something, you assume that, because it exists, it is part of the natural order, and therefore struggle against it is either futile or wrong. Although the stability provided by essentializing existing patterns offers many advantages, it also comes with costs. For example, some Christians use the statement, "the poor will always be with you," to essentialize an economically stratified society. Because it is futile to anguish over unjust social conditions, these Christians can ignore the economic dimension of politics, and discharge their charitable responsibility by making voluntary financial contributions. Similarly, some Marxists focus on the irreconcilable divide between those who labor to produce goods that satisfy society's material desires and those who profit from that labor, ignoring injustice perpetuated among those who labor, as well as between humans and other life forms. A postmodern perspective toward argumentation (including the definitions and justification given in Chapter 1 of this book) would suggest that its legitimacy depends on readers accepting the reason-based culture of liberal democracy.

Postmodernism, on the other hand, focuses on the existence of multiple, situated narratives of subjective experience that emerge from the fragmented identities and relationships of the evolving cultural landscape. This theory emphasizes diversity and the subversive voices of groups who have been traditionally marginalized in the production of cultural knowledge. A postmodern theory of argument attempts to bring marginalized groups into the decision-making process, at the same time it attempts to reshape that process.

The postmodernist concern for marginalized people grows out of an attempt to make sense of the information-age, service-economy capitalism with its mass culture of ferocious competition between multinational conglomerates for domination of local markets, its relentless marketing of commodities aided by advertising's creation of artificial desire, and franchises that reduce every local place to no-place and same-place. There is no longer a pristine Elsewhere. Every place has a Wal-Mart, a McDonalds, a Pizza Hut. Fashions are niche-marketed from J. Crew to Land's End to Ralph Lauren.

Postmodernism offers a critical stance on the shifting phantasmagoria of proliferating, manufactured media images and events that refer mostly to themselves, and that offer information but not meaning. It interprets people more as media consumers than producers; as the screens onto which programmers blast their entertainment and information and advertising beams. CNN offers an endless recycling of news from everywhere and thus nowhere, marketed to everyone and thus no one. The communication revolution has collapsed time and space, but fails to adequately explain what it means to be alive at this moment in time *with* each other, and *for* each other. This is something people can only negotiate in whatever is left of the private, and with whatever is left of our bodies after we go online to the Net as cyborgs. The President flies to Afghanistan or Iraq or [fill in the blank] to have his photo taken with members of the armed forces. He makes the trip, rather than simply posing with a virtual group of soldiers, so that American consumers can sense his authentic caring. War has become a photo op. In a world where California elects body builder/box office attraction Arnold Schwarzenegger as governor, it is difficult to distinguish between the virtual and the real, and even more difficult to decide if it matters.

The postmodernist observer coolly and cynically notes the cultural obsession with style, surfaces, and media. In a world where teeth-whitening, liposuction, aerobics, condoms, and modems replace prior forms of intimacy and community, people are unique matrices of narrowly niche-marketed, gene-spliced consumer choices made among a fantastic variety of cultural genres: religion, fashion, food, furnishings, residences, careers, and beverages (Caf, half-caf, or decaf? Espresso or cappucino?

Single or double? Latte?). The economic relations of producer–consumer have come to dominate all public and private interaction. For example, we regularly encounter college students who implicitly believe that their tuition buys them a "C," and whose primary question is, "What do you want us to know for the test?" Given the prevailing conditions of postmodern society, argumentation must either be reinterpreted as a process through which people constitute realities or risk irrelevance.

Dangers   If this cynical and somewhat pessimistic take on contemporary society bothers you, you are not alone. Postmodernism has prompted outright hostility from a broad range of ideological perspectives. Marxist critic David Harvey accuses postmodernism of reveling in diversity, simulation, and fragmentation that makes politics impossible (116–117). Dana Cloud accuses postmodernists of collapsing the distinction between discourse and the real, and fears that postmodernism will lead to "depolitization of political struggle" (154, 157). Thomas Goodnight worries that postmodernity weakens the public sphere, and thus democratic politics, by reducing it to "moments of detachment, disavowal, and cynicism flowing from and into a mediating code of cultural skepticism" (285). Robert C. Rowland claims that postmodernism threatens the entire system of argumentation pedagogy and scholarship. Kevin DeLuca points out that these critics share a fear that, because postmodernism lacks the unifying principle of a foundational premise (the humanist subject, reason, economic mode of production, laws of historical materialism), it will "lead to an incoherent politics that isolates and disempowers local resistances while aiding global corporate capitalism."

Opportunities   Kevin DeLuca posits, however, "that deconstructing transcendental foundations, inhabiting places, and living with incoherence offer hope for a radical democratic politics" (64). DeLuca is suggesting that a postmodern argumentation practice can provide the impetus for breaking down generalizations, truly becoming a part of (rather than apart from) the local communities, and accepting the vagaries of democracy (and thereby strengthening its practice). Ernesto Laclau explains that

> the abandonment of ultimate foundations and the widening of the field of undecidability expand the field of politics, that the subversion of structural laws by contingency creates the very possibility of radical politics. . . . This leads to a proliferation of discursive interventions and arguments that are necessary, because there is no extradiscursive reality that discourse might simply reflect. Inasmuch as argument and discourse constitute the social, their open-ended character becomes the source of a greater activism. (1993b 280; 1993a 341).

The possibility suggested by DeLuca and Laclau locates argumentation in a central position. If human society is understood as the result of a necessary unfolding of reason, argumentation is reduced to discovering what is occurring within a reality external to itself and human advocates are reduced to spectators. If, however, society is understood as groundless, argumentation can become the process through which people construct their own social reality.

Viewed from this perspective, postmodernism actually expands the possibilities for argument. Argumentation becomes constitutive of any social (or political) entity, rather than merely a technique for persuasion. An argument's sensibility involves recognizing that human consciousness is socially constructed through discourse, and this recognition opens up possibilities for new social constructions.

Feminisms

We hope you noticed our choice to use the plural form, "feminisms," to head this section. The following discussion should indicate that there is no universally accepted feminist theory. This is consistent with the feminist project to dismantle nonreflective patterns of social expectation. Jean Bethke Elshtain reminds us that, to accomplish such a goal, "the nature and meaning of feminist discourse itself must be a subject for critical inquiry" (605).

Feminist approaches to argumentation enable us to follow up on a distinction introduced in Chapter 1. Using Daniel O'Keefe's distinctions between argument1 and argument2, we described utterances or claims as fundamental products associated with the argumentation process. Feminist critiques offer at least three possibilities for using this construct as a beginning point for reinterpreting argumentation and critical decision making.

First, they critique traditional methods for evaluating communicative acts (argument1). Second, they suggest alternative descriptions for the entire process of argumentation (argument2). Third, they insist that a fruitful argumentation theory must include analysis of how gender and sex influence the reception of arguments, and how they constrain the presentation of arguments.

Despite the multiplicity of feminisms, some general tendencies can be identified. Here, we will define *feminist argumentation* as a process committed to critically analyzing patriarchal reasoning and revising argumentation (both theory and practice) to include considerations of gender. For additional clarity, we will define *patriarchal reasoning* as reasoning used to justify attitudes, beliefs, values, and policies that subordinate women to men.

The Role of Personal Testimony   One of feminism's earliest critiques of traditional approaches to appraising or evaluating arguments relates to the use of evidence, or support. Traditionally, the use of personal testimony has been relegated to subsidiary status in argumentation, with forms of support such as deductive reasoning, statistics, and expert opinion considered more persuasive. Karlyn Kohrs Campbell studied women speakers and found that they tended to use "personal experience, anecdotes, and other examples" to support their arguments much more often than did male speakers (12–13).

Catherine A. MacKinnon claims that personal testimony is not only pervasive in women's arguments, but is the most valid form of evidence women can use, because their experiences have occurred "within that sphere that has been socially lived as the personal" (535).

Linda Kauffman resists labeling personal testimony as the best form of evidence, however. She claims that it essentializes traditional women's roles, relying on the assumption that "all women share similar conditions and experiences" (163). For example, because the biological experience of bearing children is not available to males, some feminists have offered it as a fundamentally feminine experience that differentiates between forms of communication possible for women and men. This claim, however, isolates women who either cannot or choose not to bear children. Their experience has currency in neither the feminine nor the masculine category. Katrina Bell and her co-authors point out the danger of marginalizing African American women's experiences, which have been significantly different from those of most white, middle-class women. Feminist critiques such as those offered by Kauffman and Bell et al. illustrate why feminisms must remain plural, in order to avoid essentializing a grand narrative of what it means to argue as a woman.

Catherine Helen Palczewski found that when women used personal testimony to support public claims, they were pressured into describing their personal experience in the terms (claims, grounds, warrants) of the males who dominate public spaces. By bringing the personal into the public realm, women implicated themselves in the choice to submit to an expert authority. For example, if a woman is raped and chooses to press charges, she must inscribe her personal experience of the rape into the hegemonic structure of the legal system. Further, if she tells her story in court, she relinquishes control of her experience. It becomes the property of legal and medical experts who will reshape it into the story they think will be most likely to achieve a conviction. Although the experts may be male or female, they will frame the story so it fits into the masculine legal system.

Thus, feminists suggest the importance of giving credence to a broader variety of utterances used as claims, evidence, and other support. They do not agree among themselves, however, on a hierarchy of value among such utterances.

Argumentation as Cooperative Process   Feminisms also have made important contributions to our understanding of the argumentation process. The metaphor of argument-as-war pervades the conceptual system of western culture. As George Lakoff and Michael Johnson point out, even in arguments that are considered nonadversarial, "there is still a position to be established and defended, you can win or lose, you have an opponent whose position you attack and try to destroy and whose argument you try to shoot down" (63). Michael A. Gilbert argues that we cannot change the way we argue unless we develop "a mode of thinking that recognizes all communication as situated and emphasizes agreement" (108–9). He labels such an approach "coalescent argumentation."

Karen Foss and Cindy Griffin offer feminist argumentation as a solution, characterizing it as nurturing, affirmative, promoting self-determination, mutual respect, camaraderie, and viewing the audience as a friend (3–4). They propose an invitational model of rhetoric as a replacement for patriarchal rhetoric, which they characterize as dominating, controlling, competitive, and viewing the audience as an enemy. From this perspective, attempts to change someone's mind are considered patriarchal and coercive, whereas feminist argumentation refers to a friendly exchange of perspectives.

Palczewski and M. Lane Bruner, however, are concerned that this critique inappropriately emphasizes distinctions between argument processes traditionally engaged in by women advocates and those used by men, and threatens to "slip into [the same] biological essentialism" that has characterized traditional argumentation theories (Palczewski 162). For example, Karyn Charles Rybacki and Donald Jay Rybacki interpret feminism as saying "men use argumentation to make mono-causal position statements and tests of knowledge, whereas women engage in conversation, a more inclusive technique, that invites all participants to share their experiences" (2). This interpretation of feminism illustrates a danger Bruner associates with the practice of dichotomizing argumentation into masculine and feminine characteristics. Bruner writes that this practice "disempowers and unnecessarily constrains feminisms. . . . If feminist argumentation theory assumes that one cannot constrain and enable at the same time, or nurture and at the same time seek to change the perspective of another, then feminist argumentation is limited to a very narrow range of argumentative situations" (186, 187). To avoid this trap, feminist theorists have attempted to develop new processes of argument that avoid the binary opposition between male and female. This means that feminism must always struggle against the tendency to essentialize, or naturalize traditional female experience as the defining essence of woman as opposed to man (Bell, et al.).

The concern over essentializing differences between men and women does not mean feminisms cannot offer a significant critique to traditional argumentation processes. For example, Stephen Toulmin, Richard Rieke, and Allan Janik have written that some types of argument rely on consensus whereas others involve adversarial processes (254–255). They offer science and art criticism as illustrations of consensual argument, judicial argument as an illustration of adversarial argument, and business and public policy as illustrations of argument that integrates adversarial and consensus forms. A feminist critique of their perspective would say it does not move far enough beyond adversarial models. It would direct our attention to the fact that consensus in science refers not to a process, but to a temporary goal. For example, the competitive model used in the United States and Western Europe to distribute funds to conduct scientific research, as well as opportunities to publish the results of that research, is extolled as the basis for human progress. The notion that this competition will weed out the weaker proposals, leaving only the most reasonable arguments, is widely held in western society. This adversarial model positions scientists in competition against each other in a search for truth. Feminist critique can encourage public awareness of the implications of the adversarial model, as well as the possibilities for alternative models.

Gender Influences Reception and Presentation   Although feminist argumentation discourages its participants from using sex as a controlling variable, it encourages recognition that gender matters in both the theory and practice of argumentation. Feminist analyses of the judicial system illustrate how the premise of the male norm has circumscribed argumentative outcomes by limiting the scope of available arguments in legal discourse. Carrie Crenshaw demonstrates that legal constructions of neutrality "are reflective of primarily male concerns." When legal advocates argue "that women should be treated the same as men, [they make] the supposedly neutral standpoint the male standpoint" (172).

The conversational style adopted by many female advocates also influences audience reception of their arguments. Despite significant improvements in professional opportunities available to women, society continues to train females to fulfill roles traditionally defined as feminine. A trip through the infants' clothing section of any department store illustrates just how early this socialization process begins. A visitor from another planet would quickly learn that baby girls are to be dressed in pastels, generously sprinkled with lace and ruffles. Baby boys, on the other hand, should be dressed in bright, primary colors, often figured with tools, animals, and trucks. Both in terms of fabric and style, girls' clothing is more suited to sitting and observing, whereas boys' clothing is more suited to active participation. When parents dress their infants in the "wrong" attire, some observers assume the clothing is left over from an older sibling, and others worry that the children will become sexually confused. As girls and boys grow up, distinctions in the treatment of boys versus that of girls becomes increasingly marked.

We are not suggesting that the traditional model for raising boys is better than that used for raising girls. We simply want to point out that the differences have real consequences. These consequences mean that women face additional challenges when making a public argument. Audiences sometimes fail to take their conversational style seriously. In other situations, standards of objectivity and credibility pose challenges. Lorraine Code points out that the credibility of a female advocate suffers from society's tendency to believe women are more intuitive than men, and thus dismissing them as incapable of *producing* knowledge (65). On the other hand, the credibility of women who do not project an intuitive, nurturing persona suffers because they have violated their audiences' expectations.

We hope the previous discussion has demonstrated to you why we use the plural "feminisms," rather than the singular "feminism." These feminisms are most valuable to our study of argumentation when they offer new ways "to think through the forms and functions of, as well as attitudes toward, argument." Despite their differences, most feminisms encourage the search for "emancipatory forms of argument" (Allen and Faigley 162). They can help advocates and audiences recognize the constraining and enabling aspects in all forms of argumentation.

Feminist argumentation encourages recognition "both that existing argumentation is overly grounded on adversarial assumptions and binary oppositions, and that absolute abandonment of argumentation on feminist grounds may be unnecessary; . . . attempt to engage in consensus formation, coalescent reasoning, and non-dualistic thinking as they critique and theorize argument" (Bruner 188). Ultimately, feminist argumentation can be conceptualized as a perpetual critique of the limits imposed by gender stereotypes. This critique puts advocates in a stronger position for undertaking the integrative task of asking how apparently opposing arguments "mesh with other different experience sets, different belief systems, different value codes, and even different reasoning styles" (Ayim 189).

Postmodern and feminist critiques do not signal the end of argument. Rather, they suggest ways that argumentation can be used to constitute a more just society, rather than simply buttressing existing hierarchies. Both postmodern and feminist argumentation would reject the following defense of purely rational argument:

1. "In a pure argumentative encounter, it does not matter whether you are President of the United States or a college junior; all that is relevant is what you have to say. Of course, this ideal is rarely realized, but the principle . . . is one that recognizes the fundamental humanity in all people" (Rowland 359).
2. "As a rational problem-solving tool, argument has no gender; it belongs equally to men and women. Thus, far from being a tool of patriarchal oppressors, argument is one tool with which to free women and other oppressed groups from all forms of domination" (Rowland 362).

Postmodern and feminist approaches to argumentation encourage you to resist the urge to retreat behind a principle of equality that "is rarely realized," and instead to engage in discourse for the purposes of changing existing patterns of privilege. They offer the surprisingly optimistic possibility that argument can do more than change people's ideas on a particular topic. It can alter the very context within which those ideas take shape.

Alternative Dispute Resolution

Ideas developed from postmodern and feminist approaches to argument have motivated some people to explicitly apply argumentation theory to a wide variety of conflicts. Ordinary argument seems unable to resolve some particularly thorny disputes. Researchers have labeled these vexing conflicts as intractable, meaning that they are long running, and have been resistant to multiple attempts at resolution. W. Barnett Pearce and Stephen W. Littlejohn describe them as *moral conflicts.* They suggest that attempts to broker such conflicts should focus on altering the political context, rather than changing people's minds. Their goal is to discover ways of "managing moral disputes in a way that allows expression and without the violent, disrespectful, and demeaning outcomes of open clash" (6). Their work is part of the growing field of research and practice called *alternative dispute resolution* (ADR).

Deborah Kolb described alternative dispute resolution as a set of procedures rooted in the belief that it is essential to "bring a different kind of process to the problems of overcrowded and unsympathetic courts; to changing, conflict-ridden communities; and to the stalemates that accompany long and contentious struggles over public policy and international affairs" (2). One of the most broadly accepted ADR processes is *mediation.* Although mediations vary, all share the feature of having a third-party *facilitator* (known as a mediator) who assists disputants in reaching agreement. Another unifying characteristic is the privileging of participatory conflict resolution as empowering the disputants, and allowing them to deal directly with neutral facilitators rather than with adversarial judges and lawyers. Mediation has become a standard complement to legal systems of jurisprudence.

The rapid growth of ADR's popularity has resulted in a wide variety of processes. They range from approaches that are explicitly grounded in postmodern theory (Pearce and Littlejohn 168–216) to locally grown community groups that learn as they go

(Peterson 148–57). Some explicitly include argumentation and debate in their practices (Daniels and Walker), while others seek consensus (Arthur, Carlson, and Moore; Susskind, McKearnan, and Thomas-Larmer). As you might expect, facilitators also run the gamut from those who have studied the theory behind the Public Dialogue Consortium (Pearce and Littlejohn 197–210) to those who simply have the knack of communicating well in difficult situations. High-profile groups such as the Harvard Negotiation Project (Fisher and Ury; Ury, *Getting Past No; The Third Side*) have developed procedures that have been used in successful international negotiations. For example, U.S. President Jimmy Carter used processes from the Harvard Negotiation Project as a guide to facilitating the Camp David agreements between Israel and Egypt (Fisher and Brown). It is important to note that, in the Camp David agreements, as in most other international ADR "successes," the conflict was not resolved, but reformed in a way that made it more amenable to humane management.

Conclusion

When you critically approach argumentation, your choices and evaluations will be influenced by your history as well as your current circumstances. The interaction between you, other participants in the dispute, and the larger political structure within which all of you engage will influence both your ability to present an argument and its reception. This does not mean that the outcomes are controlled by external forces. In fact, it suggests that the discursive patterns you choose have the power to fundamentally alter the available possibilities.

Every situation has established patterns of criteria that help participants evaluate the possibilities for argumentation. Common patterns such as good reasons, science, and storytelling have evolved to help people make and justify critical decisions and argumentation. Understanding and using these patterns will help you argue effectively in most settings.

During the last half of the twentieth century, new patterns of criteria that responded to social and political changes began to emerge. These patterns are rooted in postmodern and feminist thought, and bring an explicitly critical edge to the theory and practice of argumentation. These patterns are especially useful to you if your goal is to change existing configurations of power. They also provide a theoretical basis for an explicitly nonadversarial approach to argumentation known as alternative dispute resolution.

P R O J E C T

Select an editorial from your local newspaper. Revise the editorial twice. First, write a version of the editorial that is persuasive from a scientific perspective. Be sure to use Pine's essential elements in your revision. Second, write a version of the editorial that uses either a feminist or a postmodern sensibility to make the same argument.

CHAPTER

4

Analysis in Argumentation

KEY TERM

Finding a proposition
question
objectives and values
costs and risks
biases
uncontroversial matter
alternatives

argumentative case
analysis of a proposition
determining issues
stock issues
comparative advantage
analysis of claims
criteria

Not all communication is an argument, as we have already noted. But, much of it is when you and others with whom you communicate seek to justify claims. This process can be a simple one of interpersonal exchange about what video game to play, or whether to go to Saturday's football game. Many other situations produce claims that require more extensive justification.

Argumentation can even be a lengthy and involved process with hundreds of arguments and issues developing around a single proposition of fact, value, or policy. Consider, for instance:

There is a God. (fact)
Democracy is a superior form of government. (value)
Individual freedom should be guaranteed to all persons. (policy)

On such claims there are potentially an infinite number of related arguments because by one chain of reasoning or another all potential arguments can be related. Certainly, that is the assumption of the theologian who looks at the factual proposition, "There is a God." But, even the theologian will select from all the potential claims those that will build the best case for the proposition, "There is a God." The propositions that you argue will be based on a limited number of claims. To find the proposition you wish to argue, and the claims that support it, requires *analysis: the examination of an argumentative situation for its claims and opposing claims to discover the issues and what arguments and support (evidence, values, and credibility) are most important.*

Analysis of argument is necessary, no matter at what point you enter the argumentation process. It may be your intention to seek the adherence of someone else to a claim or to refute another's claim. You may also want to evaluate your own or someone else's argumentation.

Analysis should be undertaken systematically and in advance of presenting arguments to decision makers. Analysis is not just a matter of acquiring knowledge. It is a process whereby all the constituents of the argumentative situation are examined in such a way that what needs to be argued and what it will take to gain adherence is known. With careful analysis, you can develop more effective arguments supported by evidence, values, and credibility. And even more, analysis involves learning about the others with whom you will argue. What arguments might they make that could damage your position with the appropriate decision makers?

Analysis has two somewhat distinctive parts. One part deals with developing claims from questions, when you realize that some problem requires resolution but you are not sure what that resolution is—what Charles Sanders Peirce called a "feeling of doubt." The second part is used after the proposition has been identified from the analysis of a general question. Then the objective of analysis is to find the crucial issues, understand their relative importance, and examine the claims to see what you must prove to decision makers. These two can overlap and interact if changes occur in the proposition. A single analysis may move back and forth from one to the other, but we will treat them separately because they are rather different approaches. We will first look at how to develop the proposition you wish to argue from a general question.

Critical Analysis to Find a Proposition

When you realize that there is some kind of a problem, when you have a feeling of doubt, you frequently aren't sure what to do about it. Critical decision making can be used to help you discover the proposition you will argue. If you only express your feeling of doubt you may gain the adherence of some others who are equally frustrated, but to solve the problem you need a clearer statement of the proposition. Statements like the following have to be refined into propositions to which decision makers can respond:

> Something is wrong with the library fine system.
> How serious is sexual harassment on this campus?
> Why can't the city coordinate traffic lights?
> When will the United States recognize the needs of people with disabilities?

Argumentation takes place in a broader societal context of decision making. There are stages that individuals, groups, and even whole societies go through to deal with problems. The stages in critical analysis are intended to determine a proposition.

These stages of critical analysis involve the dialectical process of posing questions and searching for answers and the rhetorical process of finding claims and support for them so that others may grant adherence to your claims (Rieke, "The Judicial Dialogue" 42–43). There are eight stages to the selection of a proposition.

An arguable proposition may appear at any stage and you need not go through each stage. Your analysis should help you to decide at what point to enter the process. If no one recognizes that a problem exists you must develop claims about the problem. But, if everyone agrees that there is a problem, you may skip that stage. Suppose everyone agrees the library fine system is unfair. If everyone is agreed on the unfairness, you can slight the analysis of the problem and search for a proposition in the solution. Therefore, you will usually not need all eight stages, depending on how advanced your knowledge is about the controversy in the question.

Identify the Question

The feeling of doubt that you have needs to be refined into a clearly stated question that represents the problem. In order to do this you must entertain genuine doubt (Dewey; Peirce). Ask yourself, "What are the potential meanings to my concern?" Entertain the possibility of alternatives. From these, identify and face squarely the question that represents that feeling of doubt (Browne and Keeley; Ruggiero 92; Millman 45). Let us use your generalized concern over library fines as an example. Here are some examples of the thoughts you might have about the library that could set the basis for you to ask the question, "What is actually the problem with library fines?"

> I forgot the due date last quarter and it cost me $16.
>
> Fines are stupid. People ought to be trusted.
>
> Many students complain that the statement of the fines system is confused and confusing.
>
> Fines cost more to enforce than they bring in.

Can you phrase a question from one of these, or some other statement, that will define the problem and provide a basis for further critical analysis?

Survey Implicated Objectives and Values

From your experience, research, and thought, identify those objectives and values that seem to be related to the question that concerns you. You need to ask: What problems seem to need addressing? What might an ideal system look like? What values do you wish to see embodied in such a program? Knowing what is sought in the decision making and the values to be served sets up the criteria upon which arguments will be tested (Janis and Mann 11). This includes your values and those of others involved as decision makers or critics. On the library question, you might consider what the objectives of a library should be; what values, such as knowledge and service, should govern the situation. The library values having books available when people want them. People value finding the books they want when they want them. No one likes to pay fines, but we often need books beyond the due date or we carelessly forget to return them. Notice how values tend to come into conflict.

Canvass Alternative Decisions

Sometimes people look for alternative decisions only long enough to find the first one that fits; sometimes they look only for the alternatives that seem most attractive. Sometimes they use a small list of handy criteria and eliminate alternatives until one is left, and sometimes people just muddle through, choosing by hit or miss (Janis and Mann 21–41; Ruggiero 92). To be critical means to examine the widest range of alternative propositions, including some that you are tempted to dismiss at once. You might consider ending all library fines, adapting them more to specific situations, or basing fines on ability to pay. Or you might decide the library should have more copies of important books, put all material online and eliminate hard copies, or find another punishment for delinquent patrons.

Weigh the Costs and Risks

Being critical means looking at the negative as well as the positive arguments on all alternative decisions (Janis and Mann 11). *Cost* means more than money; it means values and goods sacrificed by rejecting one alternative for another. *Risk* includes the degree of uncertainty involved and the strength of the worst-case scenario. So, what are the costs and risks of the possible solutions to the library fine problem? Would books be returned if there were no fines? Is it too expensive to buy multiple copies or go online? Are other punishments more onerous than fines?

Search for New Information

Using words like *facts* or *data* often masks the complexity of information seeking. Information means overcoming ambiguity in language, developing a measure of the quality of evidence, searching for errors in discovery or measurement of data, and thinking about significant information that is missing (Browne and Keeley). What kind of information do you need to convince you that people would return books without fines? Or that going online is expensive?

Criticize the Alternatives

Each alternative claim must be tested against the objectives and values sought in the decision and the relevant information (Ruggiero 92; Millman 46–47). This testing includes reexamination of the positive and negative consequences of each alternative proposition, even when the process puts originally attractive alternatives at risk (Janis and Mann 11; Browne and Keeley).

Note Your Biases That Block Alternatives

The brain has been called a "variably synchronized illusion organ" (Regal 48–69), which means that people can create their own reality and feel confident about it while others perceive them as wrong. One extreme case is of three people in Ypsilanti, Michigan, who were each certain they were Christ, even when confronted by the others making the same claim (Rokeach "Three Christs").

You are not likely to have that problem, but everyone has blind spots. You must notice what biases and prejudices are driving you toward or away from some alternatives (Browne and Keeley). This area is where your awareness of the thinking of others is most useful. It is not reasonable to hold to positions simply because *you* feel strongly about them. Remember the library fine example? Perhaps you are bothered by the library fine system because you had to pay. Perhaps others will see this as your problem, not the library's. It is not necessary that you change your position just because others disagree with it, but a careful examination of others' views will help you to check your biases.

Select a Proposition

Using the results of the earlier stages, you are ready to select the proposition you find most reasonable. Perhaps you will discover that many people believe the statement of the library fine policy is confusing, so you decide the policy should be rewritten. Or, finding that, unlike other libraries, yours has no grace period, you might then decide that the library fine system should provide for a seven-day grace period for all except reserve books. Perhaps you will discover that there is no arguable problem and, therefore, you have no proposition.

These eight stages of critical decision making are used to find a proposition from a feeling of doubt when you believe there is a problem but do not know what to do about it. Perhaps you went through such stages wondering what to do when you graduated from high school. You may be going through them right now as you try to decide what your major should be. You may be familiar with this process from your job. It is a system widely advocated by management experts.

Traditionally, after you have selected a proposition, you will be expected to consider three other steps: (1) Make plans to implement the proposition, (2) Prepare contingency plans, and (3) Build a case for your decision. These will be covered in Chapter 5, Case Building.

Critical analysis, as we will consider it in this chapter, involves a first stage, finding a proposition, and a second stage, analyzing it for issues. You will not always go through the first stage to find a proposition. Frequently, the proposition has already been identified. That is true of most public propositions. You have probably already heard of such propositions as:

> Abortion should be illegal.
> Medical marijuana should be legalized.
> Affirmative action programs are unnecessary.
> Same-sex marriages should be legal.

You may even have considerable information and a position for or against each of these propositions. Even so, you would be wise to go through the stages to give yourself a better understanding of the proposition and its alternatives, to make yourself a more valuable participant in the discussion. Whether you found your proposition by critical appraisal or had it presented to you through public debate, the process of identifying your supporting claims begins. That requires the second stage: critical analysis of a proposition.

Critical Analysis of a Proposition

Any proposition is analyzed by identifying the various claims (fact, value, and policy) that are available to support or oppose it. Take note of what others are saying and what you can think of about the proposition, then state the claims that are both expressed and implied. Search out the crucial issues. These issues are generated by looking to the clash of arguments, as in a debate. Not all argumentative situations are debates, but each is potentially a debate. If you wish to advance arguments, you must be prepared to answer objections to them. You need to meet even unstated objections that are likely to be known by decision makers. Therefore, it is best to treat every argumentative situation as a potential debate.

In Chapter 1, we spoke of the internal dialogue through which you engage in a mini-debate in your own mind. That debate should involve imagining how others would react to your proposition. You should pursue both sides of the proposition with equal vigor. Critical decision making requires that you find the issues and you will only find issues if you study both sides of a proposition.

Determining the Issues

A simple method for determining the issues is to make a list of arguments for and against the proposition and then match them up. For instance, in November of 2002 voters in the state of Nevada had an opportunity to vote on State Question No 9: "Shall the Nevada Constitution be amended to allow the use and possession of three ounces or less of marijuana by persons aged 21 years or older, to require the Legislature to provide or maintain penalties for using, distributing, selling or possessing marijuana under certain circumstances, and to provide a system of regulation for cultivation, taxation, sale and distribution of marijuana?" In the official sample ballot there were statements for and against Question 9 (Figure 4.1). These statements are the basis for

FIGURE 4.1

For	Against
1. Proposal "will allow law enforcement and the courts to focus resources on more serious crimes."	"Decriminalization will lead to more crime, more substance abuse."
	a. The tourism industry in Nevada will be negatively impacted."
	b. "Nevada will become the nation's marketplace for drug sale and usage."
2. "Marijuana has fewer harmful side effects than alcohol and tobacco, which are already legal and regulated by the state."	"Savings resulting from refocusing law enforcement resources will be outweighed by increased health costs."
3. "The system of regulation and taxation required by the proposed amendment could generate tax revenue for the state."	The increased tax revenue will "be outweighed by the cost" of "another state agency to regulate the cultivation, sale, taxation, and distribution of marijuana."
4. "State control may replace the current illegal market for marijuana."	
5. Proposal would "require the legislature to authorize appropriate methods of supply and distribution of marijuana for medical purposes at low cost."	"Because production and distribution of marijuana is illegal under federal law, effective regulation will be impossible to enact and enforce."
a. "Seriously ill patients" who cannot afford it now will be able "to enjoy the medical benefits of marijuana."	Nevada law already allows for the medical use of marijuana.
	6. "Marijuana is a 'gateway' drug."
	a. Decriminalization will increase the number of marijuana users who will likely move on to "drugs like heroin and cocaine."
	7. "It is not appropriate to amend the Nevada Constitution to create a right to use and possess marijuana."

you to see how a proposition is analyzed. Before you begin to examine the arguments for and against this proposition, you should realize that you are looking at real-world argumentation, which is not always as clear or well-developed as you would like.

Above are the main arguments (not necessarily in the order they were made). The numbers identify the main claims made by each side. The unnumbered statements are claims made in opposition to the numbered claims. This matching up of claims and counterclaims can help you set the issues.

These arguments, matched up for and against, are organized to determine issues—the places where opposing claims clash. First, look at the opposing claims that do not suggest an issue because they agree with one another. In this case there are none. But sometimes there will be claims that are called *uncontroversial matter.* Both sides agree to the claim. It is not an issue. Argument 4 could be an example of un-controversial matter. The argument is so weak ("State control *may* replace . . .) that it will not be contested. Later in the debate if it is strengthened it may become an issue. It may also be used as support for another issue.

Two claims of the opponents to the proposition are not specifically agreed to by its supporters, but those claims are also not opposed. They might be opposed later in the election campaign but now do not constitute issues:

6. "Marijuana is a 'gateway' drug. Decriminalization will increase the number of marijuana users who move on to drugs like heroin and cocaine."
7. "It is not appropriate to amend the Nevada Constitution to create a right to use and possess marijuana."

Argument 6 is the most interesting of these seeming non-issues. Although there is no mention in the arguments for decriminalization about controlling drug use, one would expect either or both of the arguments that marijuana does not lead to hard drugs or that marijuana use will not increase under decriminalization. Could it be that people who favor decriminalization agree with argument 6 and it is uncontroversial matter? Perhaps when they consider the voters, the decision makers in this case, they will need to oppose this argument and make it an issue.

Argument 7 is not uncontroversial matter. Those who oppose decriminalization surely believe that amending the Nevada Constitution is appropriate. However, it is a technical claim and, perhaps, not worth spending time on.

If you eliminate arguments 4 and 7 as not constituting issues (though we real-ize that they may come into play as a part of another issue) and keep argument 6 be-cause it is central to the case against decriminalization, there are five issues:

1. Will decriminalization decrease crime?
2. Is marijuana less harmful than alcohol and tobacco?
3. Will decriminalization produce greater revenue for the state?
4. Will decriminalization improve the distribution and cost of medical marijuana?
5. Will decriminalization increase the number of marijuana and drug users?

There were more arguments raised during the campaign, but these five from the ballot arguments are a reasonable summary of the issues. They reflect the fundamen-tal questions to be addressed in order to make a critical voting decision.

Rank-Order the Issues

The first stage in this process of locating the issues more specifically is to rank-order them based on their importance to the decision makers. Permit us to illustrate how you might examine these issues based on what we know from following the topic.

The decision about which issues are more and which are less important deter-mines your strategy for building a case. From the arguments and issues developed in this analysis, it appears that issue #1 (Will decriminalization decrease crime?) and issue #5 (Will decriminalization increase the number of marijuana and hard drug users?) are most important and they are related. They could almost be combined, for if decriminalization would decrease arrests for possession of three ounces or less but increase the number of users of marijuana and hard drugs, a person might oppose the proposition on the basis that it would cause *greater* harm. The resolution of these issues would answer issue #3 (Will decriminalization produce greater revenue for the state?), as well. Because issue #3 is dependent on issues #1 and #5, we see it as relatively less important than the other issues.

The second most important issue, it seems to us, is the issue of harm, #2: "Is marijuana less harmful than alcohol and tobacco?" The distribution and possession of marijuana is a federal crime because it is generally considered dangerous to one's health and to the public welfare because it leads to crime. Large numbers of voters, perhaps a majority, will want *proof* that it is not harmful before they consider decriminalization. So issue #2 is close in importance to issues #1 and #5.

Issue #4, on the distribution and lower costs for medical marijuana, might influence some people who find it difficult to get the medical marijuana they believe they need, though it is not likely to be the most important issue for the public at large. However, the argument *against* the distribution for medical reasons (see the summary of arguments, Figure 4.1) raises a question that could be an additional vital issue: Is it impossible to have effective regulations because marijuana is illegal under federal law? If the answer is yes, that calls into question many of the arguments for the proposition, including the entire last clause asking the legislature "to provide a system of regulation for the cultivation, taxation, sale, and distribution of marijuana."

The process of rank-ordering the issues requires you to consider not just what you think, or what an opponent might think, but the preconceptions of the decision makers. Such speculation can lead to a number of different conclusions, but our analysis so far produces the following rank order:

Increase or decrease in crime. (#1)

Increase or decrease in the number of users. (#5)

Harm from marijuana. (#2)

Increase or decrease in revenue (#3)

Improve or not distribution and cost of medical marijuana. (#4)
(But watch here for an issue of federal versus state action.)

Assuming this is the order of importance, you will want your case to emphasize the issues in the same order. If you believe that the revenue issue #3 is the most important one, you would need to realize that it will take a lot more argumentation to raise it in the consciousness of decision makers.

The arguments over Nevada State Question No. 9 are complex and sometimes implied, but there are five issues here that are probably at the center of the controversy, and are the questions on which the decision makers should be expected to decide. In Chapter 5 we will discuss case building. We will show you several ways of organizing your case. Two of these case formats are useful in analysis as you try to understand the issues, regardless of what case you build: stock issue and comparative advantage analysis.

Stock Issue Analysis

Many people use *stock issue analysis* as a means of understanding the issues in a policy claim. They are called *stock* because they serve as a generic guide to policy analysis. Users of stock issue analysis say that to gain adherence to a policy claim you have to get a positive response from decision makers on three questions:

1. Is there a need for a change from the status quo?
2. Is the proposed change practical?
3. Is the proposed change desirable? (Will its advantages outweigh its disadvantages?)[1]

Here are the potential issues from Question 9 organized by stock issues.

Need for a change
Is marijuana harmful to one's health?

Practicality
Is the proposition inappropriate for a constitutional amendment?
Is the proposition impossible to enact because of federal law?

Desirability
Will the proposition decrease or increase crime?
Will the proposition increase or decrease the number of users?
Will the proposition increase or decrease revenue?

There are a few interesting points about these issues. All of these are issues of fact that support a policy proposition. There are value claims that support some of the issues but they are probably uncontroversial matter. For instance, in the need issue, "Is marijuana harmful to one's health?" both sides agree that good health is positive, so this value claim is not part of the debate. A similar situation exists with the issue of the increase or decrease of crime. Crime is a negative value for both sides.

At least two of these issues, "Is marijuana harmful to one's health?" (need) and "Is the proposition impossible to enact because of federal law?" (practicality) are straightforward issues of fact. Either side can argue using medical studies, studies of

---

[1]The stock issues of policy as we have identified them here are the most traditional. Others have used some variation of (1) Ill (need), (2) Blame, (3) Cure (the proposed change), (4) Cost/Benefit (Warnick and Inch 240–43; Ziegelmueller, Kay, and Dause 38–46; Lee and Lee 163–64). See Robert O. Weiss 76–77 for an example of a writer who uses stock issues as we do.

the relationship between marijuana and hard drug use, exact attention to federal law and court rulings. A third issue, "Is the proposition inappropriate for a constitutional amendment?" (practicality again) depends on the definition of the word *inappropriate*. Is there some legal statement by which the inappropriateness of a constitutional amendment may be judged? Or, is this almost a value issue, where "inappropriate" means the violation of some societal value?

The three issues of desirability are all issues of future fact, making them more difficult to prove. To support the decriminalization of marijuana one might argue by analogy, for instance, that crime decreased when the prohibition against alcohol ended, or that crime or health is better or worse in other countries that have decriminalized marijuana. However, it is much more difficult to prove a claim of future fact than it is to prove one of present fact. The issues of desirability will probably be the most contested issues and the most difficult to prove.

Dividing the issues by stock issue analysis will help you to see what you need to prove and where the emphasis should be. It will also help you to see what kind of evidence, values, and credibility you need to make that emphasis, and, as we shall see in Chapter 5 (Case Building), this technique can be used to organize your case.

Comparative Advantage Analysis

When a need is agreed to and only questions of practicality and desirability remain, analysis usually proceeds on a comparative advantage basis. Comparative advantage means that you analyze the advantages and disadvantages of the proposal against the *status quo,* Latin for "the way things are now," or some other alternative. Suppose your analysis revealed that Question No. 9 had these possible advantages and disadvantages:

Advantages	*Disadvantages*
It is no more harmful than alcohol or tobacco.	It is harmful to one's health.
It will decrease crime.	It will increase crime.
It will increase revenue.	It will decrease revenue.
It will provide appropriate methods of supply.	It will be impossible to enact because of federal law.

There is an additional, hidden advantage to decriminalization. Those in favor probably favor decriminalization because they see the current law as unfair to current users. However, they do not argue this claim because of a possible negative reaction in the general population. That does not mean that it won't be in the minds of some decision makers and may need to be considered in building a case.

What becomes most interesting in this comparative analysis is that the last disadvantage listed, if upheld, can detract from all the advantages (except for health) because decrease in crime and increase in revenue both depend on an alternate means of distribution through the state. So, if such action could not be taken because of federal law, then all the advantages melt away. The ability of the state to set up a method of supply and distribution could be the central issue in a case against decriminalization.

Analysis of Claims

When the proposition is reduced to a workable series of issues of fact and value, you must further refine your analysis by focusing on each fact or value claim used to support or oppose the proposition. Your objective here is to develop a plan for assessing the strength with which the claims resolve the issue.

Identify the Most Significant Claims

We have discussed the ordering of issues on pages 64–66 and will not repeat that here. But as we already observed, the most significant claim may be about the practicality of a state program to regulate marijuana. If so, opponents will need to concentrate much of their argument on that issue. Note, however, that the possibility that federal action might make state action impossible is not in the original arguments in favor of Question No. 9. The proponents of decriminalization don't want to bring that up. They concentrate on what they see as their advantages. But, they still will need to be prepared for the claim in a rebuttal argument that federal law preempts their advantages. It may be the most significant issue even if not publicly acknowledged by those who favor decriminalization. If it is in the minds of the decision makers it cannot be ignored.

Clarify What Each Claim Asserts

At this point you have a rank-ordered series of issues, you know their significance to the stock issues, and you have recognized the comparative advantages of each. Next, you need to analyze each of them to locate the specific nature of the issue. For instance, on the issue "Is marijuana less harmful than alcohol and tobacco?" what does less harmful mean?

While there are no stock issues of fact or value because values change with decision makers and spheres, there are some guidelines for such analysis.[2] Those guidelines involve establishing criteria for evaluating each claim and then finding the point at which the claim is most vulnerable to rebuttal. Disagreements may arise over the criteria themselves, the relationship of the claim to the criteria, or the relationship of the support to the criteria.

[2]Some writers have called something similar to what we are suggesting here the four stock issues of propositions of value. For instance:

1. What are the definitions of the key terms?
2. What are the criteria for the values?
3. Do the facts correspond to the definitions?
4. What are the applications of the values? (Freeley 55: Warnick and Inch 218–22).

Each claim has a subject term and a judgment term. For instance, on the claim "Marijuana is less harmful than alcohol or tobacco," there is little difficulty in understanding the subject term. The subject of this sentence is marijuana. However, the judgment term, *less harmful,* presents a problem in definition. That is where the criteria come in. What criteria can you use to define less harmful? Does it include the harm from hard drugs? It is only after you know the criteria for making a judgment that the judgment can be verified.

Let us use this claim as a basis for the next problem in the analysis of issues of fact and value: what is the specific point of clash that makes this claim an issue?

Locate the Points of Disagreement

To evaluate a claim you must locate the points of disagreement over it. As you do this work, you will be setting up the basis on which to evaluate the strength of the claim. We will suggest four locations for disagreement:

LOCATION I: By what criteria should the claim be judged?
LOCATION II: Which criteria are the most important?
LOCATION III: To what extent does the claim satisfy the criteria?
LOCATION IV: What is the strength of support for the claim?

By What Criteria Should the Claim Be Judged? Those who oppose Question No. 9 could argue that since marijuana leads to hard drugs, it is more harmful than alcohol and tobacco. With that argument they would be using the strongest available criterion. Those who argue for decriminalization could claim as the criterion that only marijuana health costs compared to alcohol and tobacco be used. Thus, there would be an issue over criteria.

Which Criteria Are the Most Important? Even when criteria are agreed upon there can still be a disagreement over which criterion is most important. For instance, suppose that proponents and opponents agree on three criteria for judging a claim that the proposition is "impossible to enact because of federal law." They are:

1. Statements in federal narcotics laws
2. Federal court rulings
3. Basic rights of states under the U.S. Constitution

They still could disagree over which is most important. Proponents could argue, for instance, that states' rights principles are most important. Opponents could argue that federal court rulings define what the states' rights are.

To What Extent Does the Claim Satisfy the Criteria? The three criteria identified above, even if accepted by all parties to the dispute, may not resolve the disagreement over the claim that the legalization of marijuana is "impossible to enact because of federal law." The federal law may be vague on the question of state action or there may be conflicting court rulings. The claim that such a legalization would be "impossible to enact" could be subject to qualification and, therefore, have less force than the arguer would want.

What Is the Strength of Support for the Claim?   Every argument must ultimately rest on some kind of support (evidence, values, or credibility). We mentioned earlier that the arguments in the November 2002 *Nevada State Sample Ballot* are not supported. To fully argue the case there must be more than assertion. Therefore, it is necessary to find the available support, and evaluate it as a part of the case.

Particularly on factual claims, the support necessary will usually emphasize evidence (examples, statistics, testimony). An arguer needs to find the strongest possible evidence for a position. Though values and credibility can be strong bases to support arguments, they are most effective when linked to evidence.

What evidence is most trustworthy to decision makers on the effects of marijuana: Personal examples? Scientific studies? Testimony of experts?

Conclusion

People determine where argumentation begins. They discover problems and determine how these problems will be resolved. They frequently do this in a hit-or-miss fashion from limited knowledge and analysis. The adherence of others can be more easily developed if the analysis of problems takes place systematically rather than haphazardly.

To understand how to engage in such analysis, some terms need to be understood. Because any statement may be linked to any other statement and thus generate an infinite number of claims, the number of arguments must be reduced to some workable basis. This is achieved in two parts: first, the critical process of finding a proposition when only a general problem (a "feeling of doubt") is recognized; and, second, the process of finding the crucial issues in the argumentation after the proposition has been identified.

Propositions are discovered through a process of analysis involving eight potential steps: identify the question, survey implicated objectives and values, canvass alternative decisions, weigh the costs and risks, search for new information, criticize the alternatives, note your biases that block alternatives, and, then, select a proposition.

Once a proposition has been determined, it can be more specifically analyzed. A policy proposition is analyzed by looking for the clash of arguments as in a debate, rank-ordering the issues, applying stock issue analysis, and examining comparative advantages. Thus, by looking at both sides of the proposition, the arguer can discover the issues of fact or value that are likely to be most crucial. Each value and factual claim is analyzed by finding criteria for the judgment term in the claim with which to measure the subject term. Issues about fact and value claims will be found in one of four locations:

1. The formation of appropriate criteria
2. The relative importance of various criteria
3. Whether or not the claims meet the criteria
4. The strength of support for the criteria

When the proposition is identified, the issues discovered, and their specific natures identified, the arguer can then determine what must be argued and how best to build a case for it.

P R O J E C T

Many newspapers, including *USA Today,* have a regular feature of printing two opposing editorials on current topics. *Congressional Quarterly* also features such exchanges and, of course, they can be found in ballot pamphlets such as we have used in this chapter. Find one of these exchanges and find the issues in the controversy.

5   Case Building

KEY TERMS

presumption	clarity
burden of proof	significance
prima facie case	relevance
burden of rejoinder	inherency
brief	consistency
contexts	chain of reasoning
counterargument	problem–solution
convincing vision	criteria

In our discussion of the steps in argumentation analysis in Chapter 4, we closed with the mandate to build an argumentative case for the proposition you want to be adopted by the decision makers. We also explained analysis, which forms the backbone of case building. In this chapter, we tell you how to build a case.

Sometimes we hear people condemn the argumentative effort involved in presenting a well-prepared case with the claim that the truth needs no defense. Looking back over thousands of years of history and noting the frequency with which poor decisions have been made, we can only conclude that people who believe truth needs no defense are dangerously naive.

A lawyer approached the annual meeting of her firm's salary committee with the belief that she was outperforming many of the male attorneys but was not being rewarded accordingly. She was aware of an "Old Boys" network that operated during the firm's daily basketball games and discussions that followed in the locker room among the male partners, so she decided to prepare a case for herself.

When she went to the salary committee meeting, she had charts demonstrating her performance in each of the firm's criteria for rewards: billable hours, new clients brought to the firm, revenue generated, pro bono work, successful overall performance, and so on. Her charts demonstrated a growth curve in each criterion and compared it with the firm's standards to reveal that she was, indeed, one of the top producers.

The response was disappointing. The senior and managing partners said it was unseemly to make such a "case" out of the annual salary review. One was expected to be more sedate and cool about the whole thing and let the true qualities of one's performance emerge quietly.

Does that mean that preparing a case was a mistake? No. If she had waited for her true qualities to emerge on their own, they might never have been recognized. It does say, however, that cases must be adapted to the sphere in which they will be presented. In this law firm, cases for salary and other professional rewards were expected to emerge subtly through interpersonal interaction throughout the year. The annual salary meeting was designed as an opportunity to present a relaxed and confident summary of a case already made.

If the women in the firm do not choose to play basketball at noon, or if they do not feel truly welcome to do so, they must find other opportunities for interaction with senior partners or those on the salary committee through which to make their case according to the cultural rules of the firm. And, in spite of the resistance to formal presentations to the salary committee, it still makes sense for those in less powerful positions to prepare a formal case, because they have to confront the power establishment with the reasonableness of their positions.

So when we talk about making an argumentative case, we are referring to preparing a plan, a strategy, a comprehensive series of arguments that combine to support a decision persuasively. In a sense, a case is a complete story that helps others see that your proposed decision is the right and sensible thing to do. The context in which a case is communicated and the manner of communication will vary according to the argumentative or decision rules of the particular sphere in which the decision will be made.

In this chapter, we discuss the preliminary steps toward building cases, the process of briefing arguments, developing a vision of the case, and communicating the case to specific decision makers. We aim our discussion toward more formal situations, in the belief that if you can handle the complex cases you can surely adjust downward toward less formality (an argument using the commonplace *a fortiori* as we explain in Chapter 2).

Preliminary Steps in Case Building

As academic debaters, business executives, lawyers, legislators, or scientists will tell you, good cases are the result of both thorough preparation and knowing how to build them. No matter how clever you are at argumentation, you will have a tough time defending a position against others who have done more and better research, assuming they are also accomplished in argumentation. The preliminary steps in case building are vital and must not be overlooked.

Follow Critical Decision Making

In Chapter 4, we set out a series of steps in critical decision making. This process constitutes the bulk of the preliminary work to be done in the preparation of a case. Even though you begin wanting to defend a certain point of view or specific decision, you are wise to set that aside momentarily and analyze the situation with as open a mind as possible. Looking seriously at all alternatives with as much knowledge and as little prejudice as possible will strengthen your position in one or more of the following ways: (1) You will have available the strongest possible statement of your case; (2) You will have a realistic knowledge of the strengths and weaknesses of other alternatives (we often assume weaknesses that do not exist); (3) You will be able to modify your position to avoid weaknesses and maximize strengths; (4) You will be able to abandon your position entirely if you find it not worthy of your support.

Identify the Nature of the Proposition

Having worked your way through the steps in critical decision making, you should be ready to advance the point of view or outcome of your research. You will be required to establish adherence to a series of specific claims that, when combined, will add up to support for your more encompassing claim, which we call a proposition (legislators call it a resolution or bill; lawyers call it a cause of action, claim, or motion; scholars call it a thesis, hypothesis, or theory; and people in business call it a presentation, pitch, or sales message). Propositions are explained in Chapter 4.

Suppose you are thinking about buying a new car. Like almost everyone, you would like to get the best car for the least amount of money, but you are not entirely confident of your ability to do so. *Consumer Reports* is a magazine dedicated to helping people make critical decisions, and they have prepared a case designed to convince you to subscribe to their "New Car Price Service." Let's see how their arguments are presented. Their proposition is that car buying can be less of an ordeal for you if you subscribe to their service.

    I. To negotiate effectively for a new car, you must know what the dealer paid for the car.
      A. The "sticker" price represents what the dealer wants you to pay.
      B. The "invoice" price is a guide to what the dealer paid.
      C. The New Car Price Service will provide you with the following:
         1. Invoice and sticker price for the car.
         2. Invoice and sticker price for all factory installed options and packages.
         3. Current rebates, unadvertised dealer incentives, and holdbacks.
    II. To negotiate effectively for a new car, you need to understand how cars are sold.
      A. Salespersons want to bargain down from the sticker price, but you should bargain up from the invoice price.
         1. If the car you want is in tight supply, you may have to pay full price.
         2. Otherwise, 4 to 8 percent over the invoice price for popular models is reasonable.

  B. Salespersons want to sell extras that increase the price.
   1. For example, rustproofing, undercoating, fabric protection, extended warrranty, windshield etching, and so on are generally overpriced or worthless.
  C. New Car Price Service will provide solid advice on how to negotiate your best deal.
   1. With invoice and sticker price comparisons, you have your negotiating room.
   2. You will have step-by-step professional car-buying advice.
   3. New car buyers who use New Car Price Service save an average of $2,200 on their purchases.
   4. The cost of the service is $12.[1]

Did the arguments in this case sound convincing? Can you think of ways the case could have been made stronger? Would you seriously consider using this service before buying a new car?

Assess Presumptions and Burden of Proof

In Chapter 2 we introduced you to presumptions which, alongside shared interpretative strategies, facts, probabilities, and commonplaces, are starting points of argument. Now we extend the concept of presumption to include decision makers' state of mind regarding your proposition and introduce the concept of burden of proof to describe the challenge to overcoming presumption.

Presumption In 1828, Richard Whately defined a presumption in favor of any proposition as the "preoccupation of the ground, which implies that it must stand good till some sufficient reason is adduced against it; in short, that the burden of proof lies on the side [that] would dispute it" (Whately 112). This says nothing about the truth or quality of that position. Presumption identifies the state of mind or prejudice people hold regarding some proposition.

Because propositions emerge from the basic concepts of fact, value, and policy, you can usually expect to find decision makers presuming that what they now regard as fact, value, and policy will continue to be so regarded unless and until someone undertakes the burden of proving otherwise. Frequently, this means that there is a presumption in favor of the *status quo,* but not always.

The only presumption that matters, however, is what is actually in the minds of those who will ultimately make the decision. To find presumption, then, you must go to the decision makers and listen carefully. They will not always tell you the truth. Because we extol open-mindedness, people are often reluctant to confess their prejudices.

---

[1]This ad (case) appears regularly on the back cover of *Consumer Reports.* We have drawn our example from the September 2003 edition.

Everyone has prejudices or established world views, as we describe in Chapter 2 in the discussion of argumentation and critical appraisal. You must build your case on your best analysis of your decision makers' genuine presumptions.

In the debate over affirmative action, which we will discuss later, the presumption is hard to figure. Because affirmative action policies have been in place for many years, you might assume they benefit from the usual presumption in favor of the status quo. But, in June of 2003, the U.S. Supreme Court declared University of Michigan undergraduate admissions unconstitutional and its law school admissions constitutional, both with regard to affirmative action and on the same day. So, presumption is unclear, at best.[2]

If presumption favors your proposition, your case need only be aimed at maintaining and reinforcing it. You may need no case at all if no one is arguing for another proposition. The best case often consists of few words. If you were already familiar with *Consumer Reports'* New Car Price Service and planned to use it to buy your new car, their case could have consisted of the name plus the 800 number. If, however, you never heard of *Consumer Reports,* and consider yourself a pretty savvy negotiator, their case would need to be hardhitting and persuasive.

Burden of Proof   Burden of proof identifies the responsibility to initiate argument and set out a case sufficient in argumentative strength and breadth to bring the decision makers to doubt their presumptions and then see themselves, at least potentially, able to adhere to your proposition. From a communicative perspective, fulfilling a burden of proof means moving decision makers to the point that if no further argument were to occur, they will grant adherence to your proposition. In that way, you will have shifted the initiative to your opponents, who now have the burden of rejoinder. If they do not reply to your case, their position will erode.

Prima Facie Case   What we have just described, a case that provides sufficient argument to justify adherence to its proposition if no counterargument occurs, is called a *prima facie* case. This is a Latin term still used in law that says, in essence, the case is sufficient on its face or at first glance to justify adherence. *Consumer Reports* could argue endlessly about the advantages of their new car price service, but if they never succeeded in convincing you, at the very least, to *consider* using the service, they would have failed to pass the first test. They would lack a prima facie case.

A prima facie case does nothing more than shift the burden of carrying the argument forward from you to those who previously were protected by presumption. They now have the *burden of rejoinder:* they must supply counterargument to stay in contention. You should not expect that just because you have made a prima facie case you will win the adherence of the decision makers. It just means you are now a vital part of the decision process. Remember, also, that all these technical terms become meaningful only in what goes on in the decision makers' minds. In some abstract

---

[2]See *Gratz et al. v. Bollinger et al.; Grutter v. Bollinger et al.*

sense, you may have every reason to believe you have set out a prima facie case, when the decision makers remain unmoved.

We were discussing the abortion question with a colleague one day, when he finally announced the discussion was over. When we asked why, he said, "I cannot refute your arguments, but I will not change my mind. So there is no point in talking further." We felt we had done all that was needed to make a *prima facie* case, but our case was to no avail if it did not bring the colleague's presumptions into doubt. A common saying is, "If you don't want to change, don't listen." Our colleague chose to listen no longer.

The preliminary steps in case building, then, include following the critical decision making process, identifying the nature of the proposition, assessing the presumptions and burden of proof, and deciding what will be needed for a prima facie case. Now you can proceed to prepare a brief of available arguments.

Briefing Arguments

There are two significant responsibilities in case building: (1) clear, well-supported, and defensible arguments; and (2) a convincing vision of the rightness of your cause. Neither is sufficient alone.

Old-fashioned law professors used to tell their students that knowing the law and doing their homework was all that was needed. Advocacy was both unnecessary and rather shady. On the other hand, some trial lawyers used to say a convincing vision (a "theory of the case") and powerful advocacy was all that was needed. The law isn't the law until some judge is moved to say so, they proclaimed.

Scientists often say that science speaks for itself, and it is unnecessary and even improper to become a scientific advocate. Technicians, however, may reply that science is just "blue sky" until someone translates it into practical terms.

It is a mistake to act as if reason and advocacy are at odds. When a lawyer enters court knowing the law thoroughly and able to communicate a compelling vision of justice as well, the other one-dimensional attorneys often fail to understand why their arguments are rejected. Scientists who combine powerful research with eloquent presentation of their work become the giants of their time. Charles Darwin is an example of one who combined solid science with rhetorically powerful advocacy (Campbell). His compelling vision of evolution was so effective that many who disagree with it are trying, more than a century later, to prevent children from learning about evolution in school. In this section, we describe how to brief the arguments, and in the next we talk about developing a convincing vision of your case.

The concept of a *brief* comes from the act of reducing mountains of information to manageable proportions. A brief sets out in argumentative outline form the essential elements of the proposition, including likely counterarguments. An argumentative outline form differs from other types of outlines in the sense that it identifies the lines of argument and support for the claims stated. It does not represent subdivisions of major concepts, and thus you might have only one subitem identifying support under a stated claim. The brief also demonstrates the various reasoning strategies that might be used to strengthen the case.

The Elements of the Brief

A fully developed brief should contain the following elements.

Identification of the Decision Contexts   Within a single decision-making sphere, there are frequently many contexts in which argumentation functions. Dennis Jaehne has found many different and complex contexts for argumentation just within the bureaucratic system of the U.S. Forest Service. An environmental group that wants, for example, to stop helicopter shooting of coyotes must carry its case from local Forest Service personnel all the way through several administrative levels ending in Washington, DC. The debate over turning millions of acres of public land into wilderness areas is even more complicated, involving many government bureaucracies, commercial interests, and citizen groups.

Before any idea such as expanding the wilderness becomes law, it will probably need to be argued among interested citizens, special interest groups, legislative research personnel, legislative committees, lobbyists, in formal floor debate, and among executive bureaucrats who must translate law into administrative policies. Each context is likely to bring up different arguments and issues, and all should be accounted for in the brief.

Statement of the Proposition   Sometimes you may be assigned a proposition by someone else and sometimes it will be your job to state the proposition. In either case, as you move through time and contexts, it may be necessary to modify the proposition, however slightly.

Statement of Uncontroversial Matter   Definitions of terms, shared criteria, admitted facts, and shared claims should be stated explicitly. These are the starting points of argument discussed in Chapter 2.

In debating extension of wilderness areas, most people agree with the value of protecting nature as well as the importance of economic activity and the availability of good jobs. Such points of agreement must be made clear so that they can be used to support other arguments and ultimately contribute to a joint critical decision. Unless you know these uncontroversial starting points, you will have problems finding issues.

Statement of Potential Issues   The propositional analysis we discussed in Chapter 4 provides you with a series of issues that seem to be the most important. You will use these to build this part of the brief. However, these are only the *potential issues,* those most likely to become central to the decision. Furthermore, as you examine these issues in the light of the significance of various contexts, issues will probably change.

In business, for example, you may start with a presentation to your manager for whom staying within the budget is a major issue. Having obtained your manager's support, you next go to the assistant vice president, for whom meeting schedules is prime. If you are successful at that level, you may present to the regional vice president, for whom distribution and quarterly return on investment count most. And if that is successful, your presentation to the CEO may need to focus on issues of company vision and market share, with cost, schedule, distribution, and even quarterly return being of less importance.

Statement of Arguments and Counterarguments   For each issue, you need to state the claims you intend to support with argument and the possible opposing claims or refutations that might detract from them. At this point in your preparation, you are trying to cast the widest net for all claims that tend to support your proposition. For each context, you will select those arguments that are most relevant to the decision makers at hand.

An Example of a Brief

The best examples of briefs will be found in the hands of people engaged in real argumentation, those in law, business, scholarship, government, politics, and so on. If possible, interview such a person or secure an internship to work on a proposition. This will give you the best example of what we have been talking about. Short of that, we will present a highly compressed example that does not go as far in detail as to state explicitly the forms of support. We have chosen to look at the debate over affirmative action policies in higher education.

Decision Contexts   In the middle of the twentieth century, the Supreme Court of the United States declared an end to racial segregation in education. That decision generated a succession of laws and policies aimed first at ending segregation, and then at redressing the harm that had been done by the process. By the end of the twentieth century, a debate had emerged over the future of such policies as affirmative action (designed to facilitate integration in education and elsewhere) that had resulted from the ban on segregation. The prevailing U.S. Supreme Court decision at the start of the twenty-first century was the 1978 ruling on *Regents of the University of California v. Bakke,* which said that colleges could use race and ethnicity as a factor in admissions decisions but could not designate certain numbers of spaces for members of specific ethnic and racial groups. However, between 1978 and 2003, a series of court opinions had refined and limited affirmative action, and public opinion polls reported an increasing tendency by citizens to believe affirmative action had achieved its goals and should be ended. Those who felt affirmative action had begun to discriminate unfairly against members of nonprotected groups particularly supported this opinion. The immediate decision contexts with which we will be concerned are these:

1. Jenifer Gratz and Patrick Hamacher sued the University of Michigan when they were denied admission as first-year undergraduates. Both were residents of Michigan and were Caucasian. They claimed the admissions policy that

automatically granted members of "underrepresented minorities" (African American, Hispanics, and Native Americans) 20 points toward a possible 150 points violated the Equal Protection Clause of the Fourteenth Amendment to the U.S. Constitution and Title VI of the Civil Rights Act of 1964.

2. The University of Maryland had a scholarship program reserved for black students that was declared unconstitutional.

3. The University of California system began phasing out its affirmative action in admissions, hiring, and contracting in 1995. Opponents claimed the number of minority students in California declined as a result of this action.

4. Because Congress has the power to decide on laws and appropriations relevant to affirmative action, legislators formed a decision context.

5. To the extent that opposition to affirmative action constituted a reason to vote for or against a candidate for public office, the entire electorate formed a decision context.

State the Proposition   The specific proposition under consideration changes from context to context. In California, the proposition was that all parts of the higher education system should eliminate policies giving preferences to women and minorities in admission and hiring decisions. In other states, the propositions dealt with various alternatives to the established affirmative action practices.

Courts only consider specific cases involving specific legal issues. So their propositions are likely to be stated as in a case that became influential in the debate, *Adanan and Constructors v. Pena.* Here the Court supported the proposition that federal affirmative action programs involving the use of race as a basis for preferential treatment are lawful only if they can withstand federal courts' "strict scrutiny." This term means that the courts give the highest possible presumption against any preferential treatment based on race or gender, and those who would advocate affirmative action bear the highest possible burden of proof.

Throughout the higher education establishment, both private and state colleges and universities reexamined their practices. They weighed a commitment to diversity against potentially harmful law suits and political objections to admissions, faculty hiring, and scholarship programs reflecting affirmative action criteria.

Uncontroversial Matter   The concept behind affirmative action programs rests on key values that do not come into contention. As you will see when we turn to potential issues, the debate centers on how the values are carried into practical application. Here are some of the points that remain uncontroversial.

1. No practice in higher education should be in violation of federal and state law or court orders.

2. Society should be "colorblind."

3. Affirmative action should continue only as long as it is needed to overcome past or present discrimination, or to produce an educational benefit stemming from a diverse student body.

4. All people should be treated fairly.
5. In college admissions, there should not be quotas set on the basis of race, gender, or ethnicity.
6. Increasing the number of people who are the first generation in their family to attend college is a good thing.
7. Affirmative action should rest only on a compelling government interest to remove barriers to higher education and increase the diversity of students.
8. Affirmative action should be narrowly tailored to meet a specific, actual need.

Potential Issues   Potential issues can be found by examining carefully the arguments used by people already involved in the question of affirmative action. You will see that some of the issues stated below are broad in scope while others are narrow, and some of the narrow ones are really implied in the broad ones. We will list them all, because as the debate goes on, there will be shifts in issues that need to be anticipated. When we present examples of arguments, you will see that some subordinate issues identify potential arguments in support of the broader issues.

1. Is affirmative action in higher education inherently unfair?
2. Does affirmative action in higher education lower the bar on qualifications for admission?
3. Does affirmative action limit educational resources and opportunities for non-minority students?
4. Are race- and gender-specific scholarships and fellowships illegal?
5. Has affirmative action achieved its goal of redressing the effects of past discrimination?
6. Will policies aimed at helping only the disadvantaged fulfill any continuing affirmative action needs?
7. Is affirmative action in higher education necessary to achieve a colorblind society?
8. Does higher education require a diverse student body?
9. Are diverse student bodies a significant source of increased social and professional diversity?
10. Does affirmative action on campuses open avenues to employment as faculty and staff to women and minorities?
11. Will the United States face critical shortages of talent in crucial jobs in science, education, and professions if college graduates do not come from all sectors of society?
12. Does automatically granting points for admission to underrepresented minorities discriminate against other applicants?

Potential Arguments and Counterarguments   What we present below is a highly shortened version of what arguments and counterarguments should look like. The important point to note is that we have tried to put arguments that develop opposing claims on the same issue opposite each other.

Arguments Supporting the Ban	Arguments Opposing the Ban
I. Affirmative action in higher education is unfair.	I. Affirmative action promotes fairness.
A. Admissions should be based on merit alone.	A. Admissions must consider many criteria to yield a qualified but diverse student body.
B. Giving minorities automatic preference denies admission to qualified candidates. 1. Virtually all minorities are admitted.	B. To control enrollment and keep high standards, some qualified candidates must be rejected. 1. Fewer minority students apply. 2. Minority students self-select; only the best apply.
C. Automatic preference points constitute an unlawful racial quota. 1. *Regents v. Bakke* rules out quotas.	C. Automatic preference do not constitute an unlawful quota. 1. *Regents v. Bakke* spoke of setting aside separate seats held back for minorities; Michigan does not do this.
2. Automatically granting preference points to all underrepresented minorities is not narrowly tailored to meet the desired government interest in a diverse student body.	2. Administrative difficulty in considering thousands of applicants makes individual evaluation of each applicant impracticable.
II. There is no longer a need for affirmative action.	II. Affirmative action is still needed.
A. Minorities today have not specifically been discriminated against. 1. The law has removed discrimination in education: *Brown v. Board of Education.* 2. The Civil Rights Act has had over 30 years to correct discrimination.	A. Discrimination is still practiced. 1. The schools are segregated by neighborhood and income. 2. There is discrimination despite the law.
B. To discriminate on the basis of race, even for purposes of helping, is to demean minority people. 1. Race is alien to the U.S. Constitution. 2. Successful minorities lose individual credit for their work.	B. It is more demeaning to deny a person access to education because of race, ethnicity, or gender. 1. Equality of opportunity is central to the Constitution. 2. There are plenty of people who receive credit.
C. Special help to the disadvantaged will do all that needs to be done. 1. Minorities who are disadvantaged are the ones deserving special help. 2. Disadvantaged people represent all races and genders.	C. There is not enough data to support this claim.

Arguments Supporting the Ban	Arguments Opposing the Ban

III. Affirmative action in higher education is illegal.
  A. Courts say a race-based scholarship is not legal at U of Maryland.
  B. Other decisions have denied affirmative action laws.
    1. *Adanan and Constructors v. Pena*
    2. *City of Richmond v. J. A. Croson Company*
	III. The courts have not definitively decided this point.
	  A. U.S. Supreme Court did not consider this case.
	  B. These cases did not address higher education affirmative action plans.
	    1. U.S. Supreme Court approved U of Michigan law school admissions that consider race (*Grutter v. Bollinger,* 2003).

IV. Higher education will be diverse enough without affirmative action.
  A. All qualified students will be admitted.
  B. Diversity is not needed in higher education.
	IV. Higher education must have diversity through affirmative action.
	  A. No affirmative action means a drop in minority students.
	  B. Education must reflect the larger society, which is diverse.
	  C. The United States will see a shortfall of qualified professionals if affirmative action is eliminated.

V. Standardized testing is needed to maintain the quality of education.
  A. Test scores provide vital data for placement.
	V. Standardized tests do not reflect students' levels of achievement.
	  A. Test scores result in discrimination.

Developing a Convincing Vision

A brief provides you with a set of fully developed arguments. But, as Karl Llewellyn observed about lawyers arguing before appellate courts, something more than fully developed arguments is required. He said that while courts accept a duty to the law, they also hold a vision of justice, decency, and fairness. So the obligation of a legal case is to combine what Llewellyn calls a technically sound case on the law (which the other side will probably also have) with a convincing vision that will satisfy the court that "sense and decency and justice require . . . the rule which you contend for. . . ." He says:

> Your whole case must make *sense,* must appeal as being *obvious* sense, inescapable sense, sense in simple terms of life and justice. If that is done, a technically sound case on the law then gets rid of all further difficulty: it shows the court that its duty to the Law not only does not conflict with its duty to Justice but urges along the exact same line (182).

Reread his statement. Notice that it is the vision that moves the decision maker in your direction, while the arguments merely dispel doubts that the vision is correct and provide a rationale for its promulgation.

What is sensible, just, decent, or right is a function of the world view of the decision makers. To make a case is to engage and shape that world view on behalf of your cause. As Richard Rorty says, truth, goodness, and beauty are not eternal objects that we try to locate and reveal as much as artifacts whose fundamental design we often have to alter ("Philosophy" 143). Rorty believes that we satisfy our burden of proof by offering "sparkling new ideas, or utopian visions of glorious new institutions. The result of genuinely new thought . . . is not so much to refute or subvert our previous beliefs as to help us forget them by giving us a substitute for them" ("Is Derrida" 108–09).

Robert Branham says that policy propositions necessitate imagination "of the alternative worlds in which the proposed actions would operate." They entail a comparison of alternative visions of the future emerging from policy alternatives. "At minimum," he says, "debaters must articulate a vision of the future world in which the plan exists and a future in which it does not" (247). Review the discussion on storytelling and narrative in Chapter 3 to see what it means to articulate a vision.

Learn the Decision Makers' Vision

In our discussion of critical appraisal in Chapter 2, we explained the role of narratives, scripts, and scenarios in evaluating argument. We said that decision makers evaluate arguments in terms of their personal vision. To make a convincing vision of your case first requires an understanding of the vision of your proposition now held by the appropriate decision makers.

People on both sides of the affirmative action debate share a vision of an America where everyone is judged on the basis of their individual merits, and race, gender, or ethnicity play no part in the equality of opportunity. At that point, however, the visions separate. One vision is of America, the land of individual opportunity, with nothing standing between you and the presidency but your abilities and ambitions.

Another vision is one of America where white men dominate and where, without the force of law, others will never have an equal chance for success. That vision includes the fact that there has never been a president who was not a white man. No matter what vision your decision makers hold, they will likely dismiss arguments predicated on visions they find ridiculous.

Some people find a vision of heaven in which angels wear white robes and wings and play harps unbelievable, while others take it quite seriously. An Internet search for the word *angel* produces extensive and elaborate variations on its meaning. It is prudent to sound out decision makers on their vision before trying to attach your case to one.

Tell the Story of Your Vision

The *Oldest Living Confederate Widow* tells us that, "Stories only happen to the people who can tell them" (Gurganus 256). Reality rests upon the stories we take as accurate characterizations of the way things truly are. Visualization serves to intensify the feelings of the decision makers toward your proposition; it vividly projects them into a state in which your proposed decision is effectively in operation (Gronbeck et al. 128). When you tell the story of your vision, you make your proposed decision real.

Telling the story of your vision allows you to take your decision makers on a trip through time. Wayne Beach says people regularly engage in "time-traveling" in their communication through the medium of telling stories, or "storifying," as he calls it (1). To make sense of the future, we must often turn to the past and consider the present, says Beach.

In legal contexts, decisions almost always turn on a characterization of the past: did the accused run from the murder scene; was the contract actually agreed to by all parties even though it had not been signed; was the car exceeding the speed limit at the time of the accident?

To make a sound policy decision, as in the question of affirmative action, decision makers must be taken on a trip through past American history, and then given a vision of the future as it would function under the proposition. The more effectively these stories are told, the more real the vision will be and the more motivated the decision makers will be to support your proposition.

Consider an Example

A member of the U.S. House of Representatives submitted a bill (proposition) asking that the Custer Battlefield National Monument in Montana be renamed the Little Bighorn National Battlefield Park and that a Native American memorial be erected. He had prepared his case carefully, but he also had to address a well-established vision of what happened between people coming to live in North America from the sixteenth century on and those who were already living there. Unless he could inspire members of Congress with his new vision, his proposition stood little chance of passing.

Randall Lake observes that contemporary civilizations make themselves legitimate by grounding their origins in historical processes, and that is the case in the United States today. Lake says there is a powerful and well-developed Euramerican narrative in place that renders Native Americans relics of the past and thus absent from the present and irrelevant to the future. In brief, the Euramerican narrative follows a "time's arrow" metaphor, suggesting events moving in a line from past to present to future. The Europeans arrived in North America, encountered a savage that had to be "civilized" and "saved," and ultimately produced a "vanishing red man." In this vision, the Battle of the Little Bighorn is merely an anomaly, a glitch in the steady movement toward the inevitable triumph of the Europeans. So it makes sense to honor Custer, a martyr in a great cause. Since the Native American has vanished, there is no point in a memorial.

Those who would sustain a case for a Native American memorial must take the decision makers on a time-traveling expedition to establish an alternate vision to the time's arrow notion. They offer a "time's cycle" vision instead. Tribal life, says Lake, moved not along a linear chronology but in a cyclical pattern associated with the seasons and cardinal directions: the circle, not the line, is important. Thus, there is no beginning or end, but a constant cycling. We approached a young boy at the Taos Pueblo one time and asked, "How old are you?" He replied, "I do not measure my life with numbers."

In the Native American vision, the cycle now comes around to memorializing *all* those who fought at the Little Bighorn. The proposition to change the name of the memorial was proposed by then U.S. Representative Ben Nighthorse Campbell of Colorado (he shortly became a U.S. senator), whose great-grandfather fought against General George Armstrong Custer and the Seventh Cavalry at Little Bighorn River. In his vision, Native Americans did not vanish and become irrelevant, they have been here all along and were just made invisible by the Euramerican story.

Ben Nighthorse Campbell, by his very presence in the U.S. House of Representatives, represented the circle—what goes around, comes around—a Native American, whose ancestor fought and defeated Custer, stood before the nation as a symbol that there is no vanishing red man. The case would have been infinitely weaker had a Euramerican argued it.

The Congress chose Campbell's vision: a Little Bighorn National Battlefield Monument (Public Law 102–201), with monuments to both sides, such as we have at sites of Civil War battles. The once invisible army that attacked Custer appears now as the victor in the battle.

Communication to Specific Decision Makers

Preparing a brief and a vision of the case are part of the overall planning and strategy in case building. They represent the vital research phase. However, each time a specific decision-making context is encountered, a specific adaptation of the case must be made. Is the case to be presented in writing, orally, or both? Will others present counterargument? What format of argument will be followed: discussion, presentation, debate, negotiation, mediation? What sphere-based rules apply? Will a decision be made immediately or after deliberation?

What Are the Communication Constraints?

Having done all the research on your case, there is a powerful temptation to present everything you have at every opportunity. Lawyers once wrote such long briefs that the appellate courts set page limits. In almost every situation, time limits will apply, even if only by implication. The important point to remember is this: say what you need to say to make your point, and no more. Do not expect the decision makers to hear or read volumes of material and select what is most relevant to them. It is your job to do the selecting and to make the difficult decision to leave out much material that is good but not the best for this group.

Use different media effectively. Because some people feel more comfortable writing their case than presenting it orally, they choose to bypass oral presentations. The reverse is also true. It is a mistake to presume that writing or speaking alone is as effective as a combination of the two plus any other appropriate nonverbal means, such as charts, graphs, films, models, slides, or transparencies. Each medium of communication can serve a role in making a case and should be used.

What Counterargument Will Occur?

In formal debates like trials or legislative deliberations, speakers are followed by someone taking another point of view and likely to refute what has been said before. In other situations, such direct advocacy may be avoided. There are times when a speaker has been invited to present a case, only to learn later that others have also been invited to present alternative cases. On some television magazine programs such as *60 Minutes,* people are interviewed individually, and later their remarks are edited together to make the interview appear to have been a debate.

The presentation of a case must be adjusted to meet the needs presented by counterargument. The more powerful, direct, and sustained the counterargument, the more carefully the case must be adjusted to withstand such criticism, to bolster weakened points, and to engage in counter-refutation. If there is to be such direct counterargument, it is important that you know that in advance, secure specific permission to respond to the attacks, and come prepared with backup support.

What Argumentative Format Will Be Used?

Veteran advocates do not walk into a decision-making situation without plenty of advance notice of the order of the speakers, how long they will speak, how frequently they will speak, what the agenda will be, how the physical surroundings will be set up, what materials will be appropriate, who will attend, and so forth. Read the history of debates among candidates for major political office to see how much attention they pay to such details.

Lawyers, using their image of courts as a model, often walk into an arbitration only to discover the rules are quite different. They raise objections to witnesses and evidence, they demand recesses or postponements, they try to speak at great length, only to be told by the arbitrator that it is not done that way here. Arbitrations are informal: people sit around a table and discuss a problem. The arbitrator may not admit certain evidence or may admit evidence that would be rejected in a court. Formal speeches are rarely made, and an effort is made to keep the proceedings short and simple. Lawyers who do not bother to learn these differences tend to make a poor case presentation.

Political candidates carefully work to keep "debates" more on the order of press conferences in which a panel of reporters alternate in asking questions. They toss coins to see who speaks first and last, because they know these are important speaking positions. They like to turn a reporter's question into an opportunity to make a short speech rather than answer the question, and they earnestly avoid any direct interaction with each other that might force them to address specific issues while on the defensive.

In business presentations, it is often the case that day-long sessions will be scheduled with one presenter after another coming to the front. It is also common in business presentations to present many transparencies or slides in a darkened room. This means that unless you are one of the first presenters, your audience is likely to be lulled into a soporific stupor by the time your turn comes. If you follow the pattern of all the others, you will be unlikely to make much of an impression.

To bring the decision makers back to life, it will be necessary for you to violate the established pattern. It may be smart to turn up the lights, turn off the projector, and talk directly to the audience. Using other forms of visual aids such as DVD or hand-outs may also help. The important point is this: do not let obedience to an established pattern work to your disadvantage.

As we said earlier, in some situations direct advocacy of a case is considered in bad taste. When the format is more on the order of investigation, analysis, or general discussion, it may be necessary to get your case across indirectly while paying plenty of consideration and deference to other points of view.

What Are the Rules of the Sphere?

Among the mass of argument and support for your proposition, some will be quite in-admissible in certain spheres. Admissibility is most clearly defined in law, where some arguments, witnesses, documents, or comments simply will not be heard. On the other hand, many scholars become disturbed when their scientific research is presented in court in abbreviated form, without the careful documentation required in science. Many legal arguments would never survive scholarly scrutiny. Of course, a scholarly argument that wins praise in one discipline might be considered nonsense in another discipline.

What counts as the starting point for argument and what counts as proper sup-port will vary from sphere to sphere. In selecting your specific case for presentation, you must know what rules apply. A corporation may make a decision based on solid arguments within its context that would never win the adherence of government reg-ulators. One case would have to be defended before company executives, with quite another ready for presentation before a regulatory agency. This is not to say that the company is being two-faced or devious; it merely recognizes that arguments and sup-port that lead to a business decision may need to be combined with different argu-ments and support adjusted to another sphere. Amateurs at case making frequently argue successfully before their supporters and then expect the same case to be as ef-fective in convincing neutrals or opponents.

How Will the Decision Be Made?

Rarely does a single case presentation lead to immediate decision. Typically, some time passes between argumentation and decision making. The questions for case se-lection are how much time will pass, how many other deliberations will take place, how much of the ultimate decision will be made outside your presence?

The more time that will pass between your case presentation and the decision, the more your case must be designed to make a lasting impression. A complex case with many claims may be effective for relatively short-term recall, but the more time that will pass, the more the case must be encapsulated in a few memorable points that will stay in decision makers' minds.

It is here that vision, language, and focused argument come together to make powerfully memorable arguments. Few remember the legal intricacies of Justice Holmes's argument in *Schenck v. United States,* but many firmly "know" the prohibition against "falsely shouting fire in a theatre and causing a panic." He boiled his case down to a memorable statement that was combined with another: this speech act would present a "clear and present danger," which government has a right to punish, and thereby made a case for an interpretation of the First Amendment to the U.S. Constitution that retains currency well into another century. The more deliberations that will occur prior to the decision, the more your case must be designed to endure close scrutiny. If you have weaknesses that are sure to be exposed, it makes sense for you to bring them up first, acknowledge them, and then show why they do not fatally damage your case. Use a two-sided approach, giving full credit to other proposed decisions while showing clearly why they are not the best, and use more neutral language, which is unlikely to offend anyone.

What Critical Values Will Be Applied?

Because different demands will be placed on your case as you move from one context or sphere to another, it makes sense to pay attention to the way each set of decision makers approaches the decision task. We will identify five generic values usually relevant to decision making that can guide your analysis of each situation.

Clarity   It may be belaboring the obvious to say your case should be clear to the decision makers, but clarity is tricky. Language meaning is socially based. If you ask people, "Is what I have said clear?" they may say it is when their understanding is not at all what you hoped it would be. What you need to understand is what interpretative strategies are typical of these decision makers, and then try to express your case so that it will be clear in a joint sense—satisfying you and them.

Significance   What is highly significant to you may be less so to your decision makers. We all have hierarchies of concerns. Special interest groups such as environmentalists or abortion opponents often seem to think that everyone shares their fervor, which is often not the case. For example, if someone asks you if world peace is significant to you, you may say it is, but not significant enough to donate money to the cause or attend a conference. When presenting a case, it helps to have an idea of where your significance coincides with that of the decision makers.

Relevance or Salience   One way you can decide what parts of your brief should be presented to a particular set of decision makers is by learning what is relevant to them;

what is salient at the moment. In the debate over affirmative action, we have included issues related to legality or constitutionality. While everyone is probably concerned with those issues their relevance is most likely to be found within the legal system. People may say that they certainly want to act within the law, but that question will not become salient unless and until the courts take up a case in which that question will be considered.

Inherency Decision makers might agree with the substance of your case but feel unmoved to action because they do not believe you have identified inherent problems—problems so deeply embedded that action is required. For years, proponents of a balanced budget amendment to the Constitution claimed that deficit spending was inherent to the U.S. Congress. Then opponents pointed to balanced budgets achieved without the amendment, and supported their claim that deficits are not inherent. But when deficits returned in full force, the inherency argument regained strength. Try to learn how your decision makers perceive your concerns in relation to inherency.

Consistency Gidon Gottlieb says, "One of the demands of rationality most often emphasized is the requirement of consistency" (171–72). "In our culture . . . there is a clear notion that the charge of inconsistency is a winning argument" (Sillars 3). Unfortunately, one person's consistency is another's confusion as different argument elements are identified as needing to be consistent with one another. While you will want your decision makers to believe your case is consistent, it will be important for you to learn their standards of consistency.

What Sequence of Claims Is Most Appropriate?

Remember, the purpose of a case is to generate adherence to your proposition by the immediately appropriate decision makers. That means the series of claims included in the case must combine to move the decision makers from where they are to where you want them to be. If you propose to coworkers after a particularly tough job, "Let's order pizza for the whole crowd," and everyone agrees, your case is made. If, however, your proposition stipulates that the boss pay for the pizza and the boss does not cheer, you need to make a more elaborate case. The boss clearly agrees everyone should get pizza but is reluctant to pay, so what set of claims could you make to get the boss to pay? How should you sequence those claims? There are many different patterns by which cases may be structured, and the same case might usefully be structured differently for different decision contexts. We will illustrate a few of the most commonly used patterns.

Chain of Reasoning You might use a series of claims that starts with ones on which the decision maker is virtually certain to agree (identify a starting point) and move in small steps of adherence to the proposition itself. In the pizza case, it might look like this:

CLAIM ONE (a starting point): The boss wants workers who are highly productive. This should elicit an immediate "yes" from the boss. In fact, this case pattern has been called the "yes, yes" format because its power lies in securing an increasingly encompassing series of affirmations from the decision maker. It may be used in direct interaction or may be used rhetorically.

CLAIM TWO (still virtually a starting point): Happy and satisfied workers are the most productive.

CLAIM THREE (starting to draw the boss toward the proposition): Workers who are given treats when they do good work are happy and satisfied. The boss can see the pattern now moving inexorably toward the proposition, but affirmation of the previous claims makes it hard to pull out now.

CLAIM FOUR (starting the curve ball toward the plate): This group has just finished doing a good job.

CLAIM FIVE (this is the kicker): Now is the time for a treat as an investment in higher productivity by this work force.

Problem–Solution   A common approach to case structure is a problem–solution format. It is widely used in journalistic writing and policy decision making. One of the most enduring formats for public speaking, called the *motivated sequence,* rests on this pattern. Kathleen German and her colleagues claim that it approximates the normal processes of human thinking and will move an audience toward agreement with a speaker's purposes. They describe the following sequence of claims:

ATTENTION: An opening claim aimed at generating the active involvement of decision makers

NEED: A claim that identifies a condition in need of correction

SATISFACTION: A claim that identifies a way the condition can be corrected

VISUALIZATION: A claim that sets forth the vision of the case: the world in which the condition is corrected through the proposed method

ACTION: A claim that calls for specific measures to put the proposed action into being (266–70)

Winnie Stachelberg used a motivated sequence format in her case in favor of passage of the Hate Crimes Prevention Act (HCPA). Her arguments were aimed ultimately at members of the U.S. Congress who were approaching a final vote on the bill. She published her case in the newspaper, however, intending to influence citizens who might then communicate their support to the appropriate members of congress. To get our attention, she opens with a narrative involving real, specific individuals—an effective attention-getting technique.

ATTENTION: "Although they never met each other and lived more than a thousand miles apart, University of Wyoming student Matthew Shepard and Alabama textile worker Billy Jack Gaither had one ritual in common. On weekends, they would both often drive several hours to find refuge in big-city gay bars to escape momentarily the stifling anti-gay attitudes in the small towns where they resided."[3]

NEED: "Like many gay and lesbian Americans, Gaither and Shepard took these long treks because they understood the potentially dangerous ramifications of getting identified as gay in places where the label makes one a target for violence." The author goes on to report that the two men were "murdered in a grisly fashion," because of hatred against them, and many others are in danger of the same fate.

SATISFACTION: Fortunately, the HCPA offers the promise of preventing such crimes. "If passed, the HCPA will add sexual orientation, gender and disability to the categories already protected. . . ."

VISUALIZATION: "In the 21 states that have hate crime laws that include sexual orientation, all the dire predictions of the far right have not come to pass. Free speech has not been limited. The Hate Crimes Prevention Act would actually promote free speech by protecting entire groups from being intimidated into silence. The right to free speech belongs to all Americans, not just those who spread hate."

ACTION: "A vote for the Hate Crimes Prevention Act is a vote to correct this grave injustice and protect all citizens fairly and equally."

In Chapter 4, we spoke of a stock issues case that asks: Is there a need for a change? Is there a practical plan to meet that need? Is the plan advantageous? This case format is essentially the same as the problem–solution one just described.

Criteria   A case pattern particularly well suited to propositions of value is one that essentially involves three steps:

1. Establish adherence to a set of criteria.
2. Establish adherence to claims of fact relevant to the criteria.
3. Use the criteria to gain adherence to a value judgment about the factual claims.

Robert Pear and Erik Eckholm illustrate the criteria case structure in a discussion of physician ownership of profit-producing medical facilities and equipment. They cite the argument of Dr. Arnold S. Relman, editor of the *New England Journal of Medicine.*

CRITERIA CLAIM: "When you earn money by referring to a facility where you are an investor, you're just using your patient as a economic commodity." Relman thus claims that one criterion [measure or test] of improper behavior on the part of physicians is whether a patient referral produces a profit that involves a conflict of interest such that the action is more for greed than for good health.

---

[3]Winnie Stachelbert, "Does America Now Need Federal Legislation to Deal with Hate Crimes?" for the Knight Ridder News Service, *The Salt Lake Tribune,* Sunday, October 17, 1999, AA7. This was published as a debate, with Stachelbert taking the affirmative position.

FACTUAL CLAIMS: Pear and Eckholm claim (1) there has been a rapid rise in ownership of magnetic resonance imaging (MRI) machines by physicians who use them as a diagnostic tool; (2) ten percent of physicians have invested in businesses to which they refer patients; (3) physicians who share ownership of laboratories and other health care businesses order more services than other physicians.

VALUE-JUDGMENT CLAIM: Since each of these factual claims identifies an instance in which the referring physician will earn more money with more referrals, this behavior is improper.

The final claim uses the criterion established first to make a judgment on the factual claims. The case structure is effective by separating a criterion or principle of value to which adherence can be gained in the abstract, and only then applying it to a specific case for which adherence to a value judgment is sought.

The criteria format can work with propositions of policy and fact as well. In the physician example, some advocates have gone on to argue for laws that prohibit physicians from referring patients to business ventures in which they have a financial interest. The case would merely add one more step:

POLICY-ACTION CLAIM: Since that which is improper should not be allowed, government should legislate against physician referral to business ventures in which they have an interest.

To use this pattern for a proposition of fact, one simply first establishes the criteria for what counts as fact and then advances the factual claims that show consistency with the criteria. A human skeleton was discovered in remarkably sound condition even though scientists estimated its age at more than 9,000 years. Native American tribes claimed the remains were of one of their ancestors and demanded the right to dispose of them according to their funeral traditions. Scientists wanting to study the skeleton claimed it was not related to the Native American tribes. At issue was a question of fact: is this skeleton related to Native Americans?

CRITERIA: If the DNA of the skeleton can be related to current Native Americans, it is one of their ancestors and should be turned over to them for burial. If the DNA cannot be related to Native Americans, they have no claim to the remains.

FACT CLAIM: Analysis of DNA shows no relation to Native Americans or European Americans. In fact, it relates most closely with certain Japanese groups. Therefore, the Native Americans have no claim on the skeleton and it can be turned over to scientists for study.

Conclusion

Case building rests on thorough research and preparation. Before you are ready to support any proposition, you should have worked through the steps in critical decision making and have a wide appreciation for the problem and the various alternatives. You should phrase your proposition to express your position clearly in relation to the particular decision context or sphere at hand. And you should fully understand the status of presumption and burden of proof for each set of decision makers.

A full brief that surveys the various decision contexts, notes the uncontroversial matter, states potential issues, and then outlines all available arguments alongside potential counterarguments should be prepared well in advance of decision making. At the same time, a convincing vision of the case that will help drive home your position and make it memorable should be conceived. Finally, a specific case presentation must be prepared for every set of decision makers to whom it is to be presented. Three possible sequences of claims in a case are chain of reasoning, problem–solution, and criteria.

PROJECT

Interview a politician, scientist, lawyer, or businessperson. Ask your specialist how a case is made within the specialty. Ask to see a sample of one used in the past.

PART TWO

Tools

Aristotle said, "State your case, and prove it." In this section, we discuss how people do that. What is the nature of arguments and what counts as proof? Proof, called support here, consists of evidence, values, and credibility. How do people subject arguments to critical evaluation in the process of refutation, including the analysis of fallacies?

6 The Nature of Arguments

KEY TERMS

grounds	argument by cause to effect
warrant	argument by effect to cause
backing	argument by sign
qualifier	argument by analogy
rebuttal	argument by authority
reservation	argument by definition
argument by generalization	analyzing arguments

You will find argumentation used in all spheres of life. Argumentation can be seen in the philosopher's careful step-by-step pursuit of a single claim with all of its ramifications. It can be found in the give-and-take debate of a corporate boardroom or the state legislature. It is found in your everyday conversations with others. Given such a wide variety of situations, it is impossible to explain a single system for understanding argumentation. It is different from sphere to sphere but there are also similarities that we will begin to examine in this chapter.

In western culture everyone is expected to give reasons to justify their claims. If a judge simply said to a defendant, "I think you are as guilty as sin and I intend to lock you up and throw away the key," the judge would be making an argument about the defendant's moral state and what should be done about it, but it would be a legally unacceptable argument. So, the decision must be based on evidence and reason within certain carefully defined limits. While the standards of reasonableness will differ from sphere to sphere, all will have standards by which decision makers will expect arguers to act. Even conversational argumentation has its standards of reasonableness (Jackson and Jacobs).

A second similarity in the nature of reason giving is the types of arguments. Certain spheres will emphasize one type of argument over another. In the Judeo-Christian tradition, the emphasis is on reasoning by analogy from sacred text as authority to contemporary understandings and actions. Scientists argue for general principles from observing natural phenomena. Lawyers argue from legal statutes, customs, and precedents, but taken together, all use a limited number of argument types.

A third similarity among these argument spheres is that the argument types all can be examined using a single model. This model provides you with an analytical tool for judging the reasonableness of an argument. In Chapter 4 we discussed how you might analyze a controversy to find the important issues. In Chapter 5 we explained how these issues can be built into an organized system of argumentation: a case. In this chapter we will show you how each argument can be examined through the Toulmin model of argument, the major types of arguments, and some principles for developing your own arguments and examining the arguments of others.

The Model of an Argument

In this chapter we will look intensively at individual arguments using a modification of a model developed by Stephen Toulmin (1958 iii) to help you understand the parts of an argument and their interrelationships. The model we are using is useful to analyze an argument. But do not be confused; the model does not represent the order in which you should organize your argument. Depending on the decision makers, you may choose to leave out some parts or organize them differently than we describe here. The model explains all the parts you might use and provides a basis for analyzing an argument.

Here is a summary of an argument that has been made about global environmental issues:

> The petroleum industry is causing widespread environmental destruction, particularly in poor and minority communities, in countries as different as the United States and Nigeria. In the Niger Delta (Nigeria), oil is taken from and processed on lands inhabited by an aboriginal group known as the Ogoni. Industrial practices in Ogoniland are not consistent with those practiced in other locations. For example, Shell, which is one of the major oil extraction companies, operates in more than 100 countries, yet 40 percent of its spills have occurred in the Niger Delta. Oil spills and oil dumped into waterways have polluted the Ogoni water supply and destroyed the aquatic life and mangrove forests that previously served as natural filtering systems. One study found petroleum hydrocarbons in a stream at 18 parts per million, which is 360 times higher than levels allowed in Europe. In 1993, Ken Saro-Wiwa led a protest of 300,000 Ogoni against the Nigerian government and Shell. The group accused the government of marginalizing the Ogoni, and Shell of environmental degradation. It also demanded a change in these practices. The leaders of the protest were captured, tried by a military tribunal, and hanged. In the face of worldwide publicity, Shell withdrew its staff from Ogoniland. The petrochemical industry, however, has continued the same practices in the Niger Delta to this day. By 1998 it was estimated that oil companies had extracted more than 30 billion dollars worth of petroleum from Ogoniland. The Ogoni have not shared in this prosperity.
>
> Louisiana (United States) ranks first in the nation in per capita toxic releases to the environment. This pollution burden is further skewed toward poor and minority communities. A Geographic Information Systems (GIS) analysis of toxic releases showed a clear pattern of siting polluting facilities near predominantly African American commu-

nities. Further, enforcement of federal regulations has been lax in these communities. Activities at Shell's Norco plant (located in an area populated by African Americans) illustrate this problem. Despite multiple violations of permits at Shell's Norco plant, the Louisiana Department of Environmental Quality has resisted taking action, even when residents have documented illegally high levels of toxic substances in the air. Shell also skillfully uses U.S. tax exemption programs. For example, in 1988 an explosion that resulted from "deficient pipe inspection, insufficient monitoring and testing . . . and deficient engineering design" killed seven employees, injured several others, and caused a general evacuation of the area. As a result of the explosion, Shell was fined $3,630. The fine was more than offset, however, by a $450 million tax exemption because of damage to the plant, as well as a $2,500 tax credit for each employee it hired to replace the seven who were killed in the blast. During the 1990s, Norco residents learned to take air samples and have consistently detected cancer-causing chemicals that exceed state and national health standards. They are attempting to secure a hearing by the United Nations Commission on Human Rights, arguing that their treatment violates the *International Convention of the Elimination of All Forms of Racial Discrimination,* to which the United States is a signatory (Wright).

Let's look at this argument and see what its parts are and how they are put together. You probably have realized that this argument really contains two major claims, with one focusing on the general relationship between the petroleum industry and environmental degradation, and the other focusing on unequal distribution of this degradation. We will use the first of these two possible claims to illustrate how Toulmin's model can provide the basis for analysis.

Claim

In the very first sentence, as is often the case, you find the *claim.* It is a value claim: (Claim) The petroleum industry is causing widespread environmental destruction.

Grounds

But a claim alone is only an assertion. To make a claim believable, one must have a reason. The arguer must provide *grounds, a statement made about persons, conditions, events, or things that says support is available to provide a reason for a claim.* In this argument the grounds for supporting the claim are a series of subclaims of fact. In certain areas, the natural environment has been damaged by accidental oil spills, purposeful dumping of wastes, and releases of toxic gases into the air.

(Grounds) ⟶	(Claim)
Where the petroleum industry is active, the environment has been damaged by oil spills, dumping, and toxic releases into the air.	[Therefore] The petroleum industry is causing widespread environmental destruction.

Warrant

To make this a good argument, the grounds must have a basis for justifying the claim. There must be *a warrant, a general statement that justifies using the grounds as a basis for the claim.* It is the warrant that makes the movement from grounds to claim reasonable. In many, perhaps most, arguments, the warrant is not stated, it is implied. In this case it is stated or implied several times.

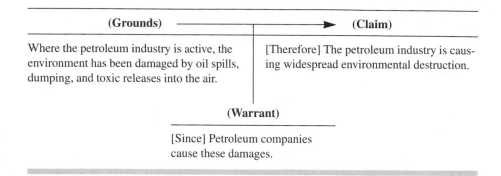

(Grounds) ────────────▶	(Claim)
Where the petroleum industry is active, the environment has been damaged by oil spills, dumping, and toxic releases into the air.	[Therefore] The petroleum industry is causing widespread environmental destruction.

(Warrant)

[Since] Petroleum companies cause these damages.

Backing

For some people, "claims, grounds, and warrant" are all an argument would need. They would accept the reasoning and find the claim acceptable. Others, however, particularly on controversial questions, would want more. They would require backing for either the grounds or the warrant. *Backing is any support (specific instances, statistics, testimony, values, or credibility) that provides more specific data for the grounds or warrant.* In this case, examples provide specific backing for the grounds and the warrant is backed (although unstated) by the value of the natural environment.

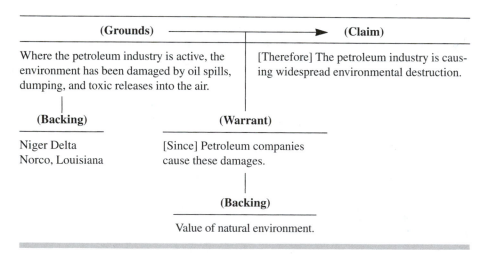

(Grounds) ────────────▶	(Claim)
Where the petroleum industry is active, the environment has been damaged by oil spills, dumping, and toxic releases into the air.	[Therefore] The petroleum industry is causing widespread environmental destruction.

(Backing)

Niger Delta
Norco, Louisiana

(Warrant)

[Since] Petroleum companies cause these damages.

(Backing)

Value of natural environment.

Qualifier

To be reasonable, an argument must have a claim and grounds for that claim, and the link between the two must be justified by a warrant. The grounds or warrant may need backing, depending on the level of questioning by decision makers. Sometimes, you have to look very carefully at the claim to see how much is being claimed. Some claims will have a *qualifier, a statement that indicates the force of the argument.* As we noted in greater detail in Chapter 1, words such as *certainly, possibly, probably, for the most part, usually,* or *always,* show how forceful a claim is. The qualifier in this case, "usually," is limited but still indicates a forceful claim.

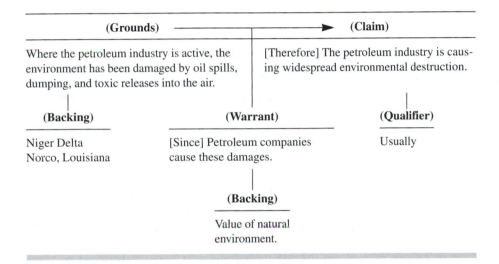

(Grounds) ⟶	**(Claim)**
Where the petroleum industry is active, the environment has been damaged by oil spills, dumping, and toxic releases into the air.	[Therefore] The petroleum industry is causing widespread environmental destruction.

(Backing)

Niger Delta
Norco, Louisiana

(Warrant)

[Since] Petroleum companies cause these damages.

(Qualifier)

Usually

(Backing)

Value of natural environment.

Rebuttal and Reservation

The actual strength of this argument has to be judged as well by possible *rebuttal, the basis on which the claim will be questioned by decision makers,* thus requiring of the arguer more or less support, or more or less qualification. In this case the main rebuttal is identified as the uses to which society puts petroleum-based resources. You recognize that objections to this claim probably will not be about its correctness but its relative importance. The rebuttal itself is another claim, for which you could develop an entire argument.

Sometimes arguers will have a *reservation, a statement of the conditions under which the claim would not apply.* There is no reservation here but there might have been if, for instance, the arguer had said, "The petroleum industry is causing environmental destruction *in the developing world.*" Since there is no reservation, the arguer has the burden of providing backing, or support, for the claim that environmental damage caused by the petroleum industry is a global problem.

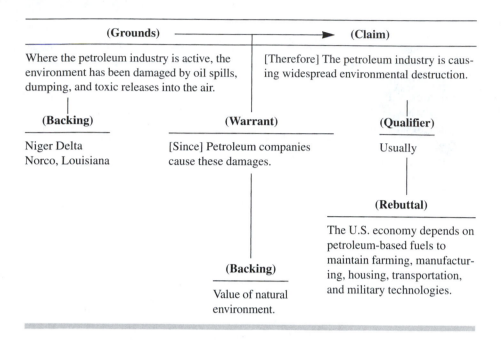

Not all arguments are the same. Some will be found reasonable without backing. Some parts will not be stated; some will be carefully developed. Some claims will be subject to significant rebuttal, others to little. Some warrants will be specific; others will be vague. You will find some arguments much easier and others more difficult to diagram than this one on global environmental damage. However, the Toulmin model should help you evaluate the argument when someone asks, "Is this argument reasonable?" It will be the basis for examining the problems with arguments in Chapter 11. It will also be useful to you in understanding the different types of arguments.

Types of Arguments

In Chapter 2 we identified the commonplaces of arguments: those principles that are used to generate starting points of argumentation. Among the commonplaces were certain principles of reasoning: generalization, cause, sign, analogy, and authority. These constitute the basis for most arguments. The purpose of this section is to look at those principles more carefully to see how they are applied in all but the most specialized situations and how they differ in the nature of their grounds, claims, and warrants.

The Parts of an Argument

Claim: A single statement advanced for the adherence of others

Grounds: A statement made about persons, conditions, events, or things that says support is available to provide a reason for a claim

Warrant: A general statement that justifies using the grounds as a basis for the claim

Backing: Any support (specific instance, statistics, testimony, values, or credibility) that provides more specific data for the grounds or warrant

Qualifier: A statement that indicates the force of the argument (words such as *certainly, possibly, probably, usually,* or *somewhat*)

Rebuttal: The basis on which the claim will be questioned by a decision maker

Reservation: A qualification of the original claim that answers a rebuttal

There is no natural superiority of one type of argument over another. However, their relative usefulness will vary from sphere to sphere. Authority is a crucial form of argument in religion, but is less significant in science. Analogy, a strong force in political argumentation, is frequently considered suspect by social scientists. The economist may consider a sign argument useful but not nearly so useful as does the weather forecaster. Nonetheless, each type of argument has its use and the chances are that not a week goes by that you do not use them all.

Argument by Generalization

Generalization, or rhetorical induction, is an argument in which a series of similar instances are assembled to show the existence of a general principle. A good example is a public opinion poll. For instance, in 1999 a National Communication Association-Roper/Starch Poll asked a national sample of U.S. residents how comfortable they felt in various communication situations. Over 60 percent felt comfortable in face-to-face interpersonal communication and a similar percentage felt comfortable speaking on the phone. Slightly over 50 percent felt comfortable communicating in writing, while only about 25 percent felt comfortable in public speaking ("Americans Feel . . . "). But the pollsters didn't ask all adults in the United States; they asked a sample of 600 and reasoned that they could generalize about all people from that group. So, the sample becomes the grounds for generalization about all U.S. citizens.

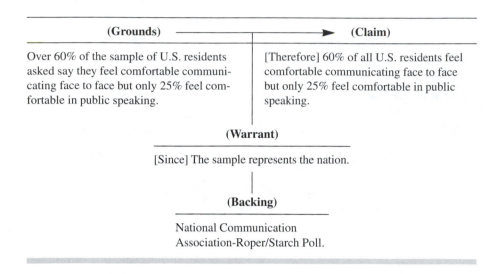

(Grounds) ⟶	(Claim)
Over 60% of the sample of U.S. residents asked say they feel comfortable communicating face to face but only 25% feel comfortable in public speaking.	[Therefore] 60% of all U.S. residents feel comfortable communicating face to face but only 25% feel comfortable in public speaking.

(Warrant)

[Since] The sample represents the nation.

(Backing)

National Communication
Association-Roper/Starch Poll.

Generalizations also can be made from individual cases. Jodie T. Allen argues that there is a significant interest nationally in controlling urban "sprawl." She supported this generalization with these examples: "[F]rom Portland, Ore., to Baltimore, Md.—with stops at Denver, Salt Lake City, Austin, Detroit, Chicago, and Atlanta—smart-growth strategies are growing. . . . More than half of state governors from both parties, mentioned smart growth in state of the state messages this year" (23).

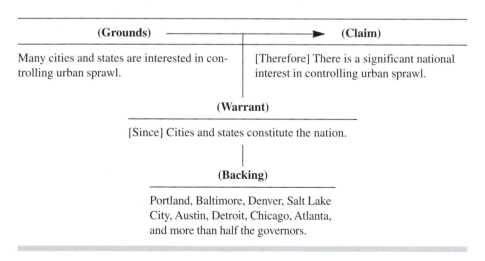

(Grounds) ⟶	(Claim)
Many cities and states are interested in controlling urban sprawl.	[Therefore] There is a significant national interest in controlling urban sprawl.

(Warrant)

[Since] Cities and states constitute the nation.

(Backing)

Portland, Baltimore, Denver, Salt Lake
City, Austin, Detroit, Chicago, Atlanta,
and more than half the governors.

You will note that this argument contains a qualifier, *many* cities and states, not all. This is a forceful claim to say there is a national interest. It requires strong backing for decision makers to accept it, but not so much as if she had said, "overwhelming national interest," for instance.

Argument by Cause

In western culture we tend to believe that people, things, and ideas cause events to take place. If the economy is good, then the president or Congress is believed to have caused it. If you don't feel well, you expect a physician to tell you the cause. An argument by cause can reason from cause to effect or from effect to cause.

In an argument from *cause to effect* the grounds function as a cause for the claim. In 1999 a number of cities filed lawsuits against gun manufacturers for damages caused by guns used in the commission of crimes. The first such suit was won by the city of Brooklyn, New York, on behalf of six homicide victims and a severely wounded man. The case was based on a cause to effect argument.

The plaintiffs in the Brooklyn case argued handgun makers "oversupply" gun-friendly markets, mainly in the South, aware that the excess guns flow into criminal hands via illegal markets in New York and other states with stricter anti-gun laws (Gun Industry . . .).

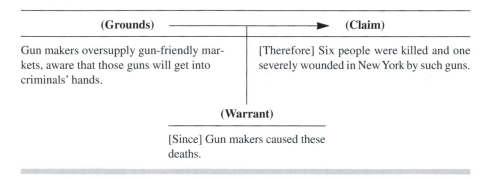

In *effect to cause* reasoning the grounds function as the effect of the claim. When people find that something is a problem they seek to find a cause for it. This is substantially the basis of medical diagnoses. You have a headache and you wonder about cause: "Was it something I ate?" "Stress?" "Lack of sleep?" "A problem with my eyes?"

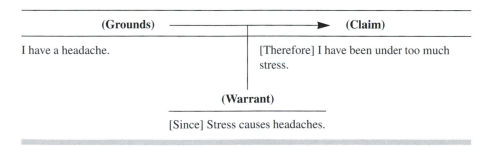

The opponents of gun control argue that gun manufacturers are not responsible for crimes with guns. Shortly after the mass shooting at Columbine High School in

Colorado, gun advocates argued that if school officials had had guns they could have prevented the killings. The National Rifle Association used a study by two criminologists at Florida State University, Gary Kleck and Marc Gertz, to show that every year almost a million people protect themselves from criminals with fire arms. "Those data clearly indicate," says Paul H. Blackman, "that using a gun for protection decreases the likelihood that a violent crime (particularly robbery and assault) will be completed or that the intended victim will be injured, compared to taking some other protective measures or taking no protective measures" (1–2).

   That is an argument from effect to cause.

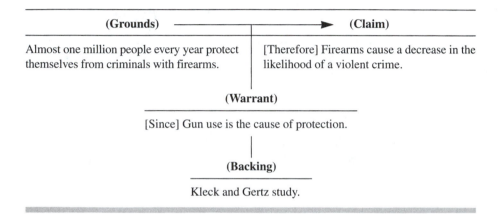

(Grounds)	**(Claim)**
Almost one million people every year protect themselves from criminals with firearms.	[Therefore] Firearms cause a decrease in the likelihood of a violent crime.

(Warrant)

[Since] Gun use is the cause of protection.

(Backing)

Kleck and Gertz study.

Argument by Sign

Argument by sign is closely related to causal argument but is different. A sign argument is based on a warrant that every thing, condition, or idea has characteristics that will tell you whether or not it is present. You see a "For Sale" sign on a car, and you believe you could buy the car if you cared to.

   Look back at the argument presented at the beginning of this chapter. It is rarely possible to actually demonstrate that toxic substances are coming out of a smokestack. Many of them are not visible and have no odor. Communities that are plagued with dirty industries usually must rely on circumstantial evidence. For example, Norco residents have learned that they should take air samples when they sense unusually high levels of irritation to their eyes and mucous membranes. They have been able to use the results of sample analyses to argue that industries in their town are emitting toxins they have failed to report. For example, in 1999, Norco air samples that were analyzed in an EPA-approved laboratory showed high levels of methyl-ethyl ketone in several locations. Methyl-ethyl ketone is a health hazard. It would not be expected to occur naturally in this region, but is stored in tanks at the Shell's Norco plant. Norco residents continue to take air samples, and analysis consistently detects multiple cancer-causing chemicals (including toluene, benzene, carbon disulfide, styrene, methyl tert-butyl ether) at rates far above state and federal health standards. Norco residents used all of these grounds as signs to argue that Shell was endangering the public health.

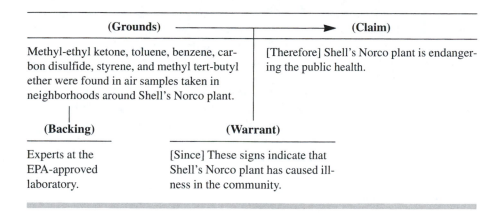

(Grounds) ——————————→ (Claim)

(Grounds)	(Claim)
Methyl-ethyl ketone, toluene, benzene, carbon disulfide, styrene, and methyl tert-butyl ether were found in air samples taken in neighborhoods around Shell's Norco plant.	[Therefore] Shell's Norco plant is endangering the public health.

(Backing)	(Warrant)
Experts at the EPA-approved laboratory.	[Since] These signs indicate that Shell's Norco plant has caused illness in the community.

Weather forecasts are sign arguments. A ridge of high pressure is a sign that there will be no rain or snow, while low pressure or unstable upper level disturbances are signs that rain or snow may develop.

1999 was an unusually active season for hurricanes. These hurricanes were predicted better than in previous years because of what Colorado State University (CSU) meteorologist William Gray calls "climate signals." Among them:

1. "Warmer than normal sea-surface temperatures in the North Atlantic."
2. "Above-average West African rainfall."
3. "Eastward-moving stratospheric equatorial winds."
4. "La Niña, another cyclical phenomenon that is marked by a mass of cold water in the eastern equatorial Pacific."

Professor Gray's "climate signals" are all used in an argument by sign ("What's breeding . . .").

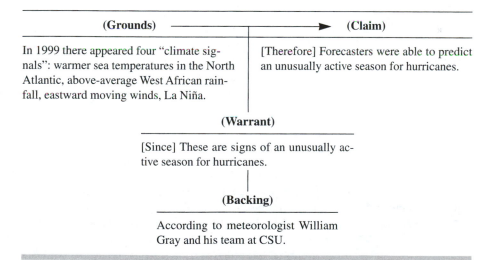

(Grounds)	(Claim)
In 1999 there appeared four "climate signals": warmer sea temperatures in the North Atlantic, above-average West African rainfall, eastward moving winds, La Niña.	[Therefore] Forecasters were able to predict an unusually active season for hurricanes.

(Warrant)
[Since] These are signs of an unusually active season for hurricanes.

(Backing)
According to meteorologist William Gray and his team at CSU.

For many years the American bald eagle was rarely seen. Consequently, the bird was placed on the Endangered Species List. In 1999 it was removed from the Endangered Species List and has been seen in greater numbers in more places. Both its removal from the Endangered Species List and the increased sitings are signs that bald eagles are no longer endangered.

It is important to differentiate causal and sign argument. The shortage of bald eagles was a sign that they were endangered, but, it was not the cause. The cause most argued was the pesticide DDT that got into the eagles' systems and made them unable to reproduce. The causal link was strengthened when eagles increased after the use of DDT was outlawed. A sign is not necessarily a cause, and vice versa.

Argument by Analogy

In *arguing by analogy,* you compare two situations that you believe have the same essential characteristics and reason that a specific characteristic found in one situation also exists in the analogous situation.

It has been traditional to differentiate between literal and figurative analogies. The literal analogy is presumed to be based on factual comparisons of situations, and the figurative analogy is based on more fanciful relations. No two situations can be *literally* alike. However, some comparisons are more material than others. The most important factor for you as an arguer, however, is not the materiality of the cases but how the decision makers will see the quality of the relationship argued.

North Carolina Governor Jim Hunt and Bob Chase, past president of the National Education Association, argue against school vouchers to provide money for poor children to attend private schools. Hunt says, "Vouchers are like leeches. They drain the lifeblood—public support—from your schools." Having a system of vouchers, says Chase, would be like "bleeding a patient to death" (Peterson 29).

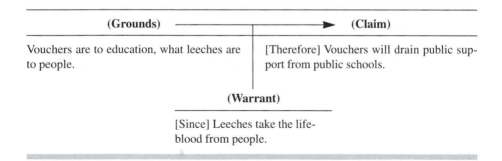

(Grounds) ——————————▶	(Claim)
Vouchers are to education, what leeches are to people.	[Therefore] Vouchers will drain public support from public schools.

(Warrant)

[Since] Leeches take the life-blood from people.

A more literal analogy, perhaps, would be the comparison made in the argument at the beginning of this chapter. According to this argument, the situation in Louisiana and the Niger Delta are very much alike. In both cases a multinational corporation has taken advantage of groups of people characterized by poverty and minority group status. The corporation has caused environmental degradation and human rights violations in both communities. In this case, the environmental justice advocate attempts to emphasize the horror of Shell's treatment of U.S. citizens by comparing a U.S. setting with a Nigerian setting. Many Americans know that, although Nigeria has valuable natural resources (such as petroleum), most of its population live in dire poverty. Additionally, U.S. citizens who identify themselves as environmentalists or human rights advocates also may be aware that pressure from Shell and other petroleum companies contributed to the Nigerian government's decision to hang Ken Saro-Wiwa. This analogy adds urgency to the argument for environmental justice by directing attention to similarities between Shell's effects on the living conditions of African Americans in Norco and the Ogoni people in Nigeria. It suggests that this treatment can happen anywhere in the United States.

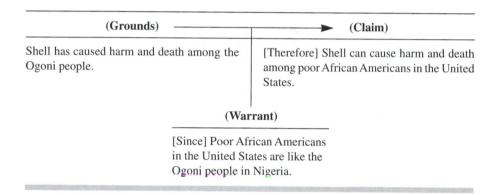

(Grounds)	⟶	(Claim)
Shell has caused harm and death among the Ogoni people.		[Therefore] Shell can cause harm and death among poor African Americans in the United States.

(Warrant)

[Since] Poor African Americans in the United States are like the Ogoni people in Nigeria.

Argument from Authority

In Chapter 9 we will discuss how your credibility can support the adherence decision makers give to your argument. Even persons of high credibility, however, frequently use the credibility of others to argue a claim. In *argument from authority* you argue that a claim is justified because it is held by a credible person; ordinarily someone other than yourself. The most common way of presenting such an argument is to cite an authority.

Scott Stossel argues that although the United States leads the world in scientific research, this record is in danger because young Americans are discouraged from entering the sciences because of the competition for jobs. Foreign nationals are more and more becoming the scientists in our research laboratories. "Nearly a third of all students who earned their doctorates in the sciences—and more than *half* of all students who earned their doctorates in engineering—in this country between 1991 and 1995 came from foreign countries." How do we know this is true? Because the figures come from the National Science Foundation (17). This is an argument from authority.

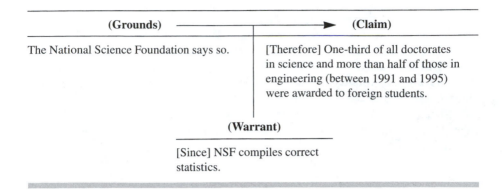

The warrant of authority is crucial to the success of this argument. The decision makers must believe that NSF is an authority. Such authority might also be argued based on an individual rather than an organization. Later in his argumentation, Stossel cites Professor Sharon Levin of the University of Missouri and Paula Stephan of George State University (18). Remember in the example of argument from sign about the "climate signals?" We cited Colorado State University meteorologist William Gray. That was an argument from authority within a sign argument.

The argumentation from authority depends for its power on how expert and unbiased the decision makers believe the authority to be. For that reason you frequently need to explain the credentials of the person or organization as backing for the warrant. That argument would be diagramed this way:

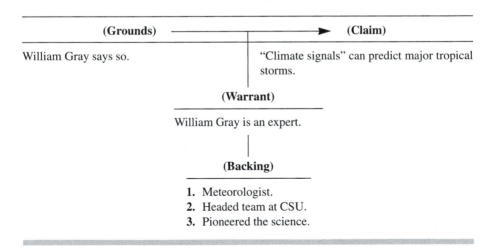

There is another kind of argument from authority that is considered more questionable. It is called *bandwagon* or *ad populum*. It says that a claim is good because people believe it. Although it is considered a fallacy by many, its acceptability depends on the sphere in which it is used. In science, for instance, an argument that most people believe there is global warming so it must be true, is unacceptable. However, in a democratic society it is a powerful kind of political argument. It rests on the authority of majority opinion, a strong political value. Or it could rest on the authority of those most involved. In the argumentation of Paul Peterson supporting a voucher system for poor and minority children to attend private schools, he argues: "According to a recent survey undertaken at Stanford University, 85% of the inner-city poor favor a voucher plan, compared with 59% of more advantaged parents who live in the suburbs."

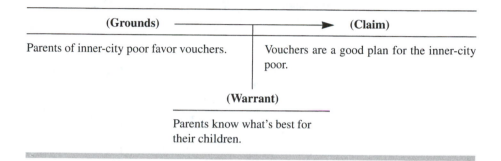

This is a powerful political argument because it argues that a majority of those who might be expected to use vouchers support them. These people are not experts, as a meteorologist is an expert, but decision makers may believe they know what is best for their children.

These five types of argument (generalization, cause, sign, analogy, and authority) constitute the arguments you are most likely to find in your own argumentation and that of most others, though there are special variations on these in some spheres. If you concentrate on them, diagram them to see their parts and the reasoning that holds them together, you can better evaluate the quality of the arguments. Later in this chapter we will look more carefully at how to analyze the arguments you encounter. First, however, you should consider an important special kind of argument: argument by definition.

Definitions as Argument

Definitions are an essential part of any argumentation. They serve to identify exactly what is being argued. Even in situations of strong disagreement, disputants should try to agree on the subject of the disagreement. Definitions are claims that must be supported by effective argumentation, because meanings are based on consensus. Value-laden terms such as *love, knowledge, justice,* or *God* clearly have no single precise definition. Neither do such apparently straightforward terms as *climate change, gun control, abortion,* or *economic prosperity.* When you use words, you cannot appeal to a single correct definition. You must present a convincing argument to support your interpretation. Definitions can be used as support for your arguments only if you have a common interpretation with the decision makers and hopefully with opponents as well. There are several common ways to build an argument in support of your definition, and we will discuss some of them.

Formal Definition

A formal definition involves the development of a deductive logic-based argument (see Chapter 3) where a term is located within a general class for which there is a high probability of a common audience interpretation, and then differentiating it from other aspects of the class. The formal definition is usually the first one given in a dictionary.

> A *democracy,* as Americans use the term, is a form of government [general class] in which the people either directly or through elected representatives exercise power [differentiation].
>
> *Climate change* is change in temperature on the surface of the earth [general class] influenced by the greenhouse effect [differentiation].
>
> *Fundamentalism* is a movement in American Protestantism [general class] based on a belief that the Bible is a literal historical record and incontrovertible prophecy [differentiation].

Definition by Example

Just as examples (see Chapter 7) can serve to support an argument and are essential to argument by generalization, they can define an unknown idea. In *definition by example,* you identify examples that decision makers are likely to know, and relate your concept to them.

> *Holocaust* is mass murder of Jews (and others) by the Nazis in World War II, any whole-sale destruction, especially by fire, a great slaughter, or massacre.
>
> The *New Deal* is characterized by, for example, such programs as Social Security, the Federal Deposit Insurance Corporation, and the Securities and Exchange Commission.
>
> To *proselytize* is, for example, what the Mormons do when they send two young people around knocking on doors to talk about their religion.

Functional Definition

Sometimes a good way to make a convincing definition is to illustrate how a concept functions.

> *Spark plugs* ignite the fuel mixture in an internal combustion engine.
>
> *Dental floss* cleans the areas between your teeth.
>
> A *heuristic device* gives students a guide to use for learning on their own.

Definition by Analogy

You can establish a clear meaning for a concept by using argument by analogy to show how a term is like or unlike other familiar concepts. Remember, arguments by analogy work by placing a concept under study alongside one on which there is agreement. If they can be shown to have significant similarities, the unknown concept can take on meaning from that which is already agreed upon.

Definitions by analogy resemble formal definitions, but they are subtly different. In formal definitions, concepts are identified logically as part of a class. In definition by analogy, concepts are explained by their similarity to a more familiar concept.

> *School vouchers* are like business vouchers that can be exchanged for goods and services. They differ in that they can be exchanged for private school attendance.

> A *historical novel* is like a history book in that it is based on the study and interpretation of the past, but it differs in the fact that the author is free to include imagined characters, conversations, and events.

> An *oboe* is like a clarinet in that it is a slender woodwind musical instrument, but it differs in that it has a double-reed mouthpiece.

Definition by Authority

Arguments based on authority are common in definition. The most obvious authority is a dictionary, which for many situations is all the authority you need. Resist being entrapped, however, by a veneration of authority leading you to believe that the dictionary is the final or only authority on word meanings. Often, it is the worst because dictionaries cannot possibly be published fast enough to keep up with the dynamics of language. However, they will give you a general guide to three factors that will strengthen your argument in many situations.

Usage identifies how a word commonly appears in our communication; what people usually mean. Widespread use of a word for a certain meaning provides some authority for that meaning or definition.

Etymology reports the history of a word from the earliest languages. In the past, an argument for a definition that was based on what the root of a word meant, for instance in Greek or Latin, was more powerful than it is today. Today, such an argument is mostly effective with people who still believe that words possess inherent meaning.

Wordsmiths, or the people who create or modify words, can be used authoritatively to support a definition. When physicists theorized the existence of subatomic particles as the fundamental units of matter, they needed a new word for them. They turned to literature in James Joyce's *Finnegan's Wake:* "three quarks for Mr. Marks," and named their particles *quarks.* Academics, adolescents, gangs, ethnic groups, musical groups, and others commonly create new words and can serve as the authorities on definitions.

The Analysis of Arguments

You can see from the examples we have discussed in explaining the types of arguments that people do not organize their arguments exactly according to our model or any other model. That is because arguments are aimed at decision makers who know things about the subject, share values and credibility assumptions that the arguer need not mention, and respond to language structures that change the order of the model in actual use.

Consequently, the Toulmin model is a useful analytical tool to check your own arguments and the arguments of others for the kinds of problems discussed in Chapter 11. In this section we will explain some of the characteristics of arguments that make the application of the model difficult, and then some guidelines for using the model to help you analyze an argument.

Characteristics of Arguments

Arguments are difficult to analyze, but if you recognize why that is the case it will help you to use the model more effectively. They are difficult because they usually have parts missing, the order of the parts may vary, and they may overlap with one another.

Parts Missing   Most arguments have parts left out. If the arguer believes the decision makers accept the grounds, then he or she will sometimes provide no backing, as is the case of the argument by analogy about school vouchers. Warrants are frequently omitted because they are clearly implied by the other statements the arguer makes. An example of this is the argument with the claim that many cities and states are interested in controlling urban sprawl.

It is not the lack of a stated warrant that poses a problem for decision makers. The warrant is clearly implied. The real concern is on the level of adherence the decision makers give to the implied warrant.

In the argument about predicting the 1999 hurricane season on page 107, there is no data from the Gray study to support the four climate signals. The argument is based only on the decision makers accepting Professor Gray as an authority. Do the decision makers believe that these data exist? Do they trust that he knows the data? The fact that the data are unstated assumes that they do.

Sometimes even claims are not stated. This is particularly true of argumentation that follows a strategy of telling stories. You could tell stories about people who defended themselves from assault by having a weapon in their possession without ever stating the claim that people should carry a weapon for self-protection. The claim is not stated but the decision maker knows that is the claim because the overall orientation of the argument clearly implies it.

Order in Arguments   Arguments do not necessarily follow the order: grounds, warrant, claim. Indeed, they most frequently, and clearly, begin with the claim. Scott Stossel argues that although the United States leads the world in scientific research, young Americans are discouraged from entering the sciences. He might have placed the specific evidence from the National Science Foundation before the claim.

Such an approach is the standard of argumentation in the sciences and social sciences where the grounds are always developed first and the claim then developed from those grounds. Such an approach is seen by many as objective. The arguer wants to imply that the evidence is studied before a claim is made, though it is, of course, an argumentative strategy. The arguer knew the claim all along but chose to delay revealing it to decision makers.

Overlapping Arguments   Frequently, two or more arguments are developed in the same paragraph because the arguer sees them as linked. That is the case of the argument by Paul H. Blackman. He argues from effect to cause that firearms cause a decrease in the likelihood of violent crime. However, he also argues from authority that the Kleck and Gertz study proves that nearly one million adults each year use firearms for protection from criminals. The argument about environmental justice also uses several approaches. It argues from generalization, providing many examples of Shell's violation of laws and ethical norms. It argues from cause to effect when claiming that certain chemicals cause cancer (note that it did not explicitly provide backing for this assertion; relying on the audience to assume that the arguer was following recognized expertise). As mentioned earlier, it argues by sign and analogy. In both the example about firearms and the example about environmental justice, you should analyze the individual claims separately and then together to see how well each argument is developed.

Guidelines for Analyzing Arguments

Frequently, arguments are linked to one another, their parts do not appear in any particular order, and parts are left out. Consequently, you may have trouble seeing in an article, television commercial, or speech what an argument is and what its parts are. Here is a useful sequence of guidelines for analyzing an argument:

1. Discover and state the claim or claims. What is it the arguer wants you to believe, value, or do? Claims may appear anywhere in the argument but most likely at the beginning or the end.
2. Look for the subclaim of the grounds. It can best be determined if you know the claim first and then ask yourself "On what basis am I supposed to give adherence to the claim?"
3. Look for the warrant. Since it will most frequently be the part omitted, it will be the most difficult to find. But if you know the claim and the grounds you can find even an unstated warrant because it is the statement that would justify the movement from grounds to claim. If stated, it will frequently be identified by words such as *for, because,* or *since.*

4. Examine the warrant to determine the kind of argument you are analyzing. Look back over the examples we have used and you will see it is the warrant that identifies the kind of argument by identifying the commonplace (or principle) behind it. Here are a few of the warrants we have used:

"The sample represents the nation. . . ." [generalization (representative, comprehensive, overall)]

"Gun makers caused these deaths." [cause (effect, generate, because, lead to, result in)]

"These signs indicate that Shell's Norco plant has caused illness in the community." [sign (indication)]

"The Ogoni People in Nigeria are like poor African Americans in the United States." [analogy (parallel, like, alike)]

"The parents of inner city children know what's best for their children." [authority (expert, knowledgeable, trustworthy, skillful)]

5. Look for backing (evidence, values, credibility).
6. Look for qualifiers. What limits are put on the claim? Look for words like *usually, sometimes,* and *frequently,* which modify the force of the claim.
7. Look for refutation and reservation. Given the argument you have diagramed, to what potential rebuttal has the arguer adapted the claim?
8. Evaluate the quality of the argument by asking how well the elements of the argument meet decision makers' possible rebuttals.

Conclusion

Arguments appear in a wide variety of situations, and they differ in their nature from one context to another. Yet all arguments can be diagramed by a variation of the Toulmin model, which illustrates how a claim can be justified only by showing that there are warranted grounds for it. In addition, grounds and warrants may need backing; claims may need to be qualified and stated with a reservation to avoid rebuttal.

Although the model provides a basis for the analysis of all arguments, not all arguments are alike. Certain types of arguments (commonplaces) can be observed. Argument by generalization attempts to draw a general claim from a series of instances. It is a rhetorical induction, the argument form closest to pure induction. Arguments may claim cause and effect relationships either of cause to effect or effect to cause. They may claim the existence of one condition as a sign of another. Arguments may claim that one condition is analogous to another, and they may be warranted by the credibility of an authority.

It is frequently necessary to develop an effective argument in support of a definitional claim before using it as part of the larger argumentation. Definitions can be formal or functional, by example, analogy, or authority. Definitions should be agreed to by decision makers and, if possible, by opponents.

The Toulmin model is an analytical tool. People do not organize their arguments according to the model because decision makers already know something about the subject. So, with most arguments, parts are missing, the order is different than the model, and arguments overlap. To analyze such arguments, start by stating the claim(s) and then find the grounds. Once this is complete, you should be able to find the warrant (frequently unstated) that justifies the supporting relationship between grounds and claim. This should also tell you what kind of argument is at hand.

Finally, take notice of the materials that serve as backing, qualifiers, refutation, and reservation. These pieces of information will permit you to evaluate the quality of the argument for the decision makers.

PROJECT

Bring to class one example of each of the types of arguments. Look for these in contemporary publications such as newspapers, magazines, advertising flyers, or Internet sites. Be prepared to explain each argument by relating its parts to the Toulmin diagram. Your instructor may assign different types of arguments to different class members.

7 Support: Evidence

KEY TERMS

example

hearsay evidence

reluctant evidence

statistics

central tendency

trend

probability

testimony of fact

testimony of opinion

sphere dependence

hypothetical example

negative evidence

documented evidence

assertion

expert evidence

It should be clear from the previous chapter that an argument is a series of subclaims that support a claim and if decision makers find these subclaims and the connections among them reasonable, they accept the argument for the claim. Each of those subclaims serves as what we will call *support* for the claim. In addition, sometimes a subclaim has backing that also supports it and, therefore, the claim.

For you to understand the nature of support in argumentation we will examine a controversial issue in American politics: gun control. Those who argue for greater restrictions on the private ownership and use of firearms argue that police statistics show that guns are the major source of the contemporary increase in violent crime. They point to the increase in students taking guns to schools. They use estimates by researchers that by the year 2004 the annual number of firearm deaths will be greater than automobile accident deaths. They argue that state records show that gun restrictions under the Brady Bill have kept guns out of the hands of felons and mentally unstable people. Additional restrictions, they say, will further stem the violent atmosphere in America.

Those who oppose restrictions on gun ownership and possession argue that it is a basic right protected under the second amendment to the Constitution. They say that the National Rifle Association opposes such restrictions because it wants to protect people's natural rights. Total violent crime, according to the FBI Uniform Crime Report, they say, is highest in states that are more restricted. Guns are needed so that law-abiding citizens may protect themselves and, they say, guns don't commit crimes, criminals do. Lenient judges and plea bargaining attorneys who put criminals out on the street are the problem, not guns in the hands of honest citizens.

In these arguments for and against gun control we can see that support (backing) is available in three forms: evidence, values, and credibility. The arguer chooses which to use and emphasize.

CREDIBILITY: Are organizations like the FBI, police agencies, cited researchers, and the NRA trustworthy? Are they competent to judge the situation? Is the maker of the original argument credible?

VALUES: How important is the control of violence? Is gun ownership a constitutional right? A natural right? How important is self-protection?

EVIDENCE: Are there increased examples of children taking guns to school? How good are the statistical projections on firearm deaths? What is the relationship between restriction and violent crimes?

When decision makers ask these questions they are asking for backing for the grounds and warrants of the arguments generated by the controversy. The next three chapters deal with these three types of support: credibility, values, and evidence. This chapter will examine evidence in the form of examples, statistics, and testimony. In Chapter 8 we will examine values as support, and in Chapter 9 we will see how credibility supports a claim.

Evidence, as we will use the term in this chapter, is *the support for a claim that the arguer discovers from experience or outside authority: examples, statistics, and testimony.* As we stated in Chapter 2, different spheres have different definitions of what counts as evidence and which forms have the most significance. In some spheres, evidence plays an extremely important role while in others values and credibility are more important. However, there is substantial empirical data and centuries of commonsense observation to support the idea that, when properly presented, most decision makers are influenced by evidence.

Forms of Evidence

Evidence (examples, statistics, and testimony) supports a claim in such a way as to cause the decision maker to give adherence to that claim. Evidence need not be a part of the spoken or written argument in order to contribute to adherence, however. The simplest form of an argument is the statement of a claim: an assertion. Assertions are not usually considered good arguments, but they can gain adherence when decision makers already know the evidence.

CAROL: "Pick me up at 5:00 so we can get to Sam's early and make sure we
   get to the game on time."

DON: "Okay. Sam is always late, so that's a good idea."

Carol's assertion receives instant adherence from Don because of previous experiences with Sam's tardiness. If called upon, Carol could provide examples such as
the time they were late for the barbeque because of Sam. The specific examples are in
the mind of the decision maker and, thus, stated evidence is unnecessary.

   In addition, the arguer cannot ignore evidence in the minds of the decision makers that runs counter to the argument. The unstated negative evidence in the minds of
the decision makers must be met as surely as the evidence of an outspoken opponent.
Although the emphasis in this chapter is on the way in which you may strengthen arguments through the use of evidence, you should always consider possible responses
to unstated evidence held by decision makers.

Example

Examples may refer to *undeveloped instances used in an argument by generalization.*
Such examples may be short. Bruce Luecke argues that the U.S. Space program has
produced "30,000 spin-off products and technologies since its inception in 1958."

> . . . to name a few that NASA lists there are: new fire-fighting suits with better breath-
> ing systems; a device that can warn of pending heart attacks; digital imaging that enables
> a more accurate medical diagnosis; a longer-lasting running shoe; and scratch resistant
> contact lenses (684).

He uses five short examples to illustrate the large number that he and NASA claim.

   An extended example, or *illustration,* usually means *an extended instance that
illustrates a general principle* (Perelman and Olbrechts-Tyteca 357). David Grann
begins his article about the "Knowledge to Power Program" (KIPP) at "a middle
school in the heart of the South Bronx" across the street from the Andrew Jackson
Housing Project with an extended example contrasting the regular students leaving
in the afternoon with the KIPP students who continue working, chanting rhymes
about reading, going "back to basics," and getting high success rates on academic
tests (24). That extended example is used to support the claim that this is "a public
school that works."

   Examples aim at confronting others with what they will accept as bits of reality, things that happened. One of the most compelling and probably most commonly
used examples occurs when you remind others of their own experiences.

   Remember our earlier example of the argument of Carol and Don and the examples they might have used to support their claim about Sam? Those examples were
of their own experiences. Such examples abound in interpersonal argument.

> "Let's go backpacking this summer. We had such a great time last year on the
> Kern Plateau and in the Wind Rivers."

"Don't buy beets. I've never had beets cooked a way I like them."

"Let's go see the new Sean Penn movie. I really liked him in *Dead Man Walking, I Am Sam,* and *Mystic River.*"

Even in public argument it is common for a speaker to use examples taken from the experiences of decision makers.

In 1999, the National Association for the Advancement of Colored People (NAACP) adopted a resolution calling on all U.S. citizens to boycott the state of South Carolina until the state ceased to fly the Confederate battle flag over the South Carolina State House. A debate in *The Crisis* magazine of the NAACP in October of 1999 featured an African American state senator who argued against the boycott. He used his own experiences of protesting the flag as background for his changed position: he now believes that the flag should be flown along with a "liberation flag" honoring African Americans. In support of the boycott, Anthony B. O'Neill, an African American lawyer from Charleston, South Carolina, argued for the boycott using examples that were personal to his largely African American audience.

> Senator Ford worries that African Americans living in South Carolina will pay for the boycott. We suffered from the bus boycott. We suffered from membership in the NAACP. We suffered for trying to register to vote. We suffered when we sent our little children to school. We suffered when we sought enrollment in colleges and universities. We suffered when we were blown to bits on Sunday morning while trying to worship the Creator. We suffered when we petitioned our employers for better wages and working conditions. Black people have suffered for every inch of ground that has been gained since first being brought to these shores.

In Chapter 3, we described how good stories function in argumentation. All examples, and particularly extended examples, need the characteristics of good stories. The story should ring true for the decision makers. The illustration must have characters, action, motives, and outcomes that make sense to them. In the case of a possible classroom argument about a change in the course registration system students must use, you might ask students to create their own stories. The scenarios of long lines, faulty telephone and computer instruction, failure to get classes, preferences for others, and payments that must be made just before payday, is a "story" that rings true to them.

In most public argumentation and many interpersonal argumentative situations, the specific instances you use will be outside the experience of the decision makers. Indeed, they will most frequently be outside your experience. In those situations it is important to make the specific instances as believable as possible, to make them seem real. Specificity of details and the citation of credible sources promote the idea that the instances are real because they can be verified by the decision makers.

Remember how Bruce Leucke argued that the space program had spun off 30,000 products and he gave examples of five of them? There is also a credibility argument, in that he says that the list came from NASA. Part of the power of these examples comes from how well decision makers trust NASA.

Specific details help examples seem more real because detail makes it easier for a decision maker to visualize. Even pictures can help. In the late 1800s logjams were cleared from America's rivers to make navigation easier. Now logjams are being rebuilt in the rivers to shade the waters, preserve spawning temperatures, and produce food for fish. To explain the logjam, Kathleen Wong used a photo of one in the Stillaguamish River in Washington and this verbal description:

> In the summer of 1998, Tim Abbe, a University of Washington fluvial geomor-phologist, . . . trucked fallen trees up to 90 feet long . . . and built five jams. "Like open-heart surgery, it's really gruesome while its going on," says Abbe. "You've got some of the biggest bulldozers Caterpillar makes in the stream bed trying to lift the trees as fast as possible. . . ." Despite Abbe's description, the finished product appears amazingly natural. "People say it looks just like a pile of wood," says engineer Tracy Drory. . . . "And I say that's exactly the point." Snorkeling expeditions this month have revealed pools beneath the dams sheltering chinook waiting to spawn.

A special kind of specific instance, called the *hypothetical example,* is used where real examples are not available or when the available real examples are not close enough to the decision makers' experience. It is important that a hypothetical example be perceived as equivalent to a real example. That is, it must have the detail and credibility to give it the characteristics of a real example.

Here is a hypothetical example that you might use to illustrate the problems of auto repair rip-offs:

> Here's a not-very-far-fetched description of what you might be involved with. You take your Ford escort in for repairs; there's something wrong in the engine or transmission. It's making a lot of noise that it didn't make before. You learn that the repair should take about ten hours and the charge is $30 an hour. The bill is $300 for labor. Sounds like simple arithmetic, right? Wrong! The actual work took only seven hours and that should save you $90. But, the service manager tells you they go by the *Flat Rate Manual* that says this repair should take ten hours, so you pay for ten hours of labor, even though it took only seven.

Statistics

Statistics are essentially a numerical compacting of examples. Statistics provide a means for talking about a large number of examples without citing every one. This means of compacting examples is found in various forms in argumentation: raw numbers, central tendencies, probabilities, and trends.

Raw Numbers   Some statistical references are clearly intended to emphasize significant numbers of examples. The publication *Investment Forum* is intended to persuade professionals to invest retirement and other discretionary income with TIAA-CREF. In 2003, portfolio stability was a major concern among investors. One article ("TIAA-CREF's Tenets") listed five key factors that contributed to the company's stability. The second factor was diversity. "The CREF Stock Account, for example, holds over 4,500 securities—much more than most other companies' equity funds, which in some cases can have as few as 20 stocks" (4).

Another article also built on the diversification argument, explaining that "the TIAA General Account [avoids being too closely tied to any single economic downturn] by investing in foreign bonds and real estate" (p. 6). The article then provided statistical evidence in the form of raw numbers to support its claim. As of the end of the second quarter of 2003, "$7.9 billion was invested in investment-grade international bonds and private placements, $2.1 billion was invested in emerging market bonds and private placements, and $1.2 billion was invested in directly owned international real estate" (p. 6).

The 30,000 products NASA claimed as spin-offs of the space program offers another example of raw numbers. Raw numbers also are used to provide evidence of general health conditions in the United States. Haney supported the claim that cases of humans getting rabies from bats are "exceedingly rare" by citing "federal health statistics" that there were four cases in 1995, two in 1996, four in 1997, one in 1998, and none by October of 1999. At the turn of the century about 100 people a year died from rabies (Haney).

There are a number of points worth observing about these examples of raw numbers. First, where the numbers are large, they are rounded off to make them easier to understand without essentially damaging their accuracy: The *Investment Forum* article stated that "The CREF Stock Account holds over 4,500" securities. These are not exact but rounded numbers. That is undoubtedly true of the 30,000 spin-offs. Second, the raw numbers are compared with other possibilities so the decision maker can tell, for example, that holding 4,500 securities is substantially different from holding 20 stocks. Decision makers also can tell, not just that the four or fewer cases of rabies from bat bites describe the situation in recent years, but that this number is substantially different from the 100 who actually died of rabies at the turn of the century.

Comparison is strongly influenced by the statistical measure you use. For instance, in 1995, when some argued that the United States was spending too much money on foreign aid, the statistics showed that the United States was second only to Japan in the dollars spent on foreign aid (Japan $11.3 billion, United States $9.7 billion). However, as a percentage of the nation's gross national product the United States was last among developed nations, with 0.15 percent. Twenty other countries gave a greater percentage of their gross national product in foreign aid, led by Denmark, Norway, and Sweden with 1.03 percent, 1.01 percent, and .98 percent ("Soft Touches").

One adaptation of statistics that none of these arguments used (because they are national arguments), but that you should consider, is to localize or personalize statistics. For instance, while national sources will tell you the average cost of a used 2002 Hummer, what price comparison could you get by calling your local General Motors dealer or checking the web page? Statistics must be rounded and compared for easier comprehension of their magnitude, and perhaps localized and personalized for greater impact.

Central Tendency   Some statistics go beyond raw numbers to provide an indication of what is normal in a larger population. Central tendencies are frequently called *averages*. In 1999, the following argument used averages to claim that Latino students are less likely to go to college than other students, and that this result is caused, in part at least, by lower expectations.

> A study done in 1999 by the Educational Testing Service, the organization that developed the SAT, compared Latinos 18 to 24 years of age with the same age group in the general population. It found that only 22 percent of Latinos went to college compared to 32 percent of the general population. Part of the reason for this, they believe, is that Latinos have lower expectations. 55 percent of Latino eighth-graders expect to go to college compared to 64 percent of African Americans, 68 percent of non-Latino whites, and 72 percent of Asians (Associated Press).

Both these sets of statistics are based on a sample of the populations studied. They also represent averages. Even if only 55 percent of Latino eighth graders expect to go to college, that doesn't tell you anything about a specific student or group of students. The figures are averages.

Statistical Probability   In Chapter 2, we talked about various meanings of the word *probability,* and statistics can represent one of them. Hilary Waldman used statistical probability to explain why doctors spent years misdiagnosing and prescribing wrong medications to Sofi Pagan, a young girl who was finally diagnosed with Batten, a genetic disease with 100 percent fatality, in November 2000. The gene for Batten disease is extremely rare, and a child must inherit one gene for the disease from each parent. The chance that two people who carry that gene "will marry and have children is about one in 25,000. Even if two carriers do find each other, their chance of having a sick child is one in four. It's so rare, in fact, that only 300 children in the United States have Batten disease" (83). The story went on to explain that Sofi's little brother, who was born before the Pagan family had any suspicion that Sofi was ill, also had Batten disease.

In another use of statistical probability, Alice Park reported that a drug known as letrozole offers additional hope to breast cancer survivors. Park explained that women who have been treated for breast cancer take the drug tamoxifen for five years to prevent recurrence. After five years, they must stop using tamoxifen, even though recurrences occur beyond the five-year mark. According to Park, a trial involving more than 5,100 women demonstrated that those who began taking letrozole after five years "experienced 43% fewer cancer recurrences than those assigned to the placebo group" (81).

The numbers in both of these examples are based on a concept of probability called *frequency.*

The statistics are an expression of the frequency with which events occur by pure chance, or the likelihood that something exceeds pure chance. That is, pure chance would predict that 30 percent of the population will get cancer by the time they are 70 years old, but if they smoke, their likelihood exceeds pure chance by a significant factor. Or, doctors are unlikely to test for Batten disease, because pure chance would not predict that a child would have it. Further, even when two carriers do have children (as with the Pagan family), there is only a one-in-four chance that any pregnancy will result in a child with Batten disease.

In the breast cancer study, pure chance would predict that the women treated with letrozole and those assigned to the placebo group would have the same rate of cancer recurrences, and changes from that seem to be related to use of letrozole. Forty-three percent is a significant movement beyond pure chance.

One of the problems of judging by statistical probability is the problem of deciding what probability is significant. The Delaney Clause of the Federal Food, Drug, and Cosmetics Act establishes a zero tolerance rule for judging additives in processed foods. Here is an argument against zero tolerance and for a higher probability requirement:

> Delaney allows no additive in processed foods that research has shown may induce cancer in laboratory animals—zero tolerance. "Pesticides are considered additives if they concentrate at all in the food during processing. Furthermore, under Delaney a substance can be defined as inducing cancer even if the incidence only happens at high doses, causes only benign tumors or despite negative results from other animal-feeding studies" (Thompson 13).

Statistical Trends   Many times statistics are used to compare a situation over time, to discover a trend. Genaro C. Armas noted that, in the United States, "the number of women 15 to 44 forgoing or putting off motherhood has grown nearly 10 percent since 1990, when roughly 24.3 million were in that class" (A11). Armas went on to explain that these numbers "reflect the well-established" trends of women attending college, entering the workforce, choosing to adopt rather than conceive a child, or choosing not to have children at all. Armas cited David Popenoe, "co-director of the National Marriage Project, a research group at Rutgers University" to support her statement that this last trend was particularly pronounced among wealthy women, who "had the highest childless rates, in part a reflection of the increased professional options available to them." Armas reported a smaller trend in the overall birthrate among U.S. women in this age group, with "61 births per 1,000" in 2002, and "67 per 1,000 in 1990." During the same years, the "birth rate for women 15 to 19 rose from 40 per 1,000 to 56 per 1,000" (A11). Because women aged 15 to 19 are unlikely to have extensive college or other professional training, this apparent aberration supports Armas's interpretation that the larger trend among women from 15 to 44 is explained by the availability of increased professional options.

The direct comparisons in the article on childlessness among U.S. women are based on census data accumulated between 1990 and 2000. Direct comparison cannot extend before 1990, because the census bureau did not track childbearing among women under 18 until 1990. The claim of a trend, however, is based on similar data accumulated over several decades. The statistical strength of Armas's claim is further strengthened because the report was based on data from 50,000 homes spread across the United States.

Combining Forms of Evidence

Few arguments rely on only one form of evidence. Instead, successful arguments demonstrate careful use of several different forms. Las Vegas showman Roy Horn (of the duo Siegfried and Roy) was mauled by a tiger while performing at the Mirage hotel in October 2003. The attack led to a spate of news coverage about private ownership of tigers. Michael D. Lemonick argued that private ownership of tigers was widespread, cruel, and dangerous. He used several forms of evidence to make his point. He began by telling the story of a tiger kept in a Harlem apartment house until police rappelled down the outside of the building, tranquilized the tiger, and relocated it to an animal sanctuary. He encouraged readers to identify with his claim that private residences are too small for tigers by placing a photo of the Harlem tiger at the beginning of his story. The tiger's face is pressed against heavy metal bars, and its eyes cry out for release. Lemonick followed with additional examples, then with statistics. He offered raw numbers, stating that between 1998 and 2001 the United States saw seven fatal tiger attacks "and at least 20 more that required emergency care" (63). He introduced statistical probability into his argument by claiming that these numbers should not be surprising, since there are about 10,000 privately owned tigers in the United States; twice as many as live in the wild. Thus, the statistical probability of being near a "pet" tiger in the United States is greater than it is anywhere in the wild. Lemonick relied on the expert testimony of Richard Lattis, director of New York City's Bronx Zoo, to clinch his argument. According to Lattis, tigers always remain wild animals, and private owners subject themselves and everyone else to unwarranted danger. In response to those who claim to keep pet tigers because they love the animals, Lemonick quoted Lattis as stating that private ownership of tigers is "a selfish, self-centered way of treating animals" (64).

So, statistics are compacted examples that sometimes appear as raw numbers, are sometimes averaged, frequently rounded off, and usually compared if they are to have maximum force for decision makers. From the point of view of evidence, however, you must remember that no matter how much counting and predicting has gone into statistics, they still rely on the response of the decision makers to have value in argumentation. Lots of people acknowledge the statistical relationship of smoking to cancer and heart disease, for instance, but do not apply it to themselves.

Testimony

Testimony is the statement of another person or agency that is used to support a claim. It may be used with examples or statistics as backing for the grounds of an argument. It may also serve, as we noted in Chapter 6, by itself as the grounds for an argument by authority. Testimony adds the credibility of its source to the grounds or warrant of an argument.

Traditionally, testimony has been divided into two types: *testimony of fact* and *testimony of opinion*. Obviously, all testimony represents the opinion of the person or agency cited. However, testimony about facts that provide examples or statistics is seen by many as stronger than testimony that only expresses the opinion of the source. Indeed, there is a general view among the researchers in this area that example and statistical evidence are more powerful than opinion evidence (Reinard 38–40). This is in line with the commonsense notion that testimony of fact is preferable to testimony of opinion.

Testimony of fact adds to examples or statistics the credibility of the source of the testimony. Daniel S. Turner argues that "America's infrastructure is crumbling." "It will take," he says, "more than a trillion dollars to upgrade roads, bridges, mass transit, airports, schools, dams, water purity, and waste disposal facilities in the next century." In each of these areas he argues that a series of facts exist that cannot be overlooked. On roads and bridges, for instance,

1. More than half of the roads in the United States are "substandard."
2. Substandard roads, bridges, and pavement are responsible for 30 percent of fatal accidents.
3. Passenger travel doubled between 1970 and 1995 and will increase nearly two-thirds by 2015.
4. Thirty-one percent of bridges are structurally deficient.
5. Eighty billion dollars will be required to eliminate the backlog of bridge deficiencies and maintain repair levels.
6. Full repair of the nation's roads and bridges would require $437,000,000,000.

These are not "his" facts, moreover; he presents them as the testimony of the Federal Highway Administration and the American Society of Civil Engineers (10–11). Turner makes a similar analysis of each of the areas of the infrastructure, and in each case he identifies an authority for the facts (e.g., U.S. Department of Transportation, American Association of State Highway and Transportation Officials, Federal Aviation Administration, Environmental Protection Agency, Association of State Dam Safety Officials). These are not just "facts" but testimony of fact. The power of the evidence rests in the detail of amounts and percentages but depends on the authority, not of the arguer, but of the sources of the testimony.

The distinction between testimony of fact and testimony of opinion may not always be as clear as it might first seem. These three sources provided statements of fact, but "facts" from the source organization's point of view. In truth, all these pieces of testimony represent opinion, although it is *expert* opinion. And there still is potential for bias, which is discussed later in this chapter. The crucial question for you as you use testimony is whether it will be perceived as fact and not "just opinion." That judgment will depend on the credibility of the source and the specificity with which that source develops the information.

The distinction between the two types of testimony is very important to certain specialized spheres of argumentation such as the law. A witness may testify to seeing the defendant enter the house at about 9:20 p.m. and leave about 10:15 p.m. carrying a suitcase. However, if the witness thinks the suitcase was full of valuables, that is opinion and not considered evidence by legal standards.

Some of the biases of these specialized spheres have been incorporated into our general practices. For this reason, we test factual testimony by asking about the testifier's experience, access to direct perception of the facts, and expertise on the matter at hand. As a general principle, good factual testimony comes from an expert source with direct knowledge. That source carefully delineates the fact testified to from its own and others' opinions. Even so, you must remember that the source is only testifying *about* facts and any time a human is involved, so is opinion.

General Principles for the Use of Evidence

To set down specific principles for the use of evidence is difficult because the believability of an argument is so heavily influenced by who the decision makers are and the factors they bring to the situation. However, some principles have evolved that are generally accepted by most persons in our society. These principles serve as reasonable standards for tests of evidence. They help you to see the difference between forceful and questionable evidence.

Use Representative Instances

This is another way of saying that you should choose the best examples available to prove a generalization. Remember the use of examples by Bruce Luecke on page 120? He argues that the U.S. space program has produced 30,000 spin-off products that are useful to the general population. He supports this with five examples. All seem important, having to do with improved health and safety and running shoes. Are they representative of the 30,000? That is difficult to tell. His argument would be stronger, perhaps, if each of his examples had been representative of one of the five areas where products might be identified with the space program.

There is no mathematical formula for judging representativeness, although specialists in survey research have standard rules they follow. Ultimately, the key question is, to what extent will decision makers believe that these examples are representative and, therefore, provide reason enough to warrant adherence?

Use a Sufficient Number of Instances

To form a satisfactory generalization, enough examples must be provided to convince others that the argument is believable. There is no magic number for the amount of evidence needed, but there is a long-standing "rule of three." Where a claim is in contention, use at least three examples. It is clear that some evidence is useful even when the decision makers already agree to the claim. It also is clear that the argument is seen as more powerful when more high-quality evidence from multiple sources is added. But, large amounts of evidence that is perceived as of low quality weakens an argument (Reinard 40).

One study of presidential debates indicates that "higher rates of factual evidence can lower a candidate's perceived effectiveness in a debate" if the evidence is not carefully linked to the claim or subclaim being argued. The authors of that study show how John F. Kennedy, in his first debate with Richard Nixon, successfully used extensive evidence but made sure decision makers could see the link to his claim of not being satisfied with America.

> I'm not satisfied to have fifty per cent of our steel mill capacity unused. I'm not satisfied when the United States had last year the lowest rate of economic growth of any major industrialized society in the world. . . . I'm not satisfied when we have over nine billion dollars worth of food—some of it rotting—even though there is a hungry world, and even though four million Americans wait every month for a food package from the government, which averages five cents a day per individual. . . . I'm not satisfied when the Soviet Union is turning out twice as many scientists and engineers as we are (Levasseur and Dean 139).

Account for Negative Instances

Particularly with knowledgeable decision makers, you make a mistake if you fail to account for instances that do not support the claim. The study we cited earlier that identified the trend among U.S. women to remain childless deals carefully with negative instances. In fact, it reported and explained negative instances. Recall that it reported the birthrate among women 15 to 19 actually rose between 1990 and 2000. This was explained by the presumption that such young women were unlikely to have extensive professional options. Armas also responded to the negative instance of an increase among never-married women in professional positions who chose to have a child. She pointed out that these women are economically capable of raising a child without a partner, and suffer much less social stigmatizing than in the past. Further, she pointed out that even with the increased likelihood that never-married professional women will choose to have children, the trend for women to remain childless remains strong.

Arguers who fail to account for negative instances that decision makers know about will lose credibility. Even with people who do not know the negative instances, some acknowledgment of them may strengthen an argument because it makes the arguer seem more trustworthy.

Give the Value Characteristics of Instances

It is important to let decision makers know what value judgments apply to the example. The following instances all provide a value clarifier (shown here in italics, though the words probably were not emphasized that way originally).

> "The *best* example of the increase in violence against minorities is the shooting at a Jewish day care center in Granada Hills, California."

"That 54 percent of all high school seniors have smoked marijuana is a *good* example of the widespread use of drugs."

"A *recent* example of press censorship occurred in the *New York Times*."

"A *typical* example of the efforts to clear up water pollution is the activity on the Connecticut River."

Make Instances Seem Real with Details

People tend to give greater adherence to more specific examples (Kline 412). Even hypothetical examples should be given the characteristics of real examples. Suppose you were to argue for new traffic regulations and develop a hypothetical example to explain how traffic congestion can be a serious imposition that needs new regulations. That hypothetical example might be stated like this: "Suppose you start home tomorrow night and find yourself in a massive traffic jam that delays you, and you miss an important appointment." Your example would be better if given the characteristics of a real example of streets and freeways your decision makers know: "Suppose as you leave work at 5:00 tomorrow night you turn onto the freeway at the Temple Street on-ramp. All that is needed to close down the Hollywood Freeway is one car out of gas just beyond Silver Lake Boulevard and there you are, stuck for hours in the sweltering heat, missing your important appointment."

Use Decision Makers' Experience

Although you should provide enough examples to support your claim with decision makers, the other side of that coin is also important. The tedious repetition of examples for people who already know them can injure the effectiveness of an argument. Therefore, you should remind decision makers of what they already know in support of your case. Phrases such as "as you already know," "your own experience has shown," and "as you learned last week" help strengthen your case.

Use Current Examples and Statistics

Clearly, the most up-to-date information is superior to less current information in assessing the present situation. Even for historical study, current information should be more useful because historical evidence is frequently cumulative. That is, every new piece of information makes the previous idea clearer. Also, more recent statistics may be more useful in historical argument because more sophisticated statistical measures have been employed.

Use Reliable Sources for Instances and Statistics

Avoid the bias of the source. This is important, not only because of the danger of drawing a less accurate generalization, but because such bias, when recognized, will damage the argument. Even though it is sometimes possible to win adherence through the use of biased sources that some decision makers do not recognize as biased, it is not wise to do so. Evidence from such sources can only be successful in seeking short-term adherence. Even persons who initially gave adherence will learn from others of the biased sources and, in the long term, remove adherence. Such a discovery could weaken your credibility with them on many claims.

Even information that is not biased but *appears* to be from a biased source is poor evidence because of others' reactions. A company that produces pain relievers offers a free booklet that they claim explains about pain relievers. You have no way of knowing whether the information provided is accurate but you may distrust it because it is offered by a source potentially biased by its own commercial self-interest.

For each example or statistical study that you take from someone else, ask your-self the extent to which that source is biased and the extent to which it may appear biased to others. Federal government agencies such as the Bureau of Labor Statistics are generally regarded as unbiased. But the claim cited earlier that there are 30,000 spin-offs from the space program is made by NASA and that agency may be trying to boost its image to get new funds. Whether sources are biased or not, the crucial issue is whether decision makers *think* they are or suspect that they may be.

Research foundations supported by private companies inspire varied levels of confidence. For instance, the statistics on petroleum imports published in *Petroleum Supply Annual* are accepted by virtually everyone because the petroleum industry needs accurate data on imports to do its work. The tobacco industry, on the other hand, being under fire from health advocates and agencies, is clearly perceived as biased whether or not it is. Research results by the American Tobacco Institute about the effects of cigarette smoking on health were questioned long before government agencies got involved. When you are structuring an argument, carefully consider bias and the potential for the perception of bias, because it can have a serious influence on the extent to which decision makers are willing to adhere to an argument.

Carefully Consider Statistical Measures

For our purpose, statistical measures basically answer the question: How typical are the examples? Darrell Huff in the book *How to Lie With Statistics,* presents many of the problems of statistical argument in everyday language.

One could spend a lifetime of study and become an expert in statistical argument and its errors. For the moment, however, the following are a few of the mistakes to avoid.

"The Sample with the Built-in Bias"   If you asked your classmates what they thought about the federal ban on private possession of handguns and they approved it by a vote of 15 to 5, that would be impressive, but if 10 others had refused to answer your question, you might have a built-in bias for which you were not accounting. Thus, the potential actual split was 15 to 15 or 25 to 5. The real proportions could be as great as 5 to 1 or as little as dead even. Also, suppose some of the people who opposed the ban did so because they thought it was not strong enough. That would give you another built-in bias.

"The Gee-Whiz Graph"   Graphic representation of statistical data can provide a visual clarification. It can also mislead. All graphs should be carefully examined to be sure that they provide information in a form that reflects the best interpretation of the data. Figures 7.1 and 7.2 are graphs of the percentage of high school seniors using marijuana/hashish in the twelve months prior to the survey by the University of Michigan's Institute of Social Research between 1975 and 1997. The figures could be graphed in many ways. What do these graphs show? Is there a steady and fairly consistent percentage of use, particularly between 1992 and 1997 (see 7.2)? Or, is there a substantial fluctuation in the percentage of use (see 7.1)? Does a dramatic increase occur between 1992 and 1993? Remember that graphs such as these are arguments, and they are no better than the analysis and evidence that goes into them.

"The Well-Chosen Average"   *Average* is a popular term standing for some measure of central tendency in data, but there are several ways of measuring it. One such measure is the *median,* the point above and below which 50 percent of the items fall. A second measure is the *mode,* the value that appears most frequently among the data. The third measure is the *mean,* an arithmetic average and the term most correctly applied to the term *average.* The mean is found by dividing the number of items in a series into the sum of all the items.

It's salary negotiating time at the place where you work, and the company president says that you shouldn't expect much of a raise because the average salary at this

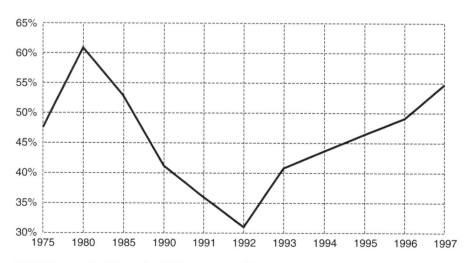

FIGURE 7.1   Marijuana/hashish use among high school seniors.

Source: World Almanac and Book of Facts, 1999. Page 878.

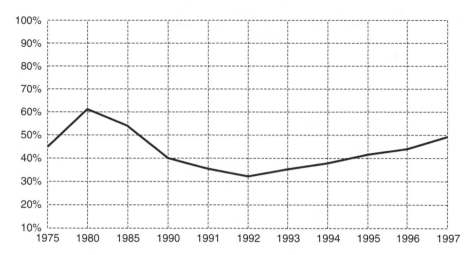

FIGURE 7.2   Marijuana/hashish use among high school seniors.

Source: World Almanac and Book of Facts, 1999. Page 878.

company is $20,000 a year, and you already earn that. The average in this case is the mode. You check it out and find that the median salary is $30,000 and the mean salary is $57,000. Here are the salaries:

$450,000 × 1
$150,000 × 1
$100,000 × 2
$57,000 × 1 Mean
$50,000 × 3
$37,000 × 4
$30,000 × 1 Median
$20,000 × 12 Mode

Has your employer chosen the measure of central tendency well?

"Much Ado About Practically Nothing"   There are groups in higher education who undertake the task of determining the quality of graduate programs in various disciplines. One hears the statement, "We are one of the top five communication [or psychology or political science] departments in the country." Statistical reports are published showing the relative ranking of all graduate programs by specialty. They make an impressive display, and people use them in arguments. The problem is that the data are gathered by randomly sending questionnaires to people in the discipline who may have only limited knowledge of work in all the institutions to be considered. The results do not control the bias in favor of the department the largest number of surveyed faculty graduated from, bias toward schools with certain popular approaches to the field, bias in favor of larger schools, and the long time between periods of productivity in a department and when the results of those periods become part of its reputation. Those who understand these factors may well see the data as "much ado about practically nothing."

Use Comparison to Clarify Statistics

We noted earlier in the discussion of statistics that they can be more useful if compared. If you lived in Albuquerque, New Mexico, you could argue that your state and local tax burden is low for a family of four with a $50,000 a year income. It averages only $6,900, according to the *Statistical Abstract of the United States*. But, $6,900 sounds like a lot of money, almost 14 percent of income, to some people. It would be best to compare it with other cities like Des Moines, Iowa, $8,200; New York, $13,200; Philadelphia, $15,200; or Bridgeport, Connecticut, $18,800 to show that the Albuquerque tax burden is the lowest surveyed in the Bureau of Census figures (310).

If you wanted to argue that government projections for the fastest-growing occupations in the country show that those occupations are in the health care area, you might cite these examples by the Bureau of the Census: the number of home health aides is expected to increase 138.1 percent by the year 2005, human service workers 135.9 percent, physical therapists 88 percent, and occupational therapists 78.1 percent. Those percentages look impressive, but they become even more impressive when compared to some that are estimated to decline in the same period: machine operators—32.8 percent, telephone installers—50.3 percent, equipment operators—60.2 percent, and frame wirers—75.3 percent (411).

Base Testimony on Credibility Measures

The purpose of testimony is to provide credibility to a claim by adding a second person or agency to its support. The trustworthiness and competence of the source of the testimony is essential to its effectiveness. We discuss credibility in greater detail in Chapter 9. We will make only a few comments here.

Before you accept testimony, ask yourself if the person was in a position to know, either as an observer or with the expertise to make an intelligent observation. Ask if the source of the testimony has anything personal to gain by the acceptance of the facts testified to. Ask if this is first hand knowledge or just a testimony about someone else's testimony.

A more specific source will add greater force than a vague one. Reports in the press are often attributed to unnamed or unknown sources, and readers have trouble assessing credibility. It is important for you to let decision makers know when testimony is from a credible source. Of course, that will influence your practices, because some sources will not be credible to decision makers and will need to be dropped. For instance, LaVarr Webb and Ted Wilson wrote that tax exemptions for credit unions violated "the first principle of fair tax policy." They went on to explain that this exemption hurts education. "Most Utah businesses, including banks, pay their fair share of taxes, contributing millions of dollars to educate Utah's children. Allowing a few large, profitable, expanding credit unions to avoid this responsibility increases the burden on all other businesses and citizens" (65). Readers might note that Webb and Wilson's article appeared in a publication that is edited by the senior vice president and public relations manager for a major bank, and is distributed at no charge to bank customers. This information might lead decision makers to judge Webb and Wilson's claims as biased in favor of the banking industry.

Sphere Dependence of Evidence

Evidence may be evaluated differently depending on the sphere in which the argumentation occurs. The evidence necessary to provide grounds or backing for a claim may well change as the sphere of argument changes. Sphere dependence in evidence does not merely mean that some evidence will be accepted in one sphere and rejected in another, but also, that one kind of evidence may be used in two spheres but valued more in one than in the other. We will note some of the more common cases of sphere dependence of evidence.

Hearsay Evidence

Legal practice does not lend credibility to *hearsay evidence,* that is, testimony a person might give about a statement made by another person. It is usually not admissible. Only what a witness directly observes is admissible. The law makes this provision because only statements from witnesses who can be held responsible are accepted. But in politics the reverse is frequently the case. When reporters say that the president of the United States (or even a "usually reliable source") told them something, it has a potential for developing a greater adherence to their arguments than if they claimed they observed it themselves.

In politics, ideas are frequently tried out on the public without requiring the arguer to be responsible for them. In addition to a "usually reliable source," you may hear of something being attributed to someone ("The secretary of state is said to have told the prime minister of Japan. . . ."). Atributions are not as strong as direct quotations, but they are still acceptable because of the sometimes circumspect tradition of political argumentation.

Ordinary and Expert Evidence

A similar situation exists in the difference between *ordinary* and *expert* testimony. In most professional spheres, the expert is preferred. In humanistic scholarship a philosopher, such as Plato, John Locke, or Karl Marx, is preferred over the observations of ordinary people. In literary criticism Jane Tompkins, Catherine Belsey, or Thomas Eagleton are expected to be more perceptive about literature than college students. In interpersonal argument people probably trust people they know better than they trust strangers. You may trust your friends to recommend a movie more than the expert critic in the local newspaper. You believe your friend "knows what you like."

Expert evidence for the behavioral social scientists is not a matter of differences in testimony. They frequently survey ordinary people, so the testimony is ordinary, but the means to draw conclusions from it is not. Behavioral social scientists draw their conclusions about human behavior through an elaborate system of statistical calculations. So the evidence becomes not just a collection of instances, but a complex expert statistical demonstration.

There is an interesting situation involving expert and ordinary testimony in the court of law. Lawyers make a distinction between ordinary witnesses and expert witnesses and the legal system has careful distinctions as to when each is most acceptable. But as far as jurors are concerned, little distinction is made between ordinary witnesses, expert witnesses, and other members of the jury who can say, "Well, I have been there myself, and believe me, this is how things are done." In fact, other jurors may be the most powerful source of testimony (Hawkins).

Reluctant Evidence

Reluctant evidence, from those who are antagonistic to one's purpose, has long been considered the best evidence in public debates. In a court of law, witnesses are under oath and required to testify against their own interests. In public argument, a person's own argument may be quoted by an opponent to attack the claim and make the person seem to have extreme views. In political argument, an advocate may use the claims of persons who have been supporters of a particular policy to point out the errors of that policy.

During the months following the September 11, 2001, attack on the World Trade Center, Congress cooperated with the Bush administration to pass numerous pieces of legislation intended to protect the United States from further terrorist attacks. The USA Patriot Act, a centerpiece of that legislation, passed overwhelmingly, with only three Republicans and sixty-two Democrats in opposition. Two years later, Michael Tomasky used the testimony of conservative Republicans to argue that the Patriot Act had gone too far in its assault on American freedom.

Tomasky first cited Bob Barr, offering as his credentials the fact that this former Republican congressman from Georgia was an avid supporter of President Clinton's impeachment, voted for the Patriot Act, and currently holds an endowed position at the American Conservative Union. In July 2003, Barr participated in an interview with staff from the *Houston Chronicle* (a newspaper with strong pro-Bush leanings). The result of the meeting was a *Chronicle* editorial stating that "John Ashcroft and other Justice Department officials assure Americans that their liberties and privacy are not in jeopardy. They say the anti-terrorist Patriot Act passed after 9/11 does not apply to U.S. citizens. Ashcroft is wrong, and he knows he is wrong" (47). Tomasky went on to state that Barr no longer thinks his decision to vote for the Patriot Act was the correct one.

Tomasky also cited James Sensenbrenner, Jr., a Republican representative from Wisconsin who chairs the House Committee on the Judiciary. The Patriot Act is scheduled to sunset (cease to be legally binding) in 2005. When Orrin Hatch (Republican senator from Utah) proposed removing the sunset provisions for the Act, Sensenbrenner responded that such action would occur "over my dead body" (47). Tomasky quoted Republican representative Ron Paul of Texas as stating that many of his GOP colleagues have "come up to me and said [voting for it was] the biggest mistake they ever made" (49). Tomasky also cited opposition to the Patriot Act by Timothy Lynch, of the Cato Institute, a long-time supporter of conservative Republican politicians. Tomasky concluded that, although "it's not likely that Republicans are going to start joining the ACLU or the Human Rights Campaign," Republican opposition to the Patriot Act indicates it has gone too far in its abridgment of personal freedom (49).

Negative Evidence

Negative evidence, or the absence of evidence, is used in all spheres of argument, but it is used differently in different spheres. It is frequently used in historical scholarship. A historian who finds no evidence of women doctors, lawyers, or professors in early America will claim from this negative evidence that the professions were male dominated.

Scientists use negative evidence in the form of the null hypothesis. They try to prove that the data may be attributable to sampling error. When they cannot prove this null hypothesis, they believe that the reverse—the hypothesis is true. So, a researcher who cannot prove that children do not grow more violent from seeing violence on TV (the null hypothesis) believes that they do (hypothesis).

Negative evidence is used in international relations. For example, the members of the Bush administration tell the world community it should join the United States in attacking Iraq because Iraq has amassed weapons of mass destruction that pose a significant threat to other nations. The world community (with the exception of Britain) turns down the invitation. The administration is more successful, however, in using the same rationale, along with claims that there is a direct link between Saddam Hussein's regime and al-Qaeda, to persuade U.S. citizens that such an effort is justified. When the United States invades and conquers Iraq, opponents of the war attack the action based on a lack of (negative) evidence. Despite the rapid and total collapse of the Iraqi government and the expenditure of vast amounts of military and espionage resources, the United States fails to discover the weapons or the links. Even after taking control of Iraq's infrastructure and selecting new leaders at both national and local levels, the United States finds neither the weapons, nor evidence of their existence. Several raids produce caches of guns and missiles, but no weapons of mass destruction. Despite combing through records and debriefing dozens of Iraqi informers (or patriots), no links between Saddam Hussein and al-Qaeda emerge. Lack of such evidence serves as grounds for the claim that the primary reason the Bush administration decided to conquer Iraq was to gain more direct control over Iraqi oil supplies, which are necessary for the continued operation of the U.S. infrastructure.

Documented Evidence

In law and in most scholarly fields of humanistic inquiry (e.g., literature, philosophy, history, theology) there is a clear bias for documented over undocumented evidence, perhaps because written or recorded evidence seems more permanent.

Traditional historical scholarship provides a reasonable example of this emphasis. There is such a bias toward documents, that elaborate methods have been defined by students of historiography to determine which documents are best and how they should be interpreted. For historians, for instance, there is a strong preference for "primary sources"—original documentary evidence. At the same time, there is a strong reservation about "secondary sources"—interpretations of evidence or events. This preference is related to the historian's interest in objective historical reconstruction (Wise 59).

Documented evidence for historians has also meant documents that came from official sources or from the reports of well-educated and, presumably, more knowledgeable people. In recent years there has been a growing interest in what has been called social history that tries to define how ordinary people were responding to events. Consequently, such persons have been interviewed (what is called oral history) and these interviews, along with diaries and letters, have been accorded greater weight. Still, there remains a strong bias for documented versus undocumented evidence.

Assertion and Evidence

Testimony as evidence means, as we indicated earlier, the testimony of someone *other than* the person making the argument. However, studies of arguments in conversational discourse reveal that people do use their own authority as grounds for claims (Willbrand and Rieke 419–23).

Children argue by assertion more frequently than adults. However, the examination of the arguments of well-known adults shows that they use assertion frequently. Sometimes such assertions gain the adherence of decision makers who trust the person making the assertion. However, arguing by assertion is a questionable practice in any situation where the arguer does not have unquestioned credibility with decision makers.

You may be an unquestioned authority on some things when you talk with your friends or you might be an expert in an area that others don't know about, in which case you will need to let them know of your expertise. Most likely you will want to provide evidence and not trust your argumentation to assertion. Remember the example we cited earlier of the debate over whether African Americans should boycott the state of South Carolina over the issue of the Confederate battle flag? State Senator Robert Ford, who argued against the boycott, felt obliged to explain his long and substantial history of opposition to the flag. In a sense, then, his argument is based on his credibility, which he knows must be established with his African American decision makers to make his assertions convincing to them.

Former Senator Mark Hatfield of Oregon presents us with another example of one who, because he is a Republican senator and conservative Christian, may not need evidence when he argues against legalizing public prayer in the schools.

> I must say very frankly that I oppose all prescriptive prayer of any kind in public schools. Does that mean that I am against prayer? No. It does not mean that at all. I am very strong in my belief in the efficacy of prayer. But I must say that there is no way [the Senate] or the Constitution or the President or the courts could ever abolish prayer in the public schools. That is an impossibility. Prayer is being given every day in public schools through this country—silent prayer, personal prayer that in no way could ever be abolished even if we wanted to.

Hatfield has no evidence to support his assertions but his argument may be accepted because of his conservative credentials and his status. So if the people hearing the claim accept the credibility of the person advancing the claim, assertion may function as if evidence were attached. It is a practice to be cautioned against because, for most people in public situations, assertion without evidence will not gain adherence.

Thus, each sphere will have its own interpretation of the degree of reliance that can be put into evidence: expert or ordinary, original or hearsay, willing or reluctant, positive or negative, documented or undocumented, substantial or asserted. There may be some general bias for one or the other in each of these pairs. You will do best to think clearly about the standards of the sphere in which you undertake to argue before you select the evidence you will use.

Conclusion

Arguments may be supported to gain decision makers' adherence using evidence, values, and credibility. *Evidence*—the traditional term for examples, statistics, and testimony—is the subject of this chapter.

Examples may be used to develop a generalization or illustrate a general principle. They can be real instances or hypothetical ones. Statistics provide a means for compacting examples, for talking about a large number of specific instances at one time. Statistical measures provide the basis for averaging and comparisons. Such measures can be simple or highly sophisticated. Testimony about fact or about opinion is a means of adding credibility to a message.

A number of general principles guide you in using examples, statistics, and testimony. All are based on the inclination of the decision makers, but the principles provide general guidelines:

1. Examples should be representative.
2. Examples should be in sufficient number.
3. Negative instances should be accounted for.
4. Value characteristics of examples should be given.

5. Detail should be given to make examples seem real.
6. The decision makers' experience should be used.
7. Examples and statistics should be current.
8. Examples and statistics should come from the most reliable sources.
9. Statistical measures should be carefully considered.
   a. Avoid the "sample with the built-in bias."
   b. Avoid the "gee-whiz graph."
   c. Avoid the "well-chosen average."
   d. Avoid "much ado about practically nothing."
10. Statistics should be made clearer through comparison.
11. Testimony should be based on credibility measures.

Some forms of evidence are sphere dependent; that is, they have different values depending on the sphere in which they are used. Hearsay evidence is suspect in a court of law but quite acceptable in political argumentation. Many fields regard the expert witness as superior to the ordinary witness, but this is not true for social scientists interested in human behavior or for interpersonal argument. Reluctant testimony depends for its value on the extent to which its author is clearly perceived to be reluctant. Negative evidence is useful in international relations but not in scientific argument. Documented evidence is preferred in most scholarly fields and in religion.

P R O J E C T

Deliver a short argumentative speech in which you state a single claim and support it with specific instances, statistics, and testimony.

8 Support: Values

stated values	concrete values
implied values	value systems
positive values	hierarchies of values
negative values	changing values
terminal values	attacking values
instrumental values	values and decision makers
abstract values	sphere dependence of values

Communication technology has made enormous strides in the past fifty years, especially in the last twenty. Television satellites, cable, computers, fax machines, cellular phones, cyberspace, and the Internet all have increased by geometric ratios the availability of information to people and their ability to communicate with one another. Many feel this has been a mixed blessing, particularly when the influence on children is measured.

Children can find sex and violence on television and by surfing online. Most people believe this is a problem, but can it be solved? And how? Should media be censored? Should manufacturers be required to put V and S chips (so parents can blackout violence and sex) into the TV sets? How about similar blocks on computers? Should the government impose the restrictions on cable that are imposed on broadcast television? Would such restrictions infringe on freedom of speech? Does government censorship lead to restrictions on knowledge?

This problem is complex and made particularly difficult because it affects children. It is, as many have noted, a question of values. Think about the arguments that are generated on this question and note the values, stated and unstated, in this brief description: knowledge (information), communication, children (family, innocence), violence, sex, restriction, freedom (freedom of speech).

Not all argumentation is so obviously based on values. But all argumentation has values in its development. Some would argue that values are the defining central factor of all argumentation (Sillars "Values"). One series of studies of unplanned reasoning by children and adults in various cultures indicates that values-based reasoning is pervasive (Willbrand and Rieke 343). In this chapter we will examine values as they serve as support for claims at the same time that we remember that claims themselves may be values.

"A *value,*" says anthropologist Clyde Kluckhohn, "is a conception . . . of the desirable that influences the selection from available modes, means and ends of action." A value may be "explicit or implicit, distinctive of an individual or characteristic of a group" ("Values" 395).

In Chapter 1 we observed there are three kinds of claims: fact, value, and policy. Value claims are those that directly involve values, and policy claims require value claims to support them. Only a factual claim, which asserts that certain conditions exist in the material world and could be observed, would seem to be value free, but it is not. Even the scientist's careful statement about laboratory observations implies the values of rationality and knowledge. Thus, values are important even to choose one factual claim over another.

Values obviously relate directly to claims of value, and they are vital to policy and factual claims as well. Values, together with source credibility and evidence, are the grounds and warrants by which decision makers judge claims to be worthy of adherence. However, understanding how values serve as support is not just a matter of observing that they do. Values differ in their characteristics and in their applications. They appear in systems, and they are adapted to spheres.

Characteristics of Values

Values, then, are concepts of what is desirable that arguers use and decision makers understand. Arguers use them with credibility and evidence to justify claims. But values have a variety of characteristics and fit together in various ways. We will examine those characteristics now so that you can better understand what goes into a value system in argumentation.

Stated and Implied Values

Some statements of value concepts are direct. People sometimes say that *freedom, health,* or *wealth* is important. These words state directly the value concepts they hold. Some value concepts may be identified by several different words as is the case with *liberty, freedom,* or *independence.* Furthermore, there can be variations of a single word as in *freedom, free,* or *freely* depending upon the nature of the sentence in which they appear.

Value concepts are not always explicitly stated, however. Frequently, they are implied. Values are general concepts that define what arguers and decision makers believe are desirable, but, many values are implied in what we call *belief statements.*

Milton Rokeach defines a belief as "any simple proposition, conscious or unconscious, inferred from what a person says or does and capable of being preceded by the phrase, 'I believe that . . . ' " (*Beliefs* 113).

Many statements of what a person believes do not directly state value concepts, but imply them.

Equality

STATED: *Equal* pay for *equal* work

IMPLIED: Women deserve the same pay as men for the same work.

Science

STATED: DNA research is a *scientific* triumph.

IMPLIED: DNA research is virtually unquestionable.

Self-Respect

STATED: Every child's well-being is based on *self-respect.*

IMPLIED: Children need to learn to like themselves.

When you directly and frequently state value concepts you are more intensive in your use of values than if you imply values only through indirect statement. The closing argument of a trial frequently is more value intensive than is the examination of witnesses. In the legal sphere, there is an attempt to be value free during the collecting of evidence. Witnesses, even expert witnesses, are supposed to report only facts tied to demonstrable sources. These are values, of course, including values of accuracy, fact, and science, but they are implied rather than stated. A witness might say under questioning, "I saw the defendant take the money from the cash register and run from the store." The negative value of stealing is only implied. The closing arguments of a trial provide more freedom for an attorney to openly attach values to the evidence.

Positive and Negative Values

Our definition of a value as "a conception of the desirable" puts a clearly positive cast on value concepts. However, for every positive concept there is at least one antithesis. So a statement of a value can be either positive or negative. Earning opposes stealing, freedom opposes restraint, thrift opposes waste, knowledge opposes ignorance, pleasure opposes pain. Depending on the strategy devised, if you argue against a specific proposal you may do so by identifying positive values that oppose it or negative values that you associate with it. As a critic of argument, you will want to note the extent to which an arguer focuses on either negative or positive values.

On October 8, 2003, Arnold Schwarzenegger—Republican, motion picture action hero, and body builder—won election as governor of California in a recall of Democratic Governor Grey Davis. Governor Schwarzenegger was identified in the campaign as inexperienced in politics and government, unable to explain what he would do as governor, guilty of sexual harassment, and a man whose movies glorified violence. These negative values (inexperience, lacking knowledge, violating woman's privacy, and violence) were used by his critics against him. Some of those negative values he turned to his own advantage. Not being a politician, his lack of experience, he argued, was a positive value, not a negative one. His motion picture stardom made him an appealing personality who could provide leadership. Leadership and common sense were the values that he matched against inexperience and lack of knowledge.

Terminal and Instrumental Values

Values will reflect the *ends* a person admires (wealth, health, happiness, security) or the *means* to attain the ends (hard work, faith, helpfulness, responsibility). Milton Rokeach called these "terminal and instrumental values" (*Beliefs* 160). He also found the terminal values to be the most central to an individual's value system (*Nature* 215).

A caution is necessary on that point, however. People frequently make a terminal out of an instrumental value. For instance, they recognize that they must work hard (means) to achieve economic security (end), but for many people hard work becomes an end in itself. Retired people with secure financial situations frequently work hard at whatever they do because work has become a terminal value for them. For the scientist, a carefully worked out experiment brings pleasure. For the religious person, faith can become more than a means to salvation; it can be an end in itself.

Instrumental values such as hard work or faith sometimes become terminal values. Even so, it is worthwhile to remember the distinction when you are building and analyzing arguments.

In his research, Rokeach identified eighteen terminal values (Figure 8.1) and eighteen instrumental values (Figure 8.2) that were prominent at the time. His lists are

FIGURE 8.1   Rokeach's "Terminal" Values.

Terminal Values

1. A comfortable life	**10.** Inner harmony
2. An exciting life	**11.** Mature love
3. A sense of accomplishment	**12.** National security
4. A world at peace	**13.** Pleasure
5. A world of beauty	**14.** Salvation
6. Equality	**15.** Self-respect
7. Family security	**16.** Social recognition
8. Freedom	**17.** True friendship
9. Happiness	**18.** Wisdom

He found these 18 values most central in an individual's value system.

(Nature 28)

FIGURE 8.2   Rokeach's "Instrumental" Values

Instrumental Values

1. Ambition	**10.** Imagination
2. Broad-mindedness	**11.** Independence
3. Capability	**12.** Intellect
4. Cheerfulness	**13.** Logic
5. Cleanliness	**14.** Love
6. Courage	**15.** Obedience
7. Forgiveness	**16.** Politeness
8. Helpfulness	**17.** Responsibility
9. Honesty	**18.** Self-control

The instrumental values in this list have been adapted from Rokeach's original list to make them all nouns like his terminal values.

not exhaustive but they illustrate terminal and instrumental value concepts that you are likely to find in your argumentation and that of others. More important here, they illustrate the difference between terminal and instrumental values.

Abstract and Concrete Values

A value is a conception, so it would seem that values are abstract. Words such as *freedom, justice,* and *truth* represent abstract value concepts in society. However, there are also times when particular people, groups, institutions, or objects serve as values. These are called *concrete values* (Perelman and Olbrichts-Tyteca 77). The flag, the family, the pope, the Star of David, and the Constitution are all concrete, yet they are value concepts. The Constitution is a good illustration. It is an actual document, but in an argument it has all the power of an abstract value.

A statement that a law is unconstitutional is as value-laden for most people as it is to say that the law denies freedom. In a court of law, violation of the Constitution is a more forceful value argument than restriction of freedom. Civil justice frequently limits freedom. You have to leash your dog, drive at 20 miles per hour through a school zone, and restrict your speech when it maliciously damages another. However, no law can acceptably violate the Constitution. The Constitution is to U.S. legal argumentation what God (another concrete value for believers) is to religious argumentation.

Abstract and concrete values work together. For instance, to use authority figures as support is to use concrete values. However, you don't say to a friend, "I believe we should study harder because my father says so." You are more likely to argue, "We should study harder. My father says it will lead to greater success." The abstract value of "success" is linked to the concrete value of "father." The realization that abstract and concrete values work together leads us to another: that values, abstract and concrete, terminal and instrumental, positive and negative, stated and implied, work in systems.

Values Appear in Systems

Values do not appear alone in argumentation. They appear in value systems, that is, as a set of linked claims. Clyde Kluckhohn calls these "value orientations . . . generalized and organized conceptions . . . of the desirable and non desirable" ("Values" 411). We hear people argue for better treatment of Native Americans, not on the basis of a single value of justice or mercy, but on the basis of a series of values that link together and reflect a unified system in which each value will be perceived as compatible with every other. Indeed, one of our major arguments over values is over the compatibility of values in a system. People are charged with inconsistency if they argue for their own freedom and discriminate against minorities. We know of people who wonder how someone can oppose legalizing marijuana and still drink alcohol. Some people consider it inconsistent to argue for morality and deny a belief in God. Others find it inconsistent to support capital punishment but oppose abortion.

These are examples of arguments about the consistency of values in a given system. They come about because values do not stand alone. They work in integrated systems. The theoretical and experimental literature supports the idea that there is a limited and distinct group of value systems. There are many potential value patterns, Rokeach says, but the number will be limited because of the social factors involved (*Beliefs* 161).

In an extensive study of the value systems across cultures, Charles Morris found a dominant pattern of American value systems, although different from the value systems in other cultures (44). A frequently cited cultural difference is between Japanese and American values in their emphasis on collectivism versus individualism. Three researchers examined the role of "commitment" in both cultures. In short, how do American and Japanese workers and family members perceive the commitment they have to the agencies of the society? What values characterize the Japanese and American value systems beyond the accepted collectivism/individualism? The values [they called them themes] found among Americans were: dedication, obligation, integrity, and determination. Among Japanese, the values were: connection, membership, responsibility, cooperation, and interest. The American values are all linked to individualism. They reveal what values an individual must have. The Japanese values are all ways of explaining a collective value system. All except "interest" which reflects the individual's interest in a person or subject (Guzley, Araki, and Chalmers). Anyone who is going to engage in argumentation before decision makers whose value system comes from another culture must recognize and adapt to such differences.

Traditional Value Systems

There are several acknowledged U.S. value systems that scholars from a wide variety of fields identify (Kluckhohn, *Mirror* 228–61; Morris 185; Ruesch 94–134; Steele and Redding 83–91; Weaver 211–32). To illustrate, we will examine one value system that is probably the dominant value system in U.S. politics and government, the enlightenment value system.

The United States became a nation in the period of the Enlightenment, a new intellectual era based on the writings of scientists such as Sir Isaac Newton and philosophers such as John Locke. The Declaration of Independence is the epitome of an enlightenment document. In many ways the United States is an enlightenment nation, and if enlightenment is not the predominant value system, it surely is first among equals.

The enlightenment position stems from the belief that there is an ordered world where all activity is governed by laws similar to the laws of physics. These "natural laws" may or may not come from God, depending on the particular orientation of the person examining them, but enlightenment thinkers theorized that people could discover these laws by themselves. Thus, people may worship God for God's greatness, even acknowledge that God created the universe and natural laws, but they find out about the universe because they have the powers of observation and reason. The laws of nature are harmonious, and one can use reason to discover them all. They also can provide for a better life.

Restraints on humans must be limited because people are essentially moral and reasonable. Occasionally, people act foolishly and must be restrained by society. However, a person should never be restrained in matters of the mind. Reason must be free. Thus, government is an agreement among individuals to assist the society to protect rights. That government is a democracy. Certain rights are inalienable, and they may not be abridged: "among these are life, liberty, and the pursuit of happiness." Arguments for academic freedom, against wiretaps, and for scientific inquiry come from this value system.

Some of the words representing concepts from the enlightenment value system are:

POSITIVE: freedom, science, nature, rationality, democracy, fact, liberty, individualism, knowledge, intelligence, reason, natural rights, natural laws, progress, information

NEGATIVE: ignorance, superstition, inattention, thoughtlessness, error, indecision, irrationality, dictatorship, bookburning, falsehood, regression

People use the enlightenment value system in a wide variety of spheres and situations. They make judgments about the desirable in science, in politics, and in everyday life. All value systems, like the enlightenment system, are a set of linked claims about desirable ends and means. But the values in a system are more than linked to one another. Their relationship to one another is defined by a value hierarchy. In a particular argumentative situation, the values in a system are graded.

Values Are Graded in Systems

A particular set of decision makers is defined by the value system to which it adheres. Many residents of the United States follow what we will call a personal success value system. For many people, family, career, health, self-respect, satisfaction, freedom of choice, accomplishment, material possessions, friendship, and similar values are most important (Gallup and Newport). The personal success value system represents U.S. citizens as success-oriented in an individual way that may not be found in other cultures (e.g., the Japanese culture).

However, as natural as such a value system is in the United States, it cannot be used in a particular argumentative situation until it has some kind of order to it. Any two values potentially contradict one another. A person may value both family and career as a part of personal success. Yet an argument can be made that career can interfere with family. In such a case, the two values are not just part of a value system; they have to be understood in relation to one another and the solution in this case involves using both.

"A particular audience," say Chaim Perelman and L. Olbrechts-Tyteca, "is characterized less by what values it accepts than by the way it grades them." If you think of decision makers' values in isolation, independent of interrelationships, you "may neglect the question of their hierarchy, which solves the conflicts between them" (81–82; Walker and Sillars 141–45). Therefore, a claim that two parents should cut back on their work schedules to spend more time with their children is a matter of emphasizing family over career without denying the legitimacy of either value. Such an argument also may mean a lower rank in the hierarchy of other personal success values, such as material possessions.

Values, therefore, are concepts of the desirable ends and actions that are stated directly or implied. They are stated positively or negatively. They are terminal or instrumental, abstract or concrete. They are found in clusters that are value systems and, when applied to a particular situation, are graded to reveal their relative significance, one to another. With this understanding you are ready to see how you may use values in the argumentative situation.

General Principles for the Use of Values

Because they are so basic to argumentation, values are essential both for criticizing the arguments of others and developing your own arguments. In this section we will examine seven principles for using values in argumentation. The first three apply most directly to criticizing the arguments of others. The last four are principles that will aid you in developing your own arguments.

Values May Be Found Anywhere in an Argument

We have already observed that there are no value-free arguments. Any part of an argument can state values. Some arguments may be made up completely of claims and subclaims that openly state values. In this example all the parts of the argument contain direct, positive values.

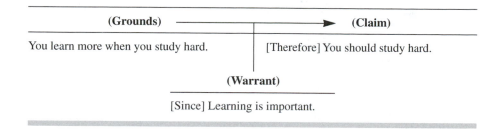

(Grounds)	⟶	(Claim)
You learn more when you study hard.		[Therefore] You should study hard.

(Warrant)

[Since] Learning is important.

Although such a value-intensive argument is possible, it is not a likely argument. In most arguments many values will be implied, not stated, and in some arguments, warrants or grounds will not be stated. Yet to function as a critic of arguments (your own or others) you will need to be aware that values may be found anywhere. You need to understand where an argument fits in a value system. You can do that only by actively looking for an argument's values.

As an arguer, you must be aware that you may be challenged at any time to state unstated values. That is a good reason for you to be aware of the values from which you argue. Two people are arguing. One says "The national economy is improving because unemployment is dropping." The other says, "The national economy is worsening because interest rates are increasing." Both claims can be supported. What is at issue is a conflict between work (employment) as a value and solvency (inflation) as a value. If you were one of these debaters, you would need to be aware of the unstated value you were defending because your opponent might call upon you to defend it.

Recognize Values in Warrants

Warrants are the most likely place to find values. Their role in an argument is to justify the reasoned movement from the grounds to the claim. Justification is clearly a value-using procedure.

The debate over the protection of wildlife has centered around the Endangered Species Act (ESA). Those who oppose the act claim that the ESA violates private property, hurts the economy, and wastes tax money. A strong argument is also made that it doesn't work. This claim is supported by a study by Charles Mann and Mark Plummer in their book *Noah's Choice: The Future of Endangered Species*. Their studies show that "by the end of 1994, only 21 species had been struck from the list, and of those 21, only 6 were delisted because they had gained enough ground to warrant removal." Others were removed from the list because they became extinct or were not endangered in the first place. Even several of those whose status improved did not do so because of the ESA (Carpenter 43). Those who argue for the Endangered Species Act claim that improvement has to be measured not only by delisting but by other factors. Their argument is really about how success is defined, and the value of success remains central to the controversy.

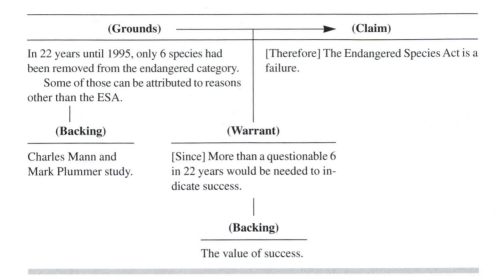

Find the Values in the Arguments of Others

Before you can decide whether to accept or refute arguments of others you need to find the values they use. Here is a specific list of tools.

1. Look for specific language that directly states values.
   a. A statement ["I believe in *honesty.*"]
   b. A word [*freedom, truth, nature*].
2. Look for negative terms [*waste, immoral, filth*].
3. Look for concrete values [*God, Constitution, Star of David*].
4. Look for indirect values ["Vaccination is essential for all children" or "A cure must be found for AIDS" (health)].
5. Look for absent values that you might expect to find ["The purpose of government is to protect life and property."] (Why have liberty and the pursuit of happiness been left out and property added to the traditional values found in the Declaration of Independence?)
6. Look for other factors that indicate values.
   a. Statistical evidence (science)
   b. Testimony of authorities who represent values [the Pope, Marx, Jefferson]
   c. Heroes and villains of stories
   d. Stylistic evidence [biblical, African American, or scientific style]

When you examine someone's argument with these tools you will have a good idea of the values in the arguer's value system.

Recognize the Limits of Value Change

Before you develop a case, you must think seriously about exactly what value changes you wish decision makers to make. Nicholas Rescher has pointed out that value changes usually take place by: (1) making a value more or less widely distributed within the society; (2) changing its relative importance to another value; (3) altering the range of a value's application; and (4) raising or lowering what one expects a particular value to mean when applied to a specific belief (14–16). These four options all have to do with shifts in the hierarchy, in application, or in the meaning of a value. None involve the almost impossible act of changing values by adding a new one or dropping an existing one.

The current public controversy over abortion is irresolvable as long as it is seen as a conflict between two prominent values in our society—life ("pro-life") and freedom ("pro-choice").

It is virtually impossible for the pro-life forces to accept the pro-choice position, and vice versa. Yet neither side denies the other's value. The pro-life position says a woman had a choice when she got pregnant, and the pro-choice group argues that quality of life must be considered, not just physical life. But, it can be argued, a woman did not have a choice in the case of rape, and the life of the mother is important. Also, there are arguments about when life actually begins.

Although the abortion debate is a rare case of two values in direct clash, there are modifications. Two proposed solutions have been to limit abortions to the first trimester or to cases of rape, incest, health of the mother, or severe fetal deformity. If either of these was generally accepted, it would represent Rescher's third condition, altering the range of application. The first trimester proposal limits "life" to after the first trimester. The second proposal limits the freedom to choose abortion.

Some pro-choice advocates argue that life is important and abortion is wrong, but government should not interfere with the individual's right to choose. They are trying to change the relative importance of life and choice. Returning the issue from the federal arena to the states would be an attempt to change the distribution of the values of life and choice in the society. People are not likely to give up either value. Any resolution to satisfy both sides seems impossible. Perhaps it is. If there is to be general adherence to either position it will come, not with the extermination of one value or another, but by one of the four adaptations indicated above. If not, no matter what happens in courts and legislatures, the debate over abortion will continue to be unresolved.

Find the Best Point of Attack on Values

The method for analyzing claims of fact or value discussed in Chapter 4 is used to determine the best point to attack value claims. First, you must determine what values support the claim. Second, you must determine what criteria to use in judging those values. Third, you must determine how to grade the values (Tuman).

Traditional journalistic standards, such as those published in the Society of Professional Journalists' Code of Ethics, reveal a value system that has been labeled "accurate interpretation." That value system maintains that journalists should be truthful, communicate information, be objective, be fair, support freedom, and accept responsibility (Sillars and Gronbeck 68–76).

FAIR (Fairness and Accuracy in Reporting) is a liberal journalistic organization like the conservative one Accuracy in Media (AIM). (You might note that both groups use terms from this value system in their names.) FAIR published an analysis of conservative radio and television talk show host Rush Limbaugh subtitled "Rush Limbaugh Debates Reality." That he is objective even Limbaugh would deny, but he does claim to be truthful and give people information ("I do not lie on this program"). He also believes that he supports freedom. He claims to accept responsibility (" . . . if I find out that I have been mistaken . . . I proclaim it . . . at the beginning of a program—or as loudly as I can"). FAIR argues that Limbaugh is neither truthful nor fair. Those two values are the basis of their criticism of Limbaugh.

FAIR claims that Limbaugh takes factual situations and draws untruthful and unfair conclusions. For instance, they claim that he says that human use of fluorocarbons does not destroy the ozone. It is a theory, says Limbaugh, developed by "environmental wackos," "dunderheaded alarmists," and "prophets of doom." Their refutation, they believe, shows that these are unfair characterizations. To support his argument, he claims that volcanoes, like Mount Pinatubo, cause more ozone depletion by a thousand times "than all the fluorocarbons manufactured by wicked, diabolical, and insensitive corporations in history." FAIR cites the journal *Science,* to claim that chlorine from natural causes, such as volcanoes, is soluble and, therefore, rain prevents it from getting to the upper atmosphere to release the carbons. FAIR also quotes an atmospheric chemist at the University of California, Irvine, who says "Natural causes of ozone depletion are not significant." FAIR contrasts these experts with Limbaugh's expert Rogelio Maduro, who they claim only has a bachelor's degree in geology (10–11). The criterion for judging truthfulness in FAIR's analysis is clearly the quality of the scientific supporters.

This short summary of a piece of argumentation illustrates the three steps necessary to determine the best way to attack a value claim. FAIR has found the values (truth, fairness, responsibility); found a criteria (science) for evaluating the argument; and determined how to grade the values (truthfulness is primary).

Such a system, Joseph H. Tuman observes, leads to five alternative attack points on such an argument:

1. Dispute the values.
   (Ex: "Fairness doesn't apply when attacking an evil.")
2. Concede the values and hierarchy but dispute the criteria.
   (Ex: Calling people "environmental wackos" and "dunder-headed alarmists" is just a joke. It is part of Limbaugh's style. People who are offended at this should get a life.)
3. Concede the value and criteria but dispute the hierarchy.
   (Ex: "The most important criterion is supporting freedom.")
4. Concede the value but dispute the criteria and hierarchy.

(Ex: "There is a more important criterion for judging scientific truth. These so-called experts are part of the "agenda-oriented scientific community.")
5. Dispute all.
(Ex: "Fairness is an inappropriate value in this case and even were it appropriate, attacking a joke doesn't make sense and freedom is more important than either of these values.") (93)

Obviously, the first and fifth alternatives are ones people would seldom use because, as we have already noted, values change very slowly. Still, this example illustrates how to challenge value claims. The three middle attacks (dispute the criteria, dispute the hierarchy, or both) are the most likely points at which Limbaugh supporters could attack the FAIR argument.

Relate Your Values to Decision Makers

The fact that limited options are available to you in a value dispute makes it clear that you will be most successful by arguing within decision makers' value systems. Adherence is most likely when the values in your arguments are ones that relate to decision makers. To achieve this you must pay close attention to the particular social group to which decision makers belong. Values are social, shared among the members of particular groups. Indeed, to a large extent, interaction among the members of a group defines the value system and its potential hierarchy. This is true of all kinds of groups: social, political, religious. It is true of families, and it is true of gangs. The values of your family (e.g., love, respect, cooperation, security) are positive to you because you are a member of that group. You probably think that gangs who hang out, get in fights over turf, bully people, and threaten authority are negative. To much of society, they are. The gang members, however, have defined their values much as your family has, and their values are positive to them.

Gang members, and those who work with gangs to effect changes in their behavior, indicate that gang members have values that are positive to them even though the way they are acted out are negative to the general society. Gang members emphasize, among other values, the need for respect, love, progress, financial security,

FIGURE 8.3 **Questions to Use When Examining Values**

Examining a Value System

1. What *proportion* of a value system is represented by negative or positive values, abstract or concrete values, terminal or instrumental values, stated or implied values?
2. What *emphasis* does the value system have? How value intensive is it? What values are most salient?
3. How *consistent* are the values within the system?
4. How *significant* are the values in the system to the decision makers?

brotherhood, and family (Gozic). Even though they see respect gained through fear, financial security from illegal acts, and brotherhood leading to turf wars, they use these positive values. Anyone who wants to change their behavior has to begin with these positive values as starting points when gangs are the decision makers. The same principle is true of most decision makers; you have to use the values they have and move toward a revised interpretation of those values.

Use Evidence and Argument to Develop Values

We can talk about values by identifying specific words that reflect these values (e.g., *freedom, work, happiness, reason, salvation*). However, you need to keep in mind that you communicate values indirectly by the evidence and argument you use more than by direct statement. This idea is what we mean by *implied values.* Rather than telling someone that your argument is "reasonable" or "factual," demonstrate that it is. Remember the old writing dictum: "Show, don't tell." Direct statements make more value-intensive arguments. There are times when you will want to make your arguments value intensive. However, for most of your argumentation, values will usually be communicated by evidence and argument.

Recent studies indicate that although people hold values, and hold them in systems such as those we have discussed in this chapter, they do not hold them in clearly defined systems. They live in a "fragmented intellectual culture" and a "fragmented popular culture" (Bellah et al. 282–83). In the words of Conal Furay, Americans "dance around their values" (19). While individuals and groups can frequently identify values, they do not use them in a fully rational fashion. Consequently, care must be taken in stating values in too absolute a manner.

You need to make clear to decision makers that your values are their values, but if you overuse values you will make your case too obvious and open it to rejection.

Earlier we used the example of the controversy over the influence of the media on children. Newton N. Minow, the former chair of the Federal Communications Commission who labeled television a "vast wasteland," told his listeners what a child can find after school on TV programs in one week. Here are some of his examples:

> A 13-year-old girl who has slept with 20 men
> Transsexual prostitutes
> Parents who hate their daughters' boyfriends
> Girlfriends who want too much sex
> White supremacists who hate Mexicans
> A woman who tried to kill herself nine times
> Sadomasochistic couples
> Dad by day, cross-dresser by night

In this partial excerpt there are a number of negative values used and most are unstated, but they are implied by these examples: sexual promiscuity, violation of childhood, hatred, racism, suicide, violation of family.

Making value-based arguments and examining the arguments of others involves finding values, understanding the limits of value change, learning to find a point of attack, relating values to decision makers, and using evidence and argument to develop values. However, these practices are tempered by a realization that value systems will differ from sphere to sphere.

Sphere Dependence of Values

Probably no other function of argumentation defines spheres so well as values. We have defined a sphere as a group of persons whose interstructured, repetitive, and therefore predictable patterns of communicative behaviors are used in the production and evaluation of argumentation. The criteria by which a group of people in a sphere appraise arguments form a value system. People are not admitted seriously to the sphere unless they have appropriate credentials (e.g., JD, MD, a successful election, ordination, a PhD in the right discipline). The permitted evidence, as we noted in Chapter 7, is regulated by the criteria of the sphere. The preferred kinds of argument, how one argues, and appropriate language all depend on the criteria of that sphere. These criteria make up a system of values. So in one sense, a sphere is defined by its system of values.

Science and religion are two spheres that have frequently been at odds with one another. A comparison of the values in these two spheres helps to make their disagreements clearer. It is not just that their claims are sometimes at issue, but their defining values are much different.

Values in Scientific Argument

Scientific argument, as we use the term here (and in Chapter 13), refers to those disciplines that use the physical sciences as a model to explain how physical, biological, human, and social entities function and interact. Scientific argument can be characterized by the values of order, usefulness, prediction, rationality, and knowledge.

Order in Science   What we have called scientific argument assumes there is some *order* in phenomena. This means that a scientist builds "a world picture" (Toulmin, Rieke, and Janik 328–30). Thus, scientific argumentation is judged by how well it can prove that the theory explains all related phenomena. Any sign that there is an inconsistency between one explanation and another must be accounted for or the explanation is deficient.

Scientists assume an order to data when they argue that one set of data will identify the natural state of related phenomena. For example, a social scientist will claim that an experimental examination of one group of children will provide a generalization about all similar children.

It is the rupture of order that interests scientists. A communication researcher discovers that TV takes up a good deal of a child's time until age fourteen. Then viewing time drops off sharply. Why? Because other factors interfere? Because parents monitor TV viewing more? Because TV programming is less interesting to teenagers? One does not decide to develop a theory about something that is explained by current theories. Theories are developed to explain a phenomenon that is different, and by developing or revising a theory to explain the change and accommodate the previous lack of change, order is returned to the sphere.

Usefulness in Science   Closely related to order is the value of *usefulness*. If order is sustained by research, then it is useful because it can be applied at other places and other times, the assumption goes. When a theory, no matter how much order it has, ceases to be useful, it is abandoned for another theory of greater usefulness.

Anthropologists in the nineteenth century considered it useful to know if people of different races and social status had different shapes and sizes to their heads. They used calipers to measure head sizes to explain their perceived differences in achievements. They believed that head size represented brain size and, thus, factors such as intelligence, social action, and language.

Today, serious social scientists consider such measurement humorous because the theory that head size determines intelligence has been rejected. There is a similar debate today over whether the Graduate Record Examination is a useful predictor of success in graduate school. Thirty years from now the GRE may be as useless as determining graduate school admission on the basis of hat size.

Prediction in Science   Implied in both order and usefulness is the value of *prediction*. It means that the theory represented in a claim will tell one not merely about the instance under consideration but it will predict how similar instances will occur. The theory of evolution is a good example of such a claim. It does not merely claim that a particular biological species changes. It predicts that all biological species evolve. It claims that they have evolved, are evolving, and will evolve according to certain principles. It asserts a high level of predictability. It is a forceful theory.

Rationality in Science   Although an ambiguous term, *rationality* is the clearest way to explain this value. It relates directly to the assumption that order exists. Abraham Kaplan distinguishes between what he calls "logic-in-use," which describes the actual patterns of thinking used by scientists, and "reconstructed logic," which describes the discourse through which scholars justify their conclusions (8–18). In the process of discovery, says Kaplan, imagination, inspiration, and intuition play an enormous role, but the discoveries must be justified to other scientists by reconstructing the imagination, inspiration, and intuition into a rational explanation that other scientists can follow and test as an intellectually coherent commentary. The rational explanation must provide a set of refined practices based on empirical evidence for the justification of claims.

Knowledge in Science   Nonprofessionals frequently describe science as the search for "scientific truth." Medical science has had a strong influence on this kind of thinking by suggesting there are certain diseases that it is learning to conquer one by one. Curiously, there is always plenty to work on, even after hundreds of years of conquest. A better term than *scientific truth* for this value is *verifiable knowledge:* an extended explanation based upon repeated attempts to justify related claims. Scientists seek knowledge that, when lodged in theories, links to the other values. It gives order to the subject under study and predicts what other useful knowledge may be known. Knowledge, then, is not some once-and-for-all final truth. Rather science, as Toulmin puts it, makes "the course of Nature not just predictable but intelligible—and this has meant looking for rational patterns of connections in terms of which we can make sense of the flux of events" (99).

The values of science identified here (order, usefulness, prediction, rationality, and knowledge) only begin to define the scientific value system. In addition, there are adaptations in the value system from one scientific discipline to another. Nonetheless, these five identify the value system of the sphere well enough to be used to contrast it with another major sphere: religion.

Values in Religion

The Judeo-Christian-Islamic tradition of religion is examined in greater detail in Chapter 14. In this chapter we briefly discuss seven values of argumentation in the religious sphere. Not all religious argumentation will cover all seven values we will discuss here, and other values are sometimes added. These seven, however, reasonably define the theological system: God; authority; human beings; morality; faith; salvation; and the church.

God The most forceful value in the Judeo-Christian-Islamic theological value system is the concrete value of God. God is understood as an entity of some kind with complete control over the world and all who inhabit it. For some, God controls every action. For others, such as deists, God is the source of natural law who sets the system into motion. In Christianity, God is frequently understood to consist of a trinity— Father, Son, and Holy Ghost—in which the son, Jesus Christ, is seen as a primary source for the understanding of the religion. So people speak of a "Christ-centered religion" to define the value of God.

The three religions of the Judeo-Christian-Islamic tradition are monotheistic— they believe in one God—although some, such as Christian Trinitarians, have one God in three persons. This one God, therefore, is all powerful and all knowing. God is usually perceived as an eternal father figure, judge, and provider.

Authority As we note in Chapter 14, in the religions of the Judeo-Christian-Islamic tradition, the starting point of much religious argumentation is an authoritative figure (God, prophet, pope) or text (the Torah, the Bible, and the Qur'an being the most obvious examples). This explains the desire among religious writers to find the earliest texts, those that are closest to the actual statements and actions of the originators of the religion.

Conflicts over the criteria for judging texts abound in theological argument. Conservative Protestants believe the Bible to be inherently and literally true. For them, almost as important as being "Christ-centered" (the value of God) is that religion be "Bible based" (the value of authority). More liberal Protestants accept the Bible as metaphor in many cases. Roman Catholicism uses specialized analysis to explain the meaning of Biblical texts. For most Christians, the New Testament is more significant than the Old Testament. For Jews, of course, the Torah is the authoritative text. Some groups, such as Roman Catholics and Latter Day Saints, find a pope or prophet to be authoritative in some specialized situations. These differences among interpretive versions clearly illustrate the importance of authority to religious argumentation.

Humans   There is general agreement in the Judeo-Christian-Islamic tradition that humans are more important than other animals. But, do humans get this status from nature? From the ability to reason? From their possession of a soul? Thus, a persistent question in religious argumentation is about the basic nature of the human.

Despite all the disagreement about the nature of humans, the religions of this tradition clearly value humans over earth, sea, air, and all other creatures. God loves humans above all others, speaks to humans, designs laws by which humans are to live, and gives dominion to humans over everything else in the world:

> And God blessed them [Adam and Eve], and God said to them, "Be fruitful, and multiply, and fill the earth, and subdue it; and have dominion over the fish of the sea, and over the birds of the air, and over every living thing that moves upon the earth" (Genesis 2:28).

Morality   Although humans in most of the Judeo-Christian-Islamic tradition are more important than all other creatures in the natural world, they still are subservient to God. They must acknowledge God and follow the commandments God gives them. Thus, a very important value for religious persons is morality and how it is defined. Even people who have no religious affiliations have obligations because the rules of religious morality have been built into the laws and customs of the society. This general value of morality begins with texts like the Ten Commandments, which contain a series of values that govern the relation of humans to God and to one another.

Words that are spoken by God have more authority than all other statements, in textual interpretation. So, God speaks to the people in Exodus:20 stating the Ten Commandments as rules for their behavior. In those commandments, among others, are values of God, love, honor to parents, life, fidelity, and honesty. Many are stated as negative values, as in "You shall not steal" (Exodus 20:15). From sacred texts, commandments, parables, and metaphors are used by believers to identify moral principles that serve as values in religious arguments.

Faith   Faith is an instrumental value unique to religion. It extends human reason beyond rational observation. To it is linked the "power of prayer," the ability of the believer to communicate with God. Faith in God, faith in prayer, and faith in authority are vital links between God and humans. Faith provides the important function of answering questions that fill in the gaps of traditional knowledge and reinforces the authority of text and spiritual leader (e.g., Is there a God? Does God answer prayer? Is there life after death?). However one looks at it, faith that allows for this relationship of human to God is a very special and important value in any system of religious argumentation.

Salvation   For some people, salvation is the most important benefit one receives from religious belief. For others, salvation is less important or even personally nonexistent. For believers in salvation, it answers the question of immortality by not only granting it but by making it a happy existence in a post-existent state (such as heaven), sometimes with a spiritual oneness with God and sometimes with a physical resurrection in paradise. For some others it means escape from the horrible eternity of suffering known as hell. Salvation is more than a spiritual condition for those people who believe; it is an earned reward for a lifetime of following the other values in this system.

The Church   Like salvation, the concrete value of the church is a value to which some religious people give little power. In Islam, Judaism, and much of Protestant Christianity, religious leaders get their status from their ability to gain the adherence of worshippers. Religious leaders are chosen and dismissed by the congregation. The church authority is in the members of an individual congregation.

For Roman Catholics and some other Christian denominations, on the other hand, the church interprets the essential texts of the religion, provides an understanding of the traditions of the religion, and administers holy sacraments in an authoritative way. In some ways, the church is still a value, even for those who do not grant it such authority, because the church grants to the individual the right to become a part of something greater than they are. There is a sense in which all members of religions in the Judeo-Christian-Islamic tradition are members of a spiritual church. *Islam, Judaism,* and *Christianity* are terms representing more than a series of values. They see themselves as a fellowship of believers.

This discussion of religious values has been brief, but it points out that any theology is a case that must be built using a value system for interpreting and grading these values. The decisions one makes on one value will affect what is possible for another. Thus, if humans are incapable of making proper decisions, some agency, such as the church or direct fellowship with God, must be available to do so. The nature of God affects the nature of fellowship with God. How one interprets salvation relates to the nature of humans. These are only a few examples of how building a case for a particular theology involves the interrelationship of these values.

The Relation of Science and Religion

We have examined these two spheres of argumentation (science and religion) to illustrate how different two value systems can be. None of the value terms of one are found in the other. Religion, unlike science, has concrete values as four of its seven values (God, authority, humans, the church). In some ways science has the most abstract value system of all. Its five primary values (order, usefulness, rationality, prediction, and knowledge) are abstract. The only terminal value for science is knowledge and the usual terminal values for religion are God and salvation. How, then, do they coexist? An examination of the relationship between these two very different value systems provides a useful example of how values interact across spheres.

These two value systems have been the subject of controversy for many years. Early disciples of science, such as Copernicus and Galileo, found themselves in disputes with the Roman Catholic Church. In 1633 Galileo was forced to recant the publication of his belief in the Copernican theory that the earth rotates on its axis and, with the other planets in the solar system, revolves around the sun. The basis for judging the Copernican theory a Christian heresy was the authority of the Church and the Bible that, taken literally, says that the sun revolves around the earth (Genesis 114–18; Joshua 10: 12–14). This controversy between religion and science can be extended far beyond the Copernican theory. However, the controversy illustrates at least a clash between the scientific values of rationality and knowledge and the religious values for authority in sacred text, faith, and Church.

For many people the sharp contrast in value systems between science and religion makes the two fundamentally antagonistic. For a natural system of order, there is the counterpart of God and the centrality of humans. Prediction is opposed by faith and salvation. Rationality is opposed by authority in sacred texts and the interpretation of the church. Accepting one value system can make the other its secondary value system. For instance, deists acknowledge God as a first cause. For them, God created the universe with natural laws, wound it up like a clock, and set it to working. The working of the universe is rational because God's principles are rational. The scientific value system is, therefore, the dominant one for deists because humans are to be scientists continually unraveling those laws. There are no miracles, answered prayers, or moral laws that are not rational and predictable. Faith is in the process, and the church is an institution that helps us to understand this gloriously ordered system.

The second way of using both value systems is to acknowledge the existence of two spheres of argument that can complement one another. For such persons, scientific order, rationality, and predictability is maintained and explained as science. God's role with humans, morality, and salvation cannot be explained by science because it is in a different argument sphere. An occasional miracle, for instance when prayer saves someone from a predicted death from disease, is just that—an occasional event. It is to be celebrated as an act of God but it does not refute the essential validity of scientific order. Neither does scientific rationality refute God, because God, operating in a sphere where science cannot argue, is the first cause of natural law.

Such a separation between spheres is not unusual. The separation of religion and science is one of the most dramatic, having received considerable attention, but the same is true with other spheres. Literary scholarship following a humanistic qualitative orientation can be seen as a different sphere and, therefore, not in conflict with behavioral psychology. Law and morality are frequently separated. Someone may not be seen to have broken the law but to have broken a moral code. Examples abound of people avoiding conflict by separating the values they live by into spheres of argumentation.

However, when spheres of argument are seen to overlap, serious value problems occur. A. J. S. Rayl and K. T. McKinney asked scientists if science proves that God exists. Many argued that the question remains outside the sphere of scientific argumentation, but a few did not. One mathematical physicist said, "If science can't reach God, then God doesn't exist" (44). Such a point of view represents a total commitment to the scientific value system. This can be seen in his further statement: "Nature will tell us what sort of definition we have to use. . . . Physical evidence could greatly alter our view of God, but we need to redefine God in terms of physics, which won't be easy" (44–48).

Statements such as these clearly indicate that this mathematician believes that an argument about anything, even something as total as God, has to be argued by the values of science.

A similar situation occurs in the area of creation science. The Creation Science Association is a research and teaching organization that claims to provide scientific proof through research that the literal six-day creation of the earth stated in Genesis is scientifically correct. However, a careful examination of their arguments shows that the proof is clearly based on textual authority, God, and faith. David Klope shows the relationship of science and religious values in one presentation of the Institute of Creation Research's "Worldview":

> In the transcendent portion of the ICR worldview, "creation" and "revelation" have priority over "science," . . . The emphasis in this entire speech is that defense of "creation" comes first from the Bible, and the speech tries to show the ICR as acting in this manner through phrases such as "what we're saying at the Institute for Creation Research is this: look, we have a revelation from God who knows everything. . . ." Sequentially this priority is even enacted in the speech: Ham [the speaker] begins the speech by citing a Bible verse, and the entire first half of the speech involves primarily Biblical issues. Although the ICR maintains the value of "science," they are careful to prioritize theology. In this view a "creationist" must first be Biblical (123–24).

Some people, therefore, can bring these two spheres together but they do so mostly by acknowledging that each deals with different issues. When spheres come together and claim to deal with the same subject, however, it is clear that argument becomes the unusual case we noted earlier of a direct clash of values.

Religion and science are quite different spheres. They do not share values. There are many ways in which argumentation in these two spheres is quite different. They can work together if one is made secondary to the other. More likely, they will work together when they are clearly seen as being different spheres of argumentation. People must see that each has its place, subject matter, and method to answer different questions. In such a situation, textual authority and faith, for instance, give answers to questions science cannot answer about moral life and salvation. Such values are compatible with order and rationality, for they have their own order and rationality. Scientific values of order and rationality in such a situation have their own authority and faith.

When people do not accept such a separation, the clash between the two value systems can become total. As you move into arguing issues in these spheres and other spheres where conflicting values exist, you need to keep this potential clash in mind. You need to consider where your decision makers stand and in which sphere they are likely to find their value warrants.

Conclusion

Values are an essential part of the analysis of every argumentative situation. They share with evidence and source credibility the grounds and warrant for a claim. No matter what kind of claim (fact, value, policy) is being argued, decision makers use values to judge whether it is worthy of adherence. A value is a general conception of a desirable mode, means (instrumental), or end (terminal) of action. It is differentiated from a belief, which is a simple statement about a specific situation. Many times values are openly stated (freedom) or implied in statements about specific beliefs ("people should vote").

Although values are usually treated as positive (freedom), they may be stated in the negative (restraint). They are usually thought of as abstract (freedom) but they can be concrete (the Constitution).

The values and beliefs used in an argumentative situation can be seen as a value system. That is, they work together and define each other's relation to the particular claim being argued. Because values are social as well as personal, decision makers can share them with the arguer. They can, therefore, be used in arguments to gain adherence. To gain adherence, however, decision makers must believe that the values in a particular system are consistent with one another.

There are a number of traditional value systems in the United States. Each of these systems not only has to be seen as having values consistent with one another, but they must be graded. That is, the decision maker must be able to see the hierarchy of values. It has been said that more important than which values are in the system is how each is graded in relation to every other value in the system.

There are some general principles for the use of values. Values may be found anywhere in an argument, although their use as warrants is probably most important. You can find the values in the arguments of others by using six specific tools discussed in this chapter. At the same time, you need to recognize the limits of value change. Changes in value systems rarely result from adding a new value or eliminating an old one. Most often, changes will come through changing a value's distribution, rescaling it, redeploying it, or restandardizing it in the value system.

The best point of attack on a value system is found by using the procedure suggested in Chapter 4 for analyzing the claims of fact or value: determine the values, the criteria for judging them, and the grading of them. This usually results in one of three attack points: dispute the criteria, dispute the hierarchy, or dispute both.

All arguments have values in them, but the most effective are those where the values are related to decision makers. However, even well-chosen values are not simply stated; they must be developed through evidence and argument.

All spheres depend on values. This is illustrated by a comparison of science and religion. Scientific argumentation is characterized by the values of order, usefulness, prediction, rationality, and knowledge. Religious argumentation is characterized by the values of God, authority, humans, morality, faith, salvation, and church. These two spheres have frequently been in conflict with one another. There is no overlap in their value systems. Conflicts between them are resolved by making one a secondary value system to the other or by treating the two spheres as having completely different roles.

P R O J E C T

Analyze a newspaper editorial. Look for its stated and unstated, positive and negative, terminal and instrumental, abstract and concrete values. On the basis of your analysis, how would you characterize the value system the writer follows?

Support: Credibility

KEY TERMS

ethos

credibility

competence

trustworthiness

good will

dynamism

reputation

sincerity

direct credibility

secondary credibility

indirect credibility

sphere dependence

The crisis in U.S. business and finance that shook the nation in the first years of the twenty-first century was all about credibility. Greed and self-interest, while not particularly admirable, are accepted as inherent to capitalistic free enterprise, but the system also contains checks and balances designed to keep these strong motivators under control. Business leaders publish quarterly reports that presumably stick to the facts, and their boards of directors stand behind them to ensure their credibility. Beyond that, accounting firms stake their reputation on their evaluation of those reports, and financial consultants who advise potential buyers of securities in the companies add their credibility. Then, this system bit-by-bit unraveled to reveal boards of directors who did not challenge CEOs who were falsifying reports, and accounting firms that, at best, looked the other way, and financial consultants who recommended stocks they knew were not as strong as claimed. Business leaders, accounting firms, and financial institutions staggered and sometimes fell because they had lost their most valuable possession: their credibility.

James M. Kouzes and Barry Z. Posner, researchers into business leadership, argue, "Managers, we believe, get other people to do, but leaders get other people to want to do. Leaders do this first of all by being credible. That is the foundation of all leadership. They establish this credibility by their actions" (276). So, in at least one major sphere of argumentation, business, credibility is a major factor. But *credibility,* as Kouzes and Pozner argue, is not "some gift from the gods (as *charisma* is defined) but a set of identifiable (and hence learnable) practices, strategies, and behaviors" (275).

While credibility may serve as a claim in argumentation, its most important role is as a means to support a claim, just as evidence (Chapter 7) and values (Chapter 8) do. You will see as you read this chapter that credibility is closely related to evidence and values.

When Aristotle first defined credibility as one of the three forms of proof, he used the term *ethos*. For Aristotle, *ethos* is "proof" that is generated in the mind of the decision makers "whenever the speech is spoken in such a way as to make the speaker worthy of credence" (38). The likelihood that adherence will be granted is increased, according to Aristotle, as the arguer is perceived as having "practical wisdom, virtue, and good will" toward the listener (121).

It is also worth noting that *ethos* is used to refer to the spirit of a whole culture as well as to individual character. The characteristics that Aristotle defined for the speaker are characteristics that will make the speaker compatible with the group, and these characteristics, "wisdom, virtue, and good will" are values that are approved of by decision makers, at least in Aristotle's day and probably today as well.

Characteristics of Credibility

Modern social scientists have worked to find an empirical definition for credibility. Although there are differences among their studies, their judgments are not much different from Aristotle's. It is reasonable, therefore, to use Aristotle as a basis and, adapting to modern research on the subject, define *credibility* as *the support for a claim that is developed by the decision makers' perception that the arguer reveals competence, trustworthiness, good will, and dynamism.*

The first thing to observe about this definition is that it is the decision makers' perception that defines an arguer's credibility. When you say that someone has high *credibility* you mean you find that person credible. Your perception of a person's credibility may also be influenced by the context of the argument. Your friend, your mother, your religious leader, your professor, may all be credible to you but on different subjects at different times. Yet there are some characteristics about decision makers' perceptions that serve as a broad base for the judgements they make. Therefore, we will examine the most often-perceived characteristics of credibility: competence, trustworthiness, and to a lesser extent, good will and dynamism.

Competence and Trustworthiness

A primary dimension that decision makers seek out is competence. A variety of value words have been used since ancient times as synonyms for *competence: wisdom, sagacity, reliability, authoritativeness, expertise, qualification.* Common sense experience would confirm that decision makers find an argument more worthy of adherence when it is advanced by a person they believe competent on the subject.

Persons who are perceived as trustworthy also have high credibility. In the literature on credibility since classical times, other value words have been used to define the meaning of *trustworthy: virtue, probity, character, evaluative, honest, sincere,* and *safe.* Common sense is that ideas are more readily accepted from persons you trust.

Good Will and Dynamism

The first two dimensions of credibility—competence and trustworthiness—are discussed by all writers. Two other factors—each of which is accepted by some and not by other writers—are *good will* and *dynamism.* Value terms such as *open-minded, objective, impartial, kind, friendly,* and *caring* have been used to characterize the good will dimension. *Dynamism,* the only one of the four terms to be strictly modern, is characterized by words such as *showmanship, enthusiasm, inspiration,* and *forcefulness.*

It is easy to see how the research might have shown either good will or dynamism to be weak or nonexistent as separate dimensions. Good will could easily be classified as a subcategory of trustworthiness. People find trustworthy those persons whom they perceive to have good will toward them. Likewise, dynamism, when it functions in a positive manner, may well be a judgment about competence. Research shows that dynamism in a speaker increases audience retention of an idea (Schweitzer). A dynamic speaker would also appear more self-assured, and self-assurance conveys the impression that the persons who posses it "know what they are talking about." Even written argument that is direct in stating a claim with a sense of authority carries with it a dynamic quality.

President Clinton was charged and, after denying it, admitted to a sexual relationship with an intern in the Oval Office. Even after he was charged and impeached in the House of Representatives, his approval ratings in the polls remained high. A majority of Americans seemed to believe that such actions, while wrong, did not limit his ability as president. Clinton strengthened his credibility by being forceful and direct on other matters such as education, Kosovo, the economy, and race relations. He was "acting presidential," some said. We might note that in his public acts and statements he ignored the charges and acted in a dynamic way toward other problems.

However, dynamism has a feature not possessed by competence, trustworthiness, or even good will. Dynamism may be perceived negatively. The overly enthusiastic salesperson who calls at dinner time promising a way for you to save money on your long distance phone bills and persists even when you aren't interested, is dynamic ("You mean you don't want to save money?") but not credible to many people.

While individuals' definitions of credibility vary, there is enough agreement to identify decision makers' judgements of trustworthiness, competence, and good will as support for a claim. With some reservation about overdoing it, dynamism also serves as a credibility factor in support of a claim.

Forms of Credibility

What decision makers know about an arguer's reputation will influence their perceptions of the claim. For instance, at the first meeting of your argumentation class, most of the members of the class probably know little about you. Your reputation is probably minimal. As time goes on in the class they know more and more about you. You develop a reputation. An arguer's reputation is important to credibility but cannot be changed instantly. Therefore, what you do to develop credibility in your argument is most important. Aristotle, when he discussed credibility, did not include a person's reputation, position, or actions outside the argument. For him *ethos* was a product of what happened in the argument. The three forms of credibility that can be built into actual arguments are direct, secondary, and indirect credibility.

Direct Credibility

The most obvious form of credibility is what we call *direct credibility*. This is the kind of credibility that you develop by making direct statements about yourself.

Every arguer brings a reputation to the decision making process. The president of the United States, the Speaker of the House, a company executive, an embezzler, a prominent athlete, all have a reputation: the opinion that decision makers have about a person's credibility before that person begins to argue. Advertisements for products frequently feature celebrities like Tiger Woods for American Express, or Michael Jordan for Hanes underwear, because of the image they have before they make the argument: their reputations.

Hawai'i is a state separated from the rest of the world both by miles of Pacific Ocean and a distinct culture. Andrew Gomes, writing in the *Honolulu Advertiser,* says, "Being perceived as 'local' is a sensitive and valuable quality for companies doing business in Hawai'i. It's the Good Housekeeping Seal of kama'aina" (a true resident, in contrast to outsiders). This is so, Gomes reports, because the Native Hawaiian host culture is joined by an ethnically diverse population, all of whom have grown up together. If the person or company advancing an argument can provide direct evidence of local roots, credibility is likely to follow.

When Clint Arnoldus, the chief executive of Central Pacific Bank, criticized rival First Hawaiian Bank as being less than local, First Hawaiian Bank's chief executive Walter Dods, responded giving direct evidence of his local credentials. He said he was born and raised in Hawai'i, was a graduate of a prominent local high school (Saint Louis), and that, unlike Arnoldus, he had not just gotten off the boat from California. His final proof was a challenge to Mr. Arnoldus to a debate in pidgin, a language that combines bits and pieces of many languages and is not likely to be spoken by anyone who is not kama'aina. Arnoldus did not accept the challenge.

Accounting firms were among the most damaged entities in the business and financial scandals we mentioned at the start of this chapter. Some accountants, who were supposed to be the guardians of honesty, accuracy, and fairness, were exposed as co-conspirators in dishonest dealings. PriceWaterhouseCoopers, wanting to distance themselves from the discredited accounting firms, engaged in direct credibility through an advertising supplement in *Business Week* and by setting up a website, www.building publictrust.com. Under a heading of "truth as a business opportunity," they list a series of shareholder rights such as meaningful information, explanations of numbers in plain language, and the facts managers use to make significant decisions. Considering that many companies are being sued by shareholders, the accounting firm says, some might argue that less rather than more openness is called for. "Not a bad argument," they reply to their own question, "but not a good argument if the overall objective is to regain public confidence." "What would companies get for all this honesty?" the ad continues. "A clear conscience and an opportunity to build credibility and trust with the investor." By directly associating themselves with these recommendations for building business credibility, PriceWaterhouseCoopers builds its own credibility as well.

Secondary Credibility

We call another form of credibility *secondary credibility*. The arguer uses another person's credibility as the grounds for the argument, thus the term *secondary*. By associating the credibility of someone else with yourself, you strengthen your own credibility.

Mark Bowden, writing on "The Dark Art of Interrogation," asks whether the United States is torturing prisoners taken from Afghanistan and Iraq. To strengthen his own credibility he uses the secondary credibility of a former CIA officer who went to work for the State Department as a counterterrorism coordinator. Cofer Black, who testified before a congressional committee, "All I want to say is that there was 'before 9/11' and 'after 9/11.' After 9/11 the gloves came off." Bowden then further uses secondary credibility by quoting a letter written by Irene Kahn, the secretary-general of Amnesty International, and sent to President Bush: "The treatment alleged falls clearly within the category of torture and other cruel, inhumane or degrading treatment or punishment . . . prohibited under international law" (56).

Obviously, secondary credibility cuts both ways: it could diminish as well as enhance one's own credibility. If Bowden's readers, for example, consider Amnesty International a group that is always crying wolf about the mistreatment of people at the hands of governments, they might discount Kahn's letter and reduce their estimation of Bowden's argument.

A problem inexperienced arguers frequently miss is that credibility is not enhanced for decision makers simply because the argument is supported by a number of well-known people and agencies. Prominent people are not necessarily credible. The National Fluid Milk Processor Promotion Board sponsors ads that argue that people should drink milk. Each ad features a celebrity with a milk mustache and the slogan, "Got milk?" One ad features the cast of the hit TV sitcom *Frasier* and argues:

> The general populace isn't merely lacking culture, it's lacking calcium. In fact, 70% of men and 90% of women don't get enough. The enlightened among us, however, drink 3

glasses of milk a day. A practice that can prevent a Freudian condition known as "calcium envy." ("Got milk?")

The subtle references to the humorous high culture snobbery and profession of psychiatry that is typical of Frasier and his brother Niles, make the connection to the show and its cast. But, of course, the six characters pictured in the ads are not experts on calcium or milk. They draw your attention to the ads, but should you make a decision to drink milk because of them?

Think of the reputation the quoted person has with decision makers. You may want to review the discussion in Chapter 7 about testimony evidence. At this point you should be able to see the close connection between evidence and credibility as forms of support for a claim. Secondary credibility is established from the testimony of sources the decision makers respect, not necessarily from the testimony of well-known sources.

Indirect Credibility

Unlike direct and secondary credibility, you develop indirect credibility without using the testimony of authorities or direct personal statements about your experiences that illustrate your trustworthiness, competence, or good will. Credibility is developed by the way you develop, support, and argue your claims. The evidence and values you use influence decision makers' perceptions about you. The more effectively you argue, the more credible you become.

Indirect credibility is probably the most forceful kind of credibility. While decision makers might rate you lower for speaking openly about your qualifications, they will not rate you for making an argument that gains adherence. In a sense, then, this entire book is about how to gain indirect credibility.

General Principles for the Use of Credibility

The credibility you generate to support your claims—direct, secondary, or indirect—can play an important part in the response you get. However, there are no easy rules for how you should use it because this changes as decision makers and spheres change. Like beauty, it is in the eye of the beholder. Still, there are some general principles of credibility that apply to most situations.

Develop Credibility from Reputation

Reputation is the credibility you have with decision makers before you argue. It may be influenced by the success you are perceived to have (Andersen and Clevenger 73) and by the perception that you are from the same group as the decision makers (Andersen 220; Myers and Goldberg 174–79).

In 1999, St. Martin's Press suspended distribution of a book about George W. Bush, then a candidate for president, when it was discovered that the author, J. H. Hatfield, may have been convicted eleven years earlier of hiring a hit man in a failed attempt to murder his boss. "Since Hatfield's credibility has been called into serious question, we feel compelled to suspend publication," said Sally Richardson of St. Martin's Press ("Questions About Author"). This is a case of a credibility judgement being made on a matter clearly separated from what was in the book. The negative reputation for criminal acts would make the arguer suspect in his claim that George W. Bush avoided criminal action for cocaine possession in 1972.

Difficulty occurs when arguers come to the argumentation situation with little credibility—not because they are unworthy of credibility, but because it is not recognized by decision makers. What we have said thus far about reputation would seem to at least reinforce half of the line from an old song, "The rich get richer and the poor get poorer." A person who comes to an argumentative situation with a favorable reputation in the area of the argument has an advantage over one who does not. Yet the person with a good reputation can make mistakes to damage his or her credibility. So it is important to reinforce your good reputation with decision makers.

Even if your reputation is limited, it can be improved. You must make special efforts, at least indirectly and with the use of secondary credible sources, to enhance your credibility. It is not uncommon for arguers to introduce statements of direct credibility about themselves that tend to increase credibility, if they are not too self-congratulatory (Andersen 228; Ostermeier).

Men's Health is a magazine that caters to young men who perceive themselves (or want to be perceived) as masculine, adventurous, sexy, and daring. In a section called, "Men's Health Challenge–We Dare You to Try This," Bill Stump, under the title "Scull Session," wants to challenge readers to, "Leave the silly canoe at home this weekend. It's time to row a real boat." To develop his own reputation as willing to take a challenge, he begins his article by reporting his own experience: "The jockstrap full of cold river water actually relaxed me. I was learning to scull—a 50-cent word for rowing a $5,000 boat—and had been preoccupied with the thought of falling in" (103). He goes on to detail his own learning experience, which did not turn out so bad, and ends with a set of instructions for his readers to follow, his credibility strengthened by the implied, "If I can do it, so can you."

Arguer's reputations can be enhanced in a formal situation by the way they are introduced (Andersen and Clevenger 64; Haiman). For instance, the fact that Bill Stump was writing an article in this self-proclaimed "guy magazine," was writing under the subtitle "We Dare You to Try This," and in his first sentence used a "guy" term (jockstrap) introduced him to the reader as a man's man.

While it isn't likely to be a factor in your credibility right now, you should be aware of the influence of mass media on the credibility of less well-known people. The mere fact that a person is singled out of the millions of bits of information available for the six o'clock news will enhance credibility. Though persons may speak for organizations of no more than a dozen people, they gain credibility from their mere presence in the media. Never doubt that reputation is increased by an arguer being quoted in a book, reported in the daily newspaper, or seen on the *David Letterman Show.*

Take stock of your reputation. It is the starting point of your credibility. You can enhance it even if it is minimal. Your reputation is a benchmark that helps you to determine what you must do in your argument to enhance your credibility.

Be Sincere

Sincerity is probably the most commonly mentioned characteristic of credibility. It would seem a simple rule that to build credibility one should be sincere, but there is clear evidence that sincerity cannot be determined by decision makers (Andersen and Clevenger; Eisinger and Mills). But people believe they can judge sincerity.

In preparation for the presidential election of 2004, a group of Democrats were competing for the chance of opposing the reelection of President Bush. Well after everyone thought the group of nine included all who were making the run, retired four-star General Wesley Clark announced his candidacy. By waiting until later in the contest, thereby avoiding comparison with the "real politicians;" by presenting himself as a former NATO Supreme Allied Commander, thus eliciting immediate comparisons with the late General and President Dwight D. Eisenhower who had also held that post and is fondly remembered as a real patriot; and by noting that he was a former Rhodes Scholar, suggesting intelligence, Clark quickly caught public attention as one who was sincerely interested in serving his country. However, it is the appearance of sincerity that decision makers judge, and this appearance may not constitute an accurate statement about the arguer.

This caveat in no way implies that you should not be sincere. We have already noted that *sincerity* is frequently used as a synonym for *trustworthiness*. You need to be aware that sincerity alone does not mean that you will be perceived as sincere. However, your sincerity is a first step to convincing others that you are sincere.

Take care to avoid obvious signs that you mean to manipulate the decision makers. When you have a bias, and it is known, a clear and honest identification of it may actually advance your credibility. Decision makers usually put greater trust in the person who openly admits a bias. It is the decision makers' discovery of covert bias that is most damaging to sincerity (Mills and Aronson).

Identify with Decision Makers' Values

Perhaps the strongest indirect credibility is the arguer's identification with the values of the decision makers. A more complete discussion of social values and their role in argumentation is in Chapter 8, but we make a few points here that directly relate to credibility.

Unless you choose to speak or write on noncontroversial points ("Motorists should slow down in school zones," "Cancer is a dangerous disease," "Everyone should have a friend"), you will find controversy. Indeed, as we have observed before, you cannot have argumentation without issues. Those issues must be addressed as decision makers see them.

When you address issues, you will be taking some positions with which some decision makers disagree. That result is to be expected, and you will lose credibility if you try to agree with the audience on every point. Such a strategy will be transparent, and your sincerity will be questioned. A chameleon-like approach is in sharp contrast to what we mean by identification with decision makers' values.

Remember that audiences are collections of individuals. You can define a group of decision makers as an entity ("This is a Republican audience," "This is an audience of concerned parents," "This audience is pro-choice"), but this is *your* definition. The members are still individuals, and though they have some things in common, they are not identical. Furthermore, many audiences are segmented. Because it is "a Republican audience" does not mean they all agree on taxes, education, welfare, or foreign policy.

You must, of course, search for common ground with the majority of decision makers. Find as many points as you can on which to agree. Most important, show that your proposal is in keeping with their values (Reinard 44). Or construct a system of values showing clearly that while your proposal is contrary to some of their values, it is still consistent with others, and those other values are more important. In addition, show that those who would oppose your position have opted for a misleading system of values.

Consider how different members of your audience might respond to values, and address the various segments. In this hypothetical argument for building a new community medical clinic, the values are linked to segments of the audience:

> A new medical clinic should be established in Porterville because it would bring new medical specialties into the town that are not now there (health—medical people). It will provide services for people who find it difficult to drive to other cities (safety, health—elderly). People from small surrounding communities will come to town and will shop here, instead of going to Fresno or Bakersfield (commerce—business people). The new center will open up 50 new jobs (employment—youth).

None of these values is likely to be questioned by any segment of the audience, yet each has a particular appeal to a particular segment. Identifying with decision makers' values can be complex at times, but usually can be done without damage to your credibility.

The use of strong value-intensive arguments, in which heavy and repeated use of directly stated values dominates the argument, may have a negative effect on credibility. The research on fear appeals (e.g., appeals to fear of murder, rape, or mutilation) illuminates what probably happens with all value-intensive appeals. Such appeals, it seems, are accepted only from an arguer with high credibility. Strong value-intensive appeals may boomerang when used by an arguer with modest credibility (Hewgill and Miller). Credibility is weakened when invested in values that decision makers question and in too many value-intensive arguments.

You may have this problem in your class. The others probably don't know you well. It would be best, therefore, for you to be careful of using strong value-intensive arguments. People who know you better, for whom you have credibility, would be more likely to respond positively to your intensity. They are more likely to see it as dynamic, particularly if they share those values with you.

Use Evidence to Build Credibility

Evidence appears to strengthen credibility, especially of a low-credibility arguer, and particularly if the evidence is not known to the decision makers (McCroskey 175). This idea is easy to understand. A highly credible arguer is much more likely than an arguer with lower credibility to be effective using assertion without evidence.

An interesting example of this is a speech by Alan Greenspan, chairman of the United States Federal Reserve Board, to an economic conference in Washington, DC. He uses no direct or secondary credibility. His only mention of himself is at the opening of the speech when he tells what he will do in the speech ("I will offer my perspective. . . . [and] I will delve into some of the pitfalls. . . .") or when calling attention to his previous stated beliefs ("As I have indicated on previous occasions . . . "). But Alan Greenspan has a tremendous reputation on the economy and he is one of very few people who need not build credibility.

People are less likely to wonder, "Where did you get that idea?" or "How do you know that is true?" Consequently, evidence becomes more important to a person with less credibility. One study shows that with apathetic decision makers, it takes twice as much evidence for an arguer with modest credibility to produce a movement toward adherence as it does for an arguer with high credibility (Lashbrook et al. 262). Furthermore, evidence in the form of examples that are close to decision makers' experiences are more believable and, therefore, are more likely to enhance perceived credibility.

An authoritative source connected to an argument will make that argument more believable. Studies show that an authoritative group has higher credibility than an authoritative individual (Andersen and Clevenger 71; Ostermeier; Warren; Myers and Goldberg). An interesting phenomenon known as a *sleeper effect* seems to operate in the use of authoritative sources as secondary credibility. A source with high credibility tends to produce a strong initial change in peoples' views. In time that initial change weakens and a lower source gains (Andersen and Clevenger 67). This suggests that the credibility of the source has immediate impact, but for long-range adherence the quality of the argument and the evidence take on greater significance. The lesson you could learn from all this is that you need to build your competence with evidence and argument that your decision makers respect.

Use Organization to Build Credibility

Well-organized cases may not increase credibility, but disorganized ones clearly weaken it, especially for low-credibility arguers. Furthermore, showing disorganization by using phrases such as "I should have mentioned this earlier" creates the impression that speakers are disorganized and, therefore, less credible (McCroskey and Mehrley; Sharp and McClung; Baker).

In Chapter 5 (Case Building), we discussed a number of different ways that a case can be organized. It is clear that the perception of disorganization can damage credibility. But what makes argumentation appear organized? One characteristic is that the decision makers know explicitly what claims are being made. When claims are vague, decision makers restructure information to correlate with their beliefs, even perhaps in the opposite direction of that intended by the speaker (Tubbs 18). First, therefore, explicit claims are preferred.

Second, a small group of well-developed arguments is preferable to a large number of unsupported arguments. Unsupported arguments invite decision makers to concentrate on their weaknesses. Well-developed arguments imply greater competence on your part. They also should be the arguments that are closest to decision makers' experience and knowledge. Thus, you are seen as having developed the most important issues.

Finally, show that you understand issues by acknowledging both sides of an argument. Even among decision makers who tend to disagree with your proposition, such two-sided argumentation creates the impression that you are fair and are not "dodging the issues." True, some decision makers who already support the arguers' proposition and who are less well-informed respond better to being shown only one side. However, showing both sides has better long-term impact. The arguer is seen as being fair, and credibility is increased. This approach also provides the basis for what is called "inoculation." Two-sided argumentation strengthens the decision makers' resistance to later refutation. This has been demonstrated in a variety of situations, including public arguments and advertising (Pfau 27–28).

Argue Issues, Not People

It is easy, when argumentation leads to sharp differences of opinion, to believe that your opponent is not fair, is biased, or has ulterior motives. Resist this tendency. Center your argument on your claims; let *your* credibility show. Attempts to attack the credibility of an opponent have been shown to weaken, not strengthen, credibility. In one study, persons who initiated such attacks were seen by decision makers as less credible with less acceptable arguments while the credibility of the person attacked was given higher credibility (Infante et al. 1993, 188–89).

This phenomenon can be seen in political argumentation where people who raise claims about an opponent's credibility are found to be less credible, even with decision makers who agree with them on issues. Notice that most successful politicians carefully qualify attacks on opponents' credibility, emphasizing their records and positions on the issues. Direct attacks on a candidate's credibility are usually made by others, not the candidates themselves.

Understand Credibility as Dynamic

You must realize that the process of argumentation is dynamic. Decision makers reject or accept your arguments on the interaction of credibility, values, evidence, and arguments that are both internal and external to the argumentation.

After studying two decades of credibility research, Jesse Delia concludes that the lack of consistent results can be explained in part by the failure to measure what takes place during the argumentative exchange itself. He says, "It is necessary to recognize that the communicator's image will, at least in part, consist of constructions made during the interaction itself." He goes on to claim that the decision to grant credibility to someone involves mental processes in which slight changes in the situation, for example the addition of another person to the discussion, may result in a decision to raise or lower that person's credibility.

A friend had just about convinced you to see a movie that she thought was great when another friend whom you consider an expert joins the conversation to point out the many flaws in the picture. Credibility granted on the basis of the first friend's opinion dissolves in the presence of an expert (Delia 375).

Decision makers are not given neat choices between highly competent and trustworthy arguers who show good will and are dynamic, versus their opposites. Thus, credibility is a composite of responses to the dimensions, and it may change even as the message is being received. Readers may know nothing of an author, but as they read a book they develop an appreciation for the author's competence based on what they have read. Similarly, experience with an arguer can change the trustworthiness dimension. To complicate matters further, there is reason to believe that for given decision makers, low credibility is not just the opposite of high credibility but a new configuration of dimensions (Schweitzer and Ginsburg).

The whole process of decision making from the highest level down through the single minor argument, constantly changes in the interaction among the elements that make it up. What we see when we talk about particular functions of credibility are arbitrarily frozen bits of information. Decision makers see a generalization or a movement in argumentation in which all the factors are seen together and simultaneously. They are always related to a particular argument, the arguers, the circumstance, and the decision makers. In politics this is called *image*.

Your reputation is a benchmark of your credibility. No matter how limited it may be with the decision makers, it is the basis upon which credibility is built. To make your argument more credible to decision makers, be sincere, identify with their values, use your evidence and organization to build credibility, and argue issues, not people. In all of your plans to enhance your credibility and use it to support your argumentation, keep in mind that credibility is a dynamic process, not a series of set rules.

Sphere Dependence of Credibility

Credibility is a dynamic process that must be seen in relation to particular circumstances, so different spheres of argumentation develop various standards for credibility. General principles such as those we have discussed will hold for most situations. They are modified, however, by the particular sphere in which the argumentation occurs.

Gary Cronkhite and Jo Liska have observed that credibility involves not just the inferred attributes that decision makers give to a particular source of an argument but also the specific subject matter and differing criteria of source acceptability. This point of view corresponds closely to our contention that credibility is influenced by the sphere of argumentation in which it operates.

You will recall that we defined a *sphere* of argumentation as a group of persons whose patterns of communicative behaviors are used in the production and evaluation of argumentation. Credibility is subject to those criteria that people operating in a particular context or purpose agree upon.

Spheres are oriented around common needs, purposes or what Stephen Toulmin calls "doing what there is there to be done" (485). In a television hospital drama, a young woman is told that she must have a mastectomy or die. It is unfair. "Why me?" is her reasonable response. But this is a question that medicine cannot answer. It has its own evidence, values, and ways of arguing that define its sphere of knowledge. The physician has tests that show the breast tumor is malignant, and medical knowledge indicates that the only solution is to remove it surgically. The only alternative she has to death or surgery, he says, is a faith healer. It is clear that he is not serious about that alternative. The young woman eventually relies on the credibility of the physicians and has the operation.

In another part of the same drama, the hospital attorney questions a surgeon's decision to do a controversial brain operation. The physician tells the attorney he is not a doctor and is not qualified to make such a judgment. The attorney argues that he must defend the hospital from malpractice suits. Here, in one hour, three spheres are introduced: medicine, religion, and law, all with different ways of arguing and different standards of credibility. Cronkhite and Liska claim that arguers who show promise of helping spheres do "what there is there to be done" will be granted high credibility. As you may have guessed, if you didn't see the drama, in this television show the highest credibility goes to those who know and act in the medical sphere.

The old saying that "Politics makes strange bedfellows" suggests that if your sphere's purpose is electing candidates to public office, you make associations with others, no matter how offensive in other respects, who show promise of helping elect your candidates. Another cliché, "When does a gambler play in a crooked game? When it's the only game in town," suggests that even otherwise questionable activities may gain credibility when they offer the only hope of "doing what there is there to be done."

President Clinton looked the other way in 1995 when Iran, a nation of low credibility for most Americans, violated the arms embargo imposed on those fighting in the former Yugoslavia. He was willing to have Bosnian Muslims get weapons as long as the United States was not involved. So he let Iran become his silent partner. Credibility, then, may be powerfully related to doing what you must do.

While competence, trustworthiness, good will, and dynamism may be general terms that cover all uses of credibility as support, they will look different from one sphere to another. What may be competence to a scientist will differ from competence in a law court, politics, or on popular television. The three areas of credibility, and how spheres influence them, that we will examine here are the arguers' reputation, secondary credibility, and indirect credibility.

The Reputation of the Arguer

Some spheres, such as science, have firm definitions of who is competent. A beginning sign is the possession of advanced degrees (usually the doctorate) in the specific science being argued. Increased competence is assumed when a scientist's research is published in prestigious refereed journals, rewarded with research grants, and cited by other researchers.

Consider the debate between scientists and religionists over the Genesis story of creation. Scientists with all the necessary credentials argue that the biblical story of the earth's creation in seven days is inaccurate because it conflicts with the theory of evolution and the evidence of science. Some groups, such as the Institute for Creation Research, have organized to argue for the scientific validity of the biblical account. Their members, who call themselves creation scientists, argue that scientific evidence supports the biblical account of creation.

They have degrees in science, and they make arguments based on the analysis of scientific data. For some people, they have the reputation of scientists because of their professions and the fields in which they have their degrees. But for the established scientific community their reputations are suspect because of the nature of their research and their lack of credentials. Why? Some have only masters' degrees, and those with doctorates have degrees in applied fields of engineering or mineral science, rather than basic research-oriented fields such as physics or genetics, and they have no record of refereed research (Klope 124). They are, therefore, seen by those in the sphere of traditional science as not having competence.

Creation Scientists also are seen as lacking trustworthiness in the scientific community because their religious orientation is perceived to lack scientific objectivity. Although we know established scientists have assumptions of their own, they see themselves as objective and believe their research is not confounded by outside factors as is the research of creation science.

While religious affiliation does not enhance scientific argument when used counter to prevailing science, lawyers like to have a member of the clergy testify in court. Though the jury may not share many of the cleric's values and though they may not find the testimony very reasonable, they believe that a cleric is to be trusted and respected.

Sports figures and entertainment personalities, as we noted earlier, are frequently used to argue for products on television: Shaquille O'Neill for All Sport, or Michael Jordan for Gatorade, for instance, might be perceived as particularly competent to argue the qualities for sports drinks. However, Michael Jordan is not an expert on telephone systems, and the other examples we have used in this chapter, including the whole cast of *Frasier,* are no more competent than the viewer to testify for a product. In such cases, the qualification isn't competence, say Cronkhite and Liska, but something more like "likability, novelty, or entertainment" (104). Decision makers are asked to purchase a product because they "like" the person in the ad. In such a situation *competence* and *trustworthiness* take on different meanings.

Secondary Credibility in Spheres

Much of what we have noted about reputation holds as well for secondary credibility. When an arguer uses the credibility of others to support claims, those others need to be seen as credible by the standards of the sphere of the decision makers. Scientists acting as scientists need to be told about other scientists who support their views.

Lawyers frequently support their arguments with the testimony of people who are experts: psychiatrists, ballistic experts, professors of communication whose research area is freedom of speech. There are areas, however, where credibility takes a serious shift and one of them is in the court of law.

Reluctant witnesses, in most situations, are not considered trustworthy. If you pressure a reluctant friend to tell you something against his or her will the potential for a distorted story is great. Such a person has a bias, so to speak; but reluctant testimony is believable in a law court. The person giving it is forced by the potential of legal penalty to testify against personal biases and interests.

Secondary credibility is not just a product of persons. Institutions also have credibility as a part of the evidence they provide. The *New York Times,* the *Christian Science Monitor,* and the *Los Angeles Times* are respected newspapers that lend their reputations to those who write for them and those who quote them. In business, the *Wall Street Journal* and *Forbes* magazine have great credibility. In the sphere of humanistic scholarship other institutional publications such as the *American Historical Review* or the *Publication of the Modern Language Association* (PMLA) are more powerful sources of secondary credibility.

An interesting source of credibility in the human and social sciences is the number of times a particular piece of research is cited by others. For instance, the *Citation Index* provides a record of how many times a particular research article is cited and in what sources. The understanding is that research is more valuable if it is used by others who publish in the most prestigious journals.

Indirect Credibility in Spheres

Arguers gain credibility from all they do in making the argument. All that we have said about the influence of spheres of argument on evidence and values applies here. For instance, we noted that hearsay evidence is usually not admissible in a court of law and its use will decrease the credibility of a lawyer who tries to enter it. If the lawyer attempts this too often, the competency of the lawyer will be questioned by the judge. But in interpersonal argument, where such rules are not established, arguers frequently increase their credibility because they have heard the report from a prestigious secondary source.

The use of values and evidence appropriate to a sphere support the claims of arguers and provide indirect credibility for the arguer. You will learn as you study and become expert in your chosen profession how decision makers assign credibility in that sphere.

Conclusion

People give adherence to arguments because they perceive them as reasonable, as employing values with which they agree, and as coming from a credible individual or group. Credibility has an important role in argumentation. It may serve as a claim in its own right, but most often it serves as support. It is generally considered to be developed by the decision makers' perception that the arguer is competent and trustworthy and reveals good will and dynamism.

There are three forms of credibility in arguments: direct credibility, used when arguers make direct statements about themselves designed to increase credibility; secondary credibility, from associating another's credibility with the argument; and indirect credibility, when the argument is developed in a way that makes the arguer more believable. Reputation adds to the likelihood of winning adherence, but only the first three forms of credibility can be directly controlled by the arguer at the time of any specific argumentation.

Credibility is very changeable because it is so related to the perceptions of the decision makers. However, there are some general principles for the use of credibility. You should use whatever reputation you have and build on it to develop credibility. Be sincere in expressing your own ideas. Identify yourself with the decision makers' values. Use evidence and organization to build credibility, argue issues, not people, and recognize that credibility, like argumentation, is a dynamic process that is changed by what happens in the argumentative exchange itself.

Credibility will be defined differently by decision makers in different spheres. Reputations are established by criteria that are different, in medicine, religion, and law, for instance. Credibility is given to the person believed capable of "doing what there is there to be done" in a particular sphere. Reputation will be built by different credentials in different spheres. Secondary and indirect credibility will differ from sphere to sphere.

PROJECT

Spend an evening watching television with a note pad in hand. Write down all the ways you can find that advertising agencies work to build credibility for their products. Engage in a discussion with others in class who have done the same. How well did what you see correspond to what is discussed in this chapter? Did you find additional principles about credibility not mentioned in this chapter?

CHAPTER

10 Refutation

KEY TERMS

process
cooperative
faction
framework
assessment
critical decision making
goals
decision makers

burden of proof
framebreaking
momentum
support
blocking
probing
questioning
flowsheet

Criticism is inherent in critical decision making, and refutation is the term we use to describe the process through which one person or faction (group of people) involved in a decision criticizes arguments advanced by another person or faction. The criticism may be addressed to other members of the same faction, to members of other factions, or to decision makers who are not a part of any faction.

The Process of Refutation

While it is often useful to say that every issue has two sides, our concept of refutation embraces the idea of many factions subscribing to some point of view or advocating one decision over another. Refutation may need to move in several directions at once.

Some commentators have characterized refutation as a destructive process: one side tearing down the arguments of the other in a game of repartee. In our view refutation is a constructive process. Just as the sculptor must chip away stone and smooth over rough places to produce a work of art, critical decision makers must put their arguments to the most severe tests possible to make the best decisions.

It is in this vein that Douglas Ehninger and Wayne Brockriede characterize debate as a cooperative enterprise. They say a debater is "not a propagator who seeks to win unqualified acceptance for a predetermined point of view while defeating an opposing view" (vii). Instead, they say refutation serves an investigative purpose in the search for the best possible decision.

The concept of refutation as cooperative and constructive becomes clearer when we call attention to fundamental processes that have been socially constructed over centuries of practice. In critical decision making, refutation implies the following minimum essential principles:

1. All interested parties are given fair notice of an impending decision so that they can prepare their response.
2. Each faction has an equal opportunity to be heard.
3. Each faction grants the others the right to examine and criticize its arguments, including access to supporting persons and materials.
4. Decision makers hear arguments only in the presence of other interested parties.
5. People are not decision makers in their own causes.
6. Each faction accepts the delay of the final decision until the critical process has taken place.
7. All factions agree to accept the final decision no matter how far removed it is from their preference.

In Chapter 11, we will discuss a view of fallacies that is based on rules such as these. The theory is that any action that impedes progress toward critical decision is a fallacy, and violating such rules does impede progress.

The constructive and ultimately cooperative character of refutation is evident in some spheres, such as legislation, law, and science. People often become impatient with legislative decision making as Democrats and Republicans debate each other, constantly finding weaknesses in the other's positions, but they accept that such delay is a price well worth paying in the interest of making critical decisions. Totalitarian government operates much faster, but most people prefer the "agreement to disagree" that characterizes partisan legislation.

In law, attorneys are instructed to disagree and criticize each others' claims in the overall cooperative search for justice. Failure to do their best to refute the opposition is a violation of legal ethics.

In scholarship, the presentation of research findings at conventions and in journals is just one phase in ongoing criticism. To be open to refutation, indeed to seek it out, is the very essence of scholarship in the cooperative search for knowledge. *Refutation* as we use it in this book must be seen in contrast to many practices that reject opposing viewpoints uncritically. The history of political decision making is filled with examples of governments silencing the opposition by putting leaders in jail, exile, or graves. *McCarthyism* denotes uncritical rejection of opposing ideas through accusation and intimidation. Talk show hosts show themselves to be uninterested in critical interaction. They use their position to talk over or cut off callers with whom they disagree, and then the audience hears the host's side of the issue when the caller has no further chance to speak. Professors who silence student opinions are equally disinterested in critical behavior.

Refutation can be most unpleasant when it identifies weaknesses in ideas you believe in fervently, and many people lack the courage to listen to it. That is uncritical behavior.

In this chapter and the next, we set out basic processes of critical behavior. We cannot provide a "manual," and there are no litmus or pH tests of argument available, but we do provide a sequence of considerations and potential strategies from which to draw and adapt to each decision.

Approaching Refutation

Refutation requires the open expression of disagreement with an argument made by someone else. Social rules in force in many cultures discourage such expressions. It is commonly considered impolite to question or challenge others, and linguists say people have a preference for agreement. Scott Jacobs and Sally Jackson say that in interpersonal argument this preference for agreement operates like a presumption in favor of the validity of what others have said. Because of this, "disagreement requires some compelling rationale, something definite enough and significant enough to overcome this presumption" (235–36). Jacobs and Jackson say that refutation is not a general attitude of skepticism, but the application of a specific argument to a specific decision.

A general attitude of skepticism may be a useful approach to refutation at times, but incessant challenging of others' statements can be obnoxious. Benjamin Franklin reports in his autobiography that challenging and refuting almost everything others say can be an ego-building practice for bright youngsters, but it should be set aside with maturity:

> I found this method safest for myself and very embarrassing to those against whom I used it . . . but gradually [I] left it. For, if you would inform, a positive and dogmatical manner in advancing your sentiments may provoke contradiction and prevent a candid attention (25–26).

Franklin concludes his discussion of this phase of his childhood with this quote from Alexander Pope: "Men should be taught as if you taught them not, And things unknown propos'd as things forgot."

Some former championship college debaters, in response to a survey conducted by the American Forensic Association in 1981 concerning the National Debate Tournament, said debate had merely reinforced what they now consider to be antisocial behaviors. They describe a tendency "to turn every conversation, whether social or academic, into a contest [in which they] always had to have the last word." "Truth, logic, tact, and just good manners were more often than not sacrificed for the sake of argument." They describe "mindless, knee-jerk" argumentation as an "insidious habit of pushing informal discussions to the argument stage," ego gratification gained by winning, showing a superiority over others. One person says, "Debate made me over argumentative, always finding problems with others' ideas. . . . It took a long time to get over it. . . . It [debate] may have increased my inability to work well with people on an interpersonal level." They found themselves seeking to conquer opponents rather than work out decisions through negotiation. One former debater concludes this way:

> The road to agreement is not always won by argument; every encounter is not a debate. I undoubtedly applied techniques irrelevantly and inappropriately. Even in an argument, I subsequently learned, it is unnecessary, perhaps even counter-productive, to refute *all* of your opponent's case. The main points are enough, and humiliation is costly.[1]

Approaching refutation requires finding a working point somewhere between these extremes: a preference for agreement and silent acknowledgment of the validity of what others say; and the brash, hypercritical, competitive, and destructive practices described by Benjamin Franklin and some former college debaters. If you keep in mind that refutation is a cooperative part of the critical process, rather than a non-contact sport, you should fare well.

Setting a Framework for Refutation

Each decision and the arguments related to it require a new analysis from which to construct refutation. There must always be an inextricable link among the goals sought in decision making, the specific decisions proposed to meet the goals, and the arguments advanced in support of the proposed decisions. Before you can engage in refutation, then, you must lay a framework from which criticism will emerge. Just as the architect must adapt the structure of a building to meet the demands of the setting and its intended use, arguers must adjust their practices to the specifics of the situation at hand.

Assess the Argumentative Situation

Refutation is a response to the argumentative situation; unless you understand the situation at hand, you are not ready to participate in refutation. Even though people tell stories about talking the police out of tickets, for the most part interactions with police do not represent an argumentative situation. It is better to present your refutation of the charges to a judge. Dinner parties in which your politics or religion differ dramatically from everyone else are probably not the place to launch into an attack on their views. Conversely, when you are part of an impregnable majority, there is little

---

[1]All quotations cited came from an anonymous data pool shared with the authors by Ronald J. Matlon, Lucy Keele, and others associated with the National Debate Tournament and the American Forensic Association. We stress that these critical comments reflected only a minority of those responding to the survey.

point in refuting the minority arguments when those arguments stand no chance of influencing the decision.

Silence is often the most effective refutation. Remember that humiliation can be costly. But remember, too, that the decision to remain silent is always a gamble: you are resting your case on an assessment of the state of mind of the decision makers. If your judgment proves to be wrong, you will probably kick yourself for not speaking out. It's a tough choice, since speaking out can sometimes do more harm than good. Only the most insightful have the courage to use silence as a refutation.

Think of the last essay exam you took. Did you find yourself trying to put down everything you could think of, turning the booklet in only when the time was up? This technique can either help you stumble on the correct answer or muddle it up. Next time, take a look at the students who finish before the time is up. They have chosen to write their best answer and stop. They have the same kind of courage needed to use silence as a refutation (or they just didn't have much to say).

The steps in critical decision making provide a guide in assessing the argumentative situation. As you check off each step, you should become more sensitive to the potential paths for refutation.

Identify the Question or Claim   Keep your eyes on what the decision process is all about. When people lose sight of the key issues, bring them back. Constantly look at issues in relation to the proposition: if the issues are decided, will the proposition follow reasonably?

Ask about the status of the discussion. Where does the present argumentation stand in relation to deciding the proposition? During the preliminary interactions around any topic or decision, the focus of decision makers is likely aimed at gathering information and identifying and sorting relevant values. They are tuning in, paying attention, comprehending, generating relevant cognitions, and acquiring relevant skills (Trenholm 56). This is probably not the time to start refutation. It is possible that the search for a decision will move inexorably toward the decision you propose, and no refutation will be required. At this point, the best argumentative approach is to make a good impression on the decision makers: establish a rapport, obtain commitments, preview your point of view, and generally build high credibility (Rieke and Stutman 68–71, 109–16).

As alternative decisions begin to emerge and compete for the decision makers' attention, as the attractiveness of the alternatives approaches parity, forcing decision makers to struggle with discriminating among them, the time for refutation has arrived (Festinger 154–55). If you advance your refutational points too soon, the effect may be lost because the decision makers are too early in their search to appreciate your points. If you wait too long, the opportunity to reduce adherence to other positions may have passed.

Survey Objectives and Values   Inherent in each sphere are overall objectives sought from argumentation and the values that will control the process. For example, find out about the rules of procedure. Different spheres prescribe different procedures of argumentation. In law, for example, refutation is restricted to specific stages in the trial and attempts to use refutation outside those limits may be denied. In business settings, criticism of a presentation is usually restricted to questioning rather than direct attack, and often this is limited to people in a high position. A lower-level person attacking a colleague may have what they call at IBM a "career-limiting experience." Before launching into your refutation, you are well advised to know the procedures.

A young negotiator going up against a seasoned veteran was determined to get the upper hand and decided to attack the other side's arguments immediately. The negotiators entered the room and had barely taken their seats when the younger man stood and delivered an impassioned, five-minute attack on the other side. There was a moment of silence, and then the seasoned veteran said, "Does anyone want a Coke before we get started?"

What are the operative cultural values? If you are familiar with film and television characterizations of lawyers at work, you may believe it is common to trash and brutalize the other side and then go out for drinks. If you have been a debater in high school or college, you may believe that tough, uncompromising attacks on others is appropriate behavior. Loud talking, rapid speech, ridicule, and other tactics make for good drama, but they are forbidden in many settings.

In our experience, these dramas do not reflect common practice. In most business settings, professional interactions, and even government sessions, restrained language, quiet voices, courtesy, and consideration for the "face" of opponents is demanded (Lim Tae-Seop 75–86). You may deliver a devastating refutation of another's position only to find you have alienated the decision makers. In countries other than the United States, this is often even more the case. Refutation, to be successful, must not exceed the cultural boundaries of the decision making situation.

Canvass Alternative Decisions   Refutation can be powerful when it exposes the fact that little effort has been made toward testing a range of alternative decisions. Further discussion can be delayed pending research that may well uncover better approaches. A common approach in criminal defense is to expose the fact that the police, thinking they had the culprit, really didn't seriously consider other suspects.

Weigh the Costs and Risks   Proposals may seem attractive on their face but lose support when the costs or risks are made clear. There are plenty of government services people would support if they did not require increased taxes. Many people who feel that more help should be provided to the homeless lose their enthusiasm when they learn that the shelter will be built in their neighborhood. In trying to craft an acceptable national health policy, congress and the president discover great support for good health care but powerful opposition to letting the federal government run it and pay for it with taxes.

Search for New Information   Refutation does not mean merely expressing your opinion. If you have not done your homework, you're not ready for refutation. In 1999, the Kansas Board of Education decided to change the status of teaching on evolution in its public schools. Immediately, outraged refutation was leveled at the board on the charge that their behavior was an ignorant attack on modern science and a step toward mixing religion with public education. Robert E. Hemenway, chancellor of the University of Kansas, wrote an essay entitled, "The Evolution of a Controversy in Kansas Shows Why Scientists Must Defend the Search for Truth." Hemenway devoted his argument to criticizing the board for eliminating the teaching of evolution. By failing to do his homework, however, he set himself up for refutation by Phillip E. Johnson, a professor of law at the University of California at Berkeley. Johnson merely noted that the board had only removed evolution from mandatory state standards, and did not insist that students be taught Biblical or creationist interpretations. By attacking the wrong issue, Chancellor Hemenway allowed his arguments to be dismissed with the wave of a hand.

Note Biases Underlying Positions   Identifying biases is an important part of refutation in critical decision making. Roadblocks can often be pushed aside by exposing preconceived notions and biases.

In the drive to end welfare programs, as they were known at the time, Congress moved to put a disincentive on illegitimate births. They called it a "family cap." The plan was to deny benefits to women who had more than one illegitimate child. Behind this plan there were clear biases. Those favoring the cap said they did not want to "subsidize illegitimacy," presuming that illegitimate children were concentrated among welfare recipients. They further had a bias that suggested welfare mothers were consciously having children to increase their benefits and behind that bias was an implicit racism suggesting that welfare mothers were mostly African American. There was virtually no evidence or research support for any of these assumptions.

Make Plans to Implement the Decision   Often, the best refutation is to take other proposals seriously and set out precisely what will be needed to implement them. The act of implementation often proves so complex, costly, or plagued with onerous side effects that enthusiasm for the decision vanishes.

Enthusiasm for national health programs frequently starts out high only to dissipate as problems associated with implementation become clear. The American people generally favor a program of insurance, but there is wide variance in what kind of program is favored. Enthusiasm for health maintenance organizations waned when cost-cutting measures led to denial of some kinds of patient care. Everyone wants cost-efficient programs but most people also want to choose their own physician and have their medical procedures paid for. Finding a way to satisfy both values in the same program is the key problem.

Analyze the Decision Makers

How will the decision be made? The tone of refutation varies with the proximity to the decision and the likelihood of opposing points being stated after yours. If you are making the last statement, after which the decision makers will immediately make their choice, a more flamboyant, exhortative, and arousing style of refutation may be appropriate. If the decision will not be made for months or years after your refutation, as in congressional hearings, appellate courts, or businesses, the style and content of your refutation should be geared toward lasting impressions and specific recall that decision makers can use during their long deliberations.

If decision makers will not be exposed to counterargument, if they are not very well informed, if they are unlikely to raise objections to your position in their own minds, or if they clearly favor your position, you may concentrate on a one-sided, highly partisan refutation. If these conditions do not apply, however, you will probably be more effective if your refutation takes a multi-sided approach resembling an objective analysis of the alternatives (Trenholm 242).

Who Are the Decision Makers? We are constantly amazed to discover people debating each other without knowing who will ultimately make the decision. In academic debate, courts of law, and other highly formalized decision systems, this does not occur, but in the vast majority of decisions made each day, who finally decides may be obscure.

The police union was negotiating with the city government over their new contract. The city's negotiating team included a professional negotiator, the city attorney, a personnel officer, and a major of police. The union side included a professional negotiator, the president of the police union, and members of the executive committee of the union. After months of talks, the issues were narrowed to one: salary. It proved impossible to reach agreement on this issue, and at that point the question of who would really make the city's decision on pay raises became salient. The union asked for a conference with the mayor, and that produced no progress. It was only when the city's negotiator asked to leave the room every time a new proposal was presented that the police discovered it was the city director of personnel, a former aide to the governor, who was calling the shots. When she was asked to join the negotiations so she could hear the positions debated, she declined and talks broke off without agreement. It accomplished nothing to refute positions without her presence.

In many business settings, decisions are addressed and arguments exchanged with none of the participants knowing who will ultimately decide. People are asked to attend meetings without knowing their role or the purpose of the meeting. Curiously, our experience is that often the participants themselves are expected to decide, but *they do not know it.* Unless you know who will actually make the decision, you cannot generate useful refutation.

In legislation, the decision makers can be quite difficult to discover. On the surface, it is the elected representatives, senators or members of Congress, for example, who vote and thus decide. But a glance beneath the surface says the real clout may be in the hands of a few people who are recognized experts in the particular area of legislation, senior members holding party power, leaders of state delegations, or powerful lobbies (Matthews and Stimson 45). Unless your refutation gets to the real decision makers, it may have no impact at all.

What Are Decision Makers' Goals? Refutation must not focus solely on the particular strengths and weaknesses of alternative decision proposals; it must relate ultimately to what is sought from the decision. It is possible that alternatives can be rejected *as a whole* rather than attacked point-by-point simply by showing that they fail to address the objective of the decision making. In law, the defense may reject the opponent's entire position by successfully arguing that no prima facie case has been advanced. What this means, simply, is that the judge could accept everything claimed by the prosecution and still not grant a decision in their behalf. In the midst of refutation, it is easy to lose sight of what the debate is about. Tit-for-tat argumentation may obscure what it is that constitutes the objective of all involved.

In legislation, for example, the overarching objective may be to manage the national economy, and opposing bills may call for deficit reduction, tax relief, reconciling the international balance of payments, controlling medical costs, or eliminating foreign aid. While each of these proposals has specific strengths and weaknesses that need attention, the ultimate goal, an effective national economy, must be the primary criterion by which they are assessed.

In partisan bickering, refutation often is focused on trivial issues to the point that everyone seems to have lost sight of what the debate is really about. Although you should criticize the arguments within the web of sub-issues on which the primary purpose rests, refutation should be based on criticism relevant to the decision objectives.

What Are the Presumptions of the Decision Makers?   In the chapters on argumentation and critical appraisal as well as case building, we discussed the concepts of presumption, probability, and burden of proof. These concepts are also crucial to refutation. There may be formal statements of presumption, such as that of innocence in U.S. criminal law, and there may be widely accepted presumptions, such as that in favor of the status quo, but each decision must be analyzed for the actual presumption in place.

In law, jurors who can truly accept the presumption of innocence of a particular accused may be so hard to find that the court will grant a change of venue. Time may be expended on behalf of proposed legislation that seems widely popular when the real decision makers have a strong negative presumption. After years of experience with television interviews of the leaders of a state legislature, we learned to ask off camera about specific bills under consideration, and almost invariably the leaders could accurately predict the outcome. Proponents would blithely continue their campaign, ignorant of a presumption against them that had to be refuted if they were to have any chance of success at all.

The character of your refutation must be responsive to the status of presumption. If your decision carries the weight of presumption, then your refutation should consist primarily of two components: (1) constantly demanding that all other positions accept the burden of proof and defining the nature of their burden; (2) constantly showing how they have failed to meet their burden of proof. The other side of that coin is this: if your position carries the burden of proof you may attempt a refutation that shifts the burden to the others. This is successful only when the others are either ignorant of their presumption or are incompetent debaters, but it is surprising how frequently it works.

Coming into a meeting one day without having done his homework, an engineer started the discussion by asking the others how much work they had done. They became so focused on explaining their accomplishments and justifying their omissions that they failed to ask whether he had done his work. He successfully shifted the burden of proof.

Remember, both of these approaches rely on the fact that you *know the presumption of the real decision makers*. Also, at any point in decision making, presumption can change, and with it the burden of proof or rejoinder. Candidates for office have been known to shoot themselves in the foot by continuing a campaign based on early data showing a powerful lead even after research reveals that presumption has changed.

Long after the end to major hostilities in Iraq in 2003, investigators had still not uncovered any weapons of mass destruction. Since this had been a major argument in favor of war, it was a point of embarrassment to the Bush administration. Administration spokespersons regularly went on Sunday talk shows to say that just because they had not yet been found did not prove they did not exist. A *New Yorker* cartoon on March 24, 2003, gave the refutation, "I just think you're going to need a better rallying cry than 'Absence of evidence isn't evidence of absence' " (46). By then, the presumptions of the people (decision makers) had changed: They presumed no such weapons existed to be found.

Are Involved Factions Trying to Act as Decision Makers?

The problem about arguing with police is that they are actually involved in the issue: they aren't judges, they are givers of tickets. When you complain to a business or government agency about their products or services, chances are you will be talking to someone who has an interest in the outcome but who is also playing judge. You may be talking to the very person whose job it is that you are criticizing. If this is the situation, the solution is to find someone else with a smaller stake in defending the opposing point of view and more interest in resolving the dispute. Asking to talk with supervisors, managers, or a regulating agency often helps.

Similarly, such interactions may often involve question-begging tactics (see Chapter 11), such as "Our policy is that. . . ." Instead of trying to refute the policy, ask to talk with a person who has the authority to circumvent the policy.

Finally, you need to get around what Tom Wolfe calls "the flak catchers." These are people in organizations whose job it is to listen to complaints (take the flak) and send people away. They are often programmed to mislead: "I wish I could help you, but there is nothing I can do." Instead of trying refutation on such people, you must get around them to real decision makers.

A woman allowed a teenage neighbor to repair her car in the high school shop class, and with the teacher's help he managed to cause $600 worth of damage. She went to the school district and spoke with the person in charge of all shop classes. He said, "I'm sorry, but the law does not allow us to carry insurance for this sort of problem. We are legally unable to help you." The woman asked a professional negotiator to go back to speak to him. He gave the same response, but this time the negotiator simply refused to accept the explanation. The administrator asked to be excused for a moment and returned with another person who introduced himself as the district insurance officer, who proceeded to give instructions about how to make a claim. The first administrator was merely acting as a flak catcher. If the woman had stopped with her first encounter, the district would have saved money. When the flak catcher failed to put off the negotiator, he brought in a real decision maker.

Analyze Opponents

Law provides "discovery" procedures that inform opponents in advance of a trial what witnesses or evidence will be presented. Opposing counsel have a chance to talk to each other's witnesses at length and to review documentary or physical evidence. The principle is that justice will be better served if opponents have time to prepare refutation carefully. The principle should be carried into all refutation: know as much as possible about opponents and their probable arguments.

Selecting a Posture for Refutation

One of the most common mistakes of inexperienced debaters is the use of a "the more you throw, the more will stick to the wall" theory of refutation. It's the same theory we spoke of earlier in relation to students writing essay exams: not enough courage to stop when you've said enough; not enough knowledge to know when enough is enough. This is a tactic used by the inexperienced or the desperate. We will suggest a variety of postures from which refutation can be conducted, in the hope of convincing you to think before you refute and to quit when you have done what you planned, even if you still have time, space, or arguments unused.

We posit a general theory of refutation: *aim refutation at the highest conceptual level possible.* Turn the water off at the main valve, don't run from faucet to faucet trying to stem the flow. A corollary of that theory is this: *when the decision is in your hands, shut up.* We have seen times when defeat has been snatched from the jaws of victory simply because the obvious victor could not remain silent. Continued refutation actually moved decision makers to change their minds.

Refute from a Constructive Basis

Whether you are defending an established position with the protection of presumption or attacking it, refutation is most powerful when it comes from the perspective of a *viable constructive position.* It is one thing to hammer away at the prevailing policy, but its defenders are unlikely to abandon it without an alternative. In fact, defenders of the status quo will probably not even perceive your refutations for what they are because of selective perception.

Thomas Kuhn reports on what he calls scientific paradigms (sub-sets of spheres) such as Ptolemaic astronomy, Newtonian physics, and quantum mechanics. Kuhn argues that "Once it has achieved the status of paradigm, a scientific theory is declared invalid only if an alternative candidate is available to take its place" (77).

In law, the defense can technically rely totally upon refutation of the plaintiff's case, but that is less powerful than generating at least a plausible alternative theory of the case. In public policy, naysayers are often turned aside with: "We know of all the weaknesses of our system, but it's the best there is." Challenges to public policy are strongest when they emanate from persuasive alternatives.

Defend Your Position

If you have constructed a viable alternative position or if you are defending the presumed position, stick with it. Too often, the heat of debate draws attention away from your home position as you sally forth to attack others. We suggest that every communication you produce in the debate begin with a restatement of your position and a discussion of how it remains intact despite the refutation of other factions. This may require some repairs. Your position may have been damaged by refutation, so your first priority is to put it back together. Remember, other factions will be trying to pull you away from your position and get you to debate on their ground. If they have the burden of proof, they will be trying to shift it to your shoulders.

Keep the Focus on the Goals of Decision Making

The highest conceptual level toward which refutation can be aimed is the goal of decision making. Constantly return the focus of the discussion to the goals sought from the decision to be made, and demonstrate any point at which other factions fail to generate those goals.

In a proposal designed to reduce spending to balance the state budget, a governor included a reduction in money given to welfare recipients offset by a new jobs program. Under refutation, the governor admitted that the costs of administering the jobs program would more than eat up money saved in welfare payments, but he said, "I feel everyone should make a sacrifice, and some work requirements seem reasonable." Focusing on the highest level of analysis, opponents argued that whether everyone should sacrifice or whether a jobs program was reasonable was beside the point. The issue was how to reduce state spending, and the governor's proposal simply did not fit that goal. In this way, opponents were able to reject the governor's bill as a whole without ever having to refute its individual elements.

Engage in Framebreaking

Chris Argyris reports research findings that suggest that people reason differently when they think about a program simply to understand it than when they intend to make a decision. They are able to detect and understand inconsistencies, errors, and other problems with decision proposals of others, *but not their own,* when under pressure to decide and act. Moreover, when they tried to refute other positions, "they created conditions that led to escalating error, self-fulfilling prophecies, and self-sealing processes" (39).

Argyris proposes *framebreaking* as the response to this problem. Helping others break their typical frame of reference in considering decision proposals allows them to see, for the first time, the problems with their positions.

Similarly, decision makers who are not otherwise involved in the argumentation need help breaking their frames of reference to see the problems you are pointing out in your refutation. Under pressure to decide, says Argyris, people disconnect from their reasoning process. These are the usual characteristics: people do not understand when their premises or inference processes are problematic; people perceive their analyses as concrete when they actually rely on abstractions and a complex series of inferences; people rarely see a need to test their own reasoning through interaction with others because they "know" their reasoning is clear and correct.

Argyris's plan involves what he calls *double-loop learning* in which "the basic assumptions behind ideas or policies are confronted, in which hypotheses are tested publicly, and in which the processes are disconfirmable, not self-sealing" (103–04). In argumentation, that process involves bringing into the open the assumptions that lie behind the arguments of others. It is used to discuss and challenge why grounds used may not be acceptable, why warrants employed may be irrelevant or without adequate backing, why reservations are overlooked or understated.

Refutation based on double-loop learning involves challenging the argumentation of others by bringing to light the fundamental assumptions, values, or frames of reference on which they necessarily rest. In this refutation, it is possible that exposing their unstated foundation may simply reject entire lines of argument. If Argyris is correct, even those whose arguments you are refuting may be helped to see their own errors and move away from their original positions.

In a proposed statement on science standards for public schools, the Ohio State Board of Education suggested that students learn "how scientists continue to investigate and critically analyze aspects of evolutionary theory." On its face, this seems to be a reasonable expectation. The same could be said about any scientific theory. However, Laurence M. Krauss, writing in the *Chronicle of Higher Education* (November 29, 2002), noticed that this language appears *only* in the section of the standards associated with evolution.

"Its absence elsewhere," claims Krauss, "suggests that evolutionary theory alone is the subject of controversy among scientists" (B20). In other words, he brought to the surface a frame of reference held by the state board about evolution being different from other scientific theories. Then, Krauss proceeded to present argument and evidence that no such controversy exists among true scientists. His refutation concluded by saying, in essence, that the board must see evolution as experiencing the same critical analysis as all scientific theory: either take the sentence out concerning evolution or put the sentence in all statements about scientific theory.

Framebreaking has been used widely to refute laws and practices that discriminate between men and women. The traditional frame of reference—that women are weaker and less intellectually and emotionally capable than men—supported laws that were proclaimed to be protective of women. When women sought to overturn the laws, they had to expose the assumption of inferiority and attack it directly. When the assumption fell, so did the concept of "protection," and that generated a new frame of reference that sex discrimination is hurtful, not protective. Many men who had opposed the women's movement shifted their position when they saw discrimination in this new light.

Test the Credibility of Other Factions

Review the discussion of credibility in Chapter 9, and think about how challenges to others' credibility might form the basis of refutation. The credibility of key proponents may be used to damage a proposal. The credibility of evidence can be challenged by exposing bias, exclusion of important reservations, outdatedness, imprecision, or other criteria discussed in Chapter 7. Credibility of sources of support can be the object of refutation.

In the long battle between the tobacco companies and their critics, credibility of evidence has played an important role. Critics claim research shows that smoking damages health, but the tobacco interests continually reject this research by pointing out that the studies found only correlations, not causal connections. In return, when the tobacco companies produce research that suggests smoking is not the cause of health problems, critics note that researchers who are paid or otherwise supported by grants from tobacco interests are not reliable neutral scientists.

When a former lobbyist for the Tobacco Institute was diagnosed with cancer and decided to speak openly about his work, his testimony was granted high credibility. He was admitting he had participated in misleading the public by withholding information and providing inaccurate information. A former insider "coming clean" in a way that reflects badly on his own work has the highest credibility.

Understand Momentum

In decision-making groups, *momentum* describes a state of mind regarding critical attention to arguments. When a long and arduous debate has taken place over one proposition, those to follow may well pass with little or no comment because the decision makers have more or less exhausted their critical energy. The last proposition to come up just before the usual time for adjournment may whip through easily because people want to leave. It is said that during World War II, General Douglas MacArthur held back certain issues until just before 5:00 p.m. when officers were anxious to get to "happy hour," thus often avoiding scrutiny.

In refutation, you must understand momentum. Trying to get people to listen to objections when momentum is running in favor of the proposition may be futile. You may need to find some way to stop action until another meeting. Proposing amendments, calling for testimony from absent witnesses, suggesting that objections need to be heard from those unaware of the proposal, or other delay tactics may keep the question open long enough for refutation to be truly heard. Try to reschedule consideration of the proposition for the first item of business at the next meeting when momentum will not have built up. Of course, if momentum is running in favor of a proposition you support, remain silent.

Deny Support

The refutation aimed at the lowest conceptual level of analysis is a point-by-point attack on the support used by other factions. Review Chapters 7, 8, and 9 on the various means of support, and consider how they can be the basis of refutation. Essentially, you proceed by denying other factions' support through challenges of authenticity, relevance, or sufficiency and by producing countersupport that neutralizes or overcomes their material.

The problem with this form of refutation should be obvious by now: you are hacking away at the lower extremities of opposition arguments, and often they can be repaired or replaced easily. Every time Hercules chopped off one of Hydra's heads she grew two more, and every time you chop off a piece of opposition support, they can grow two more. Like Hercules, you need to find a way to cauterize the wounds so they do not grow back: relate each challenge of support to the claim it backs. Demand that the *claim* be defended, and return the argumentation to the higher conceptual levels.

Sometimes debaters sandbag the opposition by presenting their weaker support first to draw an attack that they then replace with secondary support so powerful that decision makers discount any further challenges. Pilots talk of "sucker holes"—patches of apparently clear sky that lure in pilots who then find themselves in worse weather than what they were trying to escape. Apparently weak support can be a sucker hole. Your refutational energy is drawn toward what appears to be a weakness, and later you find to your horror that you have exhausted your opportunity for refutation on trivia, having overlooked more significant refutational opportunities. Then you are confronted with powerful secondary support the others had held in reserve.

Communicating Refutation

It is exciting to read about daring feats written in ways that make them sound easy; it is quite another thing to try them yourself. In military history heroism may sound attractive, but it takes on another aspect in the midst of battle. It's not as easy as it sounds. Neither is refutation.

What we often forget when reading about battles or debate is that others will be trying to do to you what you are trying to do to them. In a Walter Mitty fantasy, you may picture yourself delivering a brilliant and powerful refutation to an opponent who cringes under your eloquence and bows to your superior analysis. When you really try it, the opponent will probably give you just as much in return.

The first time you are forced to hear or read what others think of your ideas, and their comments are not complimentary, you may find yourself gravitating toward escape from the process or giving an angry, flailing response. It will take considerable cool to stay on course. Because our society does not typically condone refutation, preferring agreement or silence instead, you may lack the emotional preparation for it. As a result, there are important steps to take in communicating your refutation. The more prepared you are, the more you will be steeled against the emotions that necessarily are involved. Simulations, practice sessions, are an absolute necessity. Even the president of the United States conducts practice sessions before major press conferences.

Here is a basic format for communicating refutation that works in most situations:

1. State the point to be refuted.
2. State your claim relevant to the point.
3. Support your claim.
4. State explicitly how your criticism undermines the overall position of those you are refuting.

These four steps make clear what is being refuted and why, and link your individual refutation to a higher conceptual level. This approach makes clear how this refutation weakens not just this one point, but the whole case. In the remainder of the chapter, we will discuss refutation processes that fall within this general pattern of communicating your refutation.

Block Arguments

Refutation can be prepared in advance by briefing opponent's arguments in a form that can readily be accessed in an actual argument. This allows you to plan your response systematically through argumentative blocks—outlines that set out the opponents' arguments one by one with your response opposite. When, in the heat of debate, an argument comes up, you can glance at your prepared block on that argument and review what you planned to say in response. Most professional advocates use the blocking system to ensure a basic refutation that is consistent with their overall position and help avoid unwise arguments made in haste.

To illustrate the concept of blocking, we will provide some sample blocks on the subject of capital punishment. If the resolution is that the death penalty should be eliminated, we will put arguments in favor on the left side of the page and those in refutation on the right. These are brief, undeveloped arguments. An Internet search under the subject reveals voluminous data and opinion with which to develop the debate.

Sample Refutation Blocks

Block # 1

I. Capital punishment is state-sponsored murder
  A. Innocent people die
    1. Justice Harry Blackmun calls it murder
    2. Since 1900, 23 known innocent people have died
    3. DNA tests have freed condemmed prisoners

I. Capital punishment saves lives
  A. Deterrence works
    1. Each execution—18 fewer murders
    2. No human system is perfect
    3. DNA tests have not freed many other prisoners

Block # 2

II. The penalty is abused	II. The penalty is fair

A. There is a pattern of racial dispari-
    ties in sentencing
	A. Recent studies do not find
	    disparities

1. A killer of a white person is 4.3
      times more likely to be
      sentenced to die
	1. The court made a
	      mistake in the
	      statistics

2. Minority defendants are sen-
      tenced to die more often
	2. Minorities commit more
	      murders

Block # 3

III. It is cruel and unusual punishment	III. It is not cruel or unusual

A. It is more cruel to keep a person
    locked up knowing death is coming
	A. The victim did not deserve
	    to die at all

1. Camus said the only equal way
      would be if the accused kept the
      victim locked up waiting death
	1. We can't know who
	      suffers more

B. Methods of execution are cruel	B. Lethal injection is not
1. It often takes 10 minutes to die	painful

Block # 4

IV. The Bible does not condone capital
    punishment
	IV. The Bible does condone capi-
	    tal punishment

A. Christ taught, "Love your enemies
    and pray for those who persecute
    you (Matthew 5:43–44)
	A. An eye for an eye and a
	    tooth for a tooth is God's
	    decree (Leviticus)

Probe Opponents

In debate, early refutation should send out tentative questions and challenges to discover where other factions are weak, where they are sandbagging, and where they are loaded for bear. Listen carefully for questionable support or repetition of original support rather than secondary support. At the same time, use a continued analysis of the decision makers to learn where they perceive weaknesses in other positions as well as your own.

Based on this probing, you can match your strength against others' weaknesses. Choose your challenges to bring together your greatest strengths opposite others' greatest weaknesses *as defined by your reading of the decision makers.* If you have already won decision makers' support on a major point, don't keep going over it; just review it from time to time to keep it on their minds. Concentrate refutation on those points in other positions that remain open in decision makers' minds and on which you have some reasonable expectation of success. Don't waste time flogging an issue you cannot win.

Use Questioning to Probe   In most decision-making situations, there is some opportunity for interrogation, and if used properly it can be powerful. The most frequent mistake is to confuse probing questions with refutation itself. Rarely do you seriously damage another's position during actual questioning. Instead, you discover weaknesses, expose contradictions, challenge credibility, and extract admissions that can then be used as part of your refutation. This will strengthen your refutation because you can remind decision makers that your point is based on what the opponents themselves have said.

Follow basic rules of questioning:

1. Prepare and practice questions in advance.
2. Phrase questions to allow a reasonably brief, preferably yes or no answer.
3. Ask questions to which you know the probable answers from prior research.
4. Be courteous in tone of voice and content of question, unless you want a dog fight.
5. Don't ask a question that demands that the other side capitulate—Perry Mason is pure fiction.
6. Ask the question and shut up; if you don't get the expected answer, move on rather than try to give your preferred answer yourself.
7. If the response is evasive, rephrase and try again, courteously.

The paradigm of ideal confrontation, according to Scott Jacobs, is for the questioner to elicit a declarative statement and then request a series of brief informative replies, followed by a rhetorical question that is, at once, a reply to the original declaration and a demonstration of its contradiction. Here is an example:

> MOTHER: I have a perfectly good will.
>
> DAUGHTER (a law professor):   Will it have to go to probate?
>
> MOTHER: I don't know.
>
> DAUGHTER: Is it subject to estate taxes?
>
> MOTHER: I don't think so.
>
> DAUGHTER: Will it adjust to your changing circumstances?
>
> MOTHER: I'm not sure.
>
> DAUGHTER: Mother, don't you think it would be a good idea to have your will checked out for these things?

Prepare to Respond to Questioning   Answering questions well is a part of refutation, though few prepare for it. Lawyers spend plenty of time preparing witnesses and politicians prepare to answer the press, but few others do so. Follow these principles:

1. Never answer until you understand the question.
2. Take your time.
3. Recognize that some questions don't deserve answers.

4. If the questioner interrupts, allow it.
5. Don't elaborate if it won't help you.
6. Ask permission to elaborate if it will help you. (If permission is denied, remain silent.)
7. Answer only those parts of the question that you believe deserve an answer.
8. Answer a question that was not asked, if that makes more sense to you.
9. If given an opportunity to repeat your argument, accept it in full.
10. Remember that during your refutation you will have a chance to explain or discount the effect of your answers; don't try to do this during questioning as it will only make you appear to be whining.

Follow Good Communication Practices

The most fundamental rules of good communication should be used in refutation, even though excitement often works against such clear practices. One way to keep yourself together even under pressure is to take notes that keep you informed at a glance on what arguments have emerged around each issue.

A flowsheet is a form of note taking or outlining that shows the progress of arguments and their various refutations. The flowsheet on pages 199–201 follows the arguments of four people debating the proposition that *A Virtual University Should Be Established.* The left column shows the arguments of the first affirmative constructive and the next column the first negative. The arrows show how the negative arguments relate to the affirmative and the flow of arguments through the second affirmative and negative speeches.

Conclusion

Refutation must come from a balanced posture that is neither too silent nor too brash. It should be approached as a cooperative, critical process important to good decision making. Before you can begin refutation, you need to assess the argumentative situation to learn the way the argumentation is functioning in the particular sphere, including who the appropriate decision makers are and what are their presumptions.

Before refutation begins, you should prepare yourself for it by assessing the situation in light of the steps in critical decision making. You should also analyze the decision makers and your opponents to gain the necessary information to select a posture for refutation.

Once refutation begins, it should be aimed at the highest conceptual level possible. Often it will include a constructive basis for your criticism that you can defend. Sometimes refutation rests on framebreaking, or helping decision makers adopt a different way of thinking about the issues. You may also test opponents' credibility, stop momentum, and deny support.

In communicating refutation it is well to follow a format of stating the point to be refuted, then your refutation and support, and finally show how it undermines the

TABLE 10.1 Proposition: A Virtual University Should Be Established

Affirmative	Negative	Affirmative	Negative
I. Expanding current universities to meet future needs is too costly.	I. You are assuming high cost needs without providing necessary data.	I. The demands on higher ed. in the future are well documented.	
A. Construction costs will be high.	A. You have not specified what will be needed. You provide no figures on the cost of establishing a virtual university.	A. John Mosley, VP for Academic Affairs, U. of Oregon, writes in *Managing and Leading the University of the 21st Century: Megatrends and Strategies* provides data.	
1. Current physical facilities are deteriorating.			
2. The number of students is increasing.			
3. Construction is expensive.			
B. Costs to students will be high.	B. You have provided no comparative data showing the differential between traditional higher ed. and a virtual university.	B. Quantitative data is provided in *Postsecondary OPPORTUNITY.* No. 36, June 1995.	
1. Living away from home is costly.			
2. Commuting long distances is costly.			
3. Tuition will be raised to pay for construction, etc.			
C. Costs to students will be high.	C. What will be the amount of increase in personnel costs? Again, you give no data.		
1. Faculty salaries will increase.			
2. Additional faculty must be hired.			

(continued)

TABLE 10.1 Continued

Affirmative	Negative	Affirmative	Negative
	II. Cost must be measured against the criteria of what is needed in higher education. A. Higher education aims at preparing people to think critically, learn effectively, interact socially, and be good citizens. B. A virtual university is not able to meet these criteria. 　1. Technology is best in giving information. 　2. Technology is worst at developing critical thinking. C. Damaging our children's education is a cost that cannot be measured in dollars.	II. The criteria for higher education must be adjusted for the 21st century. A. The criteria you list come from Plato's time, and the world has changed. B. The future will demand citizens with knowledge and skills in technical fields.	II. In a technical era, truly educated citizens will become even more important than in Plato's time. A. Technology changes quickly, and if students are only filled with current information, they will soon be obsolete. B. The most practical education is one that prepares students to think, learn, communicate, decide, and act effectively.

(continued)

TABLE 10.1 Continued

Affirmative	Negative	Affirmative	Negative

III. A virtual university will be practicable and desirable.
A. New technology is practical.
  1. Computers
  2. Video conferencing
  3. Internet tutorials
  4. Off-shelf CD-ROMS
B. New technology is preferable to spending money on conventional higher education.
  1. It will remove the need to construct new buildings.
  2. It will cost students less.
  3. There will be no need to hire new faculty.
	III. A virtual U. is impracticable and undesirable.
	A. There is no substitute for shared human spaces of a campus.
	B. Face-to-face meetings with instructors is essential.
	C. Physically going to the library and conducting research is essential.
		III. Virtual universities are now working successfully.
		A. National Technical U. represents a consortium of fifty American universities.
		B. Canada has an on-line MBA.
		C. Britain has an Open University.
		D. Many states are starting virtual universities.
		  1. Western Governors University
			III. Experience with technology-based education has not been good.
			A. We learn that hundreds of students watching TV sets don't learn much.
			B. National Technical U. is mostly talking heads and graphs.
			C. Britain and Canada are not replacing their excellent universities with these experiments.
			D. WGU has failed to attract students.

IV. There are no serious disadvantages to a virtual university. A. Interaction is possible in a virtual university: students can talk with each other and the teacher. B. The best teachers can be used no matter where they are geographically. C. Quality control in instruction will be easier, more certain.	IV. There are serious disadvantages to a virtual university. A. This is no real interaction. B. No teacher can be effective in a disembodied format. C. In fact, studying by themselves, students need not do their own work.	IV. The disadvantages have not been supported by evidence.	

opponent's position. To prepare for refutation it is a good idea to build refutational blocks that summarize each argument to be refuted and your refutation of it. A flowsheet will help you keep track of an argument and visually identify what you must refute.

PROJECT

Select a newspaper editorial with which you disagree. Prepare a refutation of it with the aim of convincing the other members of the class to sign a letter to the editor rejecting the editorial.

11 Refutation by Fallacy Claims

KEY TERMS

fallacy claim
incorrect logic
sophistry
informal logic
tu quoque
begging the question
petitio principii
authority
popularity
post hoc
ad hominem
discussion rules
burden of proof
deception

refusal to reason
cooperation
irrelevant
obfuscation
quantity maxim
conflict of interest
reckless disregard
verbal aggression
appeal to pity
modus ponens
modus tollens
ad populum
pragma-dialectical

One of the critic's tasks in refutation is to examine arguments to see whether they contain fallacies. If the critic can successfully claim that an argument is fallacious, the person making the argument has the burden to correct or abandon the position. However, looking for fallacies is not like checking the oil in your car to see if you're a quart low. It's rather complicated.

We will start with a definition. *A fallacy claim asserts that an argument must be rejected because it violates a significant rule of argumentation relevant to the appropriate decision makers.* As Ralph A. Johnson puts it, "A fallacy is an argument that violates one of the criteria/standards of good arguments and that occurs with sufficient frequency in discourse to warrant being [specifically named]" (116). Central to this concept of fallacy are four characteristics:

1. Charging that an argument commits a fallacy requires that you undertake the burden of proving it to the satisfaction of the decision makers. This is in contrast to

pointing out, for example, that a computational error has been made in solving a mathematical problem or that a word has been misspelled. In math or spelling, the error may well be self-evident once attention is focused on it. In argumentation, a fallacy claim is rarely self-evident (Lyne 3).

For example, we often hear in conversation the claim, "You're being inconsistent." And the other person merely replies, "No, I'm not." If you intend to make the fallacy claim of inconsistency, you need to say something like this: "When you argue we should reduce the power of the federal government and then call for strengthening the social security and Medicare systems, you argue against yourself. That is inconsistent." When you state the fallacy claim that directly, the other person must do more than deny the charge.

2. A fallacy claim charges significant deviance from appropriate argumentation practices; it does not make nit-picking criticisms that score debate points rather than advance critical decision making. Sometimes people trounce on a slip of the tongue, a minor error, or an overstatement as though it were a triumph. A bit of hyperbole, such as

> **WILLIE:** "Trading in the stock market is perfectly safe. Since 1945, there has been a steady rise in value."

may produce a response like,

> **MOE:** "Oh yeah, what about the dotcom debacle and the drop in 2000–2001?"
>
> **WILLIE:** "Yes, of course, there was that, but the historical net direction has been up."

This may weaken Willie's credibility but it is not what we mean by fallacy, because he can hold the claim by qualifying it with, "I meant the overall trend."

3. A fallacy claim charges a violation in argumentation rules that may not be appreciated by appropriate decision makers until it is made an issue. It opens to discussion a violation at once so significant and so subtle that appraisal itself becomes an issue. One function of a fallacy claim is to pinpoint the issue that in principle needs resolution (Lyne 3).

Elder Paul H. Dunn was widely respected among members of the Church of Jesus Christ of Latter Day Saints (Mormon) for his inspirational talks and books. He used his exploits in World War II and as a professional baseball player to make religious claims. Then it was discovered that these "experiences" never happened. He fabricated them. He was accused of the fallacies of misuse of authority and deception.

This forced public debate on a moral principle that was significant but had not been explicitly discussed: must the parables used by religious teachers be true? Some claimed that if the examples were merely intended to inspire people to live a better life, then it did not matter that they were false. Others said Dunn's work must be rejected because of the violations of trust.

The U.S. Office of Science and Technology has published a policy on research misconduct including intentional fabrication, falsification, or plagiarism in proposing, performing, or reviewing research (1999). In considering the policy, David H. Guston, writing in *Science and Engineering Ethics,* questions whether deceit must be intentional to constitute misconduct, and he wonders if scientists can be trusted to police each other. And Courtney Leatherman, writing in the *Chronicle of Higher Education,* reports on five sociologists at Texas A&M University who leveled thirty-three charges of scientific misconduct at one another, and five years later they still did not have the matter resolved. Whether there was an intent to plagiarize, and whether using language virtually identical to that of another scholar constituted plagiarism, were issues that proved the toughest to resolve.

4. While a fallacy claim rests upon a significant rule of the sphere, the appropriate decision makers must reaffirm the rule for the claim to succeed. For example, The U.S. Office of Science and Technology defines fabrication as, "manipulating research materials . . . or changing or omitting data or results such that the research is not accurately represented in the research record" (55722–55725). But over the multi-year life of a research project, there will be many instances of omitting data that were not deemed relevant and material at that point in the research. The decision makers must reaffirm and specify the rule in relation to the particular research record in deciding on a fallacy claim.

In the remainder of the chapter, we discuss competing views of fallacy and examine selected social guides to the development of fallacy claims.

Views of Fallacy

Aristotle is credited with formalizing logic, and his work in the *Sophistical Refutations, Prior Analytics,* and *Rhetoric* is cited as the origin of the concept of fallacy (Hamblin 50–88). As logicians sought to make sense of Aristotle's ideas, they did so from a world view powerfully shaped by a sense of order and certainty. They were sure that the universe is orderly and that humans possess the rational capacity to understand and deal with it. Logic was perceived to be the tool of that rationality.

Logicians believed that just as numbers and abstract symbols, such as P and Q, could be manipulated within mathematical or logical analyses with certain and consistent meaning, so could ordinary language. For most of our intellectual history, people have believed that words have precise meaning and the primary task of the arguer is one of interpretation: discovering meaning and using the correct word to say what is meant.

Fallacy as Incorrect Logic

The view of logic that has emerged over the past 500 years in Europe and ultimately the United States, is one that seeks order and certainty by removing the disorderly and unpredictable aspects of human behavior. In this view, dialogue, conversation, and human feeling are "mere nuisances" (Ong 251). Logic is a system existing outside of human discourse (Howell 350–61). It has little patience for the pragmatics of language as practiced by ordinary people where the meaning of words is negotiated through usage and may vary within a single argument.

From this world view, it is no wonder that some philosophers understand Aristotle's idea of fallacy as identifying *incorrectness* in logic. They are like old-fashioned grammarians in that respect. In traditional grammar, the task is to locate grammatical errors such as this: "The books is on the table." The error is in agreement between noun and verb, because the first is plural and the second is singular. In logic, the task is to locate logical errors, for example, the fallacy of the undistributed middle term in a categorical syllogism (described in Chapter 3):

> Japanese eat raw fish.
> Sharks eat raw fish.
> Therefore, Japanese are sharks.

The error is failing to have a premise that logically links Japanese with sharks.

In the discussion of informal logic in Chapter 3, we introduced you to the hypothetical syllogism that takes the "If A, then B" form. For example, "If it rains, then the streets will get wet." You can logically use this in two ways: (1) affirm the antecedent, a *modus ponens* (it did rain, so the streets are wet); (2) deny the consequent, a *modus tollens* (the streets are not wet, so it did not rain).

On the other hand, drawing a claim from affirming the consequent or denying the antecedent can be called fallacious because they do not yield valid conclusions. That is, if you see that the streets are wet and conclude it must have rained, you could be making an error. There is more than one way the streets can become wet. Similarly, if you know it has not rained and presume, therefore, that the streets are dry, you could be committing a fallacy.

A fundamental fallacy in the eyes of some is to mistake validity for truth (Fearnside and Holther 126). This may occur when ordinary language and real issues are presented in logical form (what we call quasi-logic in Chapter 3). For example, this argument follows a valid form: Any structure built on my property belongs to me, and your fence is on my property, so it belongs to me.

While the claim seems clear-cut and valid as stated, the real problem is with the substance of the argument, not its form. Any lawyer will tell you that fences and property lines are not simply a matter of a surveyor's report. To make good on this claim, you must successfully argue not only that the property line is where you claim it is, but that you have consistently and publicly continued to claim the property. If you have allowed the fence to stay there without asserting your claim, you may have no case. A critic who stopped with the observed validity of the argument would miss the key issues.

In one view, it is not worthwhile to study fallacies based on violations of the rules of formal logic because strengths and weaknesses in argumentation are too variable (Ehninger and Brockriede 99–100). Gerald J. Massey claims that there is no theory behind logical fallacies and the subject should be sent to psychology if anywhere (170–71). In another view, although argumentation is admittedly inexact and ambiguous, taking note of such fallacies serves as a point of reference by which arguments "might be critically analyzed" (Lyne 4).

The more knowledgeable you are on the rules of logic and the ways they can be violated, the more likely you are to sniff out some of the problems in people's arguments and come up with effective refutation. But you must keep in mind that argumentation does not conform to strict rules of logic, and logical incorrectness may not be an effective fallacy claim.

Fallacy as Sophistry

A fallacy, to some, is more than an error. It is an error that leads, or could lead, rational people toward mistaken or dangerous conclusions. Those holding to this view are dedicated to more than correctness. They seek to rid the world of sophistry, the use of plausible but fallacious reasoning. The study of fallacies is a way to protect people from being led astray by persuaders who care nothing for truth in their fervor to get their way (Informal 2–15).

A typical introduction to textbooks on fallacies predicates the study on the rising intensity in the "constant battle for our minds and allegiances that is such a distinctive feature of life . . . through the mass media particularly" (Engel 4). "The triumph of rhetoric is like the spread of a virus infection," say Fearnside and Holther, "it would be a good idea if the community could somehow develop a serum against some forms of persuasion" (1). Howard Kahane believes the study of fallacies is the serum that attempts to "raise the level of political argument and reasoning by acquainting students with the devices and ploys which drag that level down" (xi). He says persuasion is often successful when it ought not to be, and so he defines a fallacy as an "argument which *should not* persuade a rational person to accept its conclusion" (1).

For example, people may be taken in by this argumentation. When the attorney general of the state announced an investigation of the university president for possible misuse of funds because it had been discovered the president had lavishly remodeled his office, the president responded by revealing that the attorney general had recently spent $10,000 just for a new door into her office.

This *tu quoque* argument (responding to a charge by making a countercharge) is a fallacy in the eyes of some because, first, it is logically erroneous in not addressing the issue of the university president's actions and, second, it may seem plausible to the public. Some people seemed quick to forgive President Bill Clinton for his misbehavior because they knew of misdeeds of others such as President Richard Nixon for Watergate and President Ronald Reagan for Iran/Contra.

While pointing to another wrong rather than dealing with the immediate issue may be objectionable in some contexts, it may not always be so. Dennis Rohatyn notes that "He that is without sin among you, let him first cast a stone at her" (John 8:7), the New Testament quotation attributed, with widespread approbation, to Jesus Christ, is a *tu quoque* argument. Jesus used it to spare a woman accused of adultery while avoiding damage to himself for seeming to violate religious rules. We know of no one who has charged Christ with committing a fallacy. Rohatyn is not approving of *tu quoque* in general, he is merely saying it is not always a fallacy to use that argumentative form (1).

We will briefly introduce you to some commonly mentioned fallacies arising from the concern over sophistry. This is not a complete list, nor are these forms of argument always sophistic.

Begging the Question   When an answer or definition seems plausible but, upon closer examination, assumes as fact that which is not proved, it may be *begging the question* (*petitio principii*). To beg the question is to assume as true that which you are trying to prove. It is also called circular reasoning. Circular definitions fall within this classification. Douglas N. Walton says that an argument ". . . that commits the fallacy of begging the question uses coercive and deceptive tactics to try to get a respondent to accept something as a legitimate premise that is really not, and to slur over the omission, to disguise the failure of any genuine proof" (*Begging* 285). Walton says this is like pulling yourself out of the quicksand by your own hair (290). A *New Yorker* cartoon (March 24, 2003, 71) put it humorously: "It could go badly, or it could go well, depending on whether it goes badly or well."

In law, the defense may successfully object if the prosecutor says, "At what time did the murder occur?" The object of the trial is to determine if a murder occurred, and the prosecutor assumed it into fact. We may know someone is dead, but whether it is *murder* is still at issue.

Similarly, to condemn abortion as murder because it is taking the life of an unborn human being is to beg the question. The statement uses the point at issue (at what point does life begin) to support the claim, and thereby fails to carry the discussion any further along.

Appeal to Authority   To assume a claim is a fact simply because someone with high credibility says it may constitute a fallacious appeal to authority. Argumentation by its nature relies heavily on support from authority, so the fact that someone uses that kind of support does not necessarily call for criticism. A fallacy claim on authority can occur when the appeal is thought to be improper because the so-called authority is not an authority on the question at issue. One may also claim a fallacy when an appeal to expert opinion is used "as a tactical device for preventing the respondent from raising the appropriate critical questions" (*Appeal to Expert* 228). That is to say, authority may be abused if it is used to silence the dialogue. Our discussion of testimonial evidence in Chapter 7 develops these ideas.

Appeal to Popularity   Similar to the objection over uses of authority is that over appeals to popularity. Claiming that something is good because it is popular runs the risk of criticism. Modern advertising employs both authority and popularity, often with questionable justification. Douglas Walton writes that the traditional interpretation of this fallacy, under the Latin name *argumentum ad populum,* no longer can be accepted because in a democracy it is relevant and proper to take into account public opinion and preferences (*Appeal to Popular*). However, he argues, the appeal to popular opinion can still function fallaciously if it is weak or overlooks other relevant evidence that should be taken into consideration; if the claim is not "dialectically relevant" with respect to the sphere in which it occurs yet appears to be relevant; or if the argument is put forward in a way that pressures others into silence (*Appeal to Popular* 276).

Is it reasonable to say that a product is good because it is a best seller? Even those who compile the best seller lists of books caution people against assuming they will enjoy any book that has been at the top of the list for many weeks. Is the candidate who is ahead in the polls the one to vote for? The polls may have been manipulated to lead rather than reflect popular opinion, or the questions in the poll may have been designed to elicit a certain response. Are the television shows with the highest ratings the best? Again, popularity may be the result of criteria that are not relevant to you or your decision makers.

Post Hoc Fallacies   Many arguments rest on a claim of causality, as we explained in Chapter 6. A fallacy may be claimed when it is believed that a faulty causal relationship is at hand. The Latin phrase *post hoc, ergo propter hoc,* from which the fallacy gets its name, calls attention to the tendency to assume a causal relation among events because they are related in time or space.

This kind of reasoning is common in politics. When a new governor or president comes into office and shortly thereafter interest rates fall, employment is up, and the economy is booming, politicians claim that they caused these effects. As often as not, the particular leader had nothing to do with it, in which case the claim could be susceptible to a *post hoc* charge.

People are quick to ascribe causes, often with little or no justification. You come down with a cold, and your mother says, "I told you not to go outside without your coat." You get in trouble, and your father says, "I told you not to run around with that bad crowd." Your grades go up at the same time that you are frequently absent from class, and you announce, "Attending class doesn't have anything to do with getting high grades." College officials often claim that going to college will cause you to earn more money since, on average, those with a college education do earn higher salaries. Whether graduates would have done as well without higher education remains unclear. Such pat causal arguments invite close scrutiny and may deserve the label of *post hoc* fallacy.

Fallacies in Language   Following Aristotle's lead, a great many fallacy claims are based on problems with the language in which an argument is expressed. Since argumentation uses ordinary language to deal with questions within the realm of uncertainty, ambiguity is always present. Still, a critic can sometimes find instances in which language problems are of such significance as to warrant a fallacy claim.

When the U.S. Supreme Court interpreted the Thirteenth, Fourteenth, and Fifteenth Amendments to the U.S. Constitution, which were passed during the post–Civil

War period, to rule that only Congress, not state and local governments, could pass affirmative action laws, Justice Thurgood Marshall accused the majority of turning the language on its head. The language was designed, he said, to keep state and local government from harming minorities, not from helping them (*Richmond v. Crosen*).

Ad Hominem Fallacies   When people turn their criticism against a person rather than the person's ideas, they may commit an *ad hominem* fallacy. There is plenty of evidence that we do this regularly in our own minds by giving more credence to the arguments of attractive people and less to the unattractive (Rieke and Stutman 128–29). It would be as if you said, "Your argument is weak because you're ugly." While you may not be as blatant as that in using *ad hominem* arguments, you may have heard people say something like, "I reject your argument against terrorism because you are from Syria." Presumably you are saying that since the government of Syria has supported terrorism, anyone born in Syria is sympathetic to terrorism. If so, it could count as an *ad hominem* fallacy claim.

Verbal aggression constitutes another form of *ad hominem* fallacy. In conversational argument, there is a presumption (preference) for agreement (Jackson and Jacobs 253). Language choices associated with the destructive use of argument fall within the concept of *verbal aggression,* which " . . . denotes attacking the self-concept of another person instead of, or in addition to, the person's position on a topic of communication" (Infante and Wigley 60). This aggression has the effect of inflicting, and may be intended to inflict, psychological pain (Infante 51). These attacks can take many forms: questioning others' intelligence; insults; making people feel bad; saying others are unreasonable; calling someone stupid; attacking character; telling people off; making fun of people; using offensive language; yelling and screaming (Infante and Wigley 64). People can attack one's competence, physical appearance, background; they can tease, ridicule, make threats, use profanity and nonverbal emblems (Infante, Chandler, and Rudd 167).

People may resort to verbal aggressiveness because of their psychological makeup and their lack of argumentative skills (Infante, Chandler, and Rudd 164–65). All of us have at one time or another resorted to these forms of attack. However, even when decision makers think your charges are accurate, verbal aggressiveness reduces your credibility (see Chapter 9). In some cultures, even the direct expression of disagreement is perceived as in bad taste.

In western culture, what is important to emphasize is the difference between assertiveness and argumentativeness, which do not give rise to fallacy claims, and hostility and verbal aggressiveness, which do. Assertiveness involves being interpersonally forceful in expressing your ideas. Argumentativeness is characterized by presenting and defending positions on issues while attacking others' positions (Infante 52). Hostility is manifest by the use of the language of negativity, resentment, suspicion, and irritability. Verbal aggressiveness involves using language to inflict pain and weaken or destroy another's self-concept (Infante 52). When this occurs, a charge of committing an *ad hominem* fallacy is to be expected.

An editorial writer in the *Honolulu Advertiser* leveled a charge of *ad hominem* fallacy at Chuck Quakenbush, who rejected the charge. The editorial noted that Quakenbush had only recently moved from California to Hawai'i, and brought his California verbal aggressiveness with him. Hawai'i, the writer said, has a unique culture calling for a less abrasive style of argumentation. Quakenbush argued, "Were feelings hurt and sensibilities offended during the [debate]? Yes. Would the needed change have occurred without this confrontation? No way" (B3). Did he commit a fallacy or did he merely employ effective argumentation?

Appeal to Pity   Arguments that are based on the elicitation of pity, or in the Latin, *argumentum ad misericordiam,* have traditionally been considered inherently fallacious. Such a broad condemnation cannot survive within an audience-centered rhetorical approach to argumentation. As our discussion of forms of support makes clear, values, including such feelings as pity, compassion, or sympathy are important to argumentation.

Douglas Walton agrees that the traditional approach to this fallacy must be set aside in favor of a case-by-case approach. A fallacious appeal to pity might be sustained in relation to the way the argument is used in context: did it further or damage the requirements of the argumentation? In general, Walton argues that the historical and pragmatic meaning of *pity* includes negative elements: a person is pitiful because of suffering from some undeserved evil (*Appeal to Pity* 73). So, concludes Walton, while sympathy and compassion are usually appropriate in argumentation, pity may be used in an irrelevant and distracting manner that inhibits the objective of argumentation.

For example, solicitations of money to save the starving children in some remote place that show babies with flies crawling on their eyes and mouths may be designed to disarm our critical faculties. In such a case, a charge of a fallacious appeal to pity might be appropriate.

These are only a few illustrative forms of fallacies commonly mentioned in the efforts against sophistry. Other potential fallacies are appeals to fear, ignorance, force, prejudice, and the pressure of the mob.

We have discussed two theoretical foundations on which fallacies can be identified: logic and sophistry. Both of these premises have come under attack in recent times.

The relevance of logic to practical argumentation is in serious doubt. Although its patterns are still recognized and used, as we discuss in Chapter 2, as a way to structure argumentation, its rules of validity are generally seen as inapplicable. Since, in this theory, a fallacy is a violation of a logic rule, fallacies become suspect when the rules of logic are deemed irrelevant.

Sophistry has always been a difficult posture from which to identify fallacies because of the extreme ambiguity of the concept. What is sophistic to one is often acceptable to another. Who is to say an argument "ought not to be persuasive?" Who has the authority to say an authority ought not to be believed in this instance? Who decides when a *tu quoque* is okay and when it is fallacious? By what rule do we say that this *ad hominem* argument is inappropriate as used and is, thus, fallacious?

If you accept these criticisms of fallacy theory, you might wonder why the study of fallacy continues to hold interest. The concept of fallacy is useful in two respects. First, by locating frequently employed mistakes in argument and giving them a name, we make it easier for critics to keep them in mind and put them to use. Pedagogically, it is easier to teach people to be critical decision makers if we can use this memory device. Second, it is easier rhetorically to communicate to decision makers that a mistake in argumentation has occurred if there is a common vocabulary of fallacy to use. Rather than needing to delve into the broad concept of causality, you can trigger understanding by suggesting there is a *post hoc* fallacy.

Fallacies as Violations of Discussion Rules

Because of concerns with traditional approaches, contemporary scholars have sought a new and acceptable theoretical basis on which to rest the concept of fallacies. Frans H. van Eemeren and Rob Grootendorst of the University of Amsterdam have developed what they call a *pragma-dialectical* approach to argumentation. By this phrase, they mean a combination of normative rules (a philosophical ideal of reasonableness) with a pragmatic study of speech acts (what people actually say and mean in argumentation).

From the pragma-dialectical perspective, van Eemeren and Grootendorst develop a theory of fallacies that first sets out ten rules for critical discussion (see Chapter 2). They include such prescriptions as allowing everyone to speak; requiring that claims be supported; demanding relevance of arguments; calling for honesty in representing arguments presented; expecting that arguments be logically valid or capable of being validated; and avoiding confusing arguments (209).

The concept of fallacy follows directly from these ten rules: any move in argumentation that blocks critical discussion by violating one of these rules is a fallacy. They conclude their discussion by arguing that all the traditional fallacies, such as those we discuss under sophistry, can be reasonably organized under one of the ten rules of critical discussion.

More recently, van Eemeren has elaborated on the concept of "strategic maneuvering," which attempts to recognize the tension you may feel between the desire to argue with perfect reasonableness and your desire to win the debate. Remember Quackenbush who admitted that he had ruffled feathers but felt that was necessary to win. If you allow your commitment to reasonable argumentation to be overruled by the desire to be persuasive, says van Eemeren, you may, "victimize the other party. Then the strategic maneuvering has got 'derailed,' and is condemnable for being fallacious" (142). If this move to persuasiveness is intentional, van Eemeren claims, it will be necessary for arguers to reaffirm their commitment to reasonableness before they can effectively continue.

Douglas Walton generally agrees with this characterization of fallacies. His pragmatic view of fallacy differs in only two respects. First, he notes that van Eemeren and Grootendorst do not make a distinction between fallacies and simple blunders in argumentation. Second, he says the idea of fallacy should be extended beyond critical discussion to include such contexts as inquiry, negotiation, deliberation, quarrels, and information-seeking dialogue (*A Pragmatic* xii).

Walton says the concept of fallacy presumes that the concern is with moves within argumentation. Merely incorrect statements do not meet his definition of fallacy. He also claims that fallacies require a " . . . serious kind of infraction that involves a systematic technique of deceptive argumentation" (*A Pragmatic* 233–34). People may commit a blunder that does, in fact, violate a rule of dialogue, but it is not serious if it is not systematic or deceptive. He says an argument is a fallacy if it twists some aspect of argument to one's advantage (*A Pragmatic* 235). A fallacy, says Walton, is an argumentation technique used wrongly, as defined by these three criteria:

1. A failure, lapse, or error, subject to criticism, correction, or rebuttal
2. A failure that occurs in what is supposed to be an argument
3. A failure associated with deception or illusion (*A Pragmatic* 237)

Ralph H. Johnson follows Walton's lead in looking at the totality of the discourse in developing fallacy claims. Johnson directs attention at what he calls three basic fallacies: (1) Irrelevant reason—is the argument relevant? (2) Hasty conclusion—is the argument sufficient? (3) Problematic premise—is the argument acceptable (116)? Finally, according to Walton, a fallacy involves the violation of some maxim of reasonable dialogue, is a systematic kind of wrongly applied technique of reasonable argumentation, and is significantly deceptive, *not a simple blunder* (*A Pragmatic* 238).

Drawing on all of these views of fallacy as well as our own thoughts, in the remainder of the chapter we will discuss how fallacy claims are a part of refutation. You should remember that the contemporary image of fallacy is tied to the actual rules governing argumentation and the willingness of decision makers to see an argument as a violation of one of those rules.

Using Fallacy Claims in Refutation

Claims of logical incorrectness, sophistry, and violations of discussion rules must be considered in your plan of refutation. Recall from Chapter 10 that you should always aim at the highest conceptual level and that pointing out specific mistakes or embarrassing slips may not do much to criticize other positions.

The highest conceptual level can usually be found by looking for the ultimate purpose sought from the argumentation. In debating the pros and cons of the death penalty, Jonathan D. Salant claims racism plays a significant role in deciding guilt.

While the same number of blacks and whites are murdered, murderers of white people are more likely to receive the death penalty. Since 1977, he says, 80 percent of the people executed were convicted of killing a white person. Kent Scheidegger, legal director of the pro-death penalty Criminal Justice Legal Foundation "blamed racial differences on fewer prosecutors in heavily minority areas willing to seek the death penalty" (Salant A20). He claims that prosecutors in more conservative counties use the death penalty more often. The highest conceptual level on which to base refutation must be whether the judicial process is operating fairly and properly or whether racism either in the form of convictions or the decisions of prosecutors is distorting justice.

Before using refutation by fallacy claim, be sure it is consistent with your overall critical pattern. If you decide to argue a fallacy claim, remember to communicate it clearly by following the steps listed below, which were detailed at the start of the chapter.

1. Accept the burden of proving that what you claim as a fallacy is fallacious in this circumstance.
2. Identify the significant argumentation practice that you claim has been violated.
3. Show why it is an issue worthy of consideration.
4. Charge the decision makers to reaffirm their commitment to this practice in this instance.
5. State explicitly how your fallacy claim undermines the overall position you are refuting.

Social Guides to Fallacy Claims

While it is impossible to identify inherently fallacious ways of arguing, we can list some relatively enduring patterns on which fallacy claims can be based. Like the traditional patterns of criteria for argument appraisal (logical, good reasons, scientific, good story) listed in Chapter 3, these guidelines are not universal but are widely seen as potentially problematic procedures in argumentation. You can use these guidelines in the development of fallacy claims.

Intent to Deceive

Earlier we said that simple errors or misunderstandings do not form the basis of fallacy claims because they can be brought up, discussed, negotiated, and corrected. But errors or misunderstandings that can be shown to be intentionally deceptive are commonly seen as fallacious. People may forgive the former but not the latter. Rohatyn makes an analogy between reason–deception and eroticism–pornography:

> One is loving, the other possessive. One respects both persons and flesh, the other objectifies and dehumanizes. One is dialogic: sensual, but never exploitative. . . . The other is monologic: vengeful and authoritarian. One is frank, vulnerable and open, whereas the other lusts for power (10).

When a scholar in the work of Dr. Martin Luther King, Jr., announced that parts of King's doctoral dissertation apparently were taken from other sources without credit, a debate ensued. On the one hand, plagiarism constitutes intentional use of another's work without credit with the intent that readers believe it is your own work. If so, King's behavior would seem to be fallacious. On the other hand, King's defenders have argued that King's purpose was benign: he was always a political activist, not a scholar, and when he used others' work he did so to make a point, not to deceive. Most agreed that if King did it simply to get his doctorate without doing his own work, it was unacceptable. The debate was over intent to deceive.

Chris Raymond reports that studies of patient histories suggest that Sigmund Freud suppressed or distorted facts that contradicted his theories. He rested his case heavily on the case histories of six people, of whom one left therapy dissatisfied after three months, two were never treated by Freud or any psychoanalyst, and another never really had therapy. Of the two remaining cases, Freud's claims of effecting a cure were refuted by a confession of Freud himself and a denial by one of the patients. A research professor of psychiatry at the University of Pittsburgh said, "It is clear that Freud did what euphemistically might be called editing of his case material . . . [but that] isn't tantamount to dishonesty" (4–5). Again, there was deception, leading to a debate over intent. To establish a fallacy claim, the critics must show that Freud doctored his cases with the intent to deceive.

Advertisers come in for considerable criticism because of their apparent willingness to deceive people to win them over. Communication scholars who specialize in the study of advertising, however, do not identify deception as central to advertising. They do say it relies upon the force of *our own* self-deceptions, fantasies, values, personal realities, or world views. Loose analysis may lead you to charge deception when an advertiser is merely using intense language, hyperbole, and dynamism alongside appeals to our own realities.

On the other hand, there are examples of those who have knowingly sought to deceive us in order to gain our adherence, and these become the object of fallacy claims.

Mark M. Hager, a professor at American University's Washington College of Law, as reported in the *Chronicle of Higher Education* (January 24, 2003, A7), was retained to represent clients who were considering suing the Warner-Lambert Company. The company makes a shampoo, Nix, that it claimed kills lice; the clients claimed it does not kill lice. Mr. Hager admitted that he and a co-counsel had gone to Warner-Lambert and worked out a deal in which they received $225,000 and the clients separately received refunds totaling up to $10,000 for their shampoo purchases, along with an agreement from the company to stop making the lice claim. However, he did not tell his clients about the $225,000 he and the co-counsel had received or that they had agreed not to sue Warner-Lambert.

Hager argued in court that he had not intentionally deceived anyone when he accepted the money. His lawyer said, "Mr. Hager's clients got everything they could have gotten, and no one was harmed." But the District of Columbia Court of Appeals disagreed. They found that Hager had violated rules of professional conduct, saying his actions, "demonstrated at best an ethical numbness to the integrity of the attorney–client relationship." The court suspended Hager from practicing law for a year.

Refusal to Reason

In a pure sense of the term, critical decision making means having a basis for a decision that can be examined critically. It does not demand any particular kind of rationale; it merely demands a rationale. To make a claim but refuse to give reasons in its support may give rise to a fallacy claim. Even to rely on altruism or one's own authority—"Believe it because I ask you to"—is a reason that can be critically examined. To say, "Believe it just because," or "Believe it for no particular reason," is to deny others (including yourself) the opportunity for critical appraisal.

Children around the age of three use the word *because* as a reason, when older children and adults almost never do so. This is not so much a refusal to reason as it is a childish understanding of the process of reasoning (Willbrand and Rieke 435).

By the same token, when someone over the age of four asserts a claim without any support, or with "because, just because," as a basis, we conclude it is a refusal to reason and may form the basis of a fallacy claim. Parents do their children no good by answering the multitude of "why" questions with "just because" answers. Government does citizens no good by answering challenges to public policy with a refusal to reason, hidden behind national security. Critical decision making rests upon the ability to consider reasons, so refusal to reason denies the critical process and constitutes a potential fallacy.

In the debate leading up to the 2003 invasion of Iraq, arguments about the alleged weapons of mass destruction held by Saddam Hussein were often cloaked in national security claims. Administration spokespersons frequently said that while they were prevented from revealing details, they were absolutely confident the weapons would be found. The Congress and the people were asked to go along with the war and wait until later for the full arguments.

Months later, when there was still no evidence of weapons of mass destruction, many people felt angry. They had supported the war on faith rather than argumentation. It was not a critical decision. If the administration was truly ignorant of the facts about weapons of mass destruction, they should not have made that a major justification for war. If they had arguments to support their case, they should have presented them and allowed the critical process to take its course. In either case, they may have been guilty of a refusal to reason.

Breach of Conversational Cooperation

H. P. Grice says that when people engage in argumentation they do so within a presumption that anything said is intended to be "cooperative," that it contributes toward the goal of the interaction. He posits four conversational maxims of such cooperation that govern each utterance: the utterance is topically relevant; it is expressed perspicuously (clear, easy to understand); it is sufficient for the meaning needed at that juncture, says neither too much nor too little; and it is believed to be true ("Logic"; "Further Notes"). Robert Sanders says that breaches of this process of conversational implicature may constitute the bases of fallacy claims (65). We will discuss each briefly, again focusing on intent. Innocent breaches of conversational implicature can, presumably, be repaired through further dialogue.

Irrelevant Utterance   Since the cooperative principle guides people to presume comments are relevant, it is possible to damage the critical process by making irrelevant statements with the intent that they be taken as relevant. We stopped at a small-town gas station recently, only then noticing that the price was ten cents a gallon more than the place across the street. The attendant, in response to our request for a justification for his high prices, said, "Well, you can go across the street if you are willing to put cut-rate gas in your car." We were supposed to presume that the quality of the cheaper gas was lower and even dangerous to use. An acquaintance who runs a station in the city says the difference in price was probably a function of one station being a "name" outlet and the other a cut-rate place. He says the gas at both places was probably about the same, since cut-rate stations often buy their gas from major name producers. That the other place was cut-rate was relevant, but not to gas quality.

Obfuscation   The cooperative principle leads us to presume that our interlocutors are doing their best to be clear and as easy to understand as possible. *Obfuscation*, as we use it here, is an intent to make communication unclear in order to secure adherence from those who trust in the commitment to clarity. The common paradigm case of unclarity—the IRS tax instructions and other publications of the federal government—probably would not count as obfuscation as defined. Bureaucrat-ese may be a disease, but it is usually not *intended* to confuse.

Obfuscation seems to abound in the statements of investment companies. Trying to convince people to invest in their funds but not violate government rules leads to some strange arguments. In the 1999 Annual Report of Evergreen National Municipal Bond Funds, this conclusion appears:

> Going forward, we anticipate a more stable interest rate environment than we've seen during the last year, both domestically and internationally. The moderately growing domestic economy and the solid, long-term fundamentals underlying the market lead us to a cautiously optimistic outlook (Ennis).

Today, many food products include some variation of the word *light* in their name or description. *Diet* is used similarly, as are *low-fat* and *no-cholesterol*. In these instances, there is the possibility of obfuscation by oversimplification. A diet or light product may contain a few calories or a hundred or more. A no-fat product may still be fattening, and a diet product may contain dangerous cholesterol while a no-cholesterol product may contain dangerous fat. The Food and Drug Administration tries, with limited success, to keep such practices under control, but each time it must advance a fallacy claim and sustain the burden of proof.

Violations of the Quantity Maxim   The cooperative principle says we presume that our communications say enough to make sense and no more. Violations of this *quantity maxim* seek adherence by taking advantage of that presumption while saying more or less than would otherwise be appropriate. Closely related to this potential fallacy claim is the concept of conflict of interest, in which some information that would be significant to a critical decision is withheld to mask multiple motives.

Tax advisers say that people get themselves in more trouble than necessary during audits with the Internal Revenue Service by saying too much. They advise people to answer questions with the minimum necessary to respond, and no more. The problem comes, say the advisers, when the audit seems over, people are standing up to leave, and the urge toward normal conversation returns: "Well," says the taxpayer, "I'm glad that's over, because I'm leaving tomorrow for my place in the Bahamas." "What place in the Bahamas?" asks the tax auditor. "Maybe we'd better sit back down."

There is a fine line between an honest withholding of information that is not legally required, as is recommended by tax advisers, and saying more or less than is reasonably needed for understanding just to secure adherence. In court, this took place:

> **PROSECUTOR:**   Did you sleep with this woman?
>
> **DEFENDANT:**   No.

The answer is true in one sense (they did not sleep), but untrue in the meaning communicated. If exposed, the defendant may be the subject of a fallacy claim of violating the quantity maxim. The waste disposal company that publishes data showing that a shipment contains "no hazardous waste" without saying that the shipment was originally hazardous by government standards but has barely fallen out of that definition through chemical changes, is the potential object of a fallacy claim.

This maxim can be violated by overstatement as well. The same waste disposal company may try to mask the danger of its shipment by publishing page upon page of details documenting what hazardous substances are *not* contained, just so the elements that *are* hazardous can be buried in excessive detail and thus be overlooked. This, too, may be the basis of a fallacy claim.

Conflict of Interest   Withholding of relevant information is usually the basis for charging a conflict of interest. When the ophthalmologist recommends an optical shop nearby, it is relevant to know it is owned by the ophthalmologist.

An acquaintance went to a lawyer to discuss a suit against a local company she believed had cheated her. The attorney advised her to forget about the incident and sent her away. Only later did she discover that the attorney had for many years been on retainer to represent the company in question. That discovery could count as the basis of a fallacy claim through conflict of interest.

A prominent law firm was retained by the state of Utah to defend an anti-abortion law that was under challenge by such entities as the Utah Women's Clinic. After billing the state for $170,000 in fees, the firm was discovered to represent the Utah Women's

Clinic in tax and employee benefit matters. Was it a conflict of interest to serve as attorneys for the clinic in some legal matters while at the same time opposing them in the suit over the anti-abortion law? The firm claimed there was no conflict of interest and refused to withdraw, but the state attorney general fired them.

More to the point is the question of why the firm had not notified the state at the outset about its representation of the clinic. Their failure to be "up-front" about the matter was probably more damaging than the fact of the representation itself. Knowing that the same firm had been ordered to withdraw from another case by the state supreme court because of conflict of interest simply added to their low credibility (House).

Reckless Disregard for the Truth   We have already discussed the intent to deceive; however, here we interpret the cooperative principle from a concept developed in law (see *New York Times* v. *Sullivan*). When someone participates in communication by providing information, we presume through the cooperative principle that they not only believe what they say but have some basis for that belief. In law, it may be considered malicious to communicate facts with reckless disregard for the truth, and that is the basis of this fallacy claim.

Newspapers usually make a practice of verifying stories before printing them, particularly when reporting sensitive facts such as that a banker is a heavy gambler. Independent sources are sought along with parallel confirmation. To make little or no effort to confirm a story may constitute reckless disregard for the truth, a fallacy claim. The CBS program *60 Minutes* interviewed people who claimed to have been paid as sources for news stories for which they had no information. What CBS was doing was making a fallacy claim of reckless disregard for the truth against some supermarket tabloids.

Conclusion

Fallacies are violations of significant rules of argumentation relevant to the appropriate decision makers. The notion of fallacy as incorrect logic is identified with the tradition of formal logic. While this perspective is generally not appropriate for the realm of argumentation, knowledge of specific fallacies within the system may serve as a critical guideline. Three formal fallacies are: affirmation of the consequent or denial of the antecedent; undistributed middle term; and mistaking validity for truth.

Identifying fallacies with sophistry has been a key element of informal logic. Here fallacies are seen as arguments that are persuasive when they should not be. Some specific fallacies are: *tu quoque;* begging the question; appeal to authority; appeal to popularity; *post hoc, ergo propter hoc;* fallacies in language; *ad hominem*; appeal to pity; appeal to fear; appeal to ignorance; appeal to force; appeal to prejudice; and pressure of the mob. While you cannot be sure a fallacy is present simply by noticing these argumentative forms, they can direct your attention toward such questions as whether or not an intent to deceive can be argued successfully.

Contemporary theories tend to see fallacies as violations of discussion rules. In critical interactions, there are some basic rules of rationality that can be suggested through a dialectical perspective. Fallacies occur when one of these discussion rules is violated. Mere blunders or misstatements of fact are not classified as fallacies. A fallacy must occur within argumentation and serve as a deliberate violation of accepted rules in order to gain an improper advantage.

We suggest that in making a refutation by fallacy claim, you integrate it with your overall refutation strategy. First, arguing a fallacy should make a substantial contribution to critical analysis at the highest conceptual level. Second, the fallacy claim must be effectively argued. You must accept and satisfy your burden of proving not only that a fallacy is present, but that its presence constitutes a significant and relevant consideration to the appropriate decision makers at the time.

Finally, there are enduring, socially negotiated guidelines for the development of fallacy claims that, while they do not point to certain fallacies, can be used to discern what may prove to be convincing fallacy claims: intent to deceive; refusal to reason; breach of conversational cooperation; irrelevant utterance; obfuscation; violations of the quantity maxim; conflict of interest; and reckless disregard for truth.

PROJECT

Select a letter to the editor published in a newspaper that commits what you believe to be a fallacy. Identify the fallacy and develop your argument proving why. Exchange your paper written in the first exercise with another student. Each of you write a response to the other's paper that argues one or both of these claims: (1) The alleged fallacy really is not fallacious; (2) the alleged fallacy would not be a fallacy used in another sphere.

PART THREE

Applications

Y ou know that argumentation and critical decision making occur within social entities called spheres. It is within the sphere that forms of argument are specified, criteria for their evaluation are enforced, and the character of argumentative cases is defined. While spheres are numerous and varied, there are some general areas of decision making that can be used to exemplify the way spheres shape argumentation. In this section, we discuss law, science, religion, business, and government and politics as highly generalized spheres.

CHAPTER

12 Argumentation in Law

KEY TERMS

trial

judges

jury

stare decisis

syllogism

law

analogy

relational structuring

temporal structuring

prima facie

story model

appeal

brief

presumption

appellate argument

burden of proof

decision

trial impact

Much of the argumentation practiced in a wide spectrum of spheres can be traced back to practices in law. For thousands of years, people seeking justice have understood the importance of identifying issues, clearly stating claims, and putting together cases. Knowing this, those working in other spheres have often borrowed concepts and procedures from the law to guide their own argumentation.

While the western legal tradition has a body of common argumentative practices that allows us to talk about it as a sphere, in practice there are many legal spheres or subspheres. For example, legal argumentation within the federal system has rules and procedures that differ from those prevailing in the states. And practices of argumentation in the law can vary substantially from one state to another, one locale to another, and even one judge's courtroom to another.

Furthermore, argumentation in law can vary according to the kind of case. Criminal cases call for argumentative practices that are different from those in civil cases. In criminal cases, for example, the argument must meet a greater burden of proof (beyond a reasonable doubt) than that required of arguments in civil cases (by a clear preponderance of evidence). And even within these broad concepts, argumentation in, say, a murder case can be different from that in a narcotics case. And argumentation in patent law, tax law, estate law, divorce law, labor law, environmental law, and torts (such as acts of negligence leading to personal injury) are quite different in many respects. Argumentation at the trial level is profoundly different from that before appellate courts.

So as we begin this chapter, we call your attention to the fact that while our example is fairly representative of argumentation within the legal sphere, it cannot be taken as directly applicable in all instances. It is only through experience that lawyers learn the subtle differences.

The Context

Legal decision making is usually characterized as working within a tightly controlled justice system based solely on law. But the thrust of research in legal realism and critical legal studies over almost a century argues that legal decisions are situated within social, cultural, political, psychological, and hegemonic contexts that powerfully influence how legal argument is developed and received by lawyers, juries, and judges (Aichele, Bauman; Sarat and Simon; Schlegel). Sociologist Gary LaFree argues that rape laws and their adjudication constitute a paradigm instance for considering the evolution of the law and its enforcement (13). For that reason, we have chosen a rather typical rape case (a real case we have fictionalized) as our way of describing legal argumentation.

Until fairly recently, rape convictions were difficult to obtain because prosecutors were under a heavy burden of proof. Not only did they carry the usual criminal burden of proving their case "beyond a reasonable doubt," they also had to work with a presumption that a woman's word alone could not be accepted as proof. Various forms of corroborating evidence were required and were most difficult to generate. "In 1969 New York police made 1,085 arrests for rape, and only eighteen men were convicted" (Toobin 41).

In the last quarter of the twentieth century, the situation began to change with the emergence of feminist groups charging that the laws were written and enforced largely by men who demonstrated their prejudices and sought to secure their social and political power (hegemony), particularly in the laws on rape. Today, "Feminists, with the assistance of the burgeoning victim's-rights movement, have swept away most of the legal impediments to rape convictions" (Toobin 41). So much so, claims sociologist Anne Hendershott, that the expanded definition of rape, "actually ends up removing power from women," causing them to depend on the protection of men "who attend date-rape lectures or participate in 'Take Back the Night' marches" (B7). Clearly the crime of rape reveals the many cultural forces at play.

Some specific incidents explain the widespread public interest in acquaintance rape today. Between 1993 and 2003, there were fifty-six cases of rape or sexual assault reported at the United States Air Force Academy. Air Force Secretary James G. Roche and Chief of Staff General John P. Jumper tacitly acknowledged these cases had not been handled properly when they announced that the top four academy commanders had been replaced and published an "Agenda for Change" that mandated significant improvement in handling sexual assault cases "in an expeditious, judicious, and sensitive manner . . . insuring justice both for the victim and the accused" (2003). It seems that the military-male dominance at the academy had restored presumptions thought to have been left in the past: women cadets claim that their reports of rapes were largely ignored on the presumption that a woman's testimony alone did not constitute proof.

In the history of the United States, rape and race have been closely associated. Between 1930 and 1976, there were 415 men executed for rape; 405 of them African American. And "almost all were charged with attacking white women" (Toobin 42). The highly publicized 2003 case of basketball star Kobe Bryant charged with raping a white woman who was a student at the University of Northern Colorado raised all kinds of speculation about race as well as the ability of the wealthy to defend themselves effectively in criminal proceedings. Bryant's annual income was about ten times the annual budget of the rural Colorado county prosecutor's office (Toobin 40).

It is, then, within this context that we turn to our case. Legal argumentation operates on the level of trials where fact and law are issues to be decided by juries and judges. It also operates at the level of appellate courts where questions of law are argued. We begin with the trial, and then turn to the appeal.

The Trial

John Howard Avery was charged with rape under Utah Code Ann. Sec. 76–5–402 (1991), in the Third Judicial District Court in and for Salt Lake County, the Honorable Brennan White presiding. The charge resulted from a complaint by Alberta Meyer that Avery had sexual intercourse with her without her consent. The Utah code states:

1. A person commits rape when the actor has sexual intercourse with another person without the victim's consent.
2. This section applies whether or not the actor is married to the victim.
3. Rape is a felony of the first degree.

Analysis through Critical Decision Making

You will recall from Chapter 4 that analysis should rest on the steps in critical decision making. The first opportunity for this analysis came when the prosecuting attorney learned of Ms. Meyer's claim. The question was whether or not her story was credible enough to warrant filing charges. Was it likely to convince a jury? Here is her story as reported in the appellate brief prepared by the attorney general of Utah:

> Alberta Meyer first met defendant John Howard Avery in early August 2003. Approximately a week later on August 12, 2003, they attended a wedding reception together. After the reception, [they] went to a club known as Casablanca. Throughout the evening they were friendly and even affectionate toward one another. Displays of affection consisted of brief hugging and some kissing, but there wasn't anything pushy, presumptuous or forward. They also danced and Avery ordered drinks for the two of them.
>
> Avery also spoke with some of his friends while at Casablanca whom he said he had been involved with in drug trafficking years ago. When Alberta asked defendant about these friends, he told her that they were people who were drug traffickers—dealers.

Shortly before Casablanca closed, Tony Olivera, a friend of defendant who worked at the club, invited defendant and Ms. Meyer to attend a party at his home after the club closed. They left Casablanca at approximately 1:00 to 1:30 a.m. as it was closing.

Defendant and the victim were the first to arrive at the party, along with Gale Crockett and his companion that evening, Katherine Oberer. During the party, defendant and the victim continued to be affectionate, much as they had been while at Casablanca. Although drinks were served at the party, neither defendant nor the victim consumed any alcohol while at the Olivera residence.

As other people began to arrive, defendant spoke with Gale Crockett. The victim sat down on the couch near them and defendant then sat down next to her and kissed her. Mr. Crockett and Ms. Oberer then were "going to light a bowl up," but Mr. Olivera told them not to smoke marijuana in his house and to go outside on the balcony, and they complied. Neither Gale Crockett nor Katherine Oberer saw the victim or defendant again that night.

Ms. Meyer asked Mr. Olivera where the restroom was, and he indicated that it was down the hall. Defendant said he also had to use the restroom, and so the two proceeded down the hallway. As the victim was going into the bedroom to use the main bathroom, defendant grabbed her and pulled her into the other restroom. Defendant closed the door, pushed the victim into the corner and started to undress her. The victim stated that she told defendant to stop and resisted his advances. Defendant relented only after other people started knocking on the door to use the restroom. The victim testified that she did not tell others at the party about what happened in the restroom because she thought defendant just had too much to drink; wanted to see how far he could go.

[Avery and Meyer] then went into the master bedroom where they spoke with Mr. Olivera. The defendant then used the restroom and [Meyer] continued to speak with Mr. Olivera until he was called away. Defendant came out of the bathroom, looked around the bedroom, down the hallway, closed and locked the bedroom door, and turned the light off. Defendant then went over to the bed where the victim was sitting and pushed her backward onto the bed. Despite the victim's repeated protestations, defendant proceeded to undress her. The victim testified that defendant told her to "shut up" and that she "would enjoy it."

The victim stated that she continued to resist defendant's advances, and defendant threatened to have Gale Crockett and his other friends help him rape her if she resisted or cried out for help. She stated that defendant told her, "they'll hold you down and they'll want their turn. And the only way you'll leave here is in an ambulance." The victim was afraid to scream because she did not know anybody at the party and didn't want to call his bluff. Defendant then forced the victim to have sexual intercourse.

Knowing that Utah law allows a person to be convicted of rape solely on the testimony of the victim, the prosecuting attorney could have filed charges after hearing only Ms. Meyer's statement. However, critical decision-making processes mandate a survey of the range of objectives and values implicated and a canvass of a wide range of alternative decisions. In this case, as in many others, there is always the possibility that anger, jealousy, revenge, or other motives may move someone to make false charges. It makes good sense to see how the story checks out.

In an interview with Mr. Avery, the prosecutor heard another version of the story. Avery did not deny most of what Ms. Meyer said, including the fact that they had sexual intercourse. But Avery claimed that Ms. Meyer had been very affectionate all night long, at the bar and at the party, she had encouraged him, and there were people who had observed her encouragement right up to the time they went into the bedroom. According to the Utah Supreme Court, this is what Avery claimed:

> He testified that he entered the restroom first and Meyer followed him in and initiated the sexual conduct. When people began knocking on the door, he suggested that they find a more appropriate place to continue. She agreed, and they went into the master bedroom. While in the bedroom, they spoke with Olivera. Avery asked Olivera if he and Meyer could use the room. Olivera agreed, left, and closed and locked the door behind him. Avery and Meyer then began to have sexual intercourse. Avery stated that they discussed birth control and he agreed [but failed to carry out his agreement]. His failure caused Meyer to become very angry. When defendant took her home, she was still upset.

Still following the mandate of critical decision making to search for new information and criticize alternatives, the prosecuting attorney then interviewed Jackie Sheraton, a friend of the victim's, who said that on the morning after the party (it was close to dawn when Meyer got home), Meyer told her about what happened. She said that Meyer was "distraught, confused, and kept saying something had happened and it was very wrong." Ms. Meyer then went to the hospital where a Code R (a test to verify sexual intercourse) was performed.

Within a few hours, Ms. Meyer reported to the police. Jeff Sorensen, a police officer, said that he questioned Meyer after she reported the alleged rape and her story told to the prosecutor was consistent with what she told him on the morning after the incident. Mr. Olivera told the prosecutor that he did not remember having a conversation with Avery about his using the bedroom, nor did he remember closing and locking the bedroom door.

Since Ms. Meyer's story seemed to be supported by other witnesses and evidence with sufficient force to warrant the selection of a proposition (in law, a charge), the prosecutor decided to go forward with the case. He had to build a prima facie case for the charge selected. Criminal codes are so complex and varied that prosecutors have a wide range of latitude in selecting the charge or proposition they intend to advance. Obviously, they try to choose the charge that seems most appropriate to the alleged facts, but they do so with an eye on what they believe they can realistically support in court.

The prosecutor might have chosen a less serious felony or a misdemeanor with lighter penalties, which a jury might find easier to accept. Forcible sexual abuse, for example (Utah Code Ann. Sec. 76–5–404 (1990)), is a second-degree felony. It is defined as follows:

> A person commits forcible sexual abuse if the victim is 14 years of age or older and, under circumstances not amounting to rape, object rape, sodomy, or attempted rape or sodomy, the actor touches the anus, buttocks, or any part of the genitals of another, or touches the breast of a female, or otherwise takes indecent liberties with another, or causes another to take indecent liberties with the actor or another, with intent to cause substantial emotional or bodily pain to any person or with the intent to arouse or gratify the sexual desire of any person, without the consent of the other, regardless of the sex of any participant.

This would be an easier charge to prove, and its lighter penalty might be more appealing to jurors. In this case, however, the prosecutor decided to claim that John Howard Avery was guilty of rape, a proposition of fact and law (value).

Decision Makers in the Legal Sphere   Legal arguments must satisfy two quite different kinds of decision makers. In that sense, law can be called a "multi-layered and multi-faceted" sphere (Newell and Rieke 212). The first group of decision makers consists of judges, and the second consists of jurors. There is actually a third set of decision makers, appellate judges, whom we will discuss in the second half of the chapter. As we will explain, their criteria for assessing arguments are essentially the same as trial court judges.

Judges are trained in the law and are charged with the responsibility of ensuring that lawyers' arguments satisfy the law in such areas as these:

1. Whether a particular court has jurisdiction over the case
2. Whether the case has been properly brought before the court
3. Whether a prima facie case has been advanced
4. Whether certain testimony and physical evidence can be properly admitted
5. Whether the trial has operated within the demands of due process of law
6. How the jury is to apply the law to their decision on the facts

Jurors, on the other hand, have the singular task of determining the facts: what happened in the case with which the court is concerned. In this case, they will have to decide which story to believe about the alleged rape. Lawyers will need to address both sets of decision makers and satisfy their quite different demands on their arguments.

Forms of Argument in the Law   Just as there are two kinds of decision makers in the law, there are two broad sets of argument forms required to satisfy the decision makers. Judges demand arguments that use such warrants as these suggested by former U.S. Supreme Court Justice Benjamin N. Cardozo:

1. Past court decisions (the common law) that have set precedents (*stare decisis*)
2. Federal and state constitutions
3. Federal, state, and local statutes or codes
4. History, custom, or tradition
5. Legislative intent
6. The pragmatic effect of decisions (51–180)

The arguments are usually structured along the lines of a logical syllogism as we describe in Chapter 3. The basic format is this:

| Major Premise: | This is the relevant law. . . . |
| Support: | One of the six warrants above. |

Minor Premise:	The facts of the present case are embraced within those contemplated in the law.
Support:	The jury's findings of facts in comparison with the facts of similar cases already decided.
Conclusion:	This case should be decided according to the law stated in the major premise.

When attorneys argue issues of law (value) as we have just described, they address themselves exclusively to the judge. Most often, the jury is dismissed so that they do not hear these arguments.

The judge will evaluate the arguments according to the criteria suggested by Justice Cardozo, with the strongest attention being given to previous cases that involved issues like the ones now before the court. If one side can find a case decided by the highest legal authority (see "Argument by Authority" in Chapter 6), the Supreme Court of the United States, where the facts are almost exactly the same as this case, and where the court set down a specific test stating the criteria by which the ruling is to be applied, the judge is likely to give it a high evaluation.

This is reasoning by *analogy* as we explain in Chapter 6. One or more cases are presented as essentially the same as the present case to the end that the present case should be decided the same way the previous cases were decided.

The argument is strengthened by the authority of the court that made the decision. Decisions by courts in other states are considered, but are not given as much authority as decisions made by courts in the state where the case is being tried, or by the Supreme Court of the United States.

Even when arguments are presented to the jury, they must continuously satisfy the requirements of the law. And the sequence of evidence (witnesses, documents, physical evidence, expert testimony) also tends to conform to the legal structure. Yet the jury members, as relevant decision makers, have no experience or knowledge of the law. So, attorneys must also structure arguments for them in the form of a good story, as we describe in Chapter 3, or a retrospective convincing vision as discussed in Chapter 5.

This means that jurors are exposed to arguments involving *relational structuring,* how the evidence relates to claims in the legal structure we have just described, and *temporal structuring,* how events of the conflicting stories are ordered in time. This involves coming up with a scenario that puts people, motives, causes, and effects into a satisfying structure (Schum).

The jurors conceive of the trial in terms of causal relationships—who did what to cause this? They put these causal arguments into the context of a story with a beginning, middle, and end. The jurors' stories include episodes or scenes embedded within the major story line of varying levels of significance. At the time of the verdict, juries construct a common story with episodes that match the requirements of the law as given in a judge's instructions to the jury (Hastie, Penrod, and Pennington).

The story model used by juries, which, therefore, identifies the argument form to be used by attorneys, contains three stages:

1. Put the trial evidence into meaningful structure through the addition of jury members' own sense of reality.
2. Specifically identify the requirements of the law in relation to possible verdicts.
3. Go back and revise the story in Number One so that it satisfies the requirements in Number Two (Pennington and Hastie).

The jury, therefore, evaluates arguments by testing them against their sense of how people behave and how events reasonably take place. Then they test the story against their understanding of the law. If they can find a sensible story that correlates with the expectations of the law, they have their verdict.

With this understanding of the two kinds of decision makers who must be satisfied and the argument forms they use to evaluate arguments, we can now turn to the case-building stage of this trial.

Building the Case

In law, a *prima facie* case is one that presents arguments that affirm all the essential elements of the proposition. To find what those elements are, a prosecutor looks to the wording of the law and the language of appellate courts in interpreting it. In Utah in 2003, a charge of rape required affirmation of two essential issues:

1. Did sexual intercourse occur between Avery and Meyer?
2. Did sexual intercourse occur without Meyer's consent?

The prosecutor had to work within the legal demands set and enforced by the trial judge and possibly by one or more appellate courts, but not behave in such a dry, legalistic manner as to lose the support of the jury. Because society puts the burden of proof on the state, the prosecutor must present arguments to answer yes to both these essential elements while developing a convincing vision around which the jury could construct its story.

In this instance, there was a good deal of uncontroversial matter (see Chapter 4). Avery did not deny that sexual intercourse had occurred. Although the prosecutor had to put evidence in support of that fact into the record to satisfy the appellate court, there would be no problem with it before the jury. So the only potential issue the prosecutor could foresee was whether Meyer had given her consent.

What counterarguments could be anticipated? When informed of the charges against him, Avery immediately found a lawyer, Morris Medford, to defend him. He paid him $9,000, told him his side of the story as we have already reported, and gave him the names of people who could give testimony to support his version. He mentioned Gayla Harrison, the bartender at Casablanca, who could testify that Meyer had been affectionate and quite willing while they were drinking and dancing together. He also identified Katherine Oberer and Omar Ortiz, who had been at the party. Avery said they would testify that they saw Avery and Meyer "engaging in kissing, fondling and other intense sexual play." Ms. Oberer would say she saw them "making out" quite passionately on the couch for ten or fifteen minutes before they went to the bedroom. Medford said he would proceed to prepare a defense.

Let's see how the prosecution's trial brief anticipating the counterarguments of the defense might have looked.

Prosecution's Trial Brief

I. Avery and Meyer had sex.
   A. Meyer testifies so.
   B. Avery agrees.
   C. Hospital test confirms.

I. Defense does not deny this claim.

II. Meyer did not consent.
   A. Meyer says so.
   B. Tony Olivera denies he gave permission to use the bedroom.
   C. Jackie Sheraton says Meyer was distraught; what happened was wrong.
   D. Jeff Sorensen says Meyer's story at trial is consistent with what she said the morning after the incident.

II. Meyer did consent.
   A. Avery says so.
   B. Avery says Olivera gave permission to use the bedroom.
   C. Gayla Harrison says Meyer was affectionate and willing.
   D. Katherine Oberer says they were passionate on the couch.
   E. Avery says she's just angry over a careless birth control method.

What convincing vision of this case could the prosecutor develop? The jury's presumptions had to be considered. How would they view the events? A woman going to the apartment of those identified as drug traffickers whom she did not know, with a man she had only recently met, could be viewed by ordinary people in a conservative state like Utah as asking for trouble. If the jury additionally understood her behavior as having been sexually promiscuous, they might well believe Avery.

How does the prosecutor begin the opening statement, in which the convincing vision of a legal case is set out, so as to portray Ms. Meyer as a victim, not a willing participant? Let's listen to what the prosecutor might have said.

> Jackie Sheraton was half awake, trying to convince herself to get up, when she heard her doorbell ringing and ringing. Angry at such impatience at 6:00 a.m., she shouted through the door, "Who is it?" All she heard were incoherent sobs. Now frightened at what was going on outside, she looked through the peephole in the door. She saw her friend Berty Meyer, tears washing through mascara making her face appear ghostly, collapsing against the door.
>
> Later, after a cup of coffee and lots of comforting talk, during which Berty had seemed distraught, confused, saying over and over again that something had happened and it was very wrong, Jackie learned that Berty had been a victim of acquaintance rape. Jackie knew about this; she had read about the fact that most rapes are committed not by strangers

who leap out from behind bushes but by those who are friends, family, or dating partners. She knew that just because a woman agrees to date a man it does not follow that she is willing to have sex with him, but men don't always behave according to this rule.

Jackie urged Berty to go to the police, but Berty said, as Jackie will testify, she was afraid everyone would think she was a slut, that she would be put through embarrassing and demeaning attacks. Like so many victims of acquaintance rape, she wanted to pretend it never happened. But finally, Jackie convinced her that if women don't take the initiative to come forward and see that rapists are punished, there will just be more silent victims.

John Howard Avery does not deny that he had sexual intercourse with Berty. But he will ask you to believe that Berty willingly had sex with him, went home at dawn, and then went to the home of her friend Jackie on the point of collapse, resisting the idea of making a police report until finally accepting Jackie's arguments, and then agreeing to go to the hospital for a test and then on to the police for their interrogation just because she was angry over the way he made love. He will ask you to believe Berty gave her consent and then decided to charge rape because he did not keep his word on a method of birth control.

Because the charge of rape turns almost completely on the word of the victim, it is important that the prosecutor make that word as credible as possible. Giving the jury the first impression, which is the most powerful and lasting (Rieke and Stutman 109–13), of Berty in tears, collapsing on her friend's doorstep, will shape the way they hear all the other testimony. As long as they hold the vision of her as victim, they will probably discount testimony of her affectionate behavior earlier in the evening. After all, kissing and hugging do not amount to an invitation to have sex.

At the trial, the prosecutor laid out the case; defense attorney Morris Medford cross-examined Meyer to challenge her story, called Avery to the stand to give his version, and called Gayla Harrison, who told the jury how affectionate the two had been at the bar.

Medford had not interviewed Harrison before the day of the trial, nor had he made contact with any of the other witnesses Avery had suggested. Avery was convicted of rape and was sentenced to an indeterminate term of five years to life in the state penitentiary.

The Appeal

Avery dismissed Mr. Medford as his attorney, hired another one, and appealed his conviction on the grounds that he had received ineffective assistance of counsel.

We must now consider a different form of analysis and case building as it occurs before appellate courts. Now, of course, the presumption and burden of proof have shifted. Until his conviction, Avery was presumed innocent and the burden of proof rested on the state. It was the state that had the obligation to advance and defend a *prima facie* case. With conviction, presumption shifts: Avery is held guilty of rape unless and until he advances a prima facie case to show that his conviction should be reversed or that he should receive a new trial. We will outline his brief first, then give the state's response.

Appellate Brief

At the appellate level, analysis turns to questions of law found in six sources of law mentioned on page 228. Particular attention is given to constitutions, statutes, and, most predominantly, the published decisions of appellate courts. This process resembles the brief discussed in Chapter 5. In an appellate brief, lawyers are usually required to establish their case in the following order.

Statement of Jurisdiction   The appellate court must be satisfied that it has jurisdiction over the case. A reference to the Utah Code Ann. Sec. 78–2–2(3)(h)(i)(Cum. Supp. 1989) satisfied this requirement.

Nature of Proceedings   The court wants to know the history of the case. They are told that this is an appeal from a conviction and final judgment entered against the appellant in the Third Judicial District Court, where the appellant was convicted of rape by a jury.

Statement of the Issue Presented on Appeal   The brief must identify the point of law on which the appellant asks appellate consideration. Specifically, it argues that the law guarantees a defendant effective assistance by trial counsel, and Avery did not receive that from lawyer Morris Medford.

Applicable Constitutional Provisions, Statutes, and Rules   To call attention to the applicable constitutional provisions, statutes, and rules, the brief cites the Sixth and Fourteenth Amendments to the U.S. Constitution and Article 1, Section 12 of the Utah Constitution, all of which refer to one's right to a speedy public trial by an impartial jury under conditions of due process of law and representation by counsel.

Statement of the Case   The appellant states that his lawyer's failure to interview all the potential witnesses, his failure to interview Avery and Ms. Harrison, whom he called as witnesses, until the day of the trial, and his failure to call other witnesses to testify constitute failure to render effective assistance by trial counsel, guaranteed by the constitutional provisions cited. In essence, Avery accused his lawyer of failing to conduct critical decision making procedures and thus failing to build and present an effective case.

Statement of the Facts   The brief reviews the story of the trial as we did on pages 225–227.

Summary of the Argument   The brief reviews the claims of ineffective counsel and concludes that the appellate court should reverse the trial court and order a new trial, because Avery's conviction was unfair. He might not have been convicted had he been effectively represented.

Now comes the main section of an appellate brief.

Argument   What is required to make a prima facie case on appeal? The lawyers turn to precedent—judicial decisions on previous cases with similar fact situations. In the United States, appellate courts generally follow a rule of *stare decisis,* which commands the court to let previous decisions stand and not upset that which is settled. So if the advocate can convince the court that this case is like prior cases already decided, that will constitute powerful support.

In our earlier discussion of arguments to judges, we said that attorneys try to find a case (or cases) meeting these demands:

1. Decided by the U.S. Supreme Court, the most powerful legal authority available
2. Dealing with a fact situation very close to the present case (analogy)
3. Where there is a clear statement of the rule (criteria for decision) to be followed

Appellate courts evaluate arguments according to these criteria along with judging the extent to which the rule makes sense in this case. The greater the legal authority, the more analogous the previous case(s), the clearer the rule of law or test, and the more clearly the rule seems to make good law, the stronger the argument will be in the eyes of most appellate judges.

The appellate justices' job of argument evaluation is made difficult in proportion to the strength of the other side's arguments. When the arguments are similarly strong, which is not uncommon, the decision may turn primarily on the question of which decision makes the best law—produces the most just decision—in this instance. See if you think the following argument meets those criteria.

In a case decided by the United States Supreme Court, *Strickland v. Washington,* the essential elements (the criteria for decision or the test) of a case on ineffective assistance of counsel are set forth. The court identifies these issues:

1. Whether counsel's performance was defective. This requires a showing that counsel made errors so serious that counsel was not functioning as the "counsel" guaranteed the defendant by the Sixth Amendment to the U.S. Constitution.
2. Whether the deficient performance prejudiced the defense. This requires showing that counsel's errors were so serious as to deprive the defendant of a fair trial, a trial whose result is reliable.

The Utah Supreme Court decided, in *State v. Verde,* that Utah courts are to decide ineffective assistance of counsel claims by applying Strickland's two issues. Then the brief goes on to provide a discussion of legal interpretations of these and other cases so as to show their relevance to this case.

On the question of presumption, the brief reminds the court that at trial, presumption favored Avery. It would not have been necessary to prove that Meyer gave her consent, only that there is reasonable doubt that she did not. So the argument comes down to this: Did Medford's failure to interview witnesses prior to trial, and his failure to call more witnesses to testify, constitute ineffective assistance of counsel? Might the jury have entertained a reasonable doubt about Meyer's story if they had heard other witnesses or more effective testimony?

Avery's arguments, therefore, make these responses to the essential elements.

I. Counsel's performance was defective. Medford failed to interview his witnesses before the day of the trial, and he failed to call witnesses who could have strengthened his case.

    A. He chose to call Gayla Harrison to testify to the fact that Meyer had been affectionate with Avery, and she did that with regard to the time they were at Casablanca. But it was only shortly before the trial that Medford learned that Harrison did not attend the party and could say nothing about their behavior there. So Medford learned that he lacked any evidence about their behavior at the party too late to call other witnesses. Had he interviewed Harrison earlier, he would have had time to call other witnesses.

    B. Avery gave Medford the names of other witnesses, particularly Oberer, who could have testified that Meyer was affectionate and "made out on the couch" with Avery for ten or fifteen minutes before they went into the bedroom. Medford failed to call them.

II. Deficient performance did prejudice the defense.

    A. If Medford had interviewed the witnesses Avery supplied, he probably would have called them.

    B. If the other witnesses had testified, they would have shed reasonable doubt on Meyer's claim of rape. Her ten or fifteen-minute "making out" session on the couch could well have created a reasonable doubt in the minds of the jurors.

The Attorney General's Response

The attorney general of Utah, arguing as appellee, denied the claim of ineffective assistance by counsel. The state claimed that Avery did not give the names of potential witnesses to Medford in enough time for him to check them out, that Avery was not communicative with Medford, and that Medford's decision not to call former drug traffickers as witnesses was within the range of what reasonable attorneys would have concluded. Furthermore, the state argued that Avery's story was so patently false that no amount of testimony about Meyer's behavior would have put the jury into a state of doubt. Finally, there were inconsistencies in Oberer's statement about "making out" that did not even fit with Avery's story.

The Appellate Decision

The Utah Supreme Court agreed with Avery. They said this:

> If counsel does not adequately investigate the underlying facts of a case, including the availability of prospective defense witnesses, counsel's performance cannot fall within the "wide range of reasonable professional assistance." This is because a decision not to investigate cannot be considered a tactical decision. It is only after an adequate inquiry has been made that counsel can make a reasonable decision to call or not to call particular witnesses for tactical reasons. Therefore, because defendant's trial counsel did not make a reasonable investigation into the possibility of procuring prospective defense witnesses, the first part of the Strickland test has been met.

In the instant case, the second part of the Strickland test has also been met. If called as witnesses, several of the people would have testified to the amount of consensual physical contact that occurred between Meyer and Avery at Casablanca. The most important witness would have been Katherine Oberer, who had the opportunity to observe the couple both at the club and at the party, where, according to Meyer, the rape occurred. This testimony is important for the reason that it reflects upon the credibility of Meyer, because Oberer's testimony, although not completely consistent with Avery's testimony, contradicts several aspects of Meyer's testimony. This is important in the instant case because Meyer's testimony is the only direct evidence of Avery's guilt.

In reviewing this testimony, it is important to note that because it affects the credibility of the only witness who gave direct evidence of defendant's guilt, the testimony affects the "entire evidentiary picture." It should also be noted that although it is undisputed that a person can be convicted of rape solely on the testimony of the victim, the State's case rested upon the testimony of one person. There is no independent physical evidence that supports or contradicts Meyer's testimony. The conviction, therefore, is not strongly supported by the record. There is reasonable probability that if these witnesses had been called at trial, the outcome of the trial would have been different. Since both parts of the Strickland test have been met, we hold that Avery was denied his constitutional right to effective assistance of counsel.

Reversed and remanded for a new trial.

The language in the final paragraph of the court's opinion reflects the work of defense counsel at oral argument. After only reading the briefs, the supreme court was unanimously in favor of upholding the conviction of Avery. But, during oral argument, Avery's lawyer crystallized the vision of the case: what was one person's word against another might have changed had Oberer been called to testify about the behavior on the couch. What had been a unanimous court in one direction—to uphold the conviction—changed to a unanimous court for reversal. The power of oral argument cannot be dismissed.

If you review the criteria for a judicial argument, and then read the opinion in the light of those criteria, you will see that their argument followed the criteria closely. Arguments presented by attorneys to judges and the arguments judges use in reporting their decision or opinion conform to the same set of criteria.

In this case, because the Strickland rule was well established, the appellate court finally made its decision on the extent to which the facts of this case met the test. In that sense, it was the good story or vision the appellate counsel could communicate of *how the trial might have been conducted by an effective counsel* that was crucial in deciding the case.

The Impact of the Trial

A great deal of time and money was spent on this criminal trial, only to result in an appellate court's decision that it had to be done all over again. The court would not allow a defense lawyer to fail to perform effective analysis and case building that resulted, or may have resulted, in his client being convicted and sentenced to five years to life in the penitentiary. This case serves as an excellent illustration of the importance of analysis and case building in law.

In particular, the case illustrates how following the steps of critical decision making will guide you to effective argumentation. Notice that the Utah Supreme Court finds that a decision not to engage in these steps, as Avery's first lawyer did, can never be a strategic choice. In argumentation, strategic choices of how to build and present a case must rest on the fullest possible knowledge of the relevant claims, facts, values, issues, and potential propositions.

Counterarguments or defense cases cannot rest on inadequate analysis. It may well have been that the prosecutor shifted presumption at the very beginning of the trial by communicating a convincing vision of the case that Meyer was a victim of rape, not a willing sex partner. So the defense lawyer had to have available the strongest possible support for a counterargument.

By the time the defense put its witnesses on the stand, the jury may well have developed a presumption in favor of conviction. As we said earlier, when skill at argumentation and communication are equal, the side that has done the best analysis and case building based on the best research will probably prevail.

The prosecutor was faced once again with the prospect of a rape trial against Mr. Avery. Ms. Meyer was willing to go through it once more. But Avery had already spent a total of about twenty-two months in prison, and the prosecutor did not relish the idea of a new trial. A plea bargain was struck: Avery entered a guilty plea to forcible sexual abuse, and the court credited him with the time already served and set him free on parole. If there had been a new trial, though, you can bet Avery's lawyer would have taken the case quite seriously.

Conclusion

We have examined the law as a general sphere of argument in relation to a specific trial from start to finish. The importance of thorough analysis based on the steps in critical decision making is emphasized at the trial level and in the appellate court opinion.

The two types of decision makers in the law, judges and jurors, have been discussed in terms of the argumentation that must be adapted to their special criteria. Judges demand a relational structure in which claims, evidence, and law are logically displayed. Jurors respond best to a good story that provides a temporal structure. That helps them form an image of the characters, motives, events, and causes that will form the fact situation of the case.

We have illustrated the format for a trial brief and an appellate brief, indicating how they are quite different. Finally, we have noticed how appellate courts structure their opinions along the same argumentative structure that is used by attorneys in arguing the case.

PROJECT

Go to your local courthouse—municipal, county, state, or federal—and spend at least two hours watching a trial. Courts are completely open to the public; you do not need permission. Write a report on the argumentation you observed.

13 Argumentation in Science

KEY TERMS

science	positionality
natural order	sign
fact claims	model
empirical	homology
peer	review authority
generalization	grounded claims
abduction	specific instances
hypothesis	statistical probability
theory	testimony
scientific law	replicate
conditional cause	operationalize

For many people, scientific methods stand as the most competent way to understand what is going on in the world. Scientific standards for evidence and argument are held up as the way to understand what the natural world is like. Arguments that fail such tests are easily disregarded, not only by the scientists who work in the sphere, but by lay persons as well. The sphere of science has great credibility in our society, and an examination of its understanding of evidence and argument will provide insight into the standards people frequently seek in public arguments.

First, let us define *science*. There are, after all, terms like *physical science, human science, political science, life science, natural science,* and so on. There is the distinction made by many between quantitative and qualitative science. In this chapter, we take our definition of science from physicist F. David Peat. Peat described science as "that story our society tells itself about the cosmos." It you think back to Chapter 3, you may recall our statement that stories, or narratives, are important forms of argument. The science narrative provides a supposedly "objective account of the material world based upon measurement and quantification so that structure, process, movement, and transformation can be described mathematically in terms of fundamental laws" (208). Most of the scientific endeavors that fall within this account are quantitative, using physical science as a model and mathematics as a foundation to develop explanatory theories of how entities function. Science is more than method, however, as outlined in C. P. Snow's classic book *Two Cultures,* which describes the different modes of understanding that separate science from the arts and humanities. Thus, science refers to a way of understanding ourselves and the universe that differs from humanistic (literary, historical, philosophical) inquiry. Science also differs from *research,* in which investigators seek to understand individual phenomena rather than natural laws, and in which they rely on qualitative and critical methods.

Some postmodern and feminist scholars have challenged the narrative described in the previous paragraph. Their critique argues that, because scientists cannot be neutral and objective, scientific knowledge cannot be the outcome of unbiased rational thought. Therefore, the understanding gained through science is no more accurate than understanding gained through other approaches, such as astrology or palm reading. From this perspective, science is a game with a set of rules created by scientists, and apparent successes of science in understanding the universe would not be defensible if society did not accept the rules of the scientific game. Postmodern critiques of science sometimes question whether a natural world exists outside of the mental constructs that humans erect. According to these critiques, science is no more than an elaborate social construct dedicated to maintaining existing patterns of hegemony.

On the other hand, less extreme forms of postmodernism and feminism have argued for more rigorous self-examination by scientists, an activity that is in harmony with science's basic tenets. For example, feminist critiques of science have argued that scientific theory and practice marginalize women. In response to this claim, the National Science Foundation has developed educational programs that affirmatively encourage young girls to study science and mathematics, has developed grant programs exclusively for women scientists, and has hosted seminars designed to encourage feminist scholars and traditional scientists to engage in critical discussions about the philosophy of science. The story of science, as modified by postmodern and feminist critique, has expanded to include alternative ways of asking questions about the universe. F. David Peat claimed that as long as these approaches "engage in disciplined argument and deduction, and that there is an element of careful attention to an observation, then the knowledge systems of other cultures have the right to stand as scientific viewpoints" (209). This does not mean science has given up its search for understanding, nor does it translate into science as social construct. If you fall down the stairs, you are likely to at least get a few bruises. If you spend all of Saturday and Sunday partying, you will be less able to comprehend the 8:00 a.m. lecture on Monday morning than if you obtained some sleep over the weekend. Notice that the expected results in these two examples include uncertainty—as does all scientific prediction. Although this chapter focuses on the use of argumentation in science as defined by the traditional markers of objectivity and quantification as a means of discovering fundamental laws, it is important to realize that the values of objectivity and quantification are merely markers, and that discovery is the goal.

The sphere of quantitative science can sometimes be identified by academic departments (e.g., physics, chemistry, geology, biology) in the physical and biological sciences. But many academic departments in the social sciences have some faculty members who are oriented to the quantitative while others are more qualitative in their research (e.g., anthropology, communication, linguistics, political science, psychology, sociology). The science that we discuss in this chapter is the quantitative, and it ranges over a wide variety of fields with the physical sciences as its model.

We also need to distinguish between what we call *scientific argumentation* and the political argumentation that is frequently associated with science. Scientists may be motivated to see that federal funding goes to their particular research. In addition, they may argue before public agencies for certain policy options. They may even argue that particular scientists are not competent or have falsified data. These are all part of a political role that scientists frequently play. This political role of scientists is illustrated in their public arguments over global warming, restrictions on secondhand smoke, child safety restraints in automobiles, and a host of other policy matters.

We propose to examine not this significant political role of scientists but how scientists argue as scientists: What kind of argument and evidence will they most admire in the scientific journals, research papers, and grant applications? Although we realize that scientists frequently argue in the public sphere as experts, we look here at how scientists are supposed to argue where other scientists are the decision makers. We will examine how science is integrated into political argument in Chapter 16.

The values of scientific study begin with the value of discovering order in nature through empirical and modeled rational (mathematical and logical) means. This natural order is first engaged through observation (empiricism). These observations are represented through agreed-upon procedures in numerical forms of evidence that support *hypotheses,* or tentative assumptions made in order to draw out and test their empirical and/or logical consequences. Ideally, science proceeds from hypothesis testing, to theory development, to discovery of natural law. In this context, a *theory* refers to a hypothesis that has been subjected to testing, and thus offers greater likelihood of truth. A *law* refers to a statement about how some aspects of the natural world are organized. To refer to something as a scientific law is to claim that it is invariable under the same conditions.

Even if the natural order cannot be directly observed (i.e., you cannot observe a quark, a neutron, or an attitude) scientists still require that there be *empirical adequacy.* That is, the signs of the phenomenon must be observable. The procedures for finding these claims of fact must be clearly defined so that they may be replicated or questioned. These claims of fact are linked together to provide theoretical propositions of explanation. Such propositions are in turn used to predict another specific situation that has not been observed. That is, the signs of the phenomenon must be either directly or indirectly observable.

It is stated in claims of fact combined with other claims of fact already acknowledged to provide a *proposition of cause.* In the same way, a scientist could argue that the same causes will function in the future on another phenomenon that can never be directly observed. The same assumption, of the ability of theory to predict, holds for theories about gene structure, compliance gaining among humans, or social structure.

From this perspective a theory about climate change is built from careful observation of the geological record. The case of global climate change is a useful place to begin our discussion of how the scientific method functions argumentatively, because there is widespread interest in this issue. In this chapter we will limit the discussion to argument within the scientific community. In Chapter 16, we will show how the argument changes when it moves into the sphere of government and politics.

Global climate change is a complex phenomenon that is planetary in scope and operates on a time scale that exceeds seasons, political terms, and the human life span. Global climate change differs from *weather* in both its spatial and temporal expanse. Over the twentieth century, the earth's annual mean temperature increased by about 2°F. Given this small number, you may be wondering what all the fuss is about. After all, the temperature fluctuates more than that between noon and midnight, and between winter and summer. Physiological mechanisms have evolved that enable living things to adjust to short-term (easily up to a year) and localized changes in temperature. The problem is, however, that a small change is a serious matter to the global climate system. Temperatures that continue to increase over a long time and across the entire planet influence a complex system of intertwined processes that absorb or reflect sunshine, transport heat around the globe through the atmosphere and oceans, and exchange chemicals to and from different parts of the system. And humans depend on that system to support their lifestyles, not to mention their biological survival. Thus, it is no wonder that global climate change has been the subject of extensive scientific investigation (Intergovernmental Panel on Climate Change).

The Tradition of Argumentation in Science

There are several ways that the climate change debate helps to define the tradition of argumentation in the science sphere, four of which serve as a preliminary definition of scientific argumentation. They are that science (1) deals in claims and propositions of fact; (2) searches for truth over personal gain; (3) reveals results that are complete enough to test; and (4) establishes theory that changes slowly.

Claims of Fact

First, traditional scientific argument, in its central concern, argues claims and propositions of fact. Stephen Toulmin, et al. identify four "broad and familiar issues" of science:

1. What kinds of things are there [or were there] in the world of nature?
2. How are [or were] these things composed, and how does this makeup affect their behavior or operation?
3. How did all these things come to be composed as they are [or were]?
4. What are the characteristic functions of each such natural thing and/or its parts? (315)

In the case of global climate change, scientists deal with issues like: (1) Is it occurring? (2) What has been causing it? (3) Does it pose dangers or problems to human society as a whole, as well as to specific segments of human society? (4) How serious are those dangers? and (5) What can be done to either slow or stop the warming trend?

All these questions must be answered by claims of fact. The policy questions that might come up move the argument into the realm of government and politics, which we discuss in Chapter 16.

Henry N. Pollack, a professor of geophysics who has studied global climate change for over forty years, described questions of fact that summarize the scientific debate about global climate change (216):

1. Has earth been warming over the past few centuries?
2. How has the rate of warming changed over time?
3. What is causing the warming?
4. What have been and will be the consequences of global warming?
5. What can be done to remediate the change?

By the early 1980s, most scientists had answered the first question affirmatively, and had begun to explore the details of the others. At the beginning of the twenty-first century there is a strong consensus among scientists that the earth has been warming over the past few centuries; that human activities associated with industrialization have caused a significant increase in the rate of warming since about 1850 (with another sharp increase about 1950); that consequences of this change already are being felt by some segments of society, while other consequences are expected; and that these consequences will have negative impacts on most segments of society. Scientists also tend to agree that human society can remediate this problem by reducing greenhouse emissions, particularly carbon dioxide. Note that, although climate scientists have not focused on whether society *should* take measures to reduce greenhouse emissions, their work does include explicit value statements. Scientists tend to characterize climate warming in negative ways, using phrases such as "will get *worse*," "is increasingly *severe*," and "is a growing *problem*." It would be somewhat difficult, however, to maintain completely neutral language when one is describing widespread crop failure, inundation of coastal communities, and loss of glacial water supplies.

Search for Truth over Personal Gain

Scientists are not supposed to act for personal gain. Yet public identification of discoveries has been, since the early eighteenth century, the basis on which scientific achievement is credited (Gross 90). Robert K. Merton identified the "paradox at the heart of the scientific enterprise" years ago:

> While the general progress of scientific knowledge depends heavily on the relative subordination of individual efforts to communal goals, the career progress of scientists depends solely on the recognition of their individual efforts (Gross 89).

The paradox has always been there, yet scientists are expected to have their work subject to *peer review* in which evidence and argument are tested by the scientific value of developing new knowledge, not the professional advancement of the scientist. This is one reason the scientific community is leery of climate research funded by the petroleum industry, which has lobbied successfully to prevent U.S. energy and environmental policies from responding to mainstream science on climate change. For example, Dr. Willie Soon and Dr. Sallie Baliunas presented a study that found twentieth-century warming "unremarkable compared with other climate shifts over the last 1,000 years." Other scientists were skeptical of their results, pointing out that the two researchers were funded by the George C. Marshall Institute, which "has long fought limits on gas emissions, . . . [and that] the study in Climate Research was in part underwritten by $53,000 from the American Petroleum Institute, the voice of the oil industry" (Revkin, "Politics Reasserts").

Testable Results

Science exists, according to its own rules, in an atmosphere of the free exchange of ideas, and to withhold information inhibits scientific progress. Probably most important, this argument calls attention to the fact that science is not a collection of observations or theories. Science is a comprehensive system of empirical knowledge building. So, the theory revealed, the methods followed, and the evidence used are all part of a comprehensive system. The results of climate science studies address climate questions in various ways, and those studies that pass the test of peer review are published in scientific journals such as *Science* and *Nature,* or more specifically focused journals such as *Climatic Change, Climate Research,* and *Transactions of the American Geophysical Union.* Details of the hypotheses tested and methodologies used for data analysis are provided so that other researchers can *replicate* (conduct an exact repetition) the study to determine whether the claims were sufficiently and appropriately supported.

Established Theory Changes Slowly

A theory evolves slowly over time, according to Stephen Toulmin. Even Thomas Kuhn, who used the term *scientific revolution* to characterize major changes in theory, agrees that there is no sudden overturning of theory (Suppe 135). The replacement of Newtonian physics by the theory of relativity did not come suddenly when Albert Einstein said "$E = mc^2$." There was a continual building of the theory, as one anomaly after another was found in Newtonian physics. Newtonian mechanics were being dismantled for many years before Einstein. Likewise, the theory of evolution had been around for some time before Charles Darwin. He provided evidence and the unifying explanation and got credit for it. These were not scientific revolutions; rather, they were theoretical statements that built on, and made sense of, previous theory and findings.

One reason established theory changes so slowly is that the *scientific* or *hypothetico-deductive method* requires scientists to ground any new research in past research. Unlike the descriptive method, the scientific or hypothetico-deductive method focuses on hypothesis testing and the use of a methodology (usually statistical) designed to maximize accuracy in the interpretation of research results. This approach requires scientists to move through a predetermined series of steps, all of which should be quite clearly described for fellow scientists. This method encourages scientific endeavor to focus on questions of fact and to ensure the production of testable results. It is grounded in an assumption that is remarkably similar to that found in both postmodern and feminist thought: Despite endeavors to maintain objectivity, all investigators are finite beings, positioned in time and space. They cannot observe everything all the time. Instead, what they discover will be influenced by their focus. By beginning with a specific hypothesis to be tested, investigators provide their audience with a rationale for the research focus. Or, in stating the hypothesis to be tested, investigators reveal their *positionality*.

Scientists using the hypothetico-deductive method take the following steps:

1. Identify the research problem.
2. Conduct literature review.
3. Identify broad research objectives.
4. Collect preliminary data if needed.
5. Conduct exploratory data analysis.
6. Formulate research hypotheses.
7. Formulate testable (usually statistical) hypotheses.
8. Design methodology.
9. Prepare research proposal.
10. Obtain peer review and revise.
11. Perform experiment, collect data.
12. Analyze data.
13. Evaluate, interpret, and draw conclusions.
14. Submit manuscript to peer-reviewed journal.
15. Respond to additional reviewers' suggestions, and systemically continue the analysis by repeating the process, beginning from step 5.

Scientists observe physical, biological, human, or social phenomena for factual claims. These claims are combined with existing knowledge to form theories that serve as general laws or rules about the natural condition. The theories develop in a system of peer review where others can see the claim, the evidence, and the method of argumentation and test them to confirm or deny. Since theories are built up of many subtheories and empirical confirmations, they are not, according to scientific tradition, easily overturned. New major theories are slowly infused into the system until, at some point, there is a realization among scientists that a crisis exists and they need a new theory to account for all the contradictions in the original theory. With this clearer understanding of scientific argument we will look more carefully at the roles that the different types of argument, forms of evidence, value systems, credibility, and refutation (covered in Chapters 6 through 11) play in it.

Scientific Use of Argument Types

All five of the types of arguments discussed in Chapter 6 appear in scientific argument: generalization, cause, sign, analogy, and authority. The first three, particularly cause and sign, are the most important. In addition, scientists apply each of these types by their own value system based on empiricism, logic, and mathematics.

Argument by Generalization

In one sense, all scientific argument is by generalization. The goal of such argument is to make observations that will explain a class of phenomena. Those explanations generalize about how individual cases behave or about what properties individual cases have in common. Until well into the nineteenth century, using induction or experiments to form generalizations that would serve as theories to explain the natural world was the dominant tradition of science known as Baconianism after Francis Bacon, its chief architect (Campbell 500). Generalization in modern science functions by what C. S. Peirce called *abduction*. As John Lyne explains it:

> If a given generality were true, the reasoning goes, then many particulars would be expected to turn out a certain way; if those particulars turn out in the predicted way, then the generality *may be* true. As more particular cases turn out in the predicted way, confidence in a general theory builds. . . . By statistical induction, one establishes what [the] percentage, or probability, is (184).

So the scientist begins with a hypothesis formed from limited cases. This hypothesis *may be* a valid generalization. But, the generalization must be tested for what it might be expected to show. To some extent this is a matter of replication (repetition of an experiment to see if the results are the same).

Other confirmation is based on what could be expected, or generalized, based on past research. Initially, scientific debate about climate change focused on whether the assertion that the earth has been warming was real. Climate scientists answered this question by generalizing from historical, archeological, and geological records. They reconstructed some of these records by examining materials such as the polar ice shield, samples taken from the ocean floor, and samples from the earth's core. When the hypothesis of global warming became an established theory, the debate turned to whether the warming, by then acknowledged as real, was sufficiently outside the range of natural fluctuations of climate as deciphered from these samples. Then when research indicated that the rise in temperature over the twentieth century was unusually large and fast, the hypothesis that the rate of global climate change had significantly increased became an established theory, and the scientific argument shifted to *causes* of warming.

While tests are part of the process of making the generalization acceptable, they are not argument by generalization themselves, but argument from sign, as we will explain shortly. The purpose of scientific argument is to build theories that will provide the scientific community with the most rational explanation of the natural order. This requires that extensive experimentation and evidence be assembled, but generalization is only part of the process. Perhaps more important is the examination of anomalies in the theory that might question it. Toulmin, Rieke, and Janick provide a useful example from weather forecasting:

Weather forecasting, for instance, presents some serious challenges to science, to find ways of squaring the observed course of meteorological events with the accepted principles of physical science. But that does not mean that scientists feel any responsibility for explaining every last day-to-day or minute-to-minute change in the weather. Presumably such changes are brought about in a perfectly intelligible way by some minor local fluctuation in the atmospheric conditions, but normally no real scientific interest will be served by tracking down exactly what that fluctuation was. Only if a *significant* anomaly can be demonstrated—for instance, a storm that "blew up out of nowhere" under atmospheric conditions that apparently ruled out such a possibility—will there be a genuine *scientific issue* to face (319).

Argument by generalization is, on the face of it, crucial to science. The generalizations (theories) require testing to make them more powerful. That testing is not always by replication. It will more often rely on the next two kinds of argument, cause and sign.

Argument by Cause

The assumption of science is that there is order in nature and that order is held together by cause and effect relationships. High- and low-pressure changes cause changes in the weather. Changes in the social order cause changes in the way individuals live their lives.

Once climate scientists began to focus on causes of climate change, they discovered that natural factors dominated climatic fluctuations up to somewhere between the years 1750 and 1850. From about 1850 to 1950, human factors associated with industrialization grew to sufficient potency to rival natural factors, leading to climate variability derived from a complex blend of natural and technological causes. In the latter half of the twentieth century the technologically derived causes outpaced natural factors by a large margin.

Usually, a cause comes before the effect and is both necessary and sufficient for the effect to occur. Thus, the cause must always be there. A cause is sufficient if no other factor is necessary. It takes combustion, fuel, and oxygen for there to be fire. These three together are necessary and sufficient cause for fire. Fuel alone, however, is a necessary but not a sufficient cause. The force of a scientific argument is determined by the extent to which necessity and sufficiency approach certainty.

This requirement of approaching certainty poses an increasing problem in all sciences, but particularly in the human sciences. No cases of human behavior meet certainty standards. Consequently, the human sciences use a more open statistical probability as the basis for judging cause, called a *conditional cause*. The claim is the best explanation, but it is conditional because it is supported at a statistical level that admits of some evidence to the contrary. For example, Beatrice Schultz studied several variables to see how persons who were trained in argumentation would evaluate themselves as leaders in decision making groups compared with the self-evaluation of those who had not been so trained.

Self-ratings for argumentative trainees and other participants were compared by t-test, with results showing that trainees perceived themselves as significantly more self-assured (t = 2.78; df 36; p < .01), more goal-oriented (t = 2.65; df 36; p < .01), more quarrelsome (t = 2.85; df 36; p < .01), and in the direction of significance for summarizing (t = 1.81; df 36; p = < .08). Untrained participants did not significantly alter their ratings after the second session (560).

Before the training there was no difference between the experimental group and the control group, but after the experimental group was trained, they showed a significant difference in the perception of their leadership qualities versus the control group. The only difference between the two was the training that became the necessary and sufficient cause for the change. How well do we know that? Consider one leadership characteristic: "self-assured (t = 2.78; df 36; p < .01)." A *t-test* is a statistical procedure to compare the means of two groups. The *t* value of 2.78 with the recorded degrees of freedom (df 36) tells the researcher that chance alone was unlikely to be the source of the difference they found; probably less than one time in a hundred.

If the design of the experiment was perfect, the elimination of chance as an explanation should leave only the "treatment" (training) as the cause. But this experiment does not prove that the training caused everyone to change as would be expected in a traditional understanding of cause. As a matter of fact, some participants changed, some did not, and a few probably regressed. Statistically, however, the total group changed. The change was dependent on an unknown characteristic, so we can say there is cause but the cause (training) is conditional.

Remember, however, what we noted earlier: no science is immune from uncertainty. Recall that in Chapters 1 through 3 we pointed out that uncertainty is fundamental to argumentation, and that science itself is a continual process of questioning what humanity previously had thought was certain. Many climate scientists (e.g., Lecocq, Hourcade, and Ha-Duong 1998; Tol 1999; Visser et al. 2000) have argued that even the best data analysis cannot completely dispel the uncertainty associated with different standards of evidence and risk degrees that individuals or groups participating in the debate about global warming may hold. Although uncertainty may be minimized by better measurement techniques or more sophisticated statistical analysis, it will not disappear. The ubiquitous presence of uncertainty does not, however, invalidate argument by cause. Penicillin causes illness in the form of an allergic reaction in some small percentage of the population. That does not invalidate the claim that it causes wellness by destroying bacterial infections in a much larger percentage of the population. Science is not intended to predict individual events, but to predict generalized expectations.

The Challenger spaceship disaster was caused by an O ring that failed when the temperature fell below 53°F, the minimum for which the engineers had tests (Gouran 439). A decision was made to go ahead with the launch even when the temperature fell below that level. Dennis Gouran explains that the odds were against failure in that technological system. However, as the tragedy illustrates, this conditional cause could not predict an individual case—only a probability.

Scientists look for the necessary and sufficient causes of phenomena. There is always some question, but certain causal relationships, particularly in the physical and biological sciences, come closest to producing the ideal relationship between cause and effect. For much of science a conditional relationship is the best that can be expected.

Argument by Sign

A major way to test a theory is to look for observable phenomena which the theory predicts should be there. The theory of global warming relies heavily on sign argument. Because the theory is based on propositions of past fact, the types of evidence all are signs of what has happened throughout earth's history. The Intergovernmental Panel on Climate Change noted several signs to support its argument. For example, the global average sea level rose between 0.1 and 0.2 meters during the twentieth century, global ocean heat content has increased since the late 1950s, the thickness of the Artic sea-ice has declined by about 40 percent during late summer in recent decades, and the increase in temperature in the twentieth century is probably the largest of any century during the past thousand years. These claims are not advanced as causes, but as signs, of global warming.

For another example, consider the classification of "orders" of plants and animals. Given our everyday observation of mammals (people, dogs, cats, and so on), our common sense would not put whales in the class Mammalia. Yet they are vertebrate animals that have self regulating body temperature, hair, and, in females, milk-producing mammae. These are all signs that are used to define mammals. In Chapter 6 we discussed definition in greater detail. For now, you can think of any definition as an argument from sign.

The argument from sign becomes particularly crucial in the human sciences. All survey research is a sign argument. The sample of the population is taken as a sign of the whole population. It is also an important part of experimental research in the social sciences. For instance, Cynthia Hoffner and Joanne Cantor wanted to find out what factors affect "children's enjoyment of a frightening film sequence." They studied five- to seven-year-olds and nine- to eleven-year-olds. The children viewed a sequence from *Swiss Family Robinson* in which two brothers encounter a snake. The researchers varied the introduction and the ending to provide either a threat or happy circumstances.

First, note that a video of the Robinson boys encountering a snake is taken to be a sign of a frightening film sequence. After viewing the sequence, the children were asked if they felt happy, scared, or just okay. They were also asked a number of questions such as how worried, scared, and so on, they were. Note that what the children said is taken as a sign of what they actually felt.

In addition, Hoffner and Cantor monitored skin temperature and heart rate to measure the children's "residual arousal to enjoyment." Here is one example of their sign argument on this subject: "Skin temperature changes accompany peripheral vasoconstriction, which is a measure of [sign of] sympathetic arousal" (46–48). We have simplified the procedure they used, but it should be clear that sign argument is used at every stage of the study's design.

Social scientists cannot show you "enjoyment" or "frightening," nor can they show you an "attitude," "violence," "communication conflict," or "deception." They must test their theories against things, events, or behaviors that are signs of those abstract concepts. In Chapter 2 we talked about world views that some people believe guide human mental processes. However, no one has ever seen a world view, held one up to the light, or poked it with a finger. So what makes the concept believable? World views are accepted because numerous studies using outward signs point to the existence of such organizing principles.

Argument by Analogy

Generalization, cause, and sign are the principal means by which scientists argue, but argument by analogy serves an important function also. There are two distinct phases to scientific argument: one is to provide an explanation of a phenomenon, the other is to build an empirical argument that can be tested. The first uses analogy extensively, the second only in very careful ways.

In one sense all argument is by analogy, because claims are made that are not the same as the incidents, things, or beings on which they are based. A series of examples can be thought of as analogous to the generalization it produces, or a sign can be seen as an analogy for what it represents.

Physicist Roger S. Jones uses a simple example of the basic scientific activity of measurement. To measure the length of a table top, he says:

> All I need do is decide between which two marks on the meter stick the right end of the table lies. . . . In practice, deciding whether two points are coincident boils down to making judgments about the distance between two points. Point A on the table and point B on the meter stick cannot literally be coincident, for two objects cannot occupy the same place at the same time (21).

In that sense, even measurement is an analogy.

Scientists acknowledge this limitation as a condition of their knowledge and, except for a few (like Roger Jones), argue there is a natural order about which they can develop knowledge claims even though measurement is not exact.

Analogy serves in this system as an explanation. There are quarks in physics, DNA in genetics, universes in astronomy, and attitudes in human communication. These serve as ways to explain phenomena that cannot literally be identified.

There is the analogy of mathematics, in which the rules of mathematics are used as a model of the natural world. Gene Shoemaker of the United States Geological Survey estimates that "an asteroid more than six-tenths of a mile in diameter will hit earth once every 40 million years" (Lessem 293). From this generalization you could reason by analogy that the earth is overdue for an impact that might kill three-fourths of all living things, as one perhaps did 65 million years ago in the time of dinosaurs.

Such argument by analogy includes, of course, metaphor and models (Leatherdale 1). Your biology textbook has a model of DNA. It doesn't look like DNA, but it is a way of explaining that genetic phenomenon by analogy.

In the scientific tradition we are examining here, analogy, while useful as explanation, is not as useful in making an empirical argument. Because scientists try to understand the natural world, there is a problem with the comparison of two things that are not the same. This problem applies particularly to figurative analogy, as in the example (in Chapter 6) in which North Carolina Governor Jim Hunt argued that school vouchers to pay parents to send their children to private schools "are like leeches, they drain the lifeblood—public support—from your schools" (Peterson 29). Even a literal analogy, such as the one drawn between the oil industry's treatment of poor African Americans in Norco, Louisiana, and its treatment of aboriginal inhabitants of Ogoniland, Nigeria, has its problems. There are at least as many differences as similarities between the treatment accorded the two populations. It's very unlikely that residents of Norco would be hanged for organizing a peaceful protest, even if it caused a work stoppage at the local factory. Protesters might be ignored, or even taken to jail, but few observers would equate those punishments with the hanging that occurred in Nigeria. In a scientific argument, the usefulness of this analogy would be based on a determination of what conditions are most appropriate for determining the industry's ability to influence the relevant economic, political, and legal structures so as to maximize its advantage.

While analogy is not as forceful a scientific argument as the three we discussed before, analogy *is* argued, particularly in the biological sciences. The term used for an analogous relationship in biological sciences is *homologous,* which means there are extensive similarities of structure and evolutionary origin between two biological entities. In genetics, for instance, homology means having the same linear sequence of genes as another chromosome. So for a paleontologist to claim an analogy (homology) between a dinosaur and a bird requires detailed evidence and generalization.

As early as the late nineteenth century, T. H. Huxley advanced the idea that dinosaurs were related to birds, but the theory did not hold favor because of some disparities. The theory was revived by J. H. Ostrom of Yale University in the 1970s. When J. A. Gauthier, in 1986, established that *Archeopteryx* (the ancestor of birds) had over 100 characteristics of dinosaurs, it became accepted that birds evolved from dinosaurs (Fastovsky and Weishampel 304–05). When dinosaur fossils . . . with feathers were found in China by Chinese geologist Ji Quany and confirmed by Canadian paleontologist Phil Curry, they filled in a gap in the evolutionary tree, making the claim even more powerful that birds descended from dinosaurs (Fischman).

John Lyne and Henry F. Howe use the example of E. O. Wilson, who moved far from his own area of expertise as an entomologist ("his publications prior to 1971 concern such topics as chemical communication among ants, and castes within insect societies"). In 1975 Wilson wrote *Sociobiology: The New Synthesis.* In it, and subsequently, he and his followers argue for the existence of genes for moral principles such as "altruism" (Lyne and Howe 136–40). Lyne and Howe criticize Wilson because sociobiology reveals a "superficial relationship." To say, for instance, that "certain human behavior is 'like' a certain baboon behavior" provides a basis for an analogy in public argument but not the homology necessary to a geneticist (142). It is probably most significant that sociobiology has had considerable popularity outside biology in the public sphere. Decision makers in the public sphere hold analogy to less rigid standards than scientists do.

On the other hand, scientists interested in the effect of carcinogens on rats believe there is a homology between rats and humans. To develop statistical analyses of the effects of smoking and cancer on humans when large amounts of tars and nicotines are ingested in a short period of time, rats are used rather than humans. Decisions are made about amounts necessary and periods of time based on assumptions about comparative body weights. More important is the basic assumption that humans and rats are homologous. That is, the analogy is based on extensive similarities of structure and evolutionary origin between rats and humans.

Unless a very strong analogy (homology) can be established, argument by analogy in science looks more like generalization. It serves as an explanation of a phenomenon.

Argument from Authority

An argument warranted by the authority of scientific principle is considerably different from argument from authority in public argument. In public argument, you might use authority to prove a claim ("Lower interest rates stimulate the economy, according to the chair of the Federal Reserve Board"). A scientist, however, is likely to use something more like a refutational argument. For instance:

1. The established theory has a lot of strength because of its longstanding success in predicting situations.
2. The counter theory has little evidence for its position.
3. Therefore, the established theory is still valid.

Whether as a constructive claim or a refutational one, such an argument does not look like the typical argument from authority found in public argument (Albert Einstein is a credible scientist, so we can trust his theory $E = mc^2$). For scientists making arguments in the scientific sphere, the only authority is the authority of established theory. It is probable that in private they are more likely to pay attention, if not give adherence, to arguments advanced by highly reputable scholars over unknowns, or to place greater weight on theories advanced by persons with better credentials.

By the usual rules of scientific argumentation, then, argument from authority is based on the authority of the theory, rather than of an individual. Recall our earlier claim that traditionally, scientific advancement subordinates individual effort to the search for knowledge. Individuals do have their names attached to theories (Haley's Comet, Heisenberg's uncertainty principle, Newton's laws, Darwin's theory) and scientists recognize the outstanding achievements of others, with the Nobel and other prizes. However, in the presentation of scientific arguments in scholarly papers and journal articles, you will not find the argument "X is true because Y said it."

Of course, each scientific paper includes a review of the literature in which the scientist identifies the significant findings to date and shows how the current research fits with it. The review of the literature gives the appearance of argument from authority because the most significant contributions must be by the most authoritative researchers. However, the argument advanced in the review of the literature is about the findings and theories of the research. The authority of the author is secondary. The authority of the theory is primary, yet it is not sufficient to maintain a claim in the face of conflicting empirical evidence.

There is also the authority of established theories. Earlier we noted that E. O. Wilson, takes on an extensive burden of proof because his findings challenge established theory. The assumption in science that the established theory should remain until significant evidence is generated against it gives one who wishes to overturn it a tremendous burden of proof. The presumption for the status quo is particularly strong in the sciences.

Argumentation in the sphere of science concentrates on argument by generalization, cause, and sign. Its use of generalization is somewhat different from the usual understanding of that term because it is oriented to testing theory rather than just replicating it. Scientific arguments depend particularly on cause and, to a lesser extent, sign. Argument by analogy is used mostly as a method of explanation. In empirical argument it is rare, found in a form more like generalization. Argument by authority is considered insufficient, though established principles have a kind of authority, and personal authority may play a role in private thought or discussion. Argumentation in science, as we have mentioned several times, is based on empirical evidence and we now turn to the subject of evidence.

Scientific Use of Evidence

There are three forms of evidence, as we noted in Chapter 7: examples, statistics, and testimony. All can be found in scientific argumentation. We noted earlier that science is not just a collection of observations or theories. It is a comprehensive system of empirical theory building. As we begin to examine the nature of scientific evidence we must look at that term *empirical* more carefully.

Empirically Grounded Claims

Traditionally, to be empirically grounded means that a claim must be based on sensory experience. Scientific explanations are empirical arguments when the evidence can be seen, heard, touched, smelled, or tasted. That understanding seemed reasonable in earlier centuries when our scientific theories were limited by our immediate senses, augmented by instruments such as microscopes and telescopes. Such limits are no longer applied to the term empirical because there is too much of what is known as reality that cannot be observed through even the augmented senses.

Quarks in physics, universes in astronomy, traits in biology, and the Jurassic period in paleontology are not available to the senses. "Nevertheless, science remains empirical in that its justification is in the interpretation of the material reality in which we function. In short, science makes sense of what we see, hear, and touch even though its explanation may incorporate much beyond that" (Anderson 12).

Specific Instances

Specific instances provide the empirical grounding for a scientific claim. That should be obvious. Colonies of bees, strata of rocks, actions of individuals all provide the empirical bases for forming generalizations about those phenomena that lead to hypotheses. Further examination of other instances serves to replicate, modify, or reject a theory.

A *New York Times* article about climate change research illustrates how several specific instances can strengthen, or specify, an existing claim. The instances included claims that Alaska has warmed by eight degrees over the past 30 years, today's Arctic temperatures are the highest in at least the past 400 years, and Arctic ice volume decreased 42 percent over the past 35 years. Based on these instances (in addition to other supporting evidence), the Office of Naval Research warns that it is plausible "that the summer Arctic ice cap will disappear completely by 2050" (Kristof).

Most of the scientific controversy about global warming surrounds different scenarios that are projected by computer models (Intergovernmental Panel on Climate Change). One set of scenarios assumes rapid economic development and globalization, rapid diffusion of new technologies, a global human population demographic that stabilizes, then slightly declines after 2050, and a shift in energy choices away from fossil fuels. Another set of scenarios assumes slower diffusion of new technologies, continuation of existing fertility patterns, and energy usage remaining dependent on fossil fuels. As you can imagine, each of these combinations of economic development, population trajectory, and energy choice predicts different greenhouse gas concentrations in the atmosphere and the accompanying increase of the global mean temperature. Scientists have attempted to incorporate in the climate models information from diverse disciplines including at least biology, chemistry, geology, communication, economics, and political science. Given the differences in scale, technique, and philosophy among these diverse disciplines, there is considerable controversy over both the data that are used in the models and the feedback loops that are hypothesized.

Such questioning is not unusual in science. No matter how many replications are achieved, the conditional nature of theories means that arguments are frequently based on statistical probability, and are always open to further questioning.

Statistics in Science

We noted in Chapter 7 that statistics are essentially a numerical compacting of specific instances. They provide a means of talking about many specific instances without citing every one. That approach to explanation is common for most public, even legal, argumentation. But science uses statistics in many more ways.

In scientific argumentation, statistics are not just a form of support. Ranging from relatively simple content analysis using some measure of an average, to complex computerized programs of statistical analysis, statistics become a way of reasoning.

Statistical reasoning provides the basis for generalizations about data, and arguments about the cause for the evidence assembled.

The numbers that comprise statistics serve as a sign for conditions in the natural world. Their usefulness to science is determined by the extent to which they actually are representative (signs) of what they propose to measure. No one can ever "know" many natural phenomena, as we observed in the previous section on specific instances. To use statistics, the scientist has to make assumptions about what makes a certain configuration of numbers a legitimate sign of the natural world.

The three tasks of statistics are:

1. *To quantify a set of observations into a set of numbers.* This is the descriptive use of statistics. Statistics reveal the central tendency of the numbers or the averages (mode, median, or mean), the distribution of certain characteristics, the dispersion of them, and the association among different characteristics in the set of numbers. Perhaps there are 15,000 students in your university and 54 percent of them are women. The average age is 23.7. These are all numbers that describe.

2. *To determine if the sample is representative (a sign) of the population from which it was drawn.* A poll on your campus says that 58 percent of the students favor national health insurance. Were the students questioned representative of your student body?

3. *To determine by a decision rule whether the characteristics found can be attributed to an error in sampling* (the null hypothesis) or, if not, whether an alternative explanation, usually the hypothesis, is confirmed (Anderson 175–76).

Recall the study of children and the film sequence from *Swiss Family Robinson.* The researchers used a statistical test to determine how significant the results were.

The first task is to quantify observations into a set of numbers and relationships that will tell the researcher how to describe a population. The first task concerns measurement much like the general use of statistics discussed in Chapter 7. The second and third tasks are concerned with meaning. These statistics are used to develop knowledge about a population. For these tasks, a decision rule is necessary to decide what is and what is not worth knowing. For the scientist, tasks two and three are at least as important as task one.

A look at these three tasks illustrates that there are assumptions that cannot be proven but must be taken as givens. For example, in measurement a primary assumption is that the numbers represent the phenomena. If not, then one's statistical descriptions have no real meaning. Another is that there is such a thing as a representative sample. If not, studies of public opinion, the behavior of chimpanzees, the effect of carcinogens on rats, or the physical properties of granite, would not be possible. If there is no such thing as a random sample that can be taken to be representative (a sign) of the population, the understanding of a natural phenomenon is impossible. But scientists do assume that a representative sample is possible. Another assumption is that the rate of error (the chance of being wrong) will identify the occasion of error (that the finding is false).

Statistics are important sources of evidence that link with argument by generalization, cause, sign, and analogy to form a composite system of argument.

Testimony

Testimony is a form of evidence that can stand alone as grounds for an argument from authority. For instance, you could argue that since E. O. Wilson is a respected scientist, his theory that there are genes for moral principles should be accepted. But Lynes and Howe criticize that view because his theory is outside his expertise and, more important, he does not have sufficient evidence for the theory. Is there a place for testimony in scientific argument? The answer in the human sciences is yes. In such human sciences as psychology, communication, sociology, anthropology, and political science, testimony is at least a significant basis of evidence. It is used, however, in a special way.

Testimony functions as evidence when, in surveys or experiments, people express an opinion or indicate the facts that they know about a situation. For instance, Pamela and William Benoit were interested in discovering how people account for failure or success in an interpersonal argument and how they perceived the consequences for self and other relationships. They asked twenty-seven students to write essays describing occasions of success and failure in interpersonal argument and answer questions about the consequences. Those written responses constituted the testimony that, when analyzed, provided the categories of explanations for success or failure.

Sometimes the evidence is taken from a set of categories that people judge. For instance, in Chapter 8 we introduce a series of value terms by Milton Rokeach to represent the eighteen major terminal and the eighteen major instrumental values. People are given one or both lists and asked to rank order them, and the group's composite response is taken as a hierarchy of that group's values. Like Benoit and Benoit, Rokeach used open-ended testimony to discover the values. But both studies rely on testimony in defining categories and in forming generalizations about their use by a group. The evidence is testimony (and hangs on the scientist's assumptions that the testimony is both true and real). It reflects the opinion and knowledge of the persons engaged in the experiment.

What you can see from this brief summary is that all three of the evidence forms are found in scientific argument. Statistics are clearly the most critical. Specific instances and testimony (in the human sciences) are the raw material from which statistical inferences are made. Statistical inferences are essentially linked to argument by generalization, cause, sign, and sometimes analogy.

Scientific Method as Argument

The steps of the hypothetico-deductive method are intended to guide researchers in producing the most credible argument possible. *Identifying the research problem* requires scientists to use generalization, cause, sign, and sometimes analogical forms of argument. For example, when scientists argue that increased levels of carbon dioxide lead to global warming, they are claiming that carbon dioxide is a *cause,* and global warming is its effect. When they provide evidence that glaciers in South America are retreating, that the ice sheet in arctic regions is thinning, and that sea levels are rising, they are claiming that these events are *signs* of global warming. When they explain that global climate change is a complicated system response to multiple individual events and behaviors, they are *generalizing* from the few data points they have collected. The requirement to conduct a *literature review* indicates how differently authority is used in scientific argument. Researchers do not need to review the previous research of any individual scientist so much as they need to review the primary theoretical perspectives (of course, certain names do become connected with certain theoretical claims). It they attempt to argue for something that counteracts established theory, their burden of proof is significant. Most often, they will use the literature review to identify one small weakness within existing theory, and then argue that the current (or proposed research) takes care of that small weakness.

Identifying research objectives and formulating hypotheses are fundamental to the values espoused by science. In Chapters 8 and 9 we discussed values and credibility. Science values both order, and the discovery of new knowledge. You may recall we emphasized that values function systematically, rather than individually. Without the necessity of identifying specific objectives and formulating testable hypotheses, the discovery function of science could easily destroy its orderliness. Further, without these steps, scientific replication would be impossible. Formulating hypotheses in a way that allows someone to test them also is referred to as *operationalizing* them. When you operationalize something, you provide a way to measure, or evaluate it. Most commonly, scientists operationalize hypotheses by identifying the statistical tests they will use, as well as the rejection range. The rejection range operates as a decision rule.

Suppose you wanted to know whether class attendance was correlated with the grades students earn in a class. You might hypothesize that students who attended more classes would earn higher grades. You could design a methodology that enabled you to compare daily attendance with final grades for all students. To make your hypothesis testable, you would need to decide what statistical test you would use to make this comparison. Further, you would need to designate a level beyond which you would assume that the correlation between attendance and grades should or should not be attributed to chance. That level is your decision rule. As you continue to move through the steps of the scientific method, you will rely on the value system common to most scientific endeavors to guide you in determining which forms of argument and evidence will provide the greatest credibility.

Conclusion

As examined in this chapter, science refers to the "objective account of the material world based upon measurement and quantification so that structure, process, movement, and transformation can be described mathematically in terms of fundamental laws" (Peat, p. 208). Scientists often use the physical sciences as a model and mathematics as a foundation for explanatory theories. Scientists play a significant political role, but here we are interested in how they argue to one another as scientists. Scientific study begins with the value that there is order in nature that can be discovered. Order is explained through observation, and observations are characterized in claims of fact. They are combined with other already acknowledged claims of fact to develop a proposition that is a theory about fact. That theory can then be used to predict what will happen at another time or in another place.

The tradition of argumentation in the scientific sphere can be preliminarily defined by four observations: scientific argument deals in claims of fact; it searches for truth over personal gain; it reveals results that are complete enough to test; and its theories change slowly.

Generalization, cause, and sign are the most important argument types in the scientific sphere. Generalization, in contemporary times, functions as abduction. That is, a generalization is established on the basis of its greatest probability rather than certainty.

Argument from cause is basic to scientific argumentation. When study reveals some previously unrecognized condition, the scientist wants to know its cause. To be established in theory it must be both necessary and sufficient to produce the effect. Argument from sign is important to establishing a scientific theory. Signs in biology indicate that an organism belongs to a particular species. All survey research is sign argument, as is most social science argumentation.

Argument by analogy is used primarily to explain a phenomenon. To be the basis for an empirical argument, the analogy must have extensive similarities. In biology it must be homologous. Argument from authority is the least used type of argument in science. The review of literature sections of research papers and articles and the authority of established theories function as a kind of argument from authority. Outward statements of authority as a basis for argument are not made, though they may be used in private.

Evidence in scientific argumentation is used to provide empirical grounding for claims. This relationship is indicated in the specific instances that form the base of scientific reasoning. Statistics constitute the most elaborate kind of evidence and they have three tasks: (1) to quantify a set of observations into a set of numbers; (2) to determine whether the sample is representative; and (3) to determine if the characteristics found can be attributed to an error in sampling. Testimony has a function in the human sciences, in which people are called upon in surveys or experiments to express opinions.

PROJECT

Interview a faculty member at your college or university who would be considered a scientist as we have defined a scientist in this chapter. Ask questions about the kinds of arguments and evidence he or she uses with peers (not those that might be used to convince others). Write a short paper (no more than five double-spaced pages) about what kinds of argument and evidence apply. Does the person you interviewed agree with what has been said in the chapter? How different is the interviewee's position from this chapter? Why do you suppose the difference exists?

14 Argumentation in Religion

KEY TERMS

God	church
natural theology	sacred texts
revealed theology	tradition
human beings	experience
moral behavior	revelation
evil/sin	culture
suffering	paradox
salvation	narrative

Arguments about religion are surely as old as recorded history and as recent as today's newspaper. Because we write primarily for people in western society, this chapter will be concerned with the religions in the Judeo-Christian-Islamic tradition. These religions, George Kennedy has observed, are all highly verbal religions (120). As such, they all have the primary ingredients for argumentation. But religious argumentation is quite different from argumentation in other spheres. The questions investigated and the values, evidence, and argument used to gain adherence in religious argumentation differ considerably from those of legal, legislative, or scientific argumentation, for instance. Our purpose, therefore, is to examine the factors which make religious argumentation unique.

John Macquarrie has observed that religious language can include praying, blessing, testimony, and nonverbal symbols such as crucifixes, paintings, music, and the like. "Theological language" is narrower; it "arises out of religious language as a whole, and it does so when a religious faith becomes reflective and tries to give an account of itself in verbal statements"(19). Many discussions conducted in religious situations are not much different from other public argumentation. In this chapter, we will investigate how religious argumentation is used to resolve theological issues.

In order to understand such religious argumentation we will need to look at the major questions that identify where issues and values will be found. We will then examine sacred texts, the most important source of evidence, and tradition, experience, revelation, and culture as evidence. Finally, we will see how certain forms of argument are preferred over others.

Major Questions in Religious Argumentation

The existence of a wide variety of religious groups holding different interpretations is evidence enough that religious questions abound. We will briefly identify seven questions adapted from two lists (one developed by Harry Emerson Fosdick, another by Peter C. Hodgson and Robert L. King) that constitute a fair summary of what has to be explained for a system of theology to be complete. Not all religious argumentation will cover all seven questions and other questions may arise, but these seven reasonably define religious argumentation: (1) What is the nature of God? (2) What is the nature of human beings? (3) What is moral behavior, the religious life? (4) What are sin, evil, and the meaning of suffering? (5) What is the human's relationship to God? (6) What is the nature of salvation? (7) What is the role of the church?

What Is the Nature of God?

One important distinction in religious argumentation is between natural and revealed theology. Revealed theology comes from the examination of sacred texts which reveal that there is a god and what God's relation is to humans and nature. Natural theology attempts to prove the existence of God from nature: that is, from observation and reasoning apart from revealed scripture. The arguments of natural theology began in Jewish theology (Epstein 86). Perhaps the best known example of natural theology is the five ways by which Thomas Aquinas proved the existence of God. We will summarize them here.

1. The world changes; things do not change unless some agent changes them; change cannot go on without end; there must be a first agent.
2. Patterns of cause and effect are observed in the world; it is not possible to conceive of a series of causes and effects without an initiating cause.
3. All things in the natural world are contingent on other things; nothing can be observed in the universe that is necessary. Therefore, it must exist because of something necessary: God.
4. All things have differences in value one from another. Nothing is perfect, but we cannot know the imperfect unless there is a perfect.
5. Since the natural world exhibits order and cause there is design. A universe that exhibits design must have a designer: God (Anderson 25–66).

These arguments are based on what Aquinas believed are universal natural principles; they do not depend on sacred texts.

Such argumentation about the existence of God and the logic of belief still takes place today. However, although natural theology is important in religious argumentation, it is not as prevalent as is revealed theology. Natural arguments are most frequently used, when they *are* used, to reinforce arguments about revealed religion. Even Thomas Aquinas, for instance, made his five arguments when he was already a believer.

Much of religious argumentation, says George Kennedy, begins with the authority of texts and has to do with understanding God through the clear explication of these texts (158). Probably the existence of God is easily accepted by those who engage in religious argumentation and the more difficult part of the question is the nature of God.

The religions of the Judeo-Christian-Islamic tradition are all monotheistic religions. They believe in one God. The concept of monotheism is accepted by all, but it still constitutes an area of argumentation.

In Islam the defining claim is "There is no God but Allah and Muhammad is his prophet." The inscription on the Dome of the Rock in Jerusalem, from the Qur'an says, "Praise to God, who begets no son, and has no partner. He is God, one, eternal. He does not beget, he is not begotten, and he has no peer" (Lewis, *Crisis* 44). Mormons are frequently attacked for the statement, "As man is now, God once was. As God now is, Man may be" (Smith 46). Critics interpret this to mean that there is, or can be, more than one god.

As early as the second century CE, Celsus argued that Christianity affirms three Gods: Father, Son, and Holy Ghost. Trinitarians are obliged to argue that there is only one god, but God is found in three persons. Other issues also come under the theme of the nature of God. Does God intervene in human activity? Is God jealous, revengeful, or loving? Is God a person, a spirit, a world force? Is Jesus God? Does God still reveal himself to humans? Is God found in nature?

What Is the Nature of Human Beings?

Among most arguers in the Judeo-Christian-Islamic tradition, there is a general agreement that human beings are more than other animals, as is argued in Genesis 1:28:

> And God blessed them [Adam and Eve], and God said to them, "Be fruitful, and multiply, and fill the earth, and subdue it; and have dominion over the fish of the sea, and over the birds of the air, and over every living thing that moves upon the earth."

Such a view has led some to argue that certain religions believe humans should exploit other living things, while others argue that it means that humans are called on to exercise stewardship. However it is interpreted, there is no doubt that humans are above all others, having been made in the image of God and given dominion (Genesis 1:26). But do humans get this status from God? From nature? From the ability to reason? From the possession of a soul? Thus, a persistent question in religious argumentation is about the basic nature of the human being.

There is, moreover, a longstanding and still active issue of free will versus determinism. Simply stated, it raises the issue of the extent to which human conduct is determined by God before a person is born, or is subject to individual choice. Some will choose one or the other of these positions, but much religious argumentation is addressed to combinations of the two. For instance, a religion that attempts to convert others to its view usually is a religion which believes that individuals have the ability to make the choice (free will). Islam is such a religion. Yet Islam has a strong tradition of *kismet* (fate). When a loved one dies, consolation is provided by the belief that it was fate, that the person had no control over the situation. After the tragic crash of Egypt Air Flight 990 in November of 1999 in the waters off Nantucket, relatives gathered at an interfaith memorial service for the 217 passengers who had died. Ahmed El Hattab of the Islamic Society of North America asked the mourners to submit to God's will. "Lo, we belong to God," he said, "and lo, we are returning. Let us remember it is God who grants life, and it is he who takes us back" (Chivers). Many members of other religions hold similar views. Some resolve the seeming inconsistency between free will and determinism by arguing that one has free will to accept the religion but after that, one's destiny is in the hands of God. Others argue that even the decision to choose the religion was somehow predetermined. Still others believe God gives people control over some parts of their lives but not over others.

The question about the nature of human beings also involves an issue of the extent to which humans are basically good or evil. "In Adam's fall we sinned us all," says the Puritan *New England Primer,* thus expressing the concept of original sin, which sees human beings as basically evil and unable to "save" themselves. In such a view, humans can only be "saved" by God's grace. Other people will reject such a view and see human beings as basically good, capable of making moral choices, sometimes led astray by evil forces (such as the Devil) but capable, with the support of God, of being good. Obviously, many different modifications of these positions may be argued.

What Is Moral Behavior, the Religious Life?

Knowing what is right and wrong is related to a perception of the nature of human beings. This question deals with such issues as how a person can know what is right. It may even be asked, can a person know right and wrong?

Some theologians would argue that there are specific tests which can be applied to discover what is morally right for a religion person. The *Catholic Catechism* says:

> The moral quality of our actions derives from three different sources, each so closely connected with the other that unless all three are simultaneously good, the action performed is morally bad. . . . The object of the act must be good. . . . Circumstances . . . can make an otherwise good object evil. . . . Finally, the end or purpose . . . also affects the moral situation (Hardon 283–84).

Others would argue that determining morality from a religious perspective is more complicated and more tentative than this statement implies.

There are also specific issues of interpretation. An important example is in the interpretation of the basic law, "You shall not kill" (Exodus 20:13). Is such a law an absolute injunction against any form of killing? Animals? Fetuses? Criminals? Enemies in war? The problem of interpretation is further complicated by recent translations that substitute "murder" for "kill." Practitioners of religious argumentation will differ on this and a host of other issues about what constitutes moral behavior and how the most sacred documents, such as the Ten Commandments, are to be interpreted.

What Are Sin, Evil, and the Meaning of Suffering?

One of the most complicated and perplexing questions in religious argumentation is the nature of evil and the role of sin in the production of evil. Protestant theologian John Hicks has argued that "the enigma of evil presents so massive and direct a threat to our faith that we are bound to seek within the resources of Christian thought for ways, if not of resolving it, at least rendering it bearable by the Christian conscience" (ix). Hicks calls the issue created by the concept of a loving God in the presence of evil a "dilemma."

Evil is usually defined by human self-centeredness, that leads to such negative values as cruelty, ruthless ambition, pride, murder, and adultery. In modern times, mass versions of evil such as slavery, poverty, starvation, genocide, indiscriminate war, and terrorism make it a social institution. The holocaust is the most obvious example of mass evil in modern times, but evil has existed throughout world history and in virtually all cultures.

For many religions, evil is an expression of sin, which is a "disorientation at the very center" of the human self (Hicks 300). So, the question must be answered, why has an infinitely good and loving God created sin in people and, therefore, evil in the world? The various answers provided to this question take one into many other questions. Does God grant the individual free will, and, if so, to what extent? What is a sin? For instance, is homosexuality a sin or a natural representation of human diversity? This is a growing question in the religious community today.

For some, the meaning of suffering is answered by the claim that God punishes individuals or societies for their transgressions against divine laws. Certainly, that view can be seen in the sermons and writings of New England Puritan leaders. By their view, sin is inherent in human beings ("In Adam's fall we sinned us all"). Or suffering may be a test that God provides to strengthen one's faith. Certainly, that is one meaning of the story of Job's tribulations in which the most faithful person was one the most tested by suffering.

The Book of Job is a debate among Job, his friends, and finally God, who argue various positions about suffering and God's nature and power. In the end of the story "the Lord blessed the latter days of Job more than his beginnings" (Job 42:12) because he was faithful to God even in his adversity. There are many answers to the question of suffering and all are related to the questions about the nature of God, humans, evil, and sin.

What Is the Human's Relationship to God?

"The meaning attributed to prayer," said Harry Emerson Fosdick, "is one of the most reliable tests of any religion" (201). For some people, God is unapproachable. A person's relation to God is simply that of giving praise and homage. One acknowledges God, attempts to find out as much as possible about, and stands in awe of, the deity. For others, God is very personal and through prayer and, for some people, other sacraments, a person can communicate with God. Some claim they actually talk directly with a divine being as if they were carrying on a conversation. For many people, such communication is an illusion. For others, such communication marks a human being as a special person: a prophet, for instance.

Dietrich Bonhoeffer was a German Protestant theologian. While he was in a Nazi prison in 1943, he wrote to his parents of a more socially oriented idea of the fellowship of God and humans:

> I have also been considering again the strange story of the gift of Tongues. That the confusion of tongues at the Tower of Babel, as a result of which people can no longer understand each other . . . should at last be brought to an end and overcome by the language of God, which everyone understands and through which alone people can understand each other again, . . . (Woelfel 197).

However one looks at it, this relationship of human to God is a very special and important relationship in any system of religious argumentation.

What Is the Nature of Salvation?

There are great differences of view about the question of immortality. For some it is the most important in theology because salvation is the most important benefit one receives from belief, and its absence may be the most horrible punishment. Others view this issue as less important or even nonexistent. They concentrate on the personal and social benefits of living a moral life on earth. Immortality can be seen as social, that is, the preservation of society. In such a view, individuals live on in what they contribute to others or through their children. Reformed Judaism has a concept of immortality, but it is a spiritual union with God. There is no resurrection of the body, no physical torment for sinners, no pleasures. Heaven is not a place but a state. Such a view is much less specific than the view held by most Christians, Muslims, or Orthodox Jews (Cohen 34–36).

What Is the Role of the Church?

In Islam there is no church hierarchy. Religious leaders come from the people, and they get their status from their ability to gain the adherence of others. Jews and most Protestant Christians hold a similar view. Rabbis and ministers are chosen and dismissed by the congregation. The church, when it can be called such, is either an individual congregation or a loose confederation of individual congregations. The American Baptist Convention, for instance, is such a confederation that takes theological positions, but they are not necessarily binding on individual congregations. Individuals or congregations that disagree may drop out and be unaffiliated or join another confederation such as the Southern Baptist Convention or the General Association of Regular Baptists. A similar relationship exists between an individual and a congregation.

In Roman Catholicism, on the other hand, the church is an essential agency of the religion. Tradition is very important in Catholicism. So, in order to avoid error, church authorities must interpret what God's word means. Someone who rejects interpretations sanctioned by the church may, in extreme cases, be excommunicated. In contrast, among Baptists, there is no concept of excommunication. Instead, there is the process of disfellowship. One is not removed from the sacraments of God but only from that fellowship of believers.

Other churches have varying degrees of control over the religious claims their members may hold and still be regarded as members. The stricter the church control, the more likely it may be subjected to the rebuttal that it denies the fellowship of humans with God. The more individualistic the theology, the more it is subject to the rebuttal that it has no control over ignorance and error.

In Islam, there is no concept of the separation of church and state as there is in much of Christianity. The history of Judaism is one of separation from the state until the founding of Israel in 1948. The same was true of Christianity until Constantine I was converted in the third century CE. In modern western democracies, the tradition of the separation is preserved by enlightenment thought and statements like Jesus' "Render unto Caesar the things that are Caesar's and unto God the things that are God's." But, many issues abound about how far the separation of religion from the state can or should be carried. This is a particular problem in Islam, where its founder Muhammad was both a prophet and a ruler.

Values and Themes

The themes of religious argumentation, contained in the answers to these questions, also identify the strongest values that serve as warrants of religious argumentation. Every arguer does not use all of these values. We have already noted, for instance, that Islam has a restricted concept of a church hierarchy, that some Christians reject the idea of a sinful human, and that Judaism has a restricted concept of immortality. Furthermore, the values that warrant a religion are not limited to the values contained in this limited discussion of themes. Yet, our discussion has revealed a significant set of values that are prominent in religious argumentation: God (Jesus for some), human beings (sometimes a negative value), moral behavior, evil (a negative value), sin (a negative value), suffering (sometimes a negative value), prophet, salvation, and church.

This discussion of the seven major themes and values of religion has been necessarily brief. Its purpose is to provide a basis for the analysis of religious evidence and arguments. Any theology is an argumentative case that must answer these questions to be acceptable. The decisions one makes on one question will affect what is possible on another.

Evidence in Religious Argumentation

At least in the religions of the Judeo-Christian-Islamic tradition, religious claims usually are grounded in a text: the Torah, the Bible, and the Qur'an being the most obvious examples. But the interpretation of these texts is based on interpreting them in the light of other kinds of evidence. Increasingly, in modern theology these other kinds of evidence are used alone or with one another, sometimes without text as evidence, or even in opposition to text. Thus, we can identify five forms of evidence in religious argumentation: text, tradition, experience, revelation, and culture.

Text as Evidence

Robert Grant observes of Christian theology, "the interpretation of scripture is the principal bond between the ongoing life and thought of the Church and the documents which contain its earliest traditions" (9). This explains the desire among religious writers to find the most accurate, trustworthy, and best-interpreted texts.

Accuracy   The importance of sacred documents as evidence accounts for the significant arguments over the accuracy of translation. When the Revised Standard Edition of the Bible was first published, it produced considerable controversy. Some argued that it destroyed the essential beauty of the King James version. More important for our purposes here, its translation of certain passages involved changes in wording with far-reaching implications for Christianity. For instance, in Isaiah 7:14, which many Christians consider a prophecy of Jesus' birth, the King James version says that "a virgin shall conceive," the Revised Standard version says "a young woman." The New English Bible, unlike either the Revised Standard Edition of the Bible or the King James version, even uses the term *girl* for *virgin* in Luke 1:27 in describing Mary, the mother of Jesus. These differences among three versions clearly lead to sharp differences in religious argumentation about the miracle of virgin birth.

In recent years an organization of Catholic and Protestant biblical scholars known as the Jesus Seminar have undertaken to provide a new translation of the synoptic gospels (Matthew, Mark, and Luke) and to determine the relative legitimacy of words attributed to Jesus. In this translation they employed "colloquialisms in English for colloquialisms in Greek. When the leper comes up to Jesus and says, 'If you want to you can make me clean,' Jesus replies, 'Okay—you're clean!' " instead of "I will; be clean" (Mark 1:40–41). Needless to say, this use of colloquialisms is only one practice that makes their work controversial (Funk et al. xiii).

Trustworthiness   Even when wording is agreed on, there can still be argumentation about texts. It has to do with the issue, what is the "canon"? What part of the text is acceptable as "sacred" evidence? Certain books are left out by some scholars and councils and included by others. Even some books that are included in the canon are regarded as less reliable. Books of doubtful authorship or authenticity are excluded from both the Hebrew and Christian scriptures, and are known as the Apocrypha. Even some books that are in the Bible, but whose authenticity was debated, are considered of less value than others. "Theologies," says John H. Leith, "that have depended overwhelmingly on books such as Revelation, whose admission to the canon was widely debated, have always been questioned" (235).

On the other hand, for most Christians statements have more authority if they are actually identified as the word of God. In the fourth chapter of Joshua there is a "narration of what God has done in Jewish history, put in the mouth of God himself and therefore given heightened authority." God's words are followed by Joshua's charge to the people, which is of less authority because it is an interpretation of the meaning of God's words (Kennedy 124).

In Islam a similar distinction is made between the Qur'an, which is the revelation given to Muhammad by God, and the Hadith (Sayings). The Hadith reports the actions and utterances of the Prophet and, therefore, has less authority than the revealed text (Lewis, *Islam and . . .* , 25).

Thus, in the Judeo-Christian-Islamic tradition, at least, texts are the best evidence in religious argumentation. There is, therefore, a desire to know the earliest texts, to translate them accurately, to make sure that only the inspired texts are included in the canon, and to determine the relative importance among parts of those texts, with God's own words given the highest authority.

Interpretation   After one knows, even in a general way, what texts are most accurate and which parts are to be taken more seriously, there is a further problem of interpretation. How does one know what interpretation is justified?

The first deliberate attempt to systematize a method of interpretation was probably the seven rules of the Rabbi Hillel at about the time of the birth of Jesus (Farrar 18). From the earliest times of the Christian church, this problem of interpretation was important. Paul argued from texts in his letter to the Galatians (4:21–23):

> Tell me now, you who desire to be under law, do you not hear the law? For it is written that Abraham had two sons, one by a slave and the other by a free woman. But the son of the slave was born according to the flesh, the son of the free-woman's through promise. Now this is an allegory: These women are two covenants (Galatians 4:21–23).

The Jewish scholar Philo of Alexandria observed in the first century CE that there were different ways to explain the meaning of a text. A century later, Clement of Alexandria was probably the first Christian to attempt to systematically explain the method of arguing by analogy from textual evidence. For him the scripture had meaning, but the meaning was not the obvious one.

Clement of Alexandria found five kinds of meaning in a text. They are useful, we believe, to illustrate not a complete understanding of how to interpret religious argument but as a starting point to illustrate the potential validity of textual evidence:

1. *Historical meaning:* one uses a biblical story to inform oneself about history.
2. *Doctrinal meaning:* biblical statements are taken as moral laws. The Ten Commandments are frequently treated this way.
3. *Prophetic meaning:* specific prophesies are made, as when Daniel prophesied that "the God of Heaven will set up a kingdom which shall never be destroyed" (Daniel 2:44).
4. *Philosophical meaning:* specific events or things are interpreted as symbolizing a more general principle, as when Hagar and Sarah stand for pagan philosophy and true wisdom.
5. *Mystical meaning:* specific events or things are taken to mean something quite different from what they would literally mean to the novice. In this way Lot's wife is seen to symbolize an attachment to earthly things which causes a blindness to God's truth (Grant 80).

These textual meanings are arranged in an order from the most literal to the most metaphorical. For some scholars, as religious argumentation moves down the list from the most to the least literal, it becomes more questionable as evidence. A theology grounded in historical and doctrinal meanings is the easiest to defend. Yet such a theology would face the refutation that it weakens the authority of the text by ignoring its most meaningful interpretation.

John Leith has argued that interpretation can only be made in terms of some organizing principle. "When a theologian seeks to work out his [or her] theology under the canon of scripture, he [or she] agrees to find warrant for theological assertion in the broad base of scripture, whether the datum for this theological reflection is text or symbol or theme" (237).

If, for instance, there are three repetitions in a pattern they constitute more forceful evidence. Such is the case according to Robert C. Tannenhill (42), in Mark 14:66–71 when Peter denied he had known Jesus:

> "I neither know nor understand what you mean."
> But again he denied it. . . .
> But he began to invoke a curse on himself and to swear, "I do not know this man of whom you speak."

This repetition establishes a *pattern* to give more force to the evidence that Peter denied Jesus. In addition, a new piece of evidence is introduced which creates a tension and a fuller meaning:

> And immediately the cock crowed a second time. And Peter remembered how Jesus had said to him, "Before the cock crows twice you will deny me three times." And he broke down and wept.

It is in the identification of patterns and tensions and the interaction among them that a particular text can be seen as a unified piece of evidence. Thus, whatever the emphasis of the theologian on each of the five kinds of meaning, that emphasis will be governed by some organizing principle.

Text, then, is the most important source of evidence in religious argumentation. Its accuracy, trustworthiness, and method of interpretation can be issues. In addition, text is subject to adaptation, increasingly so in modern times by tradition, experience, revelation, and culture.

Tradition as Evidence

In longstanding religious organizations—the Roman Catholic church, for instance—tradition is an important source of evidence. Over centuries, certain interpretations have been accepted, others rejected. A body of interpretations constitutes a tradition by which new interpretations must be judged. Some Protestant theologians have argued against interpreting by tradition. Each argument, they say, must return to original texts.

One Protestant writer argues that a denial of the use of tradition is seriously flawed. It is subject to the rebuttal, he says, that "none of the New Testament writings, in its present form, was authored by an apostle or one of his [Jesus'] disciples." The essential substance of Christian witness came before the scriptures (Ogden 138–51). Thus, if one is to ask what a Christian should believe, it should be realized that even the text of the New Testament is an interpretation of the meaning of Christ. So, the argument goes, tradition, the accumulated body of interpretations, is fundamental to most contemporary Christian religious argumentation.

Even the Christian theologian who rejects this argument because the Bible was inspired by God and is, therefore, a literal statement of the Christian faith, has to meet another argument. That is the argument that theologians are a product of their environment, and even when they attempt to go back to the original text they are unable to erase all traditional knowledge from their minds.

All of these arguments about tradition point to a general issue. Most theologians agree that tradition plays some part in argumentative evidence. The issue among them is: How much?

Experience as Evidence

A principle of interpretation closely related to tradition is experience. It is also a source of considerable controversy. The argument for experience is that since the text does not speak to one generation but to every generation, it must be interpreted by succeeding generations on the basis of experience. In finding the meanings of texts for contemporary times, one asks not what they meant historically but what they mean today.

Thus, the religious experiences of the individual, such as answered or unanswered prayer, or the spiritual understanding in a congregation or community, or even secular knowledge, may become evidence in a religious argument. Experience is the basis on which religion might be reconciled with science. Indeed, a theology that relies heavily on experience is frequently called "empirical theology." By such a theology one might accept religious claims that do not have a basis in scripture. Today some theologians and scientists meet to discuss the gaps in scientific thought that do not explain the cause of such phenomena as the Big Bang theory, subatomic particles, DNA, and the human genome (Easterbrook).

If religion is applicable to people's lives, as believers contend, then its principles ought to be observable there. Many are quite suspicious of experience, however, because of the danger that one may respond to secular experience which leads away from religious interpretation.

Revelation as Evidence

It is a special kind of experience when the individual is presumed to have faith to aid in understanding a text. Augustine argued, and many Christians agree with him, that God deliberately made the meaning of scripture obscure so that it could be understood only by someone who had faith (Kennedy 132). Others do not go so far, but all religious argumentation contains in it the idea that one who has faith is a better interpreter of the text than one who does not. The idea is expressed for Christians in Heb. 10:1 and 11:1:

> For since the law has but a shadow of the good things to come instead of the true form of these realities, it can never, . . . make perfect those who draw near. . . .
>
> Now faith is the assurance of things hoped for, the conviction of things not seen. For by it the men of old received divine approval. By faith we understand that the world was created by the word of God, so that what is seen was made out of things which do not appear.

Some religious groups, such as the Roman Catholic Church and the Church of Jesus Christ of Latter Day Saints, are led by individuals believed by their followers to have a special ability to produce revelations not necessarily connected to scripture. Many religious people believe that even ordinary individuals have revelations by faith. In most cases faith clarifies text. A major thesis of the reform tradition in Protestant theology is that the Holy Spirit enables one to make a correct interpretation.

Culture as Evidence

Judaism and Christianity reflect a historical culture in the sense that they see the entire cosmic process as the temporal unfolding of a divine plan with a beginning, a series of crucial events, and an end. Judaism, however, is the more historical religion. Islam is a legalistic religion in which the law is defined by the Qur'an, which was written at one time by one person.

Although Christianity has a history both before and after the life of Jesus, it is so dominated by that life that it has an ahistorical character to it. But even a person such as Martin Luther, who believed that "Christ is the point in the circle from which the whole circle is drawn" said that historical understanding is most important in giving meaning to Isaiah. For Luther, all the books of the Bible teach about Christ, but their historical context is still important (Grant 181). Interpretation that follows this line of argument will need to take into account the culture of the audience for which a text was written. For instance, was it written for Jews or Greeks or Romans, all of whom had different ways of looking at the world and, therefore, different possible rebuttals? What were the particular issues which involved people at the time? How much did they know?

Chapter 11 of the Letter to the Hebrews, quoted above, argues for faith but does so by linking it to a long series of events in Jewish history.

> By faith Abel offered to God a more acceptable sacrifice than Cain. . . . By faith Enoch was taken up so that he should not see death; . . . By faith Noah, . . . By faith Abraham, . . . And what more shall I say? For time would fail me to tell of Gideon, Varak, Samson, Jephthah, of David and Samuel and the prophets. . . .

The Letter to the Hebrews is an argument aimed at Jews and, therefore, utilizes the historical events that were a part of Jewish culture.

A major controversy in Christian theology is over the relative importance of Hebrew and Greek interpretations. "It is the characteristic of Greek thought to work with abstractions. It is not enough to know that it is a good horse or a good table, you must find out what is 'the Good.' . . . to get at reality you abstract the problem from the particular time and place, . . . Hebrew thought . . . argues . . . by presenting a series of related situation-images" (Barr 11–12). In this controversy of Hebrew and Greek interpretations is found the basic issue of the relative importance of history in understanding texts.

Islam provided rules for the proper treatment of slaves, women, Jews, Christians, and others of lesser social rank. As such these rules were a liberalization of previous practices. However, those rules still accepted slavery, plural marriage, concubinage, and second-class citizenship for nonbelievers. Similar situations have existed in Judaism and Christianity. Today, in a different culture, religious arguments abound, sometimes textually linked and some times not, rejecting slavery, supporting women's equality, calling for equal treatment of all religions, and defending gay and lesbian rights. Those who argue against such practices are likely to make some of their arguments based on the culture with or without scriptural evidence.

Thus, evidence in religious argumentation is traditionally from texts. But it is necessary to discover which texts are most accurate, and of the accurate texts, which are most trustworthy. Those texts must be interpreted for meaning and they must be defined as evidence by some organizing principle. Such texts are influenced by evidence from tradition, experience, revelation, and culture. In some cases, particularly in modern times, these four in combination or alone may function as evidence without text.

Preferred Argument Forms

The evidence developed from texts, traditions, experience, revelation, and culture form the grounds and warrants from which one makes arguments for a claim. At this point we will examine the types of arguments that are preferred in religious argumentation. The preferred argument forms are by authority, analogy, sign, paradox, and narrative.

Argument by Authority

Traditionally, the primary form in which religious arguments are found is argument from authority. God, texts, and special humans serve as a universal principle, authority, that warrants the argument, and justifies the claim:

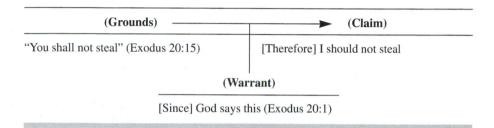

(Grounds)	⟶	(Claim)
"You shall not steal" (Exodus 20:15)		[Therefore] I should not steal

(Warrant)

[Since] God says this (Exodus 20:1)

This argument from the Ten Commandments is particularly powerful because it is warranted directly by God. Similar arguments, that are not direct statements of God's words, are warranted by the authority of the text itself, an apostle, or a prophet. Tradition, experience, revelation, and culture can also warrant an argument from authority. For instance, in the current debate over gays and lesbians as equal members, or leaders, in Christianity, the tradition of Christian love is used as a warrant. Even though specific statements in sacred texts identify the unrighteousness of homosexuals (see for instance: Leviticus 18:22 and I Corinthians 6:9), such texts are overcome, for some, by the overwhelming tradition of Christian love.

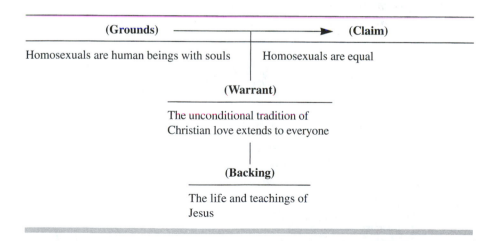

(Grounds)	⟶	(Claim)
Homosexuals are human beings with souls		Homosexuals are equal

(Warrant)

The unconditional tradition of Christian love extends to everyone

(Backing)

The life and teachings of Jesus

These are simple illustrations of argument by authority, a form that is used over and over again in varying complexities of potential rebuttal and qualification. It is the argumentation form that reflects most closely the purely logical form of the formal syllogism discussed in Chapter 3.

Where the text is taken as authoritative there is little need for verification. Consequently, generalization from sense evidence, in order to prove the value of the grounds or warrant, is less necessary than in some other kinds of argumentation. As we have seen, interpretation is not a simple process but is influenced by tradition, experience, revelation, and culture. It is quite different from argumentation in science, which frequently requires generalization to serve as warrants and observable phenomena as grounds. It is more like argument in law, where the text is accepted and interpreted. Indeed, much of Hebrew and Islamic theology is rooted in law, and Christianity is heavily influenced by its association with Roman law.

Argument by Analogy

Even the staunchest literalists do not argue that there is no metaphor in the Bible. Although they argue for a literal interpretation of the Bible, they do not argue, for instance, that when Jesus said, "You are the salt of the earth" (Matthew 5:13) he meant that his disciples were literally made of salt, nor that the parable of the prodigal son must be taken merely as a literal historical event. The very recognition that it is a parable means that it reveals a principle which can tell a person how to behave in a number of analogous situations. The main issue of most denominational argumentation is how far can one go in arguing by analogy to new interpretations of textual meaning?

Thus, while there are differences in how, and how extensively, argument by analogy is used, it is quite significant in religious argumentation. Many texts are not as straightforward in the assertion of principles from which to build claims as a law like "You shall not murder." Indeed, many are quite clearly arguments by analogy. Parables are an obvious example. When an argument is identified as a parable it means that one must argue by analogy to a useful claim:

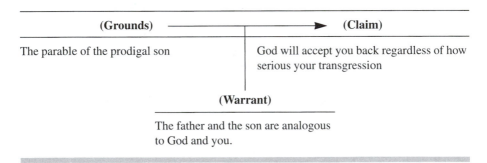

(Grounds) ────────────────▶	(Claim)
The parable of the prodigal son	God will accept you back regardless of how serious your transgression

(Warrant)

The father and the son are analogous
to God and you.

The prodigal son analogy is supported by many specific references in the biblical text to God as Father. But in religious argumentation many uses of analogy will reach far beyond such an obvious example (Perrin).

It is here that disagreements about analogy will take place. John Macquarrie puts the problem very well:

> Just how wide a gulf can this symbolism bridge? One can see that an analogy, for instance, may very well be illuminative for another situation of the same order—for instance, one legal situation may help toward understanding another analogous one. But how could an everyday situation be illuminative for another one of quite different order—or, to make the point more concrete, how could things we can say about kings, portraits or the sun be illuminating for something so remote from these relatively intelligible matters as the incarnation? (184).

One solution is to return to the literal interpretation of texts. The early church father Tertullian as well as Augustine and Aquinas argued that analogy functions appropriately only when it has a final basis in the literal statements of text (Ayers 6). This relates to a point made earlier that the text must be taken as a unified statement. That is, an analogy is justified when it reflects a general understanding of meaning. The example given above of the extensive use of "Father" for God in the text makes it easier for the prodigal son analogy to gain adherence.

However a theologian feels about a particular argument by analogy, no theologian would deny that analogy is a primary means of argumentation in religion. Paul's statement in 2 Cor. 3:6, "The letter kills, but the spirit makes alive," has been used to justify all manner of analogy. Think of all the other possibilities where metaphor (analogy) functions. Is the serpent in the Adam and Eve story literally a snake? Was the fruit of the tree literally that of the knowledge of good and evil? Did God literally kill every living creature except Noah, his family, and the creatures he took in the Ark? Consider all of these stories and many more and consider how one could argue that they are bases for an argument by analogy.

Argument by Narrative

In Judaism and Christianity much of the sacred literature is in the form of stories. The creation story, the story of Abraham, or the story of the Exodus from Egypt, when the grounding principles of both Judaism and Christianity were established, come to mind. The story of the life of Jesus, his followers and his opponents, is the central explanation of Christianity. Narratives of the Torah and the Bible can be interpreted as one of the traditional forms of argument. Earlier we identified the story of Moses and the Ten Commandments as arguments by authority, and the parable of the prodigal son as argument by analogy.

However, there are times when interpreting a narrative as a single claim is seen to weaken and oversimplify the argument. In such a case the theologian will see a story not as a piece of evidence to prove a claim but as a complex development of a theme. The Gospels of Matthew, Mark, Luke, and John tell the story of Jesus' life. But that life, for the believers, cannot be summed up in one claim or even a series of related claims. For them the narrative brings to its receivers a combination of personal experience, culture, and revelation. It is more than a literal story told. It is a narrative that links to the individual and community through a theme with a deep personal meaning.

Theologian Sallie McFague TeSelle notes that the parable of the prodigal son develops the theme of divine love (although never mentioned in the story) "through stretching the surface of the story with an extreme imagery of hunger and feasting, rejection and acceptance, lost and found, death and life" (13). For instance, the son treats the father as if he were dead. The son falls so low that he loses everything and must take the lowest job, feeding swine—unclean animals. When he returns home the father showers him with unmerited gifts. The oppositions created in this narrative develop the theme of divine love.

In some religious organizations, personal narrative is a central element in the religion. Such is the case with the Church of Jesus Christ of Latter Day Saints. At testimony meetings about once a month, members "bear testimony" (tell their stories) to elaborate the theme of the "truth of the gospel." Such a way of seeing a story permits a believer to use a narrative to reinforce the larger story of the religion. The believer looks to a personal story, or a story from sacred texts, and judges it by its consistency in developing a meaningful theme. For personal testimony one frequently judges a story by its consistency with the narratives of others. The Christian who claims to have seen Jesus relates that experience to the story of Paul on the Damascus Road, for instance. In such a case narrative provides a deep personal understanding of God, salvation, or brotherhood rather than a specific claim (Haverwas and Jones).

Argument by Sign

Closely related to argument by analogy is argument by sign. It is common to view one event as a sign of another. Miracles are taken as signs of the existence of God. It is argued that when Jesus fed the multitudes or raised a girl from the dead, it was a sign that he was God, because only God could do these things. Sign argument has its problems in determining what sign is valid. We observed in discussing experience as a factor affecting interpretation that many argue that religion should be applicable in people's lives and, thus, the principles should be observable in experience. But many signs used in popular argument would be difficult for theologians to accept. Particularly subject to skepticism is the sign argument which gets away from text. A common argument that God supports his chosen by giving them material wealth is a sign argument which is easily refuted by reference to the story of Job. Serious students of religious argumentation may accept the claim that God answers prayers but not on the sign: "I prayed for a bicycle and on my next birthday my parents give me one." Such arguments are made by laypersons but not by theologians.

Argument by Paradox

Paradox is a special kind of argument that is closely related to analogy. It is a special type of religious argument that is not mentioned in Chapter 6 (The Nature of Arguments) because it is seldom found in other spheres of argumentation. But it is a characteristic of, particularly Jewish, religious argumentation. James Barr argues that there has always been a unity in Hebrew scriptures. But, he says, Christian scholars have difficulty seeing the unity because of the failure of western educated people to "perceive the unitary though paradoxical Hebraic mind" (9).

A paradox is a riddle. The Hebrew psalmist (78:2) says: "I will open my mouth in a parable; I will utter dark sayings from of old." The Hebrew word that is translated "dark sayings" is commonly translated "riddle." "A riddle is a dark or obscure saying because it gives a deliberately obscure and puzzling description of something, a description which at first sight may well seem nonsensical but is not nonsensical when one hits upon the correct solution" (Macquarrie 29). In short, paradox is used to force a new way of thinking which makes the contradictory noncontradictory.

Religious argumentation employs such paradoxes, such riddles, frequently. Paul said, "We are afflicted in every way, but not crushed; perplexed, but not driven to despair; persecuted, but not forsaken; struck down, but not destroyed . . . for while we live, we are always being given up to death for Jesus' sake" (1 Cor. 13:12). Ignatius argued: "Of flesh and spirit, generate and ingenerate, God in man, true life in death, son of Mary and son of God, first possible and then impossible" (Macquarrie 29).

In a way, all analogy is paradoxical. Since argument by analogy compares unlike things, it is possible to have conflicting and therefore contradictory meanings. Furthermore, since religious argumentation starts from the interpretation of texts, several analogies when taken together can provide a paradox. The New Testament gives a number of images of Christ—"Son of man," "Son of God," "Messiah," "Lord," "Word." "It is impossible," says Macquarrie, "to 'harmonize' all these ideas, but from them something of the mystery of the incarnation finds expression" (228).

How does one solve the "riddle"? How is sense found in this nonsense, the parable? By looking at the paradoxical argument in its context, as a part of the complete argumentative process, it can be done. We noted above that the seemingly contradictory statements describing Christ come together to describe the mystery of something beyond language: incarnation—of God become man. Likewise, single paradoxical arguments make sense from context. So "He that loveth his life shall lose it; and he that hateth his life in this world shall keep it unto life eternal" (John 12:25) is a paradox which makes sense in the context of the greater value of eternal life which can be secured by giving up the lesser value of mortal life. Such a meaning is understandable only in the context of the other major arguments in a system of religious argumentation.

Argument by Generalization

Since most of the grounds espoused in religious argumentation are given by the text and claims are reasoned from them by authority, analogy, sign, narrative, or paradox, generalization is rarely used. Unlike scientific argumentation, that searches through specific details to find rules or laws which will predict the nature of any other case of the same kind, religious argumentation has its warrants given and reasons mostly to find specific application. The most significant exception to this rule is the idea of unity mentioned earlier. It is essential that a religious argument not be in conflict with the text *taken as a whole*. Taking the text as a whole is, in a sense, a crude form of argumentation by generalization, for one argues that all the events in the text lead to a general principle.

Natural theology, discussed on page 259, is an example of argument by generalization. The natural condition is observed and a principle drawn from it. Indeed, as we have noted, theologians frequently call this "empirical argument."

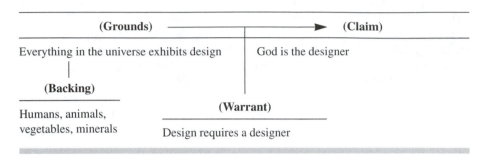

(Grounds)	⟶	(Claim)
Everything in the universe exhibits design		God is the designer

(Backing)

Humans, animals, vegetables, minerals

(Warrant)

Design requires a designer

But Thomas Olbricht has observed that most religious arguments which look at first glance like generalizations are not this at all. He found that, in his homilies, Basil the Great used the text as a source of beginning points for arguments and reasoned about specific claims by general principle. The many statements taken from the text are not for proof but for *amplification*. Olbricht cites an example from Pope Innocent III to show this amplification:

> Just as the sea is always stormy and turbulent, so the world remains always in storm and stress; nowhere is there peace and security, never is there rest and quietness, but everywhere toil and trouble. "For the whole world is seated in wickedness" (1 John 5:19). "Laughter shall be mingled with sorrow, and mourning taketh hold of the end of joy" (Prov. 14:13). With reason, therefore, the apostle laments: "Unhappy man that I am, who shall deliver me from the body of this death?" (Rom. 7:24). And the Psalmist said, "Bring my soul out of prison" (Ps. 142:7). "Man is born to labour and the bird to fly" (Job 5:7). "All his days are sorrows and miseries, *even in the night he doth not rest in mind*" (Eccles. 2:23).

In a sense this is argument by generalization, but some of the statements seem to have little to do with the main claim. So, says Olbricht, it is more like amplification of a claim already accepted rather than support for a generalization which is being argued. Early in the formation of a religion, argument by generalization may be necessary, but after its establishment it is not. It may even be considered foolish, because why should one argue a principle which is already accepted?

Generalization by statistics is especially open to question. T. Dewitt Talmage, an orthodox preacher of the late nineteenth century, used an argument from statistics to refute Robert G. Ingersoll's popular arguments for agnosticism. In his sermon, "Victory For God," he cited the increasing number of Christians in each century, the number of New Testaments distributed, the number of converts, and so forth, to prove the popularity of Christianity (290–92). Most theologians would quickly identify that as the fallacy of *argumentatum ad populum*. It is inappropriate to religious argumentation because religious argumentation does not attempt to know what is popular but what is true, and a true religion may be unpopular, as were early Judaism, Christianity, and Islam.

There are, in summary, five and occasionally six, forms of argument used in religious argumentation. Argument by authority, argument by analogy, and argument by narrative are most frequently used. Argument by sign is probably less frequently used. Argument by paradox is not as frequently used as some other forms of argument but it poses a "riddle" that can be central to the meaning of a religion. Except as natural theology, argumentation by generalization is rarely used and is open to question.

Conclusion

Religious argumentation is among the oldest spheres known to humans. The Judeo–Christian–Islamic tradition operates from an elaborate system of texts and other evidence to ground specialized theological arguments.

Theological argumentation is found in seven major questions. The explanation of most, if not all, of them will usually define a complete theology: (1) What is the nature of God? (2) What is the nature of human beings? (3) What is moral behavior, the religious life? (4) What are sin, evil, and the meaning of suffering? (5) What is the human's relationship to God? (6) What is the nature of salvation? and (7) What is the role of the church? The themes that arguers develop in answering these questions will identify the strongest values and serve as warrants for religious argumentation. These include: God, human beings, moral behavior, evil, sin, suffering, prophet, salvation, and church.

In religious argumentation, texts are traditionally the most central kinds of evidence. The theologian must first decide which texts are most accurate, which texts are most trustworthy, and how these texts may be interpreted. In the interpretation of texts, and sometimes independent of texts, tradition, experience, revelation, and culture may also serve as evidence.

Argument from authority and argument by analogy are the preferred forms of argumentation among theologians. Argument by sign is also used but less so. Argument by narrative has a special role in religious argumentation. Argument by paradox is a special kind of argument prevalent in religious argumentation but uncommon elsewhere. It involves finding a new meaning in seemingly contradictory statements. Argument by generalization is usually not used except in the sense that the text must be taken as a whole. Some of what seems like generalization is actually a kind of amplification of a claim established by some other kind of argument.

PROJECT

Choose a short text that is important to your religion. Explain what it means to you. Evaluate your own answer. On what bases did you make your interpretation? If your religion is not from the traditions discussed here, what different bases did you find?

15 Argumentation in Business

KEY TERMS

freedom and choice
transparency
booms/busts
comparison/contrast
cause/effect
sign
evidence
examples
testimony

timely innovation
competition
social responsibility
cost/benefit
change
credibility
statistics
globalization
vision

Critical decision making in business spheres has always been difficult, because taking risks is inherent in business. However, business decision making is probably more challenging today than ever before in history because of the speed with which business operates; the rapidity with which technology evolves; the changes in customer demands, expectations, and demographics; and the unprecedented need to make business transparent. To explain these changes, we will recall our discussions earlier in this book about starting points and forms of support for arguments. Remember, as in the other Application chapters in this section, "business" is far too complex a concept to count as a single sphere. At any time, thousands of spheres exist within the broad rubric of business. Our comments must be understood as being highly generalized.

Starting Points for Business Argumentation

Over the years, business spheres have developed elaborate systems designed to establish accepted facts, presumptions, probabilities, and commonplaces on which argumentation could be based. Recall that without starting points, argumentation is not possible; the greater the shared starting points, the easier it is to develop an argument.

Starting points jump-start argumentation. For example, the more facts we share at the start of our decision making, the more we will be able to use as support for our claims, and the fewer claims we will need to argue. We can reach the proposition faster with a head start.

Facts in Business Argumentation

Cornelis de Kluyver and his colleagues characterize business strategy as being different, more competitive, with a focus on value creation for shareholders, partners, suppliers, employees, and the community by satisfying the needs and wants of customers better than anyone else (3). To do this, business arguments must start with reliable facts about the needs and wants of customers and what will count as valuable for all of those stakeholders just mentioned. De Kluyver and colleagues identify learning and adaptation as the primary strategic planning value. People in business decision making are increasingly well-educated, dedicated to continuous learning, and hold in their collective memory and databases the intellectual capital that forms a major part of any firm's value. With the global nature of business, the increasing ease of communication, and the rapidity of change in almost everything, there is a constant need to check accepted facts and adapt them to current knowledge.

People outside any particular business organization also make critical decisions about the company and need good facts as starting points. Businesses need capital to start, operate, and grow, and they go to various sources to get this money: partners, venture capitalists, financial institutions, and investors. Obviously, customers need facts about price, supply, product quality and availability, delivery time, and so on.

In the summer of 2003, the Federal Energy Regulatory Commission (FERC) imposed what was called a "death penalty" on Enron Corporation, a company selling electricity and natural gas. The company was allowed to continue in business but under restrictions that weakened its competitiveness. It was already under Chapter 11 bankruptcy protection. Why was this Houston, Texas, company so severely punished? Two years earlier, in the Western United States, there was an energy crisis involving too little electricity at too great a cost. It put the state of California in such a financial crisis that in 2003 voters recalled Governor Gray Davis, at least in part because he had not handled the energy crisis well. The FERC found that Enron had manipulated the power markets by exaggerating prices and providing inaccurate facts about supply, hiding its debts, inflating its profits, and publishing deceptive accounting statements. FERC Chairman Pat Wood, in announcing the decision, said, "We send a clear signal that competitive markets must work in the interest of customers and public interest." A total of sixty-five power companies, utilities, and municipalities were asked by the FERC to justify their prices and marketing strategies during the energy crisis.

This case illustrates the critical importance of reliable facts as starting points for business argumentation. Apparently, Enron led the way in generating facts about energy that proved to be vastly in error. In essence, they committed the fallacy of intent to deceive. As a result, states such as California (i.e., customers) signed contracts for energy supplies they should not have signed. Investors, relying on inaccurate facts, bought shares of Enron stock that soon were virtually worthless. Companies that supplied Enron the energy it in turn sold were either in on the deception (the FERC singled out seven subsidiaries of Enron and five other companies for taking advantage of a warped market) or they suffered significant losses. Thousands of employees of Enron lost their jobs and found that their retirement funds and investments in Enron had lost most of their value. The FERC represented the role of government in ensuring that facts used as starting points were accurate. Government is one of the sources of *transparency,* which is achieved when agencies require businesses to open themselves to examination so that the public can rely on their reports.

Presumptions in Business Argumentation

Of the many presumptions that form the foundations on which business argumentation rests, we will discuss two: the presumption that accountants have a dedication to accurate reports independent of the companies they audit, and the presumption that analysts working in financial institutions provide reliable information about securities issued by various corporations independent of the companies being analyzed or the other departments of their own financial institution that have an interest in profiting from securities they sponsor. These are two nongovernmental agencies that participate in assuring transparency in business argumentation.

    Accounting firms stand between businesses and their appropriate decision makers as the independent agents who assure the accuracy and reliability of data and arguments published by the firm. When decision makers consider a business argument, they wisely ask, "Why should we trust what this company is saying about itself? Maybe, it is committing the fallacy of attempt to deceive so that we will think they are better, more reliable, stronger, more promising than they really are." The answer is that the reports carry an accounting firm's seal of approval. Some TV quiz shows and contests proudly announce that the questions or the votes have been under the protection of, for example, PriceWaterhouseCoopers, an accounting firm. Viewers are expected to agree that there has been no hanky-panky in the process if a reliable watchdog is protecting the data. In addition to its accounting expertise, such a firm's most valuable asset is its integrity: credibility. It is the presumption of the credibility of accounting firms that makes a great deal of business argumentation possible.

    We will illustrate this presumption with negative examples. The founder of the eighty-nine-year-old accounting firm Arthur Andersen advanced the motto, "Think straight. Talk Straight." Barbara Ley Toffler and Jennifer Reingold report in their book, *Ambition, Greed, and the Fall of Arthur Andersen,* how the firm fell from the heights of credibility to destruction through the desire to make money. Toffler, who was a specialist in ethics, says of Andersen, "I worked with people so in thrall to the great bull market of the 1990s and the power and wealth of their corporate benefactors that they completely forgot that the true purpose of their job was to protect the investing public" (7). Instead of serving as the independent agent of honesty, they became the partners to the kind of dishonesty we just described in the discussion of facts as starting points. Indeed, Arthur Andersen was involved in the Enron case as well as other similar deceptions in such companies as WorldCom, Qwest Communications, and Sunbeam. When it became apparent that Andersen was, in a way, a partner of others' greed rather than a watchdog, the firm collapsed, leaving 85,000 employees out of a job. Instead of serving as a watchdog of the ethical practice of business in the Enron case, Andersen employees, "Embarked on a frenzy of document shredding never seen before at the firm" (214).

Similarly, internal accounting is presumed by the company leaders to carry high credibility. Today, huge, global companies, often the product of many mergers and acquisitions, are increasingly the norm, making huge accounting errors possible. Andrew Backover reported in the October 22, 2003, *USA Today* that AT&T overstated its income by $125 million in 2001 and 2002. The company claimed, however, that this inaccurate reporting was not indicative of greed but only an error that employees then covered up to avoid punishment. Nevertheless, investors who purchased AT&T stock on the strength of arguments that the company was healthier than it really was were not happy. The *USA Today* article quoted Bank of America securities analyst David Barden as saying, "AT&T's 'squeaky clean' past might mean that investors give it a free pass on this one." But if AT&T says there are no more questionable accounting issues, "they better mean it" (1B).

Securities analysts, such as David Barden, are presumed to be well-informed and objective students of business performance. When they announce their arguments indicating how well a segment of industry or a specific firm is doing and is likely to do in the future, decision makers presume the claims are not being intentionally distorted by greed. Increasingly, analysts' evaluations and expectations occupy a central role in business decision making. Again, we will illustrate the point by negative examples.

On May 29, 2003, the Associated Press reported that the National Association of Securities Dealers (NASD) accused an analyst for Merrill Lynch of "deceiving investors with misleading stock research" (Gordon). The charge was a fallacy claim of conflict of interest and intent to deceive: the analyst was alleged to have gotten too chummy with a company he was supposed to be objectively analyzing. The NASD claimed that the analyst published reports about Tyco International that "contained misleading statements and exaggerated claims that differed from his own views and opinions as he privately expressed them" (8E).

But this case is one among many, and is not the worst. For example, in an advertisement for his own software investing product, Wizetrade, George Thompson claims that the presumption of objectivity of securities analysts can no longer be trusted. He supported his argument by noting that the Securities and Exchange Commission (SEC) has announced a $1.4 billion settlement with ten brokerage firms and two analysts "accused of luring millions of investors to buy billions of dollars worth of shares in *companies they knew were troubled*" because those companies were clients of theirs (Thompson, "They Lied to You" 21). Again, this was an alleged conflict of interest. Without the presumption of objectivity in analyst reports, critical business decisions become much more difficult. Thompson's Wizetrade proposes that investors gain access to raw data and do their own analysis, even though most people lack the knowledge and ability to do so wisely.

Probabilities in Business Argumentation

Among the many probabilities that provide starting points for business argumentation, the most prominent are the inevitability of cycles of booms and busts, and the expectation of upward movement in economies. Eamon Kelly, Peter Leyden and members of Global Business Network note in their 2002 book *What's Next: Exploring the New Terrain for Business,* "Busts and Booms are equally irrational" (20). By this they mean that most people, when thinking rationally, would acknowledge the probability that no matter what is happening now, boom or bust, it will be followed sooner or later by its opposite. The irrational part comes in convincing ourselves the probability will not hold true *this time.* In the late 1990s, year after year of economic expansion led many to speculate that maybe, for the first time ever, people had learned how to maintain a continuously upward economy. Arguments were predicated on the rejection of the cyclical probability: keep investing in almost anything because it will go up. Then, the dotcoms began to collapse and people realized, too late, they had been pouring money into companies that had never produced a profit and had virtually no intrinsic value. They would have been better advised to recall the old maxim, "What goes up must come down."

Then, in the middle of the bust in 2000–2003, it was hard to convince people to invest in even the most solid companies, which also was irrational. "In a bubble you can get money for anything, and in a bust you can't get money for even really good ideas. People freeze up," say Kelly and Leyden (20). Business arguments that acknowledge the probability of business cycles will be stronger. Of course, the trouble is the uncertainty of not knowing when the next cycle will come around or how high or low it will go.

But even in the face of the probability of cycles in business activity, there is also a probability of a long-term upward trend. Frequently noted is the fact that various economic measures such as those by Dow Jones show a steady rise in value since, say, the end of World War II. Even factoring in years of bust, a steady upward line in the price of securities can be shown. Thus, the probability is that in the long term, values will rise. People purchase homes on the probability that the value of the home will rise over the years of their occupation, and they hope to sell during a boom rather than a bust.

From the 1950s to the 1990s, Japan's economy steadily rose until it was one of the most dominant in the world. Then, when Japan and many of the other economic leaders in Asia suffered a downturn, they were expected to bounce back on the probability of long-term growth. Ten years later, when every other East Asian country had recovered and Japan had not, observers were perplexed. South Korea had recovered in less than two years. Fred Harmon says the difference between South Korea and Japan is not the degree of structural reform, "but the degree of vision. South Korea is still playing catch-up. Its direction is clear . . . Japan, in contrast, has enormous underutilized potential. . . . Those resources need a new national ambition" (61). It is significant, from our discussion of probabilities, that Harmon never suggests that Japan's time of economic dominance is past. Instead, he expects it will be a tougher job than South Korea's, but both will continue the predicted upward trend.

Along with the probability of booms and busts and long-term growth in business is the probability of change. Jeffrey Garten says the world is now experiencing extraordinary changes in technology and globalization that have "created a level of competition that will lead to new categories of winners and losers and for a transformation in how companies are organized and led" (19). We are now, he says, in the third such revolution. He labels England between 1750 and 1840 and the United States between the 1860s and the 1920s as the Industrial Revolutions. Now we are in the information, communication, or knowledge age, depending on who is speaking. Business argumentation uses the probability of change as a starting point for claims about what businesses and entire industries must do to anticipate and profit from the impending change, whatever it turns out to be.

Commonplaces/Forms of Argument in Business Argumentation

In Chapter 2, we define commonplaces as lines of argument, forms of argument, or places from which arguments can be built. In Chapter 3, we observe that spheres define the patterns of argument that are preferred and the criteria by which they will be evaluated. In Chapter 6, we explain various forms of argument. It is possible to identify some commonplaces that are generally characteristic of business argumentation.

Comparison and contrast can be found in much business argumentation. Adam Shell, writing in *USA Today* for October 23, 2003, reported: "On Wall Street, it's not how much money companies say they made in the past that really drives stock prices. It's how much companies say they will earn in the future—versus what analysts expect—that determines if stocks rise or fall" (1B). Shell identified two forms of comparison and contrast that feature prominently in business argumentation. First, more traditionally, companies make arguments based on comparison and contrast with past and present performance. Whether measured quarterly, annually, or over some identifiable range, the argument claims that since the present performance is better (higher, stronger, etc.) than past performance, we are in good shape. Second, increasingly decision makers pay attention to comparisons and contrasts between companies' announced expectation for the next reporting period and the expectations of presumably independent analysts. Then, at the appropriate time, the companies reveal their actual performance. The argument claims that if actual performance is near the company's prediction and equal to or higher than that anticipated by analysts, then the company is either in good shape or we have a good understanding of its shape, good or bad.

In the same October 23, 2003, issue of *USA Today*, we learn that the telecom industry, which had been ailing, reported better-than-expected results. BellSouth and Lucent Technologies both reported better than expected earnings, entering the profitable side of the ledger after a long downturn. Did this signal an end to the telecom troubles? Analysts were impressed but still cautious. They said, "After this week's lackluster results from local phone giant SBC Communications and No. 1 long-distance carrier AT&T, analysts are wary" (3B). Here, arguments are made about the health of an industry rather than individual corporations through comparison and contrast of individual firms' performance.

Cause and effect is a widely used commonplace in business argumentation. When sales decline, the cause is sought. Is it a failure in marketing? Is the competition gaining? Is the price too high or low? Are the customers changing preference? "There must be a cause," is a frequently heard claim. Like sports teams that fire the manager when the team loses too much, businesses are likely to fire CEOs. Leaders in business are regularly rewarded as the cause of success, and they usually are punished in some way as the ultimate cause of failure. *Business Week* for March 31, 2003, reported that during the downturn, some CEOs had come under unusual scrutiny: salaries were lowered and other perks such as company cars, country club membership, first-class air travel, and health club membership were restricted or eliminated. Again, the argument is cause and effect: If the company is losing money, then people at the top should feel the effect. Kenneth Lay headed Enron. Former employees of the contractor are suing him and the contractor that administered the company 401(k) plan, saying employees were improperly encouraged or even required to keep Enron stock in their accounts. Lay is widely blamed for the problems at Enron, and employees claim one effect of his action is that their retirement accounts are now almost worthless.

The Federal Reserve Board has the responsibility to control interest rates in response to economic conditions. One of the ways businesses get needed capital is to take out loans, and the rate of interest is at least as important to them as it is to a car buyer. Alan Greenspan, chair of the Federal Reserve, uses cause and effect arguments regularly in trying to decide the level of interest rates. In the March 31, 2003, issue of *Business Week,* Greenspan was quoted as saying the economic weakness then being experienced was caused by the war in Iraq, and that when the war ends, the economy will rise. But other members of the Board disagreed, saying the weakness is not only caused by Iraq uncertainty but also by, "The 90s excesses which left companies with too much capacity and consumers with too much debt" (39). When President Bush declared the end of major hostilities shortly thereafter, the economy showed only some signs of rising, but apparently there had been other causes at play. Of course, the war continued, as well.

Cost/benefit is a widely used business commonplace. In decision making, a proposition can be argued in relation to its costs and expected benefits. Obviously, if business costs would exceed benefits, the proposition will be rejected. Cost is defined variously as actual money required, the values that could have been obtained with that money by using it elsewhere, the opportunities lost by choosing this proposition, or the social, political, cultural, environmental, or other costs that will be associated with adopting the proposition. Similarly, benefit is defined many ways, including profit to be gained, money saved, or some other desired end such as increased market share, industry dominance, or improvements in ways of doing business.

The Associated Press reported on October 6, 2003, that, "Carrier Corporation is eliminating all 1,200 manufacturing jobs at its suburban Syracuse container refrigeration and compressor plant, saying it needs to shift production closer to its key markets in Asia." Ted Amyuni, the company senior vice president for operations, was quoted as saying this was a tough decision, but essential for competitiveness and growth. "These decisions," he said, "reflect, in part, market requirements. The global container market has become Asian-focused, with more than 80 percent of our container refrigeration products currently being shipped to Asia. We must be located nearer to our markets." Having identified the benefits of the move (without mentioning possible savings with cheaper labor costs), he did not stress the costs. In addition to money needed to make the move, there is the obvious cost to workers who lose their jobs and damage to the economy of Syracuse.

Sign reasoning is predominant in business argumentation. Remember, the commonplace of sign differs from that of cause in that the argument does not claim the sign is a cause or effect of a phenomenon, but that it is an indicator or a correlate. The constantly changing values on various exchanges such as Dow Jones, NASDAQ, the New York Stock Exchange, and Standard & Poors are seen as signs of broad investor confidence in the health of the economy and future performance in the business world. The actual value of any company's shares is seen as a sign of investor confidence in the future performance of that company.

Throughout a good part of 2003, the value of the dollar against foreign currencies such as the yen or euro declined noticeably. Often, monetary exchange rates are taken as a sign of the health of a nation's economy. In this case, however, there were charges made that the U.S. government was intentionally allowing the dollar to fall so that U.S. businesses could sell their products abroad at cheaper prices. If so (and the United States did not deny the charge), then allowing a cheaper dollar was taken as a sign of the Bush administration's willingness to weaken the dollar's place as the world's leading and most reliable currency in exchange for helping U.S. businesses compete more effectively outside the country.

Governments collect a variety of data to be used as signs of future movements of the economy. Increased orders for durable goods may be seen as a sign of increased consumer confidence and future demand for raw materials such as steel. When manufacturers announce increased spending on plants and equipment, it is usually taken as a sign that the firms anticipate future demand for their products. And this is taken as a sign of possible improvement in the economy as a whole. When wholesale prices fall, it may be a sign of lower levels of inflation.

Forms of Support in Business Argumentation

Evidence, values, and credibility constitute the forms of support for arguments, as we explained in Chapters 7, 8, and 9. In this section, we will discuss some of the ways evidence, values, and credibility are used in business argumentation. We will focus particularly on how business spheres shape support to their particular needs.

Evidence in Business Argumentation

You learned in Chapter 7 that the common forms of evidence in arguments are examples, statistics, and testimony. All three forms are used widely in business decision making.

Examples abound in business argumentation. Pick up any book, magazine article, or business section of the newspaper and you will find claims are constantly supported by examples of leaders, corporations, industries, or whole economies. Jeffrey A. Sonnenfeld writes about executive failures in the book *The 21st Century Executive.* His first claim is that overcoming setbacks is a characteristic of good leaders, and this is his supporting sentence: "Many contemporary business leaders, such as Robert Pittman, president of AOL/Time Warner, Bernard Marcus, founder of huge home-improvement retailer Home Depot, Steve Jobs, founder of Apple Computer, and business media mogul Michael Bloomberg, are great enterprise builders who were only momentarily traumatized when forced from major leadership positions before rebounding" (5).

Fred Harmon, writing in his book, *Business 2010,* introduces a system of quality control called "Six Sigma." The Greek letter sigma is used in statistics as a measure of deviation from the mean. For example, in university grading systems, an A grade represents three sigmas (standard deviations) above the C grade at the mean. Six Sigma suggests the highest achievable level of quality: 3.4 defects per million "opportunities," which is a term used to identify the individual steps in producing and delivering a product. It is not an easy concept to understand, so Harmon uses a hypothetical example. Suppose you are to clean a 1,500-square-foot carpet. If your quality level is three sigma, you would still have enough dirt spread throughout the carpet to cover about 4 square feet. A six-sigma quality level would leave only enough dirt to cover a pinhead. Then, Harmon goes on to use General Electric as an example of a company that has adopted the six-sigma process (135–136).

Statistics, of course, constitute the most common form of evidence in business arguments. Business runs on numbers, and virtually every aspect of decision making relies on quantified data.

McDonald's, the hamburger giant, claims to be in reasonably good shape even when many other firms are suffering from a downturn. How is that claim supported by statistics? In an October 23, 2003, report in *USA Today,* we learn that the corporation had a net income of $547 million, or 43 cents a share compared with $487 million and 38 cents a year ago. This is a 12 percent improvement. Moreover, we learn that these results were 3-cents-a-share better than analysts predicted, and as a result, optimistic investors raised the price of McDonald's stock by 16 cents, to $23.90.

Testimony as a form of evidence turns up in several places we have already discussed. Accountants and analysts provide testimonial as well as statistical evidence to support business claims. Government agencies such as the Federal Reserve, the Securities and Exchange Commission, or the Federal Energy Regulatory Commission take testimony from business representatives, economists, and other authorities, and then provide testimony in their reports that are often used in business decisions and legal proceedings.

Rob Silzer writes about how to go about selecting leaders at the top in *The 21st Century Executive.* "Executives occupy the most visible and influential positions in most organizations," Silzer says. "They have an enormous impact on the success and effectiveness of the organization. As [a] result they get a lot of attention from both employees and outside business observers" (81). It is no surprise, then, that testimony used in business arguments is most likely to be provided by company leaders. In the same article about McDonald's we discussed earlier, the claim about the company's success is further supported by testimony from CEO Jim Cantalupo, "We're in the middle of our effort, and if I were bringing home a midterm report card today, I'd say we are ahead of where we need to be in the U.S., but we still have a lot of homework to do on the international side of our business" (10B).

Values as Support in Business Argumentation

Throughout this chapter, we have been using negative examples because a series of serious violations of presumed values has occurred in U.S. business over the past few years. It is impossible to talk about business today without noticing that greed and corruption have taken center stage and a discussion of values and ethics is urgently needed. Lurking over this discussion is another, more long-term one about the costs and benefits of globalization. In this section, we will describe some of the values that support business argumentation while at the same time describing, however briefly, some of the issues of ethics and globalization.

Profit, in all its forms, is the underlying value of most business arguments. As Michael Armstrong, then chair and CEO of AT&T said, "Unless you are competitive, then all other issues are moot." And Jurgen Schrempp, chair of DaimlerChrysler, echoed the comment, saying, "Only a profitable corporation can think about being a social enterprise, too" (Garten 14). Fred Harmon, referring to a comment in the *New York Times,* says the economics and culture of the Internet reflect American values including, "A culture that celebrates risk-taking, ambition and getting very, very rich" 61).

However, some businesses and their executives tried to become very, very rich at the expense of clients, customers, shareholders, employees, and others. Wendy Tanaka, writing in the *Honolulu Advertiser* (May 4, 2003), reports that some investors are challenging current interpretations of corporate values relating to profit. She says that before corporate scandals in Enron, Arthur Andersen, WorldCom, Adelphia Communications, and others, shareholders had little influence on corporate decisions. But now, "Shareholders are starting to challenge corporate values and come up with their own values," through resolutions filed with their proxy statements. "Shareholders at the scandal-ridden Tyco International Ltd. have seen positive changes from current management. At the March annual meeting, Tyco—which saw its two former top executives charged last year with looting $600 million from the company—announced a new board of directors" (F5).

Jeffrey Garten, writing in his book, *The Mind of the CEO,* observes that, "There is a long history of business pursuing its self-interest in ways that are antiethical to the general welfare" (18). He lists oil, automobiles, pharmaceuticals, media, entertainment, and tobacco as such industries. Future CEOs should lead companies away from such practices, but the question, Garten says, is whether they can resist the "intense counter-pressures" of greed.

Globalization is now a driving value in business argumentation, and it is a negative value in the minds of many others. We just quoted the chair of DaimlerChrysler, and we can refer to that organization as an example of decisions resting on the globalization value. Two large and powerful automobile companies, one in Germany and the other in the United States, are now combined. Why would they want to do that? Globalization: they now can reach customers more quickly with a better-adapted product than they could alone. Cornelis De Kluyver and John Pearce say that political boundaries identifying countries and regions may still have some meaning, but they have almost disappeared on the "global competitive map. The ever-faster flow of information across the world has made people aware of the tastes, preferences, and lifestyles of citizens in other countries. Through this information flow we are all becoming . . . global citizens" (16). To be competitive, corporations such as Daimler-Chrysler must be global.

The other side of that coin, however, is widespread fear over loss of jobs, human rights abuses, environmental degradation, and variations in labor standards. Overarching these concerns is technophobia (fear and hatred of new technologies) and a resistance to the homogenization of culture. *Progress* was once a highly regarded value, as we noted in Chapter 8. Today, for many people, it is a hated concept. Whenever multinational conferences such as the World Trade Organization meet, there are likely to be protests. Knowing this, meeting organizers hold the meetings in more and more remote locations.

Freedom and choice are increasingly arising as values in business decision making. What Harmon refers to as an "Asian value" is the belief that economic and political freedoms are divisible. "In theory," he says, "Asian willingness to defer to authority could produce sustained growth without the political upheavals that sometimes shake western democracies" (12). But in the context of globalization, Japan, China, and other Asian economies—along with some in the former Soviet-dominated nations—are finding it difficult to conduct capitalist free enterprises within a politically controlled society. Corporations in the United States and elsewhere want to do business with these nations, but often find resistance from their shareholders and the government, who believe that refusing to do business with such countries may force them to adopt policies more in line with democracy.

In another context, workers in western corporations are demanding more freedom and choice than was previously possible. The idea of spending an entire career with one firm is long gone, and so is the willingness to be transferred every few years to new jobs in new locations. Workers demand more freedom to spend time with their families, and call for choice regarding flex-time, working from home, child-care at work, and (with the help of law) family leave. Business decisions must take these new value assertions into account.

Timely innovation frequently appears as a supporting value in business decision making. In the face of rapidly changing technology, with a customer base that is becoming older and a focus on products that are tied to the Internet, innovation is essential to profitability. Yet many companies fail to adjust to the value of innovation because their corporate culture and traditional strategic planning processes are aimed at maintaining current products and services, not creating new ones. Old command-and-control corporate structures, with many layers of organization, and corporations that are in "the aging phases of corporate life" (Burke and Morrison 63) may simply be unable to handle the demands of innovation within the time demands now in place. Dan Burke and Alan Morrison put great stress on timely innovation. "If you are going after a market niche that is currently unpopulated, you're probably in a race to be 'first to market.' " They say, "If you fail to get to market quickly, you risk becoming a 'me-too' venture with little appeal to investors and little competitive differentiation for consumers" (55). They use a bank as an example of a stodgy enterprise that took so long to consider an innovative proposal from bright employees that by the time they went to market, another product had already claimed that prized first-to-market label.

Vision toward the future has always been highly valued in business decision making, and with contemporary conditions there is less time to ponder the future before acting. Remember Harmon's comment about the difference between South Korea and Japan: they did not differ structurally. Instead he charged Japan with a lack of vision. Garten argues that it is the responsibility of corporate leaders to achieve and communicate a vision for the firm, and then to motivate employees to join in working toward it. If they are to follow your vision, "Employees have to believe that their company's top management has the interests of the rank and file at heart, that what the company is doing and how it's changing is good for them" (123).

Social responsibility regularly occurs in business argumentation. Historically, business enterprises valued profit, and arguments supported by other values stood little chance of success. Over the years, business leaders have been dragged, kicking and screaming, into the consideration of a responsibility to their employees' wages and working conditions, the interests of consumers, the effect of their business operations on their community and environment, the role of government in shaping the transparency of their policies, practices, and respect for civil rights, and today, their global responsibility. Garten quotes David Packard, cofounder of Hewlett-Packard, as reflecting the current thinking of business leaders. Packard acknowledges that making money is important to a company's existence. But, he continues, "We have to go deeper and find the real reasons for our being. . . . Our main task is to design, develop, and manufacture the finest electronic [equipment] for the advancement of science and the welfare of humanity" (131).

Thomas Friedman, writing in the *New York Times* web edition on September 25, 2003, gives an example of global responsibility. He reports that world trade talks broke down over differences between developing countries on one side, and the United States, the European Union, and Japan on the other. The issues centered on the developing countries' need to grow by exporting food and textiles while the developed nations maintain tariffs and subsidies for their farmers that make it impossible for exports to compete. Should subsidies be removed? Cost/benefit analysis suggests it would be beneficial to developing nations and to all consumers, but costly to farmers and agricultural businesses in developed nations. A World Bank study said an agreement to reduce tariffs and agrisubsidies could raise global income by $500 billion a year by 2015—more than 60 percent of which would go to poor countries, pulling

144 million people out of poverty. The developed nations' agricultural industry would suffer loss of jobs, profits, and farms, but consumers would gain by enjoying lower prices. It is a surprisingly difficult decision to make.

Credibility as Support for Business Argumentation

Credibility is defined in Chapter 9 as the perception that the arguer is competent and trustworthy, and has good will toward the decision makers. Dynamism is also frequently mentioned as a factor in credibility. In business argumentation, credibility plays a role in arguments addressed to customers, shareholders, employees, the government, other businesses, and special interest groups such as environmentalists. Consistent with our earlier comments about the ethical challenges many industries have experienced lately, the loss of credibility can be shown to damage or destroy a business' ability to advance arguments successfully, and often even the ability to stay in business.

Global competition has generated more choice for consumers, producers, shareholders, suppliers, and distributors. Increased choice produces greater demands on business to connect successfully with appropriate decision makers. It is more difficult to argue successfully when there is so much competition and a resulting increase in choice. "Increasingly, the real economic value of a corporation does not come from the assets it owns but from the domain of trust that it establishes with its customers" (de Kluyver et al. 16). This is called "branding," and it refers not simply to product brand names that are known and trusted, but corporate images that are similarly known and trusted. Arthur Andersen had an unblemished name in accounting, where credibility is virtually everything. When they lost that, they lost everything. As we have noted earlier, AT&T has a "squeaky clean" image that probably will carry them through some accounting problems, but that credibility is fragile and easily broken.

Mutual funds have held high credibility as places ordinary investors could safely put their money to work in securities without the need to study the market and be constantly on the alert for changes. The so-called little investors, without the billions of dollars needed to have staffs of experts and the big capital to move effectively in the market, have turned to mutual funds as a safe haven. Then, first little-by-little and then in a torrent, disturbing new facts emerged: mutual fund brokers were exposed as violating rules to allow special customers to make advantageous trades that the little investors were denied. Favorite clients made billions improperly. Ordinary clients did not earn as much as they might have.

Jason Zweig, writing in *Money* of October 2003, says the New York state attorney general charged that Bank of America's brokerage unit helped a hedge fund manager, "trade the bank's Nations funds at earlier prices after the market had closed. Such 'late trading' is flagrantly illegal" (51). Zweig goes on to say that while the monetary harm to any one mutual fund investor may not be so great, "The psychological damage is incalculable. The premise upon which mutual funds are sold to individuals— here's your chance to get treated just as well as a Wall Street big shot—has been exposed as a pathetic lie" (52). Credibility loss to traders was so great that some Wall Street firms, including J.P. Morgan, Lehman Brothers, and Morgan Stanley have started to hire analysts in India because of the "Heightened awareness of the need for fair and untainted research" (*New York Times* web edition, October 10, 2003).

The reputation of business leaders contributes to the credibility that supports a firm's arguments. Garten, who interviewed forty men and women at the head of many of the leading global firms, says, "CEOs are major actors in the drama called globalization." They will, he says, direct actions that will knit the world together, cause economic growth, create employment, technological development, shape the environment, and influence basic values. "However they behave, their influence will be at least as important as that of national governments and international institutions—probably more so" (6–7).

Internet websites are increasingly the point of contact between a company and its appropriate decision makers, and Burke and Morrison believe few firms are doing the right thing. The say most sites "suck." "They suck because they simply fail to communicate with the intended audience. . . . A good Web site isn't about you, it's about your customers" (11). An interactive website allows businesses to learn about those who have come to it and what their values and interests are. Then, the business can discover what credibility they have already generated and what they need to do to generate more during the interactions. The credibility so developed can be used to support future arguments. Remember from Chapter 9 that credibility exists as a perception of the appropriate decision makers. You cannot use credibility as support without knowing the decision makers' perceptions.

Credibility plays a role in argumentation within a business, and it is powerfully embedded with the organizational culture. "A corporate culture is manifested through artifacts, shared values, and basic assumptions," say de Kluyver and Pearce (40). Global knowledge companies tend to produce a culture of high energy, intellect, drive, entrepreneurship, and teamwork. They are more inclined toward consensus decision making rather than a top-down approach. In such cultures, credibility results from trust and respect generated interpersonally and plays an influential role in decision making.

Finally, credibility emanates from position—the first in the market tends to gain and retain high credibility. Business experts tend to say, "The first name in the market controls the market." You can probably name many businesses that were the first to introduce a product or service, but you will be harder pressed to name those that came in later. The first aspirin (Bayer), the first acetaminophen (Tylenol), the first long-distance carrier (AT&T), the first operating system (Microsoft), the first online bookstore (Amazon.com), the first gourmet coffee house franchise (Starbucks), the first computer chip (Intel), the first web search engine (AOL.com)—all hold high credibility largely derived from being first in the market.

Conclusion

The starting points for argument, developed in the first part of this book, consist of facts, presumptions, probabilities, and commonplaces. All are adapted to argumentation in business. Facts about business activity must be known and trusted if they are to be used as the basis of arguments. If distortions are uncovered, facts are less able to serve as starting points. Business argumentation presumes accountants provide independent analysis of facts to certify them as reliable starting points. If accountants fail to maintain their objectivity, facts become tainted and are no longer useful in argumentation. Securities analysts are also presumed to be informed and objective testers of business facts, and help to certify them as reliable. If analysts lose their objectivity, their usefulness disappears. Business arguments rest on such probabilities as the inevitable rise and fall in the economic activity referred to as booms and busts. And businesses rely on the probability of a steady rise in various forms of economic value, and the probability of change. Such commonplaces as comparison and contrast, cause and effect, cost/benefit, and sign play a major role in business arguments.

The forms of support discussed in Part Two of this book, evidence, values, and credibility, are adapted to use in business arguments. Evidence appears in the form of examples, statistics, and testimony, and such values as profit, globalization, freedom and choice, timely innovation, vision, and social responsibility are commonly used. The recent ethical challenges in business have highlighted the importance of credibility. Firms engage in "branding" to gain high credibility in the perception of appropriate decision makers, and they may lose it easily by failing to behave in a way those decision makers expect. Corporate cultures influence the way credibility works in internal decision making. Contemporary business cultures based on the knowledge era tend to be flatter, more open to innovation based on technology and intellect, and employ teamwork that allows credibility to be generated among a broader group of decision makers.

PROJECT

Find the names of at least two business leaders in your area. Make an appointment to interview them about their recent decisions. Ask to see copies of internal and external memos that contain arguments. Write a paper analyzing the arguments, focusing on what makes them especially suited to business argumentation.

16 Argumentation in Government and Politics

KEY TERMS

public sphere
political claims
political issues
the public
committee hearings
applying legal practice
using the record
good stories
majoritarianism

amendment process
credibility function
issues and images
the people
media
political debates
values and evidence
leave no shot unanswered
inoculation

Political argumentation is the oldest recorded argumentation sphere. It can be found in the ancient myths of the Babylonian King Gilgamesh, the Homeric debates of the *Iliad* and the *Odyssey*, ancient Chinese records, and the Old Testament record of the ancient Jews. One modern form of political argumentation has taken its name from an Old Testament prophet: the Jeremiad. If you could penetrate fully to the earliest actions of our species you would probably find that political discussion emerged virtually with language itself.

Wherever groups exist in the form of families, communities, organizations, states, or nations, political decisions are necessary. It is impossible to be apolitical, for inaction is also a decision. If the people who live across the street beat their children mercilessly and you do not report the fact to the authorities because you do not want to get involved, you have taken a political action based on a political reason. However, the political action we are interested in here is *political argumentation:* the process of using verbal and visual arguments among citizens, leaders, and government agencies to influence the policy decisions of a political community. This argumentation produces "consequences that are widespread and enduring; and affect persons other than oneself for good or evil" (Bitzer 230–31).

The Nature of Political Argumentation

In its broadest sense, political argumentation is synonymous with argumentation per se. However, we will be talking about argumentation that directly involves what has been called the "public's business." It is the argumentation that G. Thomas Goodnight says is characteristic of the public sphere:

> A public forum is . . . a sphere of argument to handle disagreements transcending private and technical disputes. . . . [It] inevitably limits participation to representative spokespersons [and provides] a tradition of argument such that its speakers would employ common language, values, and reasoning so that the disagreement could be settled . . . (219–20).

We define political argumentation further by examining its claims, its content, its development, and its refutation. Because political argumentation is such a universal sphere, we have chosen in this chapter to focus on refutation, which has its most distinctive role in government and politics.

The Claims of Political Argumentation

In Chapter 4 we identified three kinds of claims—factual, value, and policy. One of the defining characteristics of political argument is that it always aims at policy. A lawyer may argue the factual claim that a chemical spill was harmful to a client and, subsequently argue for a legally appropriate remedy. Both claims are treated in law as factual claims. When the same lawyer appears before a state legislative committee on the same subject, the aim is to bring about regulations that will constitute a new policy. Policy claims are argued by building a case on subclaims of fact and value, but the aim is to gain adherence to the policy claim.

The Content of Political Claims

When Aristotle referred to the relatively simple society of ancient Greece, he defined five general categories of political argumentation that are still important today: (1) finances; (2) war and peace; (3) national defense; (4) imports and exports; and (5) the framing of laws (53). Finances refers to issues emerging from consideration of fiscal and monetary policies. War and peace includes all of our foreign policy and national defense programs. Imports and exports suggest the full range of issues arising from interstate and foreign commerce—whether free trade agreements like the North American Free Trade Agreement (NAFTA) or the General Agreement on Tariff and Trade (GATT) are beneficial to the U.S. economy. The framing of laws ranges from modification of the Constitution to statutory revisions. Legislatures must set policies as general as legal rights for women and as specific as the use of "low fat," "fat free," or "diet" labels on food.

   Equal rights for women and informative food labels are good examples of the way in which Aristotle's five classifications have expanded. Decisions like these and many others that would have been personal then, are political today. We have reached the place in our complex society where every policy question is potentially political.

Political argumentation is, as J. Robert Cox says, "a normative sphere." That is, it is not defined by a specific set of claims with which it deals. Rather, the participants in political argumentation generate reasons "for a course of action and in interpreting the consequences of their decision . . . invoke a notion of 'the public' " (131). There is always implied in argumentation the idea that its policy claims are designed for the common good of some social collective that we call the public. The usefulness of such public policy is determined by the immediate needs of the community. Should local communities censor cable television? Should the federal government regulate airline prices? Should English be the official language of a state? These are all claims about what the public is and wants. However, community needs frequently have to be defined because members of the public are unaware or unclear about them. So, part of argumentation is the actual construction of the situation so the public may identify with it and respond to the specific political claims being advanced. This process of creating the community has been with us throughout political history. Christine Oravec found that the arguments for environmental conservation that emerged from Theodore Roosevelt's presidency included a subtext that constructed "the kind of public required to justify and implement" conservation policies. The needs and desires of the public constructed by this discourse provided the necessary justification for government policies designed to slow the destruction of the United States' natural resources.

The Development of Political Claims

Initially, political claims are vague. They become more specific as argumentation develops. No court of law would tolerate a claim as unclearly stated as most political claims initially are, and no scientists could proceed without a firm statement of a hypothesis. Yet most political claims begin the argumentative process in a very general form (Cobb and Elder 400):

> Air quality in U.S. cities should be improved.
> Taxes should be reduced.
> The chuckholes in Atlanta's streets should be repaired.
> The reading level of children in Denver should be improved.

These are examples of claims with which government agencies usually begin. They represent (as we noted in Chapter 4) the recognition of a problem, a "feeling of doubt." Frequently, they are almost issueless because they are claims with which everyone will agree. However, as public bodies examine these claims and interest groups argue them, they become more specific. To become a working policy, the claim must become more specific. Take the reading example. Virtually no one in Denver would object to improving the reading level of children. But how? At what cost? What will the new policy replace? and, How will improvement be measured? The answers proposed to these questions make the policy more specific and more controversial. Compare these two claims:

1. The reading level of children in Denver should be improved.
2. With funds now used for the education of children with disabilities, the Denver school board should hire fifty reading specialists to provide individualized reading programs in the fourth grade.

Issues Emerge as Claims Become More Clearly Phrased   Some people, even those who want the reading ability improved, will object to taking funds away from children with disabilities. They may argue that the money should come from other sources or new taxes, and a whole host of issues will emerge. Other people will argue that direct attention to reading is not the best way to improve reading. Rather, reading instruction should be integrated into other instruction. Issues that did not seem very important when the original general claim was advanced will arise. Some parents at a public hearing may be frustrated, saying, "I'm interested in better reading instruction for my children. Why are we talking about cutting programs for children with disabilities?" Their frustration comes from the need for claims of political argument to become specific.

Claims and Issues Will Change as Argumentation Emerges   Policies need the widest possible consensus of the members of the affected group. Therefore, claims are often amended to protect them from possible refutation. So, a school board may propose that social studies time be cut and more time allotted to reading instruction. Then they may propose greater emphasis on reading in all instruction. As a matter of fact, they may come out with a curriculum revision that seems completely at odds with the original intent to improve reading instruction. The new revision may actually cut the amount of time specifically devoted to reading instruction!

Most Claims Do Not Become Policy, and Most That Do Are Noncontroversial
Many interest groups expend great amounts of money and time researching and arguing policy claims, yet most policy claims never become policy. Even those policy claims that become legislative bills have a high rejection rate. More than 20,000 bills are proposed each session to the U.S. Congress, yet less than 6 percent of them ever become law. Of those bills that pass, two-thirds are supported by both major parties (Matthews and Stimson 6–7).

Many bills, both simple and complex, are passed without argument. While it is difficult to characterize those claims that pass easily, they most probably represent efforts to reduce conflict, reconcile varying interests, and compromise opposing goals. Political decisions that go through the modification process we have described are the product of a broad compromise-based consensus. The dramatic case of a hard-fought partisan argument on a well-defined policy claim is unusual.

In the first two years of the Clinton administration, the president and a Democratic Congress pushed through a number of controversial pieces of legislation such as the Brady Bill, restricting handgun purchases, a ban on the sale of certain assault weapons, and a budget that passed by a single vote in the Senate. Even so, all of these bills had changes from their original versions (like the exclusion of some assault weapons) in order to get the votes necessary to pass them.

Perhaps in part because of these controversial bills, the House and Senate got a Republican majority in 1994. In the election of 1994 the Republican candidates for the House argued for a series of thirty-four measures that they called their "Contract With America." However, in the first year of their control of Congress they were able to pass only those items that were agreed to by a consensus in both House and Senate (Popkin and Borger). The legislative process has more than a dozen points in committee and floor action where legislation may be delayed or defeated (Wise 22). The political party system, the presidential veto, and outside pressure all serve to make most political claims develop through continual cooperative modification until a consensus is reached.

When Contract With America Republicans tried to force some measures such as tax reduction through, they shut down the government for several days for lack of funds and they paid the price with losses in the elections of 1996 and 1998. The leader of this movement, Newt Gringrich, was forced to resign as Speaker of the House of Representatives. As further evidence of the ineffectiveness of partisan political action in Congress, a *Newsweek* magazine poll taken shortly after the impeachment hearings for President Clinton showed that 54 percent thought Republicans had hurt themselves by the way they handled the hearings and only 9 percent said they were helped. By 1999 the traditional cooperative spirit was returning, albeit with a few notable exceptions. That "Politics is the art of the possible" is nowhere clearer than in the history of the U.S. House and Senate.

To say that cooperative modification to consensus is the nature of political argumentation is not to maintain that there are no issues, no debates. The modifications necessary to consensus are discovered when issues are revealed in debate. The issues are likely to be over modifications of policy, but issues are there nonetheless.

Refutation in Government and Politics

Even in political campaigns, where conflict would seem most likely, disagreements are more likely to be over the degree or nature of a proposition rather than over a direct yes or no. On health care, taxes, foreign policy, or environmental protection, for instance, disagreements are over the degree of governmental action. In political campaigns, a diverse electorate usually makes it difficult for a politician with an absolutist position to win.

When debate is present, refutation of opposing arguments is essential to the decision-making process. Much of the legislative process is taken up with identifying potential rebuttals to a policy proposal. If the rebuttals come with political clout, the legislative policy is usually revised to accommodate them. The final draft of a bill will sometimes seem to lack clarity and coherence because it includes so many changes inserted in order to win votes by countering refutation.

The approval in 1999 of the final installment of the $1.8 trillion dollar annual budget was approved in the House on a 196–135 vote and with a vote of 74–24 in the Senate. In the Senate, 42 Republicans and 32 Democrats supported it. It was praised by both Republican and Democratic congressional leaders and President Clinton. But to get the agreement the budget had to include a number of compromises such as: an 0.38 across-the-board budget cut, a one-day delay in the September military payday, some "accounting gimmicks," and some tax credits for research and development (Toedtman; Pianin).

Argumentation in government and politics includes a variety of situations, from a televised presidential campaign commercial to a newspaper advertisement for a local city council candidate, from a congressional hearing to a mayors' debate. Although there are similarities, there are also differences. We will try to deal with these differences by looking at how refutation functions in the argumentation of three subspheres: committee hearings, legislative action, and political campaigns.

Refutation in Committee Hearings

In recent years, people have been able to see firsthand how committee hearings function. Segments have been shown on television, particularly on C-SPAN. The most dramatic, like the hearings on the federal raid on the Branch Davidian compound in Waco, Texas, the 1991 Senate Judiciary Committee hearings over the appointment of Judge Clarence Thomas to the Supreme Court and the charges of sexual harassment against him by Professor Anita Hill, the 1995 Congressional investigations of the Ruby Ridge, Idaho, eleven-day standoff between federal agents and white separatist Randy Weaver, and the 1998 House Judiciary Committee hearings on the impeachment of President Clinton, have had significant viewership. The Clarence Thomas–Anita Hill Hearings were covered live on ABC, CBS, NBC, CNN, and C-SPAN and were seen in over 14 million homes ("Viewers"). The impeachment hearings of President Clinton were seen in 4.4 million homes ("People's Choice").

Involving highly controversial charges about the actions of governmental personnel, they provided extensive examples of how refutation can function in committee hearings. The same principles apply to thousands of other hearings in Congress, state legislatures, and city and county government. Committee hearings are vital decision making scenes where the claims of argumentation are modified through refutation.

During the 96th Congress, the House Appropriations Committee and its subcommittees "held 720 days of hearings, took testimony from 10,125 witnesses, published 225 volumes of hearings that comprised 202,767 printed pages" (Davidson and Oleszek 220). Committee hearings used to get the imput of society on the scope of laws. Interested individuals, groups, businesses, and the like discuss what the law ought to be.

When you add to congressional policy and personnel hearings the many administrative hearings that administrative agencies hold to involve the public in the actual application of laws once written, you realize how important hearings are to defining and applying policy. We will look now at the characteristics of such hearings and the form that refutation takes in them.

Characteristics of Hearings

Hearings are characterized by the need to convert solutions into law to develop and focus on a record that will justify the action taken. Refutation in this setting involves the legal questioning format and telling good stories.

Hearings involve controversy over policy. Controversy leads to refutation but refutation is blunted because claims are made through a questioning process. This process resembles the type of fact-finding questions used in a court of law (Asbell 108). That is, those who hold the hearings ask questions rather than make claims. The format implies that they are gathering evidence. Frequently, it is evidence they already have. The testimony of witnesses is used to "build a record" from which specific provisions of laws or administrative decisions are justified.

Using the Record in Hearings

Although the questioning format limits how one may argue, there is still considerable potential for refutation. This refutation comes mostly from the committee members who wish to establish their position. For instance, when the Senate Environmental Protection Subcommittee held hearings on the reauthorization of the 1977 Clean Air Act, Senator Max Baucus of Montana asked questions designed to prepare arguments for refutation. He asked four presidents of health organizations what the best arguments were against their conclusions and how they would respond to them (Boynton, "When Senators" 11).

Later, Chairman George Mitchell used this record when questioning an electric utility executive who claimed there was no health problem requiring new legislation. George Mitchell asked him to read the testimony (that Senator Baucus had solicited) of the four presidents of the health organizations. Mitchell told him he would change his mind about the seriousness of the problem if he read that testimony (Boynton, "When Senators" 143).

Focus for the Record in Hearings

In most hearings (the Ruby Ridge, Waco, Thomas, and Clinton impeachment hearings are exceptions), there is little disagreement among the members of the committee. Those who serve on committees generally agree on the basic direction of legislation. Everyone on the Senate Agriculture Committee wants to help the farmer and generally they know how they want to do this and what the pitfalls are. They are there to find the best way to do it (Boynton, "When Senators" 10). This focus restricts the arguments that can be made.

Dennis Jaehne illustrates this restriction on arguments of wilderness groups in the administrative appeals of Forest Service implementation decisions. The conflict he observed between the Utah Wilderness Association and the Forest Service involved a basic value disagreement "between the idealistic concept of *preserving* land in its 'natural' state and the pragmatic concept of *protecting* land in . . . administrative rules and regulations" (496). However, in the cases he studied, the Utah Wilderness Association became pragmatic and technical in arguing modification of administrative practice in order to influence changes. He found that "rational collaboration" has problems for participants with "environmental ideals, particularly in the degree of cooptation of environmental ideals by administrative discourse. Speaking like the natives [bureaucrats] makes you rather more like the natives than not speaking like the natives" (501).

Even though witnesses might have idealistic views of the situation, they must adapt to the pragmatic questions of policy building or administration. Witnesses must follow the focus of the questioners or be without influence.

The Forms of Refutation in Committee Hearings

The questioning format that produces a focused record of testimony works from specific forms of refutation. G. R. Boynton has identified four main questions that are used ("When Senators" 145–47). They are based on the record and although questions, serve to refute the testimony of a witness.

1. The questioner reminds the witness of what he or she has said, then notes someone else's counter testimony, and asks how the witness would answer the objections. The example given earlier when presidents of health organizations were asked what opponents might say and how they would respond to these opponents is an example of such an argument. Here is a case where refutation is used on a friendly witness. The witnesses are refuted, even asked to refute their own positions, to bring out the positive answer the questioner wants.

2. The same line of questioning may be used, but it is not friendly as the witness is asked to account for the counter testimony. This form looks very much like the first but it is not friendly. Boynton gives the example of a Department of Energy witness who said that installing scrubbers on old power plants would be too expensive. Senator Mitchell noted that another witness had testified that the Germans had installed scrubbers that cost only $100 per kilowatt hour. What would they cost in this country, he asked, and why would they be more costly than in Germany? ("When Senators" 146).

3. The questioner reminds the witness of what he or she has said but claims to have counter knowledge and asks the witness to justify his or her position. This is a simple variation from the second form except that the questioner uses his or her credibility to support the refutation. This method poses a difficult problem for the witness because, for the moment at least, the person asking the question is the decision maker. Thus, it is difficult for the witness to answer that the questioner is wrong. Furthermore, the traditions of the Senate ("the world's most exclusive club") are such that open attacks on a senator will usually bring even political opponents to the senator's defense. The answer to such refutation is doubly difficult.

4. The questioner compares what the witness said at this hearing with earlier statements or actions and asks the witness to justify the discrepancy. Inconsistency, as we have discussed in Chapter 4, is a powerful basis for any refutation. Some believe it is the most powerful because it uses one's own arguments (or actions) against one's position. In the Clean Air Act hearings, Senator George Mitchell argued to the auto industry representatives:

Today you have said that the improvements we are proposing are impossible for you to meet and even if you could meet them the improved health would not be worth the cost. But, that is exactly what your industry has said every time the law has been changed from 1965 to [the] present, and despite these claims you have met the standards of each new law. Why should we take seriously what you are saying today? (Boynton, "When Senators" 146).

Telling Good Stories

G. R. Boynton's examination of the Senate Agricultural Committee hearings illustrates that all this building of a record, focus, and refutation can be put in a narrative argument:

> The "good story" told in the hearings of the Senate Agriculture Committee is "a" story. The individual narrative accounts are bits and pieces of this larger story. They do not stand alone. You cannot understand any one of these stories without understanding the larger story of which each is a part. An important role for the narratives is carrying the cognitive complexity which is the "good story" ("Telling" 437).

Many bills are omnibus measures that cover a number of subjects. A farm bill has to have narratives about potatoes, cotton, corn, and wheat; about regions; about size of farms; about methods of harvesting. These narratives have to fit together into a good story. These stories have real characters in them: farmers, workers, market specialists. They proceed through a series of events that lead to a satisfactory conclusion for all under the proposed policy. If they do not, the policy is modified to make the story right.

In a situation such as the Clarence Thomas hearings, the story is primarily about the credibility of a person. So the day after Hill and Thomas testified, their supporters came forward to confirm their statements. The *New York Times* headlined: "PARADE OF WITNESSES SUPPORT HILL'S STORY, THOMAS'S INTEGRITY." Friends of Anita Hill affirmed that as long as ten years earlier she had mentioned the sexual harassment to them. These bits of testimony supported and became a part of her story. In the same way those who testified that Clarence Thomas was completely businesslike and could never be guilty of sexual harassment, supported his story.

Committee hearings, the first of the three subspheres of political argumentation discussed here, serve as a means to clarify policy legislation, confirm participants in the process, and define administrative action. They are characterized by applied legal practice and building and using a record. These same characteristics are carried forward into the second subsphere: legislative action.

Refutation in Legislative Action

Committee hearings are a vital and time consuming part of congressional action. They serve to define a proposition from a more general question and to make that proposition (a bill) more immune to refutation. After a bill is drafted, it must pass both houses of Congress and be approved by the president (or overridden by the president's veto). In addition, public opinion, spurred on by specific events, special interest groups, and sometimes legal action can influence what will happen.

As we noted earlier, most of the problems on about two-thirds of all legislation are worked out in the committee hearings. Therefore, controversy or rebuttal in their passage through the legislative process is limited. For the one-third of the bills that are the subject of controversy, refutation is an important part of their movement through the system.

Refutation Is Usually Not Confrontational

You will recall from Chapter 13 that refutation should not be seen as an attack on an opponent to win a decisive victory. Nowhere is this principle more true than in the legislative process. It is a reflection of what has been called the first cardinal rule of politics: "Don't make enemies you don't need to make" (Dowd). More than that, however, an important value of the legislative process is majoritarianism. Sponsors of legislation try to get the greatest support that they can. They want a significant majority. The larger the better. Noncontroversial legislation is the ideal.

Refutation in this system is frequently about resolving small problems in the legislation to make it acceptable to a larger majority. For instance, a clean air act that emphasizes acid rain may be criticized for not doing enough about ambient air quality, a point of interest to more states than acid rain. The following is a paraphrase of an actual refutation. It refutes the proposed law by agreeing with it but supporting an amendment.

> We need to pass this bill to deal with the problem of acid rain. The chief sponsors of the bill have understandably, considering the problems in their New England states, emphasized acid rain. However, in the Middle West and West, ambient air quality is of greater concern. Because of the seriousness of that problem, I support the amendment to the Clean Air Act that would require modifications for ambient sulfur dioxides, sulfate, and particulate standards.

The argument is not against what is in the bill (acid rain control); it argues for an addition to the bill to regulate ambient air quality.

Refutation Is Usually Not Personal

We have noted that much legislation depends on as large a majority as possible. Such majoritarianism is important because larger majorities provide political protection. If a legislator can say that the law was supported by most Republicans and Democrats, its supporters are less vulnerable to the charge that they are "too liberal" or "too conservative." In addition, the tradition of treating one another without personal rancor is a part of the American legislative tradition.

In the floor debate over the confirmation of Clarence Thomas and in response to Republican Arlen Spector of Pennsylvania who had led the questioning of Professor Hill, Senator Edward Kennedy said, "There's no proof that Anita Hill has perjured herself and shame on anyone who suggests that she has." Senator Spector replied, "We do not need characterizations like shame in this chamber from the senator from Massachusetts." To this, Senator Kennedy responded, "I reiterate to the senator from Pennsylvania and to others that the way that Professor Hill was treated was shameful" (Apple A13). That exchange is about as personal as you will find in congressional debate.

Eric M. Uslander argued in 1993 that there is a declining emphasis in the U.S. Congress on comity. He said that there is less attention, particularly since the 1980s, to reciprocity and courtesy than was previously true (23–33). As we noted earlier, however, that was during the period of a strong Republican movement to polarize the parties. Today, while there may be a decline, there is still far less personal attack, particularly in the Senate, than might be expected of a partisan assembly.

The Amendment Process as Refutation

The amending process has always been active in committees. When a bill came to the floor of the House or Senate, amendments were usually extensions of committee hearings. However, in recent years the amendment process has been used more as a basis of refutation. Former Arizona Congressman Morris Udall noted a few years ago that the House of Representatives has become a "fast breeder reactor. . . . Every morning when I come to my office, I find that there are twenty more amendments. We dispose of twenty or twenty-five amendments and it breeds twenty more amendments" (Keefe and Ogul 208).

Many amendments are friendly. They are designed to strengthen, without changing in any significant way, the bill's essential purpose. Other amendments may look innocent enough but will actually weaken a bill and make it less likely to pass. Political scientists William Keefe and Morris Ogul explain how this can work:

> A favorite gambit in attacking a bill is to "perfect" or amend it to death. Under this plan, amendment after amendment is submitted to the bill, ostensibly to make it a "better" bill. With each amendment a new group can be antagonized and brought into opposition to the bill. Nor is it very difficult to make a bill unworkable, even ridiculous. Thus the president of the Illinois Retail Merchants Association succeeded in getting a committee in the Illinois House to adopt an amendment to a minimum-wage bill, a measure he vigorously opposed, setting up a $500,000 fund to be used in enforcement of the law. This move was calculated to stimulate new opposition to the bill. . . . Many a bill has been threatened or emasculated by a carefully drawn and skillfully maneuvered amendment (209).

By such procedures, amendments become the basis on which a bill is refuted. If an arguer is not careful, a bill can be amended to refute its original intention.

Refutation Has an Important Credibility Function

Although debate is important to a democratic society and refutation is central to it, floor debate has limited influence on legislation. A well-developed argument, a new way of looking at an issue, or a well-thought-out refutation that strikes at the center of a policy can influence undecided members. Mostly, however, floor debates, like committee hearings, are oriented to establishing a record. Speakers say what they say in supporting or refuting arguments to demonstrate their positions for their constituents.

The C-SPAN coverage of debates in the House of Representatives, though few people watch them, have aided some, like Georgia Republican Congressman Newt Gingrich who used his appearances in C-SPAN-covered speeches attacking Democratic leaders to build a record that increased his credibility among some voters, eventually leading to his election as Speaker of the House. However, as we have already pointed out, his subsequent actions and those of his partisan majority in the House of Representatives led to his downfall.

Perhaps more important than building a record or influencing a few fence sitters to move one way or another is a frequently overlooked credibility function of floor debate:

> It is a good way for members to persuade their colleagues of their competence in a public policy field; it enables them to affirm a personal position or to support or back off from a past position; it presents an opportunity to gain publicity, to consolidate old support, and perhaps to attract new followers (Keefe and Ogul 218).

Relations between Legislature and the Executive

In recent years the federal government has been characterized by what has been called "divided government," where the Congress is controlled by one party while the president is from another. In the fifty years between 1950 and 2003, a Democrat was president for only twenty-two years. The Democrats have controlled both houses of Congress for a majority of those years. In 1994 the situation was reversed and a Democrat was president while both houses of Congress were controlled by the Republicans. Although not as dramatic, similar divided government has occurred in some state governments. Even where the same party controls both legislative and executive branches, differences between the branches can occur.

In such situations, debate can be quite vigorous and even acrimonious. The president or governor has a veto that is difficult to override. So even when the opposition has a majority in the legislative branch, its power is curbed. Some presidents (Harry S. Truman holds the record with 250) earned a reputation for their frequent vetoes (Keefe and Ogul 329). The debate between a hostile majority in Congress and the president increases as an election nears.

In the autumn of 1991, there was a debate over whether or not the United States was in a recession. Much of this argumentation was definitional. This was not a depression such as the great depression of the 1930s. But was it a recession? Certain economic indicators were weak, but President George Bush assured the nation that the economy was growing out of this minor sluggishness. He proposed to accelerate that growth by repealing the tax on capital gains to stimulate investment and thus to create more jobs. The Democrats said that policy was "trickle down economics" to benefit the rich.

The Democrats wanted to extend unemployment benefits for people whose benefits had run out. President Bush vetoed that move as "budget busting." It would increase the deficit, he said. The Democrats proposed a tax cut for lower and middle income people, paid for from cuts in defense, to stimulate the economy. Bush opposed that measure because he favored his cut in capital gains.

The issues were over definition: is this a recession? They were about process: are economic conditions getting worse or better? They dealt with credibility: is the President uninterested in the poor and middle class? Do the Democrats actually want to solve the problem or just make political points? Value issues were actively involved: is the suffering serious? Will tax cuts increase economic insecurity? And, of course, there were policy issues: should unemployment insurance coverage be extended? Should the capital gains tax be repealed? The debate frequently emphasized the support and refutation of the fact and value claims behind the policy claims along with a host of other issues (e.g., limits on the military budget and restrictions on imports) linked to these policy decisions.

Eventually, some compromises were worked out between Congress and the administration. The president approved the extension of unemployment benefits, for instance, although it was not for as long as the Democrats had proposed. The lesson to be learned from observing this process is that refutation is frequently a complex problem because single issues can have implications on a wide variety of claims. Debate involves party politics, public opinion, the media, the responsibilities of government branches, the state of the economy, and the state of the world.

For the most part, problems of legislative and administrative disagreement are worked out in some system of compromises. This generality holds true at all levels of government: national, state and local. But compromise is required because there are different points of view. So political parties and individuals with different world views vie for the support of the public. This is most clear in political campaigns where candidates compete for offices and propositions are put on the ballot.

Argumentation in Political Campaigns

A political campaign is a complex mixture of activities. It includes speeches, debates, mailings, television and radio ads, sound bites for the media, person-to-person campaigning by candidates and supporters, telephone contacts, getting people to the polls, and many more activities. They all are argumentative in their nature and involve refutation. A closer examination of campaign argumentation is in order.

Campaigns Involve Issues and Images

All argumentation in the political sphere has, hidden in its attention to policy questions, an element of the personal: is this person (or party) a fit representative of his or her constituents? This dual emphasis on issue and image, present throughout the legislative process, becomes increasingly important as campaign and election time nears. The process described earlier of "building a record" becomes more focused on how that record will influence voters.

Candidates look to their opponents' record to find a basis for attack. In 2003 the Democratic Party had a bevy of presidential hopefuls, all attacking different aspects of President George W. Bush's record. For example, Howard Dean (Vermont) attacked Bush for just about everything, including the use of false information to justify invading Iraq, cutting taxes among those in the upper income brackets, and ignoring the growing number of U.S. corporations that use "temporary workers" in order to avoid providing benefits such as health insurance. John Kerry (Massachusetts) attacked Bush for providing tax cuts to wealthy individuals and corporations while the nation was trying to fight a war (in Iraq). John Edwards (North Carolina) made a pointed attack on Bush's economic elitism, claiming that Bush "wants a world where the only people who have to pay taxes are the ones who do the work" (Kusnet 24). Although these attacks all portray a negative image of Bush, they are also about issues.

In a campaign, then, questions of a candidate's image and issue positions become confused. Some argue that image takes over and the issues are pushed aside by the image constructed through short commercials and media sound bites. Even debates, they argue, emphasize the candidate's image and play down the public policy issues. Says Lloyd Bitzer, "the stuff of ordinary campaigns consists of arguments, position statements, testimonials, commercials, and other materials relating to the prudence, good character, and right intentions of the candidates—to the image. . . . Thus, discussion of issues . . . tends to be subsumed under the discussion of images" (242–43).

It is natural that political campaigns should be seen as image centered. After all, the central issue of every campaign is personal: should the candidate be elected? But, as our discussion of the Clinton and Dole ads mentioned above shows, the debate over image is not as clearly personal as many believe. Furthermore, some studies have shown that in presidential and senate races, at least, "exposure to even small doses of campaign advertising is a significant educational experience." "We conclude," say Stephen Ansolabehere and Shanto Iyengar, "that negativity does not bolster the information value of political advertising. How much voters learn about the candidates' positions and the extent to which they think about political issues when evaluating the candidates does not depend on the tone of the advertising campaign" (51).

Candidates are usually reluctant to attack an opponent directly with charges about character. In 1999 when media sources began reporting that Governor George W. Bush of Texas, the Republican front runner for president, had used cocaine, his opponents from both parties refused to comment or did little more than suggest that he clear up the issue. Questions of personal conduct can hurt a candidate but they can also backfire on the opponent who raises them. In 1992, when Gennifer Flowers said that she had had a long-term affair with Bill Clinton, he changed the image question by emphasizing the difference between private character and public character. He reinforced that claim throughout his thirteen-month campaign with statements like:

> The truth is that I have demonstrated the public character that this country needs as president. I have consistently fought for the same things for more than ten years. I fought for economic modernization, . . . education advancement, . . . to clean up the political system (Miller 349).

The 1992 and 1996 elections and subsequent polls showing positive support, despite numerous other charges about his personal character, some of which he admitted to, seems to show that the electorate can accept this distinction between public and private character. Backlash against negative advertising is less likely when negative advertisements are based on issues than on the personal characteristics of an opponent (Roberts 181).

Another image problem that has to be contended with in this era of heavily mediated campaigns is the tendency of journalists to change "the story of the election from 'who should govern' to 'who can win' " (Smith 295; Ansolabehere and Iyengar 38). The image that a candidate is a loser decreases the attention paid to the candidate and thus decreases the chance that the candidate can refute this or any other charge. Refutation obviously functions only if it is communicated, and it can only be communicated when the journalists pay attention or when the candidate has a lot of money to purchase rebuttal advertisements.

The decision of the electorate on the proposition: should the candidate be elected? looks like a simple question of image. It is not. It is influenced significantly by a candidate's record and position on issues. Credibility may be more important in political campaigns than in some other situations, but credibility is influenced by the arguments and values an audience comes to associate with a candidate. Even negative ads have more influence if the credibility of a candidate is linked to issues.

Campaign Arguments Are Linked to "The People"

A political campaign is based on an argumentative strategy. The strategy has to cast the candidate as a leader who will achieve the public policy that the people want. Terms like *the people* and *the public* are myths constructed by candidates to define the whole population as embodying the candidate's point of view (McGee). One study of the 1984 presidential debates found that both Ronald Reagan and Walter Mondale claimed to speak for *the people* although with quite different interpretations of what that meant (Werling et al. 234). Such a strategy can be seen in every campaign. Candidates defend their claims as designed to support "the people," and refute opponents' claims as attacks on "the people." Even though "the people" is a campaign myth, it is an important base for the story that a candidate must tell and maintain at the center of the campaign.

Telling the Right Story

Each campaign should add up to a convincing story of a candidate whose record shows, and statements reinforce, that he or she is in tune with the people to provide a wise public policy. Developing such a story has been transformed in many cases into "the speech" where the same arguments, values, credibility, and even examples are used by a candidate throughout a campaign. Emphasis is shifted, introductions or conclusions are changed to orient a speech to a particular audience. However, the campaign speeches turn out to be essentially one speech. The term *the speech* was first used in Ronald Reagan's pre-campaign for governor in 1966 (Ritter). It is a standard campaign procedure now. It defines the story of the campaign.

In 1992, Ross Perot was the most successful presidential candidate from an independent or third party since Theodore Roosevelt in 1912. He was a successful billionaire businessman who had never run for office but had gained some fame through Ken Follett's book, commissioned by Perot. *On Wings of Eagles* was the story of Perot's rescue of his company's hostages held in Iran at the same time that the government could not free the American embassy hostages. Perot's campaign was built around the use of half-hour infomercials where Perot used charts and interviews to tell his story.

Ross Perot's story was of a man from a poor family who rose to be a leader in business. He did this by applying the things he learned in his close-knit family. There he learned that self-sacrifice and working for others, for community, was the way to make things better, not only for others but for the individual. In this way he got things done, as he did in Teheran and in business. He is no politician, because he does not complicate and confuse things as traditional candidates do. He analyzes the situation and sees what has to be done and he does it. He will take these principles of analysis, family, self-sacrifice, and community and use them to solve the deficit, increase employment, free MIAs, and restore people's trust in the American government and confidence in themselves (Kern).

Maintaining the Story

The story does come under attack, and when that happens a campaign must use refutation to answer the charges and restore the story.

George Bush and Bill Clinton, realizing that they had more to lose than gain, did not attempt to refute Ross Perot's story.

However, after the election Perot was hurt badly and his story began to come apart when he debated Vice President Albert Gore on the NAFTA agreement in 1993. Gore attacked Perot's story that he would use the principles of self-sacrifice and community. He pointed out, for instance, that the Perot family had a tariff-free airport in Texas that they used to benefit themselves while denying the free trade advantages of NAFTA to others. Perot was unable to refute such charges. His inability to maintain his story undoubtedly contributed to his drop in popularity after the debate.

Frank Luntz is a political strategist for the Republican Party. In 2003 he was asked for advice on how to refute negative images regarding the party's environmental stance. After noting that "the environment is probably the single issue on which Republicans in general—and President Bush in particular—are most vulnerable," Luntz suggested that they should "think of environmental (and other) issues in terms of 'story.' A compelling story," Luntz wrote, "even if factually inaccurate, can be more emotionally compelling than a dry recitation of the truth" (132).

The strategy crafted by Frank Luntz responded to concerns that Republican candidates, especially George W. Bush, were having difficulty maintaining their environmental story. Luntz devoted an entire section to the issue of global warming. As we indicated in Chapter 13, the scientific community already had reached consensus that global warming was occurring, that certain human activities were a significant cause, and that the effects on society have been (and are expected to continue to be) largely negative. Scientific argument has moved on to questions of how best to address this problem. Despite strong scientific consensus, the George W. Bush administration consistently argued that global warming was not a serious issue, and opposed any regulation of emissions thought to be primarily responsible for global warming. In fact, when the Environmental Protection Agency produced a report on the state of the environment, White House editors removed most of the section on global warming, and rewrote the rest. For example, they deleted information from "a 1999 study showing that global temperatures had risen sharply in the previous decade compared with the last 1,000 years," and replaced it with information from a study financed by the American Petroleum Institute that questioned the previous study's conclusions. Science writer Andrew Revkin reported that "EPA staff members, after discussions with administration officials, said they decided to delete the entire discussion," rather than leave the selectively filtered material (Revkin, "Report by the EPA").

Frank Luntz offered a way to present a convincing story about global warming. He urged Republicans to maintain control over the argument by emphasizing scientific uncertainty: "voters believe that there is no consensus about global warming within the scientific community. Should the public come to believe that the scientific issues are settled their views about global warming will change accordingly. Therefore, you need to continue to make the lack of scientific certainty a primary issue in the debate" (137). He added that, although the Bush argument was out of line with the scientific consensus, this could be overcome with effective communication. "The scientific debate is closing [against us] but not yet closed," wrote Luntz. "There is still a window of opportunity to challenge the science" (138).

Politicians from presidents to city council members build a record through legislation and public argumentation. It is combined, in the political campaign, with the candidate's credibility, policy claims, and values to sustain a reasonable story. Defending that story is the central focus of political refutation.

Media and Refutation

Media attention is very important to defending the story. The higher the office, the more important it becomes. Many local races, like city council or state legislature, get little media attention unless something unusual happens in the campaign. Those campaigns are usually tied to the coattails of a party or higher official who does have media exposure, and to neighborhood campaigning. But at the higher level of office seekers there is a continual adaptation to media sources. Speeches and announcements are timed to make the evening news and the morning newspaper. Interviews on *Meet the Press* or *The Don Imus Show* are regular fare. Beginning in 1992 when Bill Clinton went on *The Arsenio Hall Show* and played the saxophone, it has become common for candidates for president to appear on the talk shows of hosts like Jay Leno, David Letterman, Oprah Winfrey, and Rosie O'Donnell. Similar local talk shows attract local candidates. Such appearances are used by candidates to reinforce the story and to refute the attack on it. One study of such nontraditional news sources indicates that they have more influence than traditional news sources in the early stages of a presidential campaign (Pfau and Eveland).

Such media exposure can have its negative effects. Jay Leno's monolog can keep alive issues that a candidate or officeholder doesn't want preserved, like George W. Bush's alleged cocaine use, or Bill Clinton's infidelity.

Furthermore, the press can become an adversary. In the 1988 vice presidential debate, Judy Woodruff listed prominent Republicans who had expressed reservations about Republican vice presidential candidate Dan Quayle and asked him why he had "not made a more substantial impression" on them (Weiler 215). These members of the questioning team frequently used what J. Michael Hogan calls "preemptive refutation" in debates. They attacked a candidate's position with a question. Andrea Mitchell asked Governor Dukakis this question in the third debate of the 1988 campaign:

> Governor, you've said tonight that you set as a goal the steady reduction of the deficit,. . . . No credible economist in either party accepts as realistic your plan to handle the deficit by tightening tax collection, investing in economic growth, bringing down interest rates and cutting weapons systems. . . . So let's assume, now, for argument's purpose, that it is the spring of 1989, and you are President Dukakis, and you discover that all of those economists were right and you were wrong. You are now facing that dreaded last resort—increased taxes. Which tax do you decide is the least onerous? (222)

No candidate wants to debate the reporter, particularly when she or he can say, "I was just asking a question," but that is what the candidate has to do.

The media, at every level and of every kind, also pose a problem for a campaigner who wants to refute an argument from whatever source. Media managers can control the extent to which a refutation gets covered. We have already noted the problem of local candidates in what are considered unimportant races. It is the media sources that decide that the mayor's race is important, but the second district city councilman's race isn't. They may do this because the race isn't close or because they believe nothing interesting is going on. To a lesser extent that same condition holds at every level of an election. Candidates, even for president, are restricted in how well they can reinforce and refute challenges to their story by the media's willingness to carry their copy. This is true in less visible or less highly financed campaigns. It is also part of the reason campaigns are increasingly more expensive. Candidates believe that they need expensive media campaigns to get the message out.

Media not only controls what the story will be, but may also construct a story for a candidate. Kathleen Hall Jamieson points out that media reporters such as Dan Rather, Tom Brokaw, Peter Jennings, Lesley Stahl, Lisa Meyers, Tim Russert, and newspaper reporters as well, tell voters the principles by which they should interpret the campaign. She found fifteen principles, such as "Candidates believe that symbols win more votes than substance," and "At the end of a campaign those ahead in the polls adopt the motto: 'No news is good news' " (*Dirty Politics* 163–64). All of these principles, in one way or another, tend to portray the candidate as an actor with no concern for issues, only the strategy for winning.

This discussion may seem too negative about the role of media. In a society that prizes freedom of speech and the press, the media is certainly doing its job when it asks questions that the candidate doesn't want asked, reports events that a candidate doesn't want reported, and questions the accuracy of candidates' claims. However, in a campaign the ability of a candidate to refute objections to the story is influenced by the willingness of the media to participate in the telling of the story. It is a reality to which candidates must adapt.

The Special Role of Debates

Increasingly, politics involves debates. There was a time not too many years ago when political debates were rare. Incumbents would not debate their lesser-known opponents because they had nothing to gain. The first presidential debate was between two nonincumbents, Richard Nixon and John Kennedy, in 1960. The next presidential debate was in 1976, when Gerald Ford, although an incumbent, agreed to debate Jimmy Carter because Ford was vulnerable in the polls and because he was not an elected president. Since that time, it has been an expected routine. Also since that time, debates have become an expected part of campaigning in most state and local races.

Debate experts and others have examined these debates and found them less than ideal. The general agreement is that they are not debates in the sense that candidates directly confront, question, and refute one another. Rather, they are seen as "joint appearances" with minimum exchange between candidates. The Lincoln–Douglas Illinois senatorial debates of 1858 are held up as models against which contemporary political debates are judged negatively. However, as David Zarefsky has noted, those debates had some of the characteristics we decry in contemporary political debates.

The Lincoln–Douglas debates "were often repetitive; they are characterized by the trading of charges, often without evidence; the arguments were incompletely developed . . . the moral question received scant attention in the debates,. . . . With rare exceptions, moreover, the candidates set out their own beliefs but did not grapple with the opponent's conception" (224).

Political debates are what they are because they are like the campaign, and the campaign is a reflection of the mixed political condition in the United States. A wealth of research findings points to debates as the place where people believe they can find out about the candidates and their stands on issues (Rowland and Voss 239). Campaign debates have greater attendance or viewership than any other campaign messages (Jamieson and Birdsell 121).

The status of argumentation in these debates is determined by the diverse nature of the electorate. Political parties and candidates represent voters who hold a variety of positions on issues. Some Democrats may favor better unemployment benefits, less taxes on the middle class, federal health insurance, a woman's choice regarding pregnancy, and a strong national defense, be undecided on civil rights, and support or oppose many other ideas. Other Democrats will be stronger, weaker, or ambivalent on any of these issues. Republicans will also be different in some of their views. In addition, there is a growing tendency for voters to consider themselves independent or to associate themselves with narrower special interests such as abortion, gun control, federal–state powers, or school prayer. Therefore, candidates who expect to be successful can take a strong stand on a controversial issue only where their position is in the majority or has the potential for majority support. Such a reality influences the nature of refutation in a political campaign.

Refutation in the Political Campaign

We have already discussed several implications for refutation in the political campaign, but we now look at refutation more specifically. Refutation in the political campaign is concerned with values, evidence, and credibility. It must preserve the story of the campaign and it must leave no shot unanswered.

Refutation Is Usually about Testing Proposals with Values

Favoring a controversial policy can damage a political candidate or office holder. Although eventually specific policies must be implemented, these usually come through compromise so that the controversy is muted. Candidates, even when they argue for specific proposals, make sure that they are linked to values that a strong majority of the decision makers hold.

Candidates usually argue from values they share with the public (Werling, et al. 231). But "the Devil is in the details" and so the specific proposals are difficult to argue. Bill Clinton was able to make a strong value argument that health coverage should be guaranteed for all. But as the Clinton health plan emerged and was subjected to refutation on the specifics of how it would work, it fell in popularity and was abandoned. Polls still indicated that health was an important value for most Americans but finding a plan and paying for it is no easy task. Opponents of Clinton's health plan did not argue against the idea that everyone should have good health care. In fact, they argued that public funding would reduce the quality of health care available. Years later, opponents of President George W. Bush's plan to provide partial pharmaceutical coverage for Medicare recipients did not argue against providing coverage for prescription medications. In both cases, opponents based their refutation on grounds of the best way of attaining a generically acceptable goal.

Arguments against gun control are not in favor of violence, they are about how to control it, and claim that better law enforcement will control violence and gun control will not. They will also argue on the basis of a constitutional right to "keep and bear arms." The questions abound in *which* values are the central concern of refutation. Most people oppose abortion but accept it because they believe a woman's right to the value of choice is more important. Protecting the environment is a widely held value, but we have to find a way to do it without destroying people's financial security.

Therefore, refutation in politics is usually not a matter of refuting the values an opponent develops as part of his or her campaign story. Those values are usually shared by most people. Instead, refutation usually focuses on how specific proposals violate accepted cultural values. For instance, in the later 1990s, Republicans argued for across-the-board tax cuts that are "fair" to everyone. Democrats responded that such cuts provided great benefits to the most wealthy and were not fair to the middle class and the poor.

Evidence Is Important in Refutation

In refuting the specific proposals or the attack on such proposals, campaigns generate a surprising amount of evidence. A successful campaign will provide examples, statistics, and testimony to support the value orientation of the campaign. There is considerable use of evidence in speeches and debates. Adrian W. Frana observed it in the 1988 presidential debates:

> Many examples could be provided because so much was employed. One was the use of *statistics* (Dukakis claiming the U.S. having 5% of the world's population but 50% of its cocaine use, Bush noting that taxes had been cut and that revenues were up 25% in three years). Another was the use of *examples* to personalize or illustrate a larger point (Dukakis, in talking of the 37 million Americans who have no health insurance, citing a Houston father who had been laid off and lost his coverage and now he can't let his son compete in Little League because he's afraid he will get hurt and he can't provide the health insurance; Bush using the St. Louis experience as the wrong approach to low-cost housing) (200–01).

Evidence used in political refutation can take many forms. A *USA Today* article about George W. Bush's tendency to deflect tough questions includes a series of examples. According to the article, when the Bush administration was in danger of being implicated in the Enron scandal in January 2002, Bush mounted a public relations push to divert attention from business woes. He did the same in May 2002 when investigations unearthed the fact that he had received specific warnings of terrorist hijackings before September 11, 2001. When asked about the failure to find any weapons of mass destruction (which had been used to justify invading Iraq), Bush responded by asking, "who could possibly think that the world would be better off with Saddam Husein still in power?" Bush sidestepped inquiries into the administration's involvement in leaking the name of a CIA operative whose husband had made public statements critical of the Iraq war, and the continuing deaths of U.S. soldiers occupying the liberated Iraq. He answered by stating that the threat of terrorism "has not passed," and "the terrorists who threaten America cannot be appeased. They must be found, they must be fought and they must be defeated" (Keen 4A).

Refutation in local political campaigns also includes the use of evidence. Mike Joseph wrote an article criticizing county commissioners of Centre County, Pennsylvania, for supporting a sports facility that would increase local tax rates. Joseph used statistical evidence to support his claim that the commissioners' decision was not responsive to their constituents. The "county commissioners split 2–1 in approving the allocation on Oct. 2," wrote Joseph. "In an unscientific poll of *Centre Daily Times* readers this week, more than 80 percent of respondents said they disagreed with the decisions" (A1, A6). Joseph used these statistics to support his claim that voters should not reelect the commissioners who had voted for the sports facility.

Credibility Is Significant in Refutation

In any political campaign, credibility is important because, as we have noted, the overarching proposition is about the candidate: should this candidate be elected? Therefore, all that we have said about issue and image is appropriate here. Credibility becomes important as a candidate works to sustain an image. Sometimes credibility is attacked directly, as in some examples we have noted about George Bush's characterization of Michael Dukakis as a technocrat in 1988, or the characterization of Bill Clinton as untruthful in 1996. To that we might add the most famous case, Democratic vice presidential candidate Lloyd Bentsen's 1988 remark to his Republican counterpart Dan Quayle after Quayle compared his age to Kennedy's at the time of Kennedy's election as President, "I knew Jack Kennedy. Jack Kennedy was a friend of mine. You're no Jack Kennedy."

Frank Luntz understood how essential it was for his clients to maintain credibility. In the memo on environmental argument that we discussed earlier, he explained that "the first (and most important) step to neutralizing the problem and eventually bringing people around to your point of view on environmental issues is to convince them of your *sincerity* and *concern* (italics in original)" (132). Luntz then went on to explain that no amount of logic or evidence would make up for a failure to appear sincere and caring.

It is indirect credibility, however, that most often causes problems for candidates. When candidates are seen as being on the wrong side of, confused about, or ignorant of, issues, credibility problems are serious. A candidate in danger of such credibility problems must take immediate action to refute the charges so as to restore the story crafted for the campaign.

The Story Is Significant in Refutation

When we say the candidate must "restore the story crafted for the campaign," we acknowledge refutation as more than just saying, "that's wrong." Each argument has a place in the campaign. You will recall from Chapter 13 that one needs a posture for refutation, a constructive base from which to refute the position of others. We also observed that the framework of refutation that works in most situations follows these steps: state the point to be refuted, state your claim relevant to the point, support your claim, and state explicitly how your criticism undermines the overall position (the story) of those whom you are refuting. We might add to this last point that the undermining of an opponent's position (story) should reaffirm yours.

David Kusnet argued that, while those who were campaigning for the Democratic presidential nomination in 2004 offered statements that undermined George W. Bush's position, they did not simultaneously strengthen their own positions. According to Kusnet, they failed to advance the debate, to provide new arguments, and to tell a convincing story about the positive leadership a Democratic president could provide.

Leave No Shot Unanswered

If the story of the campaign is to be sustained, then the dictum of Chris Matthews, television political commentator and a former political aide with considerable inside experience in the political campaign process, is worth remembering: "Leave no shot unanswered" (117). Perhaps no election represents this maxim so well as the election of 1988. In that election the George Bush campaign chose a strategy of devoting 50 percent of its efforts to "negative campaigning" or attacks on Michael Dukakis. It was late in the campaign when the Dukakis campaign adopted a similar strategy. Republican strategist Roger Ailes had said, "There are three things that get covered: visuals, attacks, and mistakes" (Bennett 129). The Bush campaign attacked Dukakis on conservation (the pollution in Boston Harbor), his membership in the American Civil Liberties Union (a "liberal" organization for a person who said he was not a "liberal"), on crime (the Massachusetts prisoner furlough plan that came to be known as the Willie Horton case), his softness on defense, and others. These attacks came in commercials (turnstiles of released and returning prisoners, Bush boating on Boston Harbor, pictures of medical waste in the water) speeches, and debates. And, as we noted earlier, Bush maintained the story of his opponent. In one debate, for instance, he said that one of Dukakis' answers was "as clear as Boston Harbor" (Frana 202).

Dukakis, virtually every political observer agrees, waited too long to respond. He somehow believed these were superficial charges that voters would see through and concentrated on his own "positive" campaign. He was wrong. Some negative campaigning backfires, but it always has to be refuted. Since that time candidates may have passed up a few possible responses but, in general, they have left no shots unanswered.

Refutation by Inoculation

Refutation is usually thought of as something that takes place after a candidate has had a story and the image it projects attacked. However, there is considerable evidence to show that answering the argument before it is made can have a significant effect and even prevent it from being used. Such a refutational strategy is called *inoculation*. It is a metaphor for inoculating humans against disease in which a weakened form of a virus is introduced into the body to stimulate resistance to the disease. There are two factors in political inoculation: first there is a warning of an impending attack that causes a voter to be motivated to strengthen support, and then to establish resistance to any future attack arguments (Pfau and Kenski 85).

Studies of a South Dakota senatorial race and the 1988 Bush–Dukakis presidential election by Michael Pfau and Henry C. Kenski show that inoculation "deflects the specific content of the attacks, and it reduces the likelihood that the political attacks will influence receiver voting intention. In addition, because inoculation precedes attack, it even provides defenses against attacks that are launched late in the campaign" and therefore, are particularly difficult to refute (100).

The major difficulty of such a strategy is that it brings out charges that might not have been made and is, therefore, subject to the credibility claim that the refuter is putting up a "straw man," manufacturing an argument that no one would use, in order to refute it. Still, where a candidate knows that a challenge is likely, inoculation against it is a useful refutational strategy.

Conclusion

Political argumentation is the oldest recorded argumentation sphere. It is the process of using verbal and visual arguments to influence the policy decisions of a political community. Political argumentation is characterized by the use of policy claims. The content of those claims emphasizes finances, war and peace, national defense, imports and exports, and the forming of laws, according to Aristotle, though those categories have expanded meanings in modern times. In addition, many things that would have been considered personal in other times are public now. Political claims begin in a vague form, but they become more specific as argumentation about them develops. Claims and issues also change as argumentation emerges. Most claims that are advanced do not become policy, and most that do are noncontroversial.

The first of three major subspheres of political argumentation is committee hearings. There, argumentation is characterized by applying legal practice. Arguments are developed as questions as if the questioner was only searching for facts. However, the questions are designed to build a record that can be used in subsequent hearings and legislative debates. The actual forms these questions take reveal the argumentative intent of their use. The overall objective of the questioning, record building, and refutation is to tell a good story that will stand up to criticism.

In the second subsphere, legislative action, refutation is usually non-confrontational. Under the influence of the value of majoritarianism, the objective is to get the largest possible majority. Refutation is usually not personal. The amendment process serves as a kind of refutation. Refutation has an important credibility function in building a reputation for the legislator. This process of resolving differences through the amendment process is extended to the relationship between the legislature and the executive.

In the third subsphere, political campaigns, there is a complex mixture of activities. Campaigns involve both policy issues and the images of the candidates. Campaign arguments are made in the light of an understanding of "the people" or "the public." These concepts are used as a basis for telling the right stories about the candidate and about the opponent. These stories together form the story of the campaign and its relationship to the people. That story must be maintained, not only against the refutation of opponents but that of the media as well.

Debates have a special role in political campaigns. They are probably the single most important campaign activity, despite frequent complaints that they do not involve extensive attention to the issues. Debates reflect the mixed political condition in the country.

Refutation in a political campaign tends to be about testing proposals with values. Evidence and credibility are important to refutation because they help to sustain the story propagated by the campaign. To maintain that story, a candidate and campaign must answer attacks on the story. Sometimes that refutation comes in the form of inoculation before the attack is actually made.

PROJECT

Attend a committee hearing of a campus or local government group. Write a short analysis of the argumentation used there. To what extent does it reflect the principles of committee hearings discussed in this chapter? What is your opinion of the quality of the hearings?

REFERENCES

Adanan Constructors, Inc. v. Federico Pena. United States Court of Appeals for the Tenth Circuit, No. 93–1841 (June 12, 1995). Remanded by the Supreme Court of the United States, U.S. U10252 (1995).

Aichele, Gary J. Legal Realism and Twentieth-Century American Jurisprudence. NY: Garland, 1990.

Allen, Jodie T. "Sprawl, From Here to Eternity." US News and World Report 6 Sept. 1999: 22–27.

Allen, Julia M. and Lester Faigley. "Discursive Strategies for Social Change: An Alternative Rhetoric of Argument." Rhetoric Review 14 (1995): 142–72.

"Americans Feel Less Comfortable, Less Prepared With Public and Electronic Forms of Communication." Spectra Oct. 1999: 5.

Andersen, Kenneth. Persuasion: Theory and Practice. Boston: Allyn and Bacon, 1971.

Anderson, James A. and Timothy P. Meyer. Mediated Communication: A Social Action Perspective. Newbury Park, CA: Sage, 1988.

Anderson, James A. Communication Research: Issues and Methods. New York: McGraw-Hill, 1987.

Anderson, James A. Natural Theology: The Metaphysics of God. Milwaukee: Bruce, 1962: 25–66.

Anderson, Kenneth, and Theodore Clevenger, Jr. "A Summary of Experimental Research in Ethos." Speech Monographs 30 (1963): 59–78.

Ansolabehere, Stephen, and Shanto Iyengar. Going Negative. New York: Free P, 1995.

Apple, R. W. Jr. "Senate Confirms Thomas 52–48, Ending Week of Bitter Battle; 'Time For Healing,' Judge Says." New York Times 16 Oct. 1991: A1, A3.

Argyris, Chris. Reasoning, Learning, and Action. San Francisco: Jossey-Bass, 1982.

Aristotle. "Nicomachean Ethics." Works of Aristotle. Ed. by Richard McKeon. New York: Random House, 1949: 935–1112.

Aristotle. On Rhetoric: A Theory of Civic Discourse. Trans. George A. Kennedy. New York: Oxford UP, 1991.

▪s, Genaro. C. "Record Number of Women ▪hildless, Census Shows." Deseret Morning ▪vs 25 Oct. 2003: A11.

Arthur, Jim, Christine Carlson, and Lee Moore. A Practical Guide to Consensus. Policy Consensus Initiative, 1999.

Asbell, Sally L. "Understanding the Rehabilitation Act of 1973: A Rhetorical Analysis of Legislative Hearings." Diss. U of Utah, 1989.

Asch, Solomon E. "Effects of Group Pressure Upon the Modification and Distortion of Judgments." Groups, Leadership and Men. Ed. Harold Guetzkow. Pittsburgh: Carnegie, 1951, 171–90.

Associated Press. "Low Expectations Keep Latinos From College." Salt Lake Tribune 30 Sept. 1999: A8.

Ayim, Maryann. "Violence and Domination as Metaphors in Academic Discourse." In Trudy Govier (Ed.) Selected Issues in Logic and Communication. Belmont, CA: Wadsworth, 1988, 184–95.

Baker, Eldon E. "The Immediate Effects of Perceived Speaker Disorganization on Speaker Credibility and Audience Attitude Change in Persuasive Speaking." Western Speech Journal 29 (1965): 148–61.

Barr, James. Semantics of Biblical Language. London: Oxford UP, 1961.

Bauman, Richard W. Ideology and Community in the First Wave of Critical Legal Studies. Toronto: U of Toronto P, 2002.

Beach, Wayne. "Temporal Density in Courtroom Interaction: Constraints on the Recovery of Past Events in Legal Discourse." Communication Monographs 52 (1985): 1–18.

Bell, Katrina E., Mark P. Orbe, Darlene K. Drummond, and Sakile Kai Camara.. "Accepting the Challenge of Centralizing without Essentializing: Black Feminist Thought and African American Women's Communication Experiences." Women's Studies in Communication 23 (2000): 41–62.

Bellah, Robert N., Richard Madsen, William M. Sullivan, Ann Swindler, and Steven M. Tipton. Habits of the Heart: Individualism and Commitment in American Life. Berkeley: U of California P, 1985.

Bennett, W. Lance, and Martha S. Feldman. Reconstructing Reality in the Courtroom. New Brunswick, NJ: Rutgers UP, 1981.

Bennett, W. Lance. "Where Have All the Issues Gone? Explaining the Rhetorical Limits in American Elections." *Spheres of Argument.* Ed. Bruce Gronbeck. Annandale, VA: Speech Communication Assoc., 1989: 128–35.

Benoit, Pamela J., and William L. Benoit. "Accounts of Failures and Claims of Successes in Arguments." *Spheres of Argument.* Ed. Bruce Gronbeck. Annandale, VA: Speech Communication Assoc., 1989: 551–57.

Bitzer, Lloyd F. "Political Rhetoric." *Handbook of Political Communication.* Eds. Dan D. Nimmo and Keith R. Sanders. Beverly Hills: Sage, 1981: 225–48.

Blackman, Paul H. "Armed Citizens and Crime Control." www.NRAILA.org, 7 Oct. 1999: 1–9.

Bowden, Mark. "The Dark Art of Interrogation." *The Atlantic Monthly,* October 2003, 51–76.

Boynton, George R. "Telling a Good Story: Models of Argument; Models of Understanding in the Senate Agriculture Committee." *Argument and Critical Practices.* Ed. Joseph W. Wenzel. Annandale, VA: Speech Communication Assoc., 1987: 429–38.

Boynton, George R. "When Senators and Publics Meet at the Environmental Protection Sub-Committee." *Discourse and Society* 2 (1991): 131–55.

Braine, Martin D. S., and David P. O'Brien. *Mental Logic.* Mahwah, NJ: Lawrence Erlbaum Associates, 1998.

Branham, Robert. "Roads Not Taken: Counterplans and Opportunity Costs." *Journal of the American Forensic Association* 25 (1989): 246–55.

Brockriede, Wayne. "Arguers as Lovers." *Philosophy and Rhetoric* 5 (1972): 1–11.

Browne, M. Neil, and Stuart M. Keeley. *Asking the Right Questions: A Guide to Critical Thinking.* Englewood Cliffs, NJ: Prentice, 1990.

Bruner, M. Lane. "Producing Identities: Gender Problematization and Feminist Argumentation." *Argumentation and Advocacy* 32 (1996): 185–98.

Bureau of the Census. "Civilian Employment in the Fastest Growing and Declining Occupations: 1992 to 2005." *Statistical Abstract of the United States,* 1994. 114 ed. Washington, DC 1994: 411.

Bureau of the Census. "State and Local Taxes Paid by a Family of Four in Selected Cities, 1994." *Statistical Abstract of the United States,* 1994. 114 ed. Washington, DC 1994: 310.

Burke, Dan, and Alan Morrison. *Business @ the Speed of Stupid.* Cambridge, MA: Perseus Publishing, 2001.

Business Week, Special Advertising Section, 31 March 2003.

Campbell, John Angus. "Poetry, Science, and Argument: Erasmus Darwin as Baconian Subversive." *Argument and Critical Practices.* Ed. Joseph W. Wenzel. Annandale, VA: Speech Communication Assoc., 1987: 499–506.

Campbell, John Angus. "The Polemical Mr. Darwin." *The Quarterly Journal of Speech* 61 (1975): 375–90.

Campbell, Karlyn Kohrs. *Man Cannot Speak for Her: A Critical Study of Early Feminist Rhetoric.* Vol. 1. New York: Praeger, 1989.

Cardozo, Benjamin N. *The Nature of the Judicial Process.* New Haven: Yale UP, 1921.

Carpenter, Betsy. "Is He Worth Saving?" *U.S. News and World Report* 10 July 1995: 43–45.

Chapman, Christine. "Creating Art in the Moment." *Modern Maturity.* September–October 1999, 22.

Chivers, C. J. "Mourners Seek Solace in the Rituals of Faith." *New York Times* on the Web 8 Nov. 1999.

Church, Russell T., and Charles Wilbanks. *Values and Policies in Controversy: An Introduction to Argumentation and Debate.* Scottsdale, AZ: Gorsuch Scarisbrick, 1986.

City of Richmond v. J.A. Crosen Company: 1989, 109 S. Ct. 706.

Cloud, Dana L. "The Materiality of Discourse as Oxymoron: A Challenge to Critical Rhetoric." *Western Journal of Communication* 58 (1994): 141–63.

Cobb, Roger W., and Charles D. Elder. "Communication and Public Policy." *Handbook of Political Communication.* Eds. Dan D. Nimmo and Keith R. Sanders. Beverly Hills: Sage, 1981: 391–416.

Cobb, S. "A Narrative Perspective on Mediation: Toward the Materialization of the Storytelling Metaphor." *New Directions in Mediation: Communication Research and Perspectives.* Eds. Joseph P. Folger & Trish S. Jones. Thousand Oaks, CA: Sage, 1994: 44–66.

Code, Lorraine. *What Can She Know? Feminist Theory and the Construction of Knowledge.* Ithaca: Cornell UP, 1991.

Cohen, Simon. *Essence of Judaism.* New York: Behrman's Jewish Book House, 1932.

Condit, Celeste Michelle. *The Meanings of the Gene.* Madison: U of Wisconsin P, 1999.

Cox, J. Robert. "Investigating Policy Argument as a Field." *Dimensions of Argument.* Eds. George Ziegelmueller and Jack Rhodes. Annandale, VA: Speech Communication Assoc. 1981: 126–42.

Cragan, John F., and David W. Wright. *Communication in Small Groups.* Belmont, CA: Wadsworth, 1999.

Crenshaw, Carrie. "The Normality of Man and Female Otherness: (Re)producing Patriarchal Lines of Argument in the Law and the News." *Argumentation and Advocacy* 32 (1996): 170–84.

Cronkhite, Gary, and Jo R. Liska. "The Judgment of Communicants Acceptability." *Persuasion: New Directions in Theory and Research.* Eds. Michael E. Roloff and Gerald R. Miller. Beverly Hills: Sage, 1980: 101–39.

Cronkhite, Gary. "Propositions of Past and Future Fact and Value: A Proposed Classification." *Journal of the American Forensic Association* 3 (1966): 11–17.

Czubaroff, Jeanine. "The Deliberative Character of Strategic Scientific Debates." *Rhetoric in the Human Sciences.* Ed. Herbert Simons. Newbury Park, CA: Sage, 1989.

Damasio, Antonio R. *Descartes' Error: Emotion, Reason, and the Human Brain.* New York: Avon Books, 1994.

Daniels, Steven E., and Gregg B. Walker. *Working through Environmental Conflict: The Collaborative Learning Approach.* Westport, CT: Praeger, 2001.

Davidson, Roger, and Walter J. Oleszek. *Congress and Its Members.* Washington, DC: Congressional Quarterly, 1981.

de Kluyver, Cornelis A., and John A. Pearce II. *Strategy: A View from the Top.* Upper Saddle River, NJ: Prentice Hall, 2003.

Delia, Jesse G. "A Constructivist Analysis of the Concept of Credibility." *Quarterly Journal of Speech* 62 (1976): 361–75.

DeLuca, Kevin Michael. *Image Politics the New Rhetoric of Environmental Activism.* New York: Guildford Press, 1999.

Derrida, Jacques. *The Postcard: From Socrates to Freud and Beyond.* Chicago: U of Chicago P, 1987.

Dewey, John. *How We Think.* Boston: Heath, 1910.

Dewey, John. *The Quest for Certainty.* New York: G. P. Putnam, 1928.

Docherty, Thomas (Ed). *Postmodernism: A Reader.* New York: Columbia UP, 1993.

Dowd, Maureen. "Sununu Sayonara: He Broke 7 Cardinal Rules." *New York Times* 5 Dec. 1991: A14.

Easterbrook, Gregg. "The New Convergence." *Wired Magazine* 10.12. Dec. 2002.

"Drug Use: America's Middle and High School Students." *World Almanac and Book of Facts.* Mahwah, NJ: World Almanac Books, 1999: 878.

Edelman, Gerald M. *Bright Air, Brilliant Fire On the Matter of the Mind.* New York: Basic-Books, 1992.

Edwards, Derek, and Jonathan Potter. *Discursive Psychology.* Newbury Park: CA: Sage, 1992.

Edwards, Ward, and Amos Tversky, Eds. *Decision Making.* Baltimore: Penguin, 1967.

Ehninger, Douglas, and Wayne Brockriede. *Decision by Debate.* New York: Harper, 1978.

Eisinger, Richard, and Judson Mills. "Perceptions of the Sincerity and Competence of a Communicator as a Function of the Extremity of His Position." *Journal of Experimental Social Psychology* 4 (1968): 224–32.

Elisou, Jenny. "Music Biz Misery Continues." *Rolling Stone* 7 Aug. 2003: 15–16.

Ellis, Donald G., and B. Aubrey Fisher. *Small Group Decision Making.* New York: McGraw-Hill, 1994.

Elshtain, Jean Bethke. "Feminism Discourse and Its Discontents: Language, Power, and Meaning." *Signs* 7 (1982): 603–621.

Engel, S. Morris. *With Good Reason.* New York: St. Martin's, 1986.

Epstein, Isidore. *The Faith of Judaism.* London: Soncion P, 1954: 86.

FAIR. "The Way Things Aren't: Rush Limbaugh Debates Reality." *Extra!* July/Aug. 1994: 10–17.

Farrar, Frederic W. *History of Interpretation.* Grand Rapids, MI: Baker Book House, 1961.

Fearnside, W. Ward, and William B. Holther. *Fallacy: the Counterfeit of Argument.* Englewood Cliffs, NJ: Prentice Hall, 1959.

Festinger, Leon. *Conflict, Decision, and Dissonance.* Stanford: Stanford UP, 1964.

Fischman, Josh. "Feathers Don't Make the Bird." *Discover* 20 (Jan. 1999): 48–49.

Fisher, Roger, and Stephen Brown. 1988. *Getting Together: Building a Relationship that Gets to Yes.* Boston: Houghton, Mifflin.

Fisher, Roger, and William Ury. *Getting to Yes: Negotiating Agreement Without Giving In.* Boston: Houghton, Mifflin, 1981.

Fisher, Walter R. *Human Communication as Narration: Toward a Philosophy of Reason, Value, and Action.* Columbia: U of South Carolina P, 1987.

"Footnotes." *Chronicle of Higher Education* 29 Sept. 1995: A10.

Fosdick, Harry Emerson. *A Guide to Understanding the Bible.* New York: Harper Bros., 1938.

Foss, Sonja, and Cindy Griffin. "Beyond Persuasion: A Proposal for an Invitational Rhetoric." *Communication Monographs* 62 (1995): 2–18.

Foucault, Michel. *The Order of Things.* New York: Vintage Books, 1973.

Frana, Adrian W. "Characteristics of Effective Argumentation." *Argumentation and Advocacy* 25 (1989): 200–02.

Franklin, Benjamin. *The Autobiography of Benjamin Franklin.* Ed. Gordon S. Haight. New York: Black, 1941.

Freeley, Austin J. *Argumentation and Debate: Critical Thinking for Reasoned Decision Making.* Belmont, CA: Wadsworth, 1990.

Frey, Lawrence R. "Group Communication in Context: Studying Bona Fide Groups." Ed. Lawrence R. Frey. *Group Communication in Context.* Mahwah, NJ: Lawrence Erlbaum Associates, 2003.

Fuller, Steve. *Philosophy, Rhetoric, and the End of Knowledge: The Coming of Science and Technology Studies.* Madison: U of Wisconsin P, 1993.

Funk, Robert W., Ray W. Hoover, and the Jesus Seminar. *The Five Gospels: The Search for the Authentic Words of Jesus.* New York: Scribner, 1993.

Furay, Conal. *The Grass Roots Mind in America: The American Sense of Absolutes.* New York: New Viewpoints, 1977.

Gallup, George, Jr., and Frank Newport. "Americans Most Thankful For Peace This Thanksgiving." *Gallup Poll Monthly* Nov. 1990: 42.

Garten, Jeffrey E. *The Mind of the C.E.O.* New York: Basic Books, 2001.

Gaskins, Richard H. *Burdens of Proof in Modern Discourse.* New Haven: Yale UP, 1992.

Gensler, Harry J. *Logic.* Englewood Cliffs, NJ: Prentice, 1989.

German, Kathleen, Bruce E. Gronbeck, Douglas Ehninger, and Alan H. Monroe. *Principles of Public Speaking.* New York: Longman, 2001.

Gilbert, Michael A. "Feminism, Argumentation and Coalescence." *Informal Logic* 16 (1994): 95–113.

Gilovich, Thomas, and Dale Griffin. "Introduction—Heuristics and Biases: Then and Now." *Heuristics and Biases.* Eds. Thomas Gilovich, Dale Griffin, and Daniel Kahneman. Cambridge: Cambridge UP, 2002. 1–16.

Gomes, Andrew. *The Honolulu Advertise,* 4 May 2003: A1–A3.

Goodkind, Terry. *Wizard's First Rule.* New York: A Tom Doherty Associates Book, 1994.

Goodnight, G. Thomas. "The Firm, the Park, and the University: Fear and Trembling on the Postmodern Trail." *The Quarterly Journal of Speech* 81 (1995): 267–90.

Goodnight, G. Thomas. "The Personal, Technical, and Public Spheres of Argument: A Speculative Inquiry into the Art of Public Deliberation." *Journal of the American Forensic Association* 18 (1982): 214–27.

Goodnight, G. Thomas. "The Personal, Technical, and Public Spheres of Argument: A Speculative Inquiry into the Art of Public Deliberation." *Journal of the American Forensic Association* 18 (1982): 214–27.

Gordon, M. "Ex-analyst for Merrill accused of deception," *Naples Daily News* 29 May 2003: E1–8.

"Got Milk?" *Brill's Content.* 2 (Mar. 1999): 77.

Gotcher, J. Michael, and James M. Honeycutt. "An Analysis of Imagined Interactions of Forensic Participants." *The National Forensic Journal* 7 (1989): 1–20.

Gottlieb, Gidon. *The Logic of Choice.* New York: Macmillan, 1968.

Gouran, Dennis S. "The Failure of Argument in Decisions Leading to the 'Challenger Disaster': Two Level Analysis." *Argument and Critical Practices.* Ed. Joseph W. Wenzel. Annandale, VA: Speech Communication Assoc., 1987: 439–47.

Gozic, Charles, P. Ed. *Gangs: Opposing Viewpoints.* San Diego CA: Greenhaven, 1996.

Grann, David. "Back to Basics in the Bronx." *Republic* 4 Oct. 1999: 24–26.

Grant, Robert M. *A Short History of the Interpretation of the Bible.* New York, 1963.

Gratz, et al. v. Bollinger et al

Graves, Jacqueline M. "More Americans Are Going Native." *Fortune* 26 June 1995: 30.

Greenspan, Alan. "Measuring Financial Risk in the Twenty-First Century." *Vital Speeches of the Day* 66, 1 Nov. 1999: 34–35.

Grice, H. P. "Further Notes on Logic and Conversation." *Syntax and Semantics, 9: Pragmatics.* Ed. Peter Cole. New York: Academic, 1978: 113–28.

Grice, H. P. "Logic and Conversation." *Syntax and Semantics, 3: Speech Acts.* Eds. Peter Cole and Jerry L. Morgan. New York: Academic, 1975: 41–58.

Gross, Alan G. "The Rhetorical Invention of Scientific Invention: The Emergence and Transformation of a Social Norm." *Rhetoric in the Human Sciences.* Ed. Herbert Simons. Newbury Park: Sage, 1989: 89–107.

Grutter v. Bollinger et al. U.S. (2003).

"Gun Industry Finds Itself At Wrong End of the Barrel." www.CNN.com, 7 Oct. 1999:1–5.

Gurganus, Allan. *The Oldest Living Confederate Widow Tells All.* New York: Ivy, 1989.

Guston, David H. "Policing Scientific Misconduct." *Science and Engineering Ethics.* (April–June, 1999).

Guzley, Ruth M., Fumiyo Arkai, and Linda E. Chalmers. "Cross-Cultural Perspectives of Commitment: Individualism and Collectivisim as a Framework for Conceptualization." *Southern Communication Journal* 64 (1998): 1–19.

Haiman, Franklin. "An Experimental Study of the Effect of Ethos on Public Speaking." *Speech Monographs* 16 (1949): 190–202.

Hamblin, C. L. "Imagined Interaction and Interpersonal Communication." *Communication Reports* 3 (1990): 1–8.

Hamblin, C. L. *Fallacies.* London: Methuen, 1970.

Haney, Daniel Q. "Rabies: Rare But Deadly." *Salt Lake Tribune* 21 Oct. 1999: B1–B2.

Hardon, John A. S. J. *The Catholic Catechism.* Garden City NY: Doubleday, 1975.

Harmon, Fred. *Business 2010.* Washington, DC: Kiplinger Books, 2001.

Thomas. *Hannibal.* New York: Delacorte ...s, 1999.

...vid. *The Condition of Postmodernity.* ...dge, MA: *Basil Blackwell,* 1989.

...even Penrod, and Nancy Penning-...he Jury. *Cambridge:* Harvard

Hatfield, Mark O. "Remarks on a School Prayer Amendment to the Improving America's School Act, 1994." *Congressional Record* 27 July 1994: S9894.

Haverwas, Stanley, and L. Gregory Jones. Why Narrative? Readings in Narrative Theology. Grand Rapids, MI: Eerdmans, 1989.

Hawkins, J. "Interaction and Coalition Realignments in Consensus Seeking Groups: A Study of Experimental Jury Deliberations." Diss. U. of Chicago, 1960.

Hemenway, Robert E. "The Evolution of a Controversy in Kansas Shows Why Scientists Must Defend the Search for Truth." *The Chronicle of Higher Education* 29 Oct. 1999.

Hendershott, Anne. "Redefining Rape–Expanded Meaning Robs Women of Power." *The San Diego Union-Tribune* 15 Aug. 2003: B7.

Hewgill, Murray A., and Gerald R. Miller. "Source Credibility and Response to Fear-Arousing Communications." *Speech Monographs* 32 (1965): 95–101.

Hicks, John. *Evil and the God of Love.* New York: Harper and Row, 1966.

Hodgson, Peter C., and Robert H. King. *Christian Theology: An Introduction to the Traditions and Tasks.* Philadelphia, PA: Fortress, 1985.

Hoffner, Cynthia, and Joanne Cantor. "Factors Affecting Children's Enjoyment of a Frightening Film Sequence." *Communication Monographs* 58 (1991): 41–62.

Hogan, J. Michael. "Media Nihilism and the Presidential Debates." *Argumentation and Advocacy* 25 (1989): 220–25.

Hogan, Patrick Colm. *The Culture of Conformism.* Durham: Duke UP, 2001.

Holbrook, Thomas M. *Do Campaigns Matter?* Thousand Oaks, CA: Sage, 1996.

Holy Bible: Revised Standard Version. New York: Thomas Nelson, 1952.

House, Dawn. "Law Firm Fired, But Utahns Will Still Pay Abortion-Defense Bill." *Salt Lake Tribune* 10 Oct. 1991: A1–2.

Howell, William S. *Logic and Rhetoric in England, 1500–1700.* Princeton: Princeton UP, 1956.

Huff, Darrell. *How to Lie With Statistics.* New York: Norton, 1954.

Infante, Dominic A. "Teaching Students to Understand and Control Verbal Aggression." *Communication Education* 44 (1995): 51–63.

Infante, Dominic A., and Charles J. Wigley, III. "Verbal Aggressiveness: An Interpersonal Model and Measure." *Communication Monographs* 53 (1986): 61–69.

Infante, Dominic A., Karen A. Hartley, Matthew M. Martin, Mary Anne Higgins, Stephen D. Bruning, and Ghyeongho Hur. "Initiating and Reciprocating Verbal Aggression: Effects on Credibility and Credited Valid Argument." *Communication Studies* 43 (1992): 182–90.

Infante, Dominic A., Teresa A. Chandler, and Jill E. Rudd. "Test of an Argumentative Skill Deficiency Model of Interpersonal Violence." *Communication Monographs* 56 (1989): 163–77.

Infante, Dominic A., and Rancer, Womack. *Building Communication Theory,* 2nd ed. Long Grove, IL: Waveland Press, Inc., 1993.

Intergovernmental Panel on Climate Change, *Climate Change 2001: The Scientific Basis,* A Report of Working Group I of the Intergovernmental Panel on Climate Change, 2001.

Isaacs, William. *Dialogue and the Art of Thinking Together.* New York: A Currency Book, 1999.

Jackson, Sally, and Scott Jacobs. "Structure of Conversational Argument: Pragmatic Bases for the Enthymeme." *The Quarterly Journal of Speech* 66 (1980): 251–65.

Jacobs, Scott. "How to Make an Argument from Example in Discourse Analysis." *Contemporary Issues In Language and Discourse Processes.* Eds. Donald G. Ellis and William A. Donohue. Hillsdale, NJ: Earlbaum, 1986. 149–67.

Jacobs, Scott, and Sally Jackson. "Conversational Argument: A Discourse Analytic Approach." *Advances in Argumentation Theory and Research.* Eds. J. Robert Cox and Charles A. Willard. Carbondale: Southern Illinois UP, 1982: 205–37.

Jaehne, Dennis. "Administrative Appeals: The Bureaucratization of Environmental Discourse." Diss. U of Utah, 1989.

Jamieson, Kathleen Hall, and David S. Birdsell. *Presidential Debates: The Challenge of Creating an Informed Electorate.* New York: Oxford, 1988.

Jamieson, Kathleen Hall. *Dirty Politics: Deception, Distraction, and Democracy.* New York: Oxford, 1992.

Janis, Irving L., and Leon Mann. *Decision Making.* New York: Free Press, 1977.

Johnson, Phillip E. "The Religious Implications of Teaching Evolution." *The Chronicle of Higher Education* 12 Nov. 1999: B9.

Johnson, Ralph H. "The Blaze of Her Splendors: Suggestions about Revitalizing Fallacy Theory." *Fallacies: Classical and Contemporary Readings.* Eds. Hans V. Hansen and Robert C. Pinto. University Park: Pennsylvania State UP, 1995: 107–19.

Johnson, Ralph H., and J. Anthony Blair. "The Recent Development of Informal Logic." *Informal Logic.* Eds. J. Anthony Blair and Ralph Johnson. Inverness, CA: Edge, 1980: ix–xvi.

Jones, Roger S. *Physics as Metaphor.* Minneapolis: U of Minnesota P, 1982.

Joseph, Mike. "Ballpark Plans Up for Review: Shaner Complex Expansion Swells into Campaign Issue." *Centre Daily Time* 11 Oct. 2003: A1, A6.

Kagan, Donald, Steven Ozment, and Frank M. Turner. *The Western Heritage.* New York: Macmillan, 1983.

Kahane, Howard. *Logic and Contemporary Rhetoric.* Belmont, CA: Wadsworth, 1971.

Kaplan, Abraham. *The Conduct of Inquiry.* San Francisco: Chandler, 1964.

Kauffman, Linda S. "The Long Goodbye: Against Personal Testimony, or an Infant Grifter Grows up." *American Feminist Thought at Century's End.* Cambridge: Blackwell, 1993, 258–77.

Keefe, William J., and Morris S. Ogul. *The American Legislative Process: Congress and The States.* Englewood Cliffs, NJ: Prentice-Hall, 1985.

Keen, Judy. "Bush on Offensive Over War Critics: White House Moves Fast to Manage the Debate." *USA Today* 10 Oct. 2003: A4.

Kelly, Eamonn, Peter Leyden, and Members of the Global Business Network. *What's Next: Exploring the New Terrain for Business.* Cambridge, MA: Perseus, 2002.

Kennedy, George A. *Classical Rhetoric and Its Christian and Secular Tradition.* Chapel Hill: U of North Carolina P, 1980.

Kent, Thomas. *Paralogic Rhetoric: A Theory of Communicative Interaction.* London: Associated UP, 1993.

Kern, Montague. "The Question of a Return to Basic American Values: 'My Mother and Winston Churchill' in the Heroic Narrations of Ross Perot's Infomercials." *Presidential*

Campaign Discourse. Ed. Kathleen E. Kendall. Albany: State U of New York P, 1995. 157–78.

Kline, John A. "Interaction of Evidence and Reader's Intelligence on the Effects of Silent Message." *Quarterly Journal of Speech* 55 (1969): 407–13.

Klope, David C. "The Rhetorical Constitution of the Creationist Movement." Diss. U of Utah, 1991.

Kluckhohn, Clyde. "Values and Value-Orientations in the Theory of Action." *Towards a General Theory of Action.* Eds. Talcott Parsons and Edward A. Shils. New York: Harper and Row, 1951: 388–433.

Kluckhohn, Clyde. *Mirror for Man.* New York: McGraw-Hill, 1949.

Kolb, Deborah. *When Talk Works: Profiles of Mediators.* San Francisco: Jossey-Bass, 1994.

Konner, Melvin. *The Tangled Wing: Biological Constraints on the Human Spirit.* New York: Holt, 1982.

Kouzes, James M., and Barry Z. Posner. *Credibility: How Leaders Gain and Lose It. Why People Demand It.* San Francisco: Jossey-Bass, 1993.

Krauss, Laurence M. "Words, Science, and the State of Evolution." *The Chronicle of Higher Education* 29 Nov. 2002: B20.

Kristof, Nicholas. "Baked Alaska on the Menu?" *New York Times* 13 Sept. 2003: A13.

Kristof, Nicholas. "Blood on Our Hands?" *New York Times* 5 Aug. 2003: A19.

Kuhn, Thomas S. *The Structure of Scientific Revolutions.* Chicago: U of Chicago P, 1970.

Kusnet, David. "Talking American: The Crucial First Step in Taking Back the White House," *The American Prospect,* September 2003, 22–25.

Laclau, Ernesto. "Politics and the Limits of Modernity." *Postmodernism: A Reader.* Ed. Thomas Docherty. New York: Columbia University Press, 1993a, 329–43.

Laclau, Ernesto. "Power and Representation." *Politics, Theory, and Contemporary Culture.* Ed. Mark Poster. New York: Columbia UP, 1993b, 277–96.

LaFree, Gary. *Rape and Criminal Justice The Social Construction of Sexual Assault.* Belmont, CA: Wadsworth, 1989.

Lake, Randall A. "Between Myth and History: Enacting Time in Native American Protest." *The Quarterly Journal of Speech* 77 (1991): 123–51.

Lakoff, George, and Mark Johnson. *Metaphors We Live By.* Chicago: U of Chicago P, 1980.

Lashbrook, William R., William B. Snavely, and Daniel L. Sullivan. "The Effects of Source Credibility and Message Information Quantity on the Attitude Change of Apathetics." *Communication Monographs* 44 (1977): 252–62.

Lavasseur, David, and Kevin W. Dean. "The Use of Evidence in Presidential Debates: A Study of Evidence Labels and Types From 1960–1988." *Argumentation and Advocacy* 32 (1996): 129–42.

Leatherdale, W. H. *The Role of Analogy, Model, and Metaphor in Science.* Amsterdam: North-Holland, 1974.

Leatherman, Courtney. "At Texas A&M, Conflicting Charges of Misconduct Tear a Program Apart." *The Chronicle of Higher Education* 5 Nov. 1999.

Lecocq, F., Hourcade, J. C. and Ha-Duong, M. (1998). Decision Making under Uncertainty and Inertia Constraints: Sectoral Implications of the When Flexibility. *Energy Economics,* 20(5/6), 539–55.

Lee, Ronald, and Karen King Lee. *Arguing Persuasively.* White Plains, NY: Longman, 1989.

Leff, Michael. The Relation Between Dialectic and Rhetoric in a Classical and Modern Perspective." *Dialectic and Rhetoric.* Eds. Frans H. van Eemeren and Peter Houtlosser. Dordrecht: Kluwer Academic Publishers, 2002. 53–63.

Lehrman, Sally. "From Lab to Embassy: A Plan to Get Scientists Involved in U.S. Foreign Policy." *Scientific American* March 2003: 24–26.

Leith, John H. "The Bible and Theology." *Interpretations* 30 (Oct. 1976).

Lemonick, Michael D. "Never Trust a Tiger." *Time* 20 Oct. 2003: 63–64.

Lessem, Don. *Kings of Creation.* New York: Simon and Schuster, 1992.

Levy, Leonard W. *Origins of the Bill of Rights.* New Haven: Yale UP, 1999.

Lewis, Bernard. *Islam and the Arab World.* New York: Alfred A. Knopf, 1976.

Lewis, Bernard. *The Crisis of Islam.* New York. Modern Library, 2003.

Lim, Tae-Seop. "Politeness Behavior in Social Influence Situations." *Seeking Compliance.* Ed. James P. Dillard. Scottsdale: Gorsuch Scarisbrik, 1990: 75–86.

Llewellyn, Karl N. "The Modern Approach to Counseling and Advocacy—Especially Commercial Transactions." *Columbia Law Review* 46 (1946): 167–95.

Lo, Andrew W., and Richard H. Thaler. "Two Views on Stock Market Rationality." *Investment Forum* 3 (December 1999): 13–15.

Luecke, Bruce. "Hang On For A Wild Ride." *Vital Speeches of the Day* 1 Sept. 1999: 682–85.

Luntz, Frank. *The Environment: A Cleaner, Safer, Healthier America.* The Luntz Research Companies. www.ewg.org/briefings/luntzmemo/pdf/LuntzResearch_environment.pdf, 2003.

Lyne, John R. "The Pedagogical Use of Fallacies." *Iowa Journal of Speech Communication* 13 (1981): 1–9.

Lyne, John, and Henry F. Howe. "The Rhetoric of Expertise: E. O. Wilson and Sociobiology." *The Quarterly Journal of Speech* 76 (1990): 134–51.

Lyne, John. "Argument in the Human Sciences." *Perspectives on Argumentation.* Eds. Robert Trapp and Janice Schuetz. Prospect Heights, IL: Waveland, 1990. 178–89.

MacKinnon, Catherine A. "Feminism, Marxism, Method and the State: An Agenda for Theory," *Signs* 7 (Spring 1982): 515–44.

Macquarrie, John. *God-Talk.* New York: Harper and Row, 1967.

Madsen, Arnie. "Partisan Commentary and the First 1988 Presidential Debate." *Argumentation and Advocacy* 27 (1991): 100–13.

"Making Money the Nonprofit Way." *U.S. News and World Report* 26 June 1995: 19.

Massey, Gerald J. "The Fallacy Behind Fallacies." *Fallacies: Classical and Contemporary Readings.* Eds. Hans V. Hansen, and Robert C. Pinto. University Park: Pennsylvania State UP, 1995.

Matson, Floyd W., and Ashley Montagu, Eds. *The Human Dialogue.* New York: Macmillan, 1967.

Matthews, Christopher. *Hardball.* New York: Summit, 1988.

Matthews, Donald R., and James A. Stimson. *Yeas and Nays: Normal Decision-Making in the U.S. House of Representatives.* New York: Wiley, 1975.

McCroskey, James C. "A Summary of Experimental Research on the Effects of Evidence in Persuasive Communication." *The Quarterly Journal of Speech* 55 (1969): 169–75.

McCroskey, James C., and Jason Teven. "Goodwill: A Reexamination of the Construct and its Measurement." *Communication Monographs* 66 (1999): 90–103.

McCroskey, James C., and R. Samuel Mehrley. "The Effects of Disorganization and Nonfluency on Attitude Change and Source Credibility." *Speech Monographs* 36 (1969): 13–21.

McGee, Michael C. "In Search of 'The People': A Rhetorical Alternative." *The Quarterly Journal of Speech* 61 (Oct. 1975): 235–49.

McGrath, Ben. "The Talk of the Town." *The New Yorker* 28 July 2003: 27–31.

Mead, George Herbert. *Mind, Self, and Society.* Chicago: U of Chicago P, 1934.

Meador-Woodruff, James H., Meador-Woodruff Lab: About Schizophrenia. http://www.personal.umich.edu/jimmw. 1999.

Melosh, H. J. "Around and Around We Go." *Nature* 3 Aug. 1995: 386–87.

Meyer, Herbert E. "A User's Guide to Politics." *Policy Review* 96 (Aug.–Sept. 1999).

Miller, Greg R. "Incongruities in the Public/Private Spheres: Implications of the Clinton Presidential Campaign." *Argument and the Postmodern Challenge.* Ed. Raymie E. McKerrow. Annandale, VA: Speech Communication Assoc., 1993: 345–51.

Millman, Arthur B. "Critical Thinking Attitudes: A Framework for the Issues." *Informal Logic* 10 (1988): 45–50.

Mills, Judson, and Elliott Aronson. "Opinion Change as a Function of the Communicators' Attractiveness and Desire to Influence." *Journal of Personality and Social Behavior* 1(1965): 173–77.

Minow, Newton N. "Television's Values and the Values of Our Children." Communication Policy Studies, Northwestern University. The Annenberg Washington Program Children Now Conference Keynote. 2 Mar. 1995.

Mitroff, Ian. *Smart Thinking for Crazy Times: The Art of Solving the Right Problems.* San Francisco: Berrett-Koehler Publishers, Inc., 1998.

Montgomery, Barbara M., and Leslie A. Baxter, Eds. *Dialectical Approaches to Studying Personal Relationships.* Mahwah, NJ: Lawrence Erlbaum Associates, 1998.

Morris, Charles. *Varieties of Human Values.* Chicago: U of Chicago P, 1956.

Morton, Kathryn. "The Story-Telling Animal." *New York Times Book Review* 28 Dec. 1984: 1–2.

Mukarovsky, Jan. *Structure, Sign and Function.* Trans. Peter Steiner and John Burbank. New Haven: Yale UP, 1976.

Myers, Michele Tolela, and Alvin A. Goldberg. "Group Credibility and Opinion Change." *Journal of Communication* 20 (1970): 174–79.

New York Times v. Sullivan. 376 US 254 (1954).

Newell, Sara E., and Richard D. Rieke. "A Practical Reasoning Approach to Legal Doctrine." *Journal of the American Forensic Association* 22, (1986): 212–22.

"Newsweek Poll." *Newsweek* 8 Feb. 1999: 26.

O'Keefe, Daniel J. "Two Concepts of Argument." *Journal of the American Forensic Association* 13 (1977): 121–28.

O'Neill, Anthony B. "In Support of the NAACP's Boycott." *New Crisis* Sept./Oct. 1999: 17, 53.

Oaksford, Mike, and Nick Chater. *Rationality in an Uncertain World: Essays on the Cognitive Science of Human Reasoning.* Hove, East Sussex: Psychology Press, Taylor & Francis, 1998.

Office of Science and Technology, "Proposed Policy on Research Misconduct to Protect the Integrity of the Research Record." *Federal Register* 14 Oct. 1999 (Volume 64, Number 198): 55722–55725.

Official Sample Ballot. General Election. Clark County, Nevada, 5 Nov. 2002.

Ogden, Schubert M. "The Authority of Scripture for Theology." *Interpretations* 30 (Oct. 1976).

Olbricht, Thomas H. *"Medieval Instruction in Rhetoric,"* unpub. n.d.

Ong, Walter J. "Ramist Rhetoric." *The Province of Rhetoric.* Eds. Joseph Schwartz and John Rycenga. New York: Ronald, 1965: 226–54.

Oravec, Christine. "Presidential Public Policy and Conservation: W. J. McGee and the People." *Green Talk in the White House: The Rhetorical Presidency Encounters Ecology.* Ed. Tarla Rai Peterson. College Station, TX: TAMU Press. Forthcoming 2004.

Ostermeier, Terry H. "Effects of Type and Frequency of Self Reference Upon Perceived Source Credibility and Attitude Change." *Speech Monographs* 34 (1967): 137–44.

Palczewski, Catherine Helen. "Argumentation and Feminisms: An Introduction." *Argumentation and Advocacy* 32 (1996): 161–169.

"Parade of Witnesses Support Hill's Story, Thomas's Integrity." *New York Times* 14 Oct. 1991: A1.

Park, Alice. "Cancer Fighter," *Time* 20 Oct. 2003: 81.

Parker, Richard. "Toward Field-Invariant Criteria for Assessing Arguments." Western Speech Communication Association Convention. Denver, 1982.

"People's Choice: Cable's Top 25." *Broadcasting and Cable* (129) 4 Jan. 1999: 67.

Pear, Robert, and Erik Eckholm. "When Healers Are Entrepreneurs: A Debate Over Costs and Ethics." *New York Times* 2 June 1991: 1+.

Pearce, W. Barnett, and Stephen W. Littlejohn. *Moral Conflict: When Social Worlds Collide.* Thousand Oaks, CA: Sage, 1997.

Peat, F. David. *From Certainty to Uncertainty: The Story of Science and Ideas in the Twentieth Century.* Washington, DC: Joseph Henry P, 2002.

Peirce, Charles S. "The Fixation of Belief." *Philosophical Writings of Peirce.* Ed. Justus Buckler. New York: Dover, 1955. 7–18.

Pennington, Nancy, and Reid Hastie. "Evidence Evaluation in Complex Decision Making." *Journal of Personality and Social Psychology* 51 (1986): 242–56.

Perelman, Chaim, and L. Olbrechts-Tyteca. *The New Rhetoric: A Treatise on Argumentation.* Notre Dame: U of Notre Dame P, 1969.

Perelman, Chaim. *The New Rhetoric and the Humanities.* Dordrecht, Holland: Reidel, 1979.

Peterson, Paul E. "A Liberal Case for Vouchers." *New Republic* 4 Oct. 1999: 29–30.

Peterson, Tarla Rai. *Sharing the Earth: The Rhetoric of Sustainable Development.* Columbia: U of South Carolina P, 1997.

Pfau, Michael, and Henry C. Kenski. *Attack Politics: Strategy and Defense.* New York: Praeger, 1990.

Pfau, Michael, and William P. Eveland, Jr. "Influence of Traditional and Non-Traditional News Media in the 1992 Election Campaign." *Western Journal of Communication* 60 (1996): 214–32.

Pfau, Michael. "The Potential of Inoculation in Promoting Resistance to the Effectiveness of Corporate Advertising Messages." *Communication Quarterly* 40 (1992): 26–44.

Pianin, Eric. "Congress Ends With A Flurry." *Salt Lake Tribune* 20 Nov. 1999: A1, A5.

Pine, Ronald. *Science and the Human Prospect.* Belmont, CA: Wadsworth, 1989.

Planned Parenthood. "Listen to the Anti-Choice Leaders—Then Help Us Stop Them Before It's Too Late." New York, 1989.

Plato. *Phaedrus.* Trans. William C. Helmbold and W. G. Rabinowitz. New York: Liberal Arts, 1956.

Pollack, Henry N. *Uncertain Science . . . Uncertain World.* Cambridge, UK: Cambridge UP, 2003.

Popkin, James, and Gloria Borger. "They Think They Can." *US News and World Report* 10 April 1995: 26–32.

Quackenbush, Chuck. "Letter." *The Honolulu Advertiser* April 27, 2003: B3.

Rayl, A. J. S., and K. T. McKinney. "The Mind of God." *Omni* Aug. 1991: 43–48.

Raymond, Chris. "Study of Patient Histories Suggests Freud Suppressed or Distorted Facts That Contradicted His Theories." *Chronicle of Higher Education* 29 May 1991: A4–6.

Regal, Philip J. *The Anatomy of Judgment.* Minneapolis: U of Minnesota P, 1990.

Regents of the University of California v. Bakke 438 U.S. 265 (1978).

Reinard, John C. "The Empirical Study of the Persuasive Effects of Evidence: The Status After Fifty Years of Research." *Human Communication Research* 15 (1988): 3–59.

Rescher, Nicholas. "The Study of Value Change." *Journal of Value Inquiry* 1 (1967): 12–23.

Revkin, Andrew C. "Politics Reasserts Itself in the Debate Over Climate Change and Its Hazards." *New York Times* 5 Aug. 2003: F2.

Revkin, Andrew C., and Katharine Q. Seelye. "Report by the E.P.A. Leaves Out Data on Climate Change." *New York Times* 19 June 2003: A1.

Rieke, Richard D. "The Judicial Dialogue." *Argumentation* 5 (1991): 39–55.

Rieke, Richard D., and Randall K. Stutman. *Communication in Legal Advocacy.* Columbia: U of South Carolina P, 1990.

Ritter, Kurt W. "Ronald Reagan and The Speech: The Rhetoric of Public Relations Politics." *Western Speech* 32 (1968): 50–58.

Roberts, Marilyn S. "Political Advertising: Strategies for Influence." *Presidential Campaign Discourse: Strategic Communication Problems.* Ed. Kathleen E. Kendall. Albany: State U of New York P, 1995: 179–200.

Roberts, W. Rhys. "Rhetorica." *The Works of Aristotle.* Ed. W. D. Ross. Oxford: Clarendon, 1945: 1354–1462.

Roche, James G., and John P. Jumper. *United States Air Force Academy: Agenda for Change.* Washington, DC: USAF, 2003.

Rohatyn, Dennis. "When Is a Fallacy a Fallacy?" International Conference on Logic and Argumentation. Amsterdam, 4 June 1986.

Rokeach, Milton. *Beliefs, Attitudes and Values.* San Francisco: Jossey-Bass, 1968.

Rokeach, Milton. *The Nature of Human Values.* San Francisco: Free P, 1972.

Rokeach, Milton. *Three Christs of Ypsilanti: A Psychological Study.* New York: Knopf, 1964.

Rokeach, Milton. *Understanding Human Values.* New York: Free P, 1979.

Rorty, Richard. "Is Derrida a Transcendental Philosopher?" *Yale Journal of Criticism* 2 (1989): 207–15.

Rorty, Richard. "Philosophy as a Kind of Writing: An Essay on Derrida." *New Literary History* 9 (1978): 141–60.

Rosen, Clifford J. "Restoring Aging Bones." *Scientific American* March 2003: 71–77.

Rowland, Robert C. "In Defense of Rational Argument: a Pragmatic Justification of Argumentation Theory and Response to the Postmodern Critique." *Philosophy and Rhetoric* 28 (1995): 350–64.

Rowland, Robert C., and Cary R. W. Voss. "A Structural Functional Analysis of the Assumptions Behind Presidential Debates." *Argument and Critical Practices.* Ed. Joseph W. Wenzel. Annandale, VA: Speech Communication Assoc., 1987: 239–48.

Ruesch, Jurgen. "Communication and American Values: A Psychological Approach." *Communication: The Social Matrix of Psychiatry.* Eds. Jurgen Ruesch and Gregory Bateson. New York: Norton, 1951: 94–134.

Ruggiero, Vincent R. *The Art of Thinking.* New York: Harper, 1964.

Rybacki, Karyn Charles, and Donald Jay Rybacki. *Advocacy and Opposition: An Introduction to Argumentation.* 5th ed. Boston: Pearson, 2004.

Salant, Jonathan D. "Race Study Points to Death-Penalty Imbalances." *The Honolulu Advertiser* 27 April 2003: A20.

Salzer, Beeb. "Quotable," *The Chronicle of Higher Education* 21 July 1995: B5.

Sanders, Robert E. *Cognitive Foundations of Calculated Speech.* Albany: State U of New York P, 1987.

Sarat, Austin, and Jonathan Simon, Eds. *Cultural Analysis, Cultural Studies, and the Law Moving Beyond Legal Realism.* Durham, NC: Duke UP, 2003.

Schenck v. United States. 249 US 47, 1919.

Schlegel, John Henry. *American Legal Realism and Empirical Social Science.* Chapel Hill: U of North Carolina P, 1995.

Schultz, Beatrice C. "The Role of Argumentativeness in the Enhancement of the Status of Members of Decision-Making Groups." *Spheres of Argument.* Ed. Bruce E. Gronbeck. Annandale, VA: Speech Communication Assoc., 1989: 558–62.

Schum, David A. "Argument Structuring and Evidence Evaluation." *Inside the Jury.* Ed. Reid Hastie, Cambridge: Cambridge UP, 1993: 175–91.

Schweitzer, Don A. "The Effect of Presentation on Source Evaluation." *The Quarterly Journal of Speech* 56 (1970): 33–39.

Schweitzer, Don A., and Gerald P. Ginsburg. "Factors of Communication Credibility." *Problems in Social Science.* Eds. Carl W. Backman and Paul F. Secord. New York: McGraw-Hill, 1966: 94–102.

Scriven, Michael. "The Philosophy of Critical Thinking and Informal Logic." *Critical Thinking and Reasoning Current Research, Theory, and Practice.* Ed. Daniel Fasko, Jr. Cresskill, NJ: Hampton Press, 2003: 21–45.

Sharp, Harry, Jr., and Thomas McClung. "Effects of Organization on the Speaker's Ethos." *Speech Monographs* 33 (1966): 182–83.

Shnayerson, Michael, and Mark J. Plotkin. *The Killers Within: The Deadly Rise of Drug-Resistant Bacteria.* New York: Little, Brown, 2002.

Sillars, Malcolm O. "Values: Providing Standards for Audience-Centered Argumentation." *Values in Argumentation.* Ed. Sally Jackson. Annandale, VA: Speech Communication Assoc., 1995: 1–6.

Sillars, Malcolm O., and Bruce E. Gronbeck. *Communication Criticism: Rhetoric, Social Codes, Cultural Studies.* Prospect Heights, IL: Waveland, 2001.

Sillars, Malcolm O., and Patricia Ganer. "Values and Beliefs: A Systematic Basis for Argumentation." *Advances in Argumentation Theory and Research.* Eds. J. Robert Cox and Charles Arthur Willard. Carbondale: Southern Illinois UP, 1982: 184–201.

Silzer, Ron. "Selecting Leaders at the Top: Exploring the Complexity of of Executive Fit." Ed. Ron Silzer. *The 21st Century Executive.* San Francisco: Jossey-Bass, 2002.

Simonson, Itamar. "Choice Based on Reasons: The Case of Attraction and Compromise Effects." *Journal of Consumer Research* 16 (1989): 158–59.

Smith, Eliza R. Snow. "Biography and Family Record of Lorenzo Snow." *Deseret News* 1884: 46.

Snow, C. P., *Two Cultures and the Scientific Revolution,* Cambridge UP, 1963.

"Soft Touches." *Time* 5 June 1995: 20.

Sokal, Alan D. "What the Social Text Affair Does and Does Not Prove." Noretta Koertge, Ed. *A House Built on Sand: Exposing Postmodernist Myths about Science.* Oxford: Oxford UP, 1998.

Sonnenfeld, Jeffrey A. "Deciphering Executive Failures." *The 21st Century Executive.* Ed. Rob Silzer. San Francisco: Jossey-Bass, 2002.

Steele, Edward D., and W. Charles Redding. "The American Value System: Premises for Persuasion." *Western Speech* 26 (1962): 83–91.

Stossel, Scott. "Uncontrolled Experiment." *New Republic* 29 Mar. 1999: 17–22.

Stump, Bill. "Scull Session," *Men's Health* Oct. 2003: 103–4.

Suppe, Frederick. *The Structure of Scientific Theories.* Urbana: U of Illinois P, 1974.

Susskind, Lawrence, Sarah McKearnan, and Jennifer Thomas-Larmer. *The Consensus Building Handbook: A Comprehensive Guide to Reaching Agreement.* Thousand Oaks, CA: Sage, 1999.

Talmadge, R. Dewitt. "Victory For God." *American Forum.* Ernest J. Wrage and Barnett Baskerville, Eds. New York: Harper and Bros., 1960.

Tannenhill, Robert C. *The Sword of His Mouth.* Philadelphia: Fortress, 1975.

TeSelle, Sallie McFague. *Speaking in Parables: A Study in Metaphor and Theology.* Philadelphia: Fortress, 1975.

Thompson George. "They lied to you." *The Salt Lake Tribune* 22 June 2003, A21.

Thompson, Kevin. "The Anti Clause." *California Farmer* Jan. 1995: 12.

"TIAA Strikes a Balance by Going Global," *Investment Forum* Sept. 2003: pp. 6–9.

"TIAA-CREF's Tenets for Investing in Stocks," *Investment Forum* Sept. 2003: 4–5.

Toedtman, James. "Clinton, Congressional Leaders Laud $4000 Billion Spending Deal." *Salt Lake Tribune* 19 Nov. 1999: A12.

Toffler, Barbara with Jennifer Reingold. *Final Accounting: Ambition, Greed, and the Fall of Arthur Andersen.* New York: Broadway Books, 2003.

Tol, R. S. J. "Safe Policies in an Uncertain Climate: An application of FUND." *Global Environmental Change,* 9 (1999): 221–32.

Tomasky, Michael. "Strange Bedfellows: Conservative Civil Libertarians Join the Fight," *The American Prospect* Sept. 2003: 47–49.

Toobin, Jeffrey. "The Consent Defense." *The New Yorker* 1 Sept. 2003: 40–87.

Toulmin, Stephen E. "Commentary on Willbrand and Rieke." *Communication Yearbook* 14. Ed. James A. Anderson. Newbury Park, CA: Sage, 1991. 445–50.

Toulmin, Stephen. *Foresight and Understanding.* New York: Harper and Row, 1963.

Toulmin, Stephen. *Human Understanding.* Princeton: Princeton UP, 1972.

Toulmin, Stephen E. *The Uses of Argument.* Cambridge: Cambridge UP, 1964.

Toulmin, Stephen E., Richard Rieke, and Allan Janik. *An Introduction to Reasoning,* 2nd ed. New York: Macmillan, 1984.

Trenholm, Sara. *Persuasion and Social Influence.* Englewood Cliffs, NJ: Prentice, 1989.

Tubbs, Stewart L. "Explicit Versus Implicit Conclusions and Audience Commitment." *Speech Monographs* 35 (1968): 14–19.

Tuman, Joseph H. "Getting To First Base: Prima Facie Arguments for Propositions of Value." *Journal of the American Forensic Association* 24 (1987): 84–94.

Turner, Daniel S. "America's Crumbling Infrastructure." *USA Today* May 1999: 10–16.

U.S. v Miller 307: 174 1939.

Ury, William. *Getting Past No: Negotiating with Difficult People.* New York: Bantam Books, 1991.

Ury, William. *The Third Side: Why We Fight and How We Can Stop.* New York: Penguin, 1999.

Uslander, Eric M. *The Decline of Comity in Congress.* Ann Arbor: U of Michigan P, 1993.

van Eemeren, Frans H. "Fallacies." *Crucial Concepts in Argumentation Theory.* Ed. Frans H. van Eemeren. Amsterdam: Amsterdam UP, 2001: 135–64.

van Eemeren, Frans H., and Rob Grootendorst. *Argumentation, Communication, and Fallacies: A Pragma-Dialectical Perspective.* Hillsdale, NJ: Erlbaum, 1993.

"Viewers Tune In." *New York Times* 14 Oct. 1991: A17.

Visser, H., R. J. M. Folkert, J. Hoekstra, and J. J. de Wolff. "Identifying Key Sources of Uncertainty in Climate Change Projections." *Climatic Change* 45 (2000): 421–57.

Waldman, Hilary. "Watching Lily." *Readers Digest* April 2003: 81–87.

Walker, Gregg B., and Malcolm O. Sillars. "Where Is Argument? Perelman's Theory of Values." *Perspectives on Argumentation: Essays in Honor of Wayne Brockriede.* Eds. Robert Trapp and Janice Schuetz. Prospect Heights, IL: Waveland, 1990: 134–50.

Walters, Glenn D. *Criminal Belief Systems An Integrated-Interactive Theory of Lifestyles.* Westport, CT: Praeger, 2002.

Walton, Douglas N. *Appeal to Popular Opinion.* University Park: Pennsylvania State UP, 1999.

Walton, Douglas N. *A Pragmatic Theory of Fallacy.* Tuscaloosa: U of Alabama P, 1995.

Walton, Douglas N. *Appeal to Expert Opinion: Arguments from Authority.* University Park: Pennsylvania State UP, 1997a.

Walton, Douglas N. *Appeal to Pity: Argumentum ad Misericordiam.* Albany: State U of New York P, 1997b.

Walton, Douglas N. *Begging the Question: Circular Reasoning as a Tactic of Argumentation.* New York: Greenwood, 1991.

Walton, Douglas N. *Informal Fallacies.* Philadelphia: John Benjamins, 1987.

Walton, Douglas N. *Practical Reasoning.* Savage, MD: Rowman & Littlefield, 1990.

Walton, Douglas N. *The New Dialectic.* Toronto: U of Toronto P, 1998.

Warnick, Barbara, and Edward S. Inch. *Critical Thinking and Communication.* New York: Macmillan, 1994.

Warren, Irving D. "The Effect of Credibility in Sources of Testimony of Audience Attitudes Toward Speaker and Message." *Speech Monographs* 36 (1969): 456–58.

Weaver, Richard. "Ultimate Terms in Contemporary Rhetoric." *The Ethics of Rhetoric.* Chicago: Regnery, 1953: 211–32.

Webb, LaVarr and Ted Wilson. "Understanding the Bank and Credit Union Battle." *Community* Nov./Dec. 2003: 65.

"Weed Threatens Waterways, Fish and Plants." *Salt Lake Tribune* 30 Sept. 1999: A8.

Weiler, Michael. "The 1988 Electoral Debates and Debate Theory." *Argumentation and Advocacy* 25 (1989): 214–19.

Weiss, Robert O. *Public Argument.* Lanham, MD: UP of America, 1995.

Wenburg, John R., and William Wilmot. *The Personal Communication Process.* New York: Wiley, 1973.

Werling, David S., Michael Salvador, Malcolm O. Sillars, and Mina A. Vaughn. "Presidential Debates: Epideictic Merger of Issues and Images in Values." *Argument and Critical Practices.* Ed. Joseph W. Wenzel. Annandale, VA: Speech Communication Assoc., 1987: 229–38.

Whately, Richard. *Elements of Rhetoric.* Ed. Douglas Ehninger. Carbondale: Southern Illinois UP, 1963.

"What's Breeding the Crop of Big Storms." *US News and World Report* 27 Sept. 1999: 22.

Wheeler, David L. "To Improve Their Models, Mathematicians Seek a 'Science of Uncertainty,'" *The Chronicle of Higher Education* 16 April 1999: A19. .

Willard, Charles A. "Argument Fields." *Advances in Argumentation Theory and Research.* Eds. J. Robert Cox and Charles A. Willard. Carbondale: South Illinois U P, 1982: 22–77.

Willbrand, Mary Louise, and Richard D. Rieke. "Reason Giving in Children's Supplicatory Compliance Gaining." *Communication Monographs* 53 (1986): 47–60.

Willbrand, Mary Louise, and Richard D. Rieke. "Strategies of Reasoning in Spontaneous Discourse." *Communication Yearbook* 14. Ed. James A. Anderson. Newbury Park, CA: Sage, 1991: 414–40.

Willihnganz, Shirley, Joy Hart Seibert, and Charles Arthur Willard. "Paper Training the New Leviathan: Dissensus, Rationality and Paradox in Modern Organizations." *Argument and the Postmodern Challenge.* Ed. Raymie E. McKerrow. Annandale, VA: Speech Communication Assoc., 1993.

Wise, Charles R. *The Dynamics of Legislation.* San Francisco: Jossey-Bass, 1996.

Wise, Gene. *American Historical Explanations: A Strategy for Grounded Inquiry.* Minneapolis: U of Minnesota P, 1980.

Woelfel, James W. *Bonhoeffer's Theology.* Nashville: Abingdon P, 1970.

Wong, Kathleen. "Bringing Back the Logjams." *U.S. News and World Report* 6 Sept. 1999: 60.

Wright, Beverly. "Race, Politics and Pollution: Environmental Justice in the Mississippi River Chemical Corridor." *Just Sustainabilities: Development in an Unequal World* Ed. Julian Agyeman, Robert D. Bullard, and Bob Evans (2003). Cambridge, MA: MIT Press: 125–45.

Zarefsky, David. "Criteria for Evaluating Nonpolicy Argument." *Perspectives on Nonpolicy Argument.* Ed. Don Brownlee. Long Beach, CA: Cross-Examination Debate Association, 1980: 9–16.

Zarefsky, David. *Lincoln Douglas and Slavery.* Chicago: U of Chicago P, 1990.

Ziegelmueller, George W., Jack Kay, and Charles A. Dause. *Argumentation: Inquiry and Advocacy.* Englewood Cliffs, NJ: Prentice Hall, 1990.

NAME INDEX

331

SUBJECT INDEX